We must warmly congratulate the [illegible] together this book: Joan Barber and th[illegible] transcribe the documents in the Bristol Rec[illegible] typing out the monumental journals of Flor[illegible] the originals; Mrs B. O. Fidgen for re[illegible] Beryl Chappell for typing the original m[illegible] wordprocessor and stage managing the whole [illegible] business with enormous patience and professionalism; and we mustn't forget Anton Bantock without whose dedication to the history of this (in)famous family the books would never have seen the light of day.

Denis Bristow, The Manor House, Bishopsworth
President, The Malago Society.

The work of Denis Bristow in producing the photographs and orchestrating the operation; and members of the Malago Society for publicising and distributing the copies is also gratefully acknowledged.

Anton Bantock

 ISBN. 0 9507813 4 7.

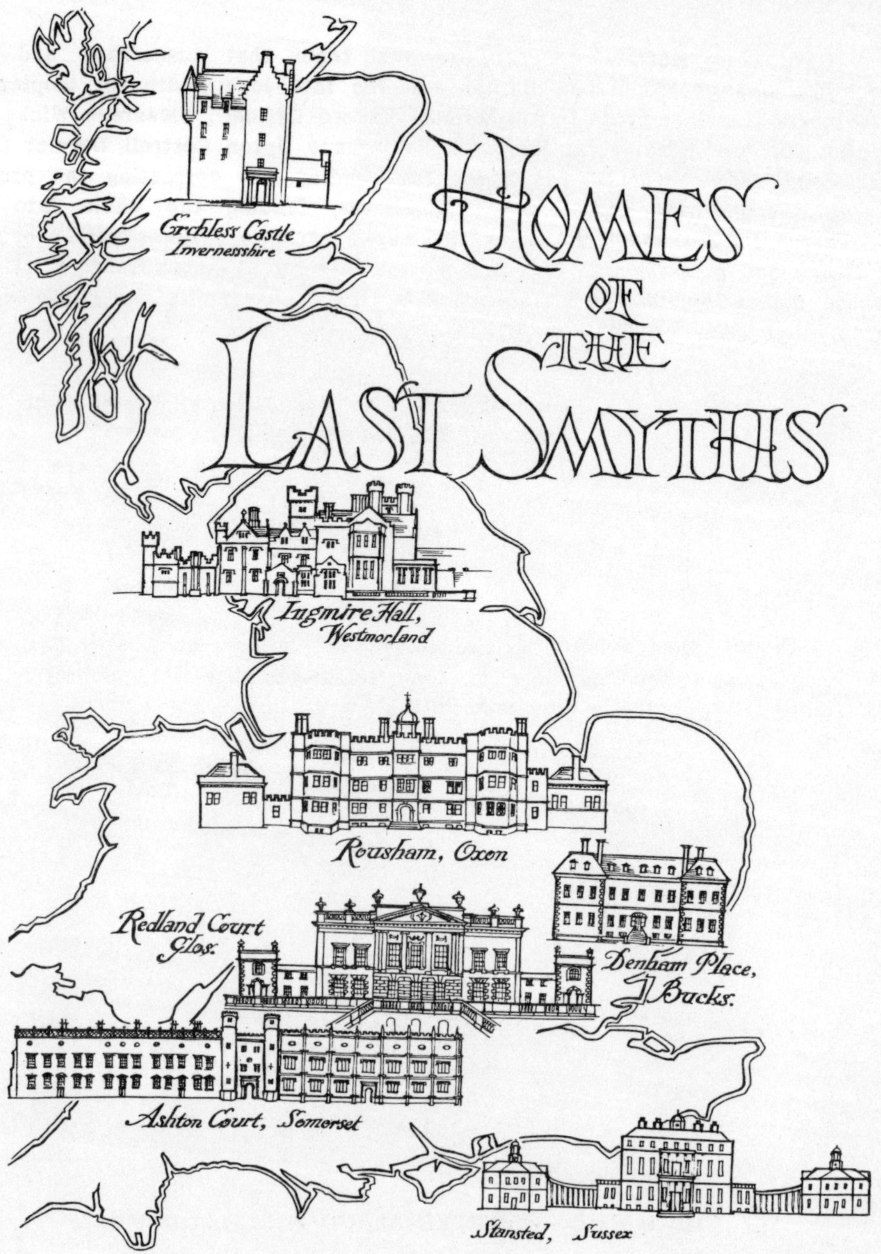
Homes of the Last Smyths
Erchless Castle
Invernesshire
Ingmire Hall,
Westmorland
Rousham, Oxon
Redland Court
Glos.
Denham Place,
Bucks.
Ashton Court, Somerset
Stansted, Sussex

The Last Smyths of Ashton Court

from their papers

Part I

1802 – 1880

ACKNOWLEDGEMENTS

I feel somewhat embarrassed in writing these notes since, in the introduction to the last book, 'The Later Smyths of Ashton Court', I promised the final part at Christmas 1984. I cannot believe that nearly seven years have passed until its arrival, but I suppose one can be forgiven when it is realised that we are trying to cover over **four hundred years** of history. And another thing: we couldn't get it all into one book so Volume Three, 'The Last Smyths of Ashton Court', has in itself become three volumes! We tried our utmost to prune Anton's text, but it would have meant leaving out so much of tremendous interest that the decision was taken to divide it into three sections. I promise that the next one will not take another seven years! It is already typeset on the computer so we are well on our way; and we've got three more volumes of fascinating reading instead of just one.

Some of the sources for this book can be found in the Bristol Record Office - namely the letters of Hugh and John Smyth under the references AC/C130/131; the account books of Arthur Way AC/E35 - AC/E52, E42 (a-c), E43 (a-n); addresses of congratulation 1957, 1884 and 1885, AC/F5/1-6; the Ashton Court Estate Annual Accounts from 1871, AC/E35 - AC/E51, E44/1-20; and the visit of the Prince of Wales 1884, AC/C126 - AC/C133, 132/1-3.

Newspapers mentioned in the text can be found in the Bristol or Bath Reference Libraries.

We are indebted to Thomas Cottrell Dormer for permission to use the unpublished journals of Mary Ann and Eliza Way, and Florence Upton Cottrell Dormer, and the original ms. of the Book of the Glen; to Dorothy North for permission to use the letters of Mary Ann Way and Florence Upton Cottrell Dormer and to consult the privately published versions of the Book of the Glen, and the journal of Florence Upton Cottrell Dormer; to Piers Cavendish for permission to use the Ashton Court Inventory of 1901; to Mrs Mont for permission to use the Way family papers; to Mr Daniels for permission to use Edgar Way's letter to John Wilkinson 1891; and to the late Mrs A. D. Collard for permission to use the papers of Private James Collard.

Photocopies of most of the relevant newspaper cuttings and all the unpublished manuscripts have been deposited in the Bristol Record Office.

CONTENTS

FOREWORD

The Last Smyths of Ashton Court were really Uptons and Ways. The direct male line died out in 1741 with the death of the second Sir John Smyth, Bart. The later Smyths were really Smiths: the sons and grandsons of Sir Jarrit Smith, who had married Florence, the sister of the second Sir John Smyth. The grandsons of Sir Jarrit left no legitimate male heirs and his two grand-daughters, Florence Upton and Mary Way, married their offspring to each other to ensure that the huge property stayed in the family. Their plan paid off, for Greville Smyth (1836-1901), the son of Thomas Upton and Eliza Way, gave Ashton Court its final and most dazzling age.

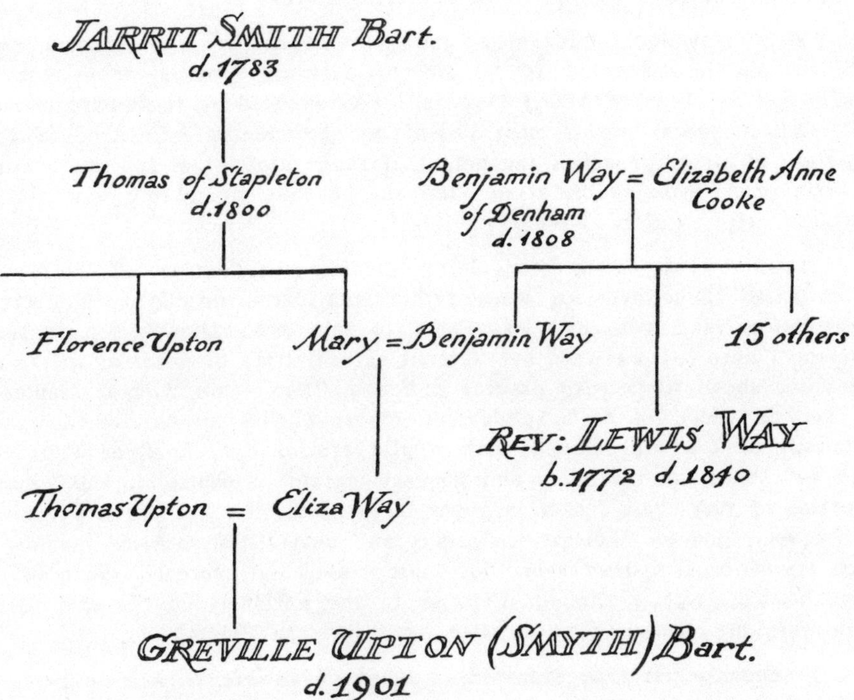

SKETCH OF STANSTED BY DRUSILLA WAY
IT WAS BURNT DOWN IN 1900

BY THE WAY

INTRODUCING THE EBULLIENT LEWIS WAY & FAMILY

In the autumn of 1822 the Rev. Lewis Way and his family left Stansted, their family home in Sussex, and began a foreign tour. Their destination was Nice (then in the Kingdom of Sardinia, not in France as it is now), for wintering on the Mediterranean was becoming fashionable among the aristocracy and the children were now of an age to benefit from the experience.

Lewis travelled first in a phaeton, driven by a coachman, with postillion, and accompanied by his eldest daughter, Drusilla, then aged 18. Drusilla and her brother Albert (17) had been exposed by their parents since their earliest years to the most liberal and broadening influences of their age, and had already reached the height of their intellectual powers. Scarcely an observation made by either of them during that memorable tour did not scintillate with worldly wisdom and wit.

Drusilla wrote, many years later, her dim recollections of their youth at Stansted: "I believe we were rather considered prodigies. Mrs Pierce taught us to read well, and Mrs Barry to talk and write French unusually well: and I dare say we were not without scintillations of paternal wit, which afterwards shone forth with greater radiance. Then came diligent studies of the Encyclopaedia on half holidays. Albert curled up on the deep oak windowsill of the Blue Room, with a pile around him, imbibing knowledge while yet small, with science and general learning dropped in, and Albert's collection of tiny chalk fossils in paper trays up in the dark dressing room of his bedroom, and his interest in insects and butterflies on pins impaled, of which I sometimes gained rainy days inspection, and secretly wondered how clever he was. Not a glimmer then as to the antiquity of the said fossils, which were all connected by us with Noah and the Flood."

Frequent visitors to Stansted in those days were William Wilberforce, George Canning and, on one celebrated occasion, the Duke of Clarence, later William IV, who showed great interest in the tapestries of the Duke of

Marlborough's wars given by Queen Anne to Lord Halifax, a former owner of Stansted. Drusilla wrote: "He explained the tapestry to my mother, who the figures were etc., with we two small ones following close, listening ...." but to Mrs Way's mortification the 'Resurrection pie' made up of left-over scraps, which was only intended to fill up the table of delicacies put before the royal visitor, was the only thing he would touch!

Drusilla was an accomplished linguist, musician and artist, and her father's inseparable companion. Albert ('Atty' to his sisters) was a brilliant scholar, with a profound interest in the antique, and a gift for describing in words and drawings the amusing incidents of their journey. Mrs Way, known affectionately to her family as 'Bombie', Atty, and his four younger sisters, travelled in 'The Heavy'. This was an enormous travelling carriage which also accommodated voluminous baggage and the family's servants. These included Albert's tutor, Mr Nosworthy, generally referred to as 'our Nos'; 'Phebsey', the governess, a very important person and a great martinet; while on the dickey were John, the butler, whom the children called 'The Duke of Puddledock', and Betty, the cook. More difficult articles, such as Mrs Way's piano, Drusilla's harp, and the children's ponies from Stansted, went by sea under the charge of Bill Drewe, Mrs Way's nephew.

The party reached Nice without mishap, and Bill and the luggage - well most of it - arrived soon afterwards. Mrs Way wrote to her mother:

"Bill arrived quite safe in the Dash last Monday, after a very quick passage, having sailed December 15th, stopp'd 7 days at Toulon by contrary wind, and arrived here Jan. 12th, a voyage of 2,000 miles. They encountered some tremendous gales; therefore have reason to be thankful for the safety of Bill and all the luggage.

"The ponies, alas, are lost, which was a great disappointment to Dill and Lewis; indeed he would never have had them sail so late in the season; he expected them to sail a month or 6 weeks before, and had they been placed in the part of the vessel usually appropriated to horses, and confin'd in the proper manner, they might in all probability have been saved, but being on the deck, they were frightened by the storm which arose Dec. 21st and lasted 4 days, that they beat and threw themselves about in so violent a manner as to endanger the ship, and the lives of all on board, and accordingly the Captain ordered them to be thrown overboard.

"The Devonshire hams arrived quite safely which I scarcely expected, being paokod 3 months and laying about in damp places, but except one (being nibbled by a mouse) which is for our Sunday dinner tomorrow, they are uninjured.

"Olivia (aged 7) is looking fat and well, and admired more than any. Lewis says he was never better and enjoys himself here. He has always occupation, delightful rides about the olive grounds, mountains etc. and pleasant Society, and has such excellent spirits he is the life of every party and everybody seems delighted with him."

Of the four little girls, Mrs Way wrote later: "Anna (aged 10) grows wonderfully tall, stout and strong" (Drusilla fondly christened her 'Length'), "she will soon be above me. I wish I could say as much of her studies as her growth; she is still voluble and disinclined to study. Olivia is much more steady; Lu (Louisa, 5) is a very steady little girl, neat and methodical in all her little concerns. She reads well, and has begun French, geography and figures, and is very fond of learning hymns and texts. Georgiana is fat and rosy, a general favourite, but she gets on slowly with her books, being disinclined to study." Georgiana was then only three!

"The complaisance and good nature of the peasants is quite their characteristic and their merry, cheerful manner of speaking makes one wish to understand patois. In walks in the gardens and orange grounds they bring their offerings of flowers, oranges etc. to 'Madame le Ministre', or 'Votre Reverence', which are my styles of address. The little ones begin to speak a little French in which they are assisted by a French nursery maid."

Albert designed for his young sisters some little story books, exquisitely handwritten and illustrated by minute sketches, each one thoughtfully incorporating incidents which he knew would amuse them. Baby Georgiana's book consisted of pictures only, mostly prevailing fashions. One shows a modish lady in a poke bonnet entitled 'Les Modes de Paris en été'.

Les modes de Paris en l'ete.

The sisters added their own contributions - the gowns of a lady's wardrobe in 1822 show the high waists, flounced skirts flounced skirts, and huge leg-of-mutton sleeves then in vogue. Only one of the pictures in Georgiana's book is a portrait, and it is entitled 'Lady Bute' - in a huge coal scuttle bonnet, and with a large nose, a cavernous mouth and sticking out teeth. These microscopic editions were sewn into bright covers and were evidently treasured for they still survive intact among the Way papers.

The company were joined in Nice by two of Lewis' sisters: Aunt Kitty (later Lady Cholmondely) and the pretty, but empty-headed Marianne and her husband, the Rev. Edward Whitby of Creswell Hall, Staffs. Mr Whitby, as a young man, had been curate at Denham and had proposed and been accepted by Marianne, but her father 'The Gruff Squire' forbade the match. For fourteen years they never met, but after her father's death she was trying on shoes in Oxford Street when she saw Mr Whitby pass the window. She ran out, with one shoe off and one on, and they were married soon afterwards.

Also of the party was a Mr Wheatly and his wife, who was described by Mrs Way as "a Cantab. who has travelled a great deal, and seems a man of general information and research, a naturalist, minerolagist and antiquarian, which will suit Albert, and I hope will be really useful to him in his studies".

In the evenings the company indulged in various intellectual diversions, one of which was a game called 'Definitions', in which each member of the party had to define an abstract idea or sentiment. For example 'The perfection of Wisdom' produced the following definitions:

Monsr.l'Abbé (a frequent guest)	"La réunion de toutes les vertus"
Mrs Way	"Is to leave it to the Gentlemen, and to know your own ignorance"
Aunt Kitty	"Even a Fool when he holdeth his tongue is accounted wise"
Edward Whitby	"To fear God; that is Wisdom"
Marianne	"I find it in my husband"
Mrs Wheatly	"In many cases, silence"
Louisa	"God"
Albert	"Stultitia caruisse" (to be lacking in in foolishness)
Drusilla	"Connoître soi-même et son créateur"
Olivia	"Peace"
Lewis Way	"To profit in future by past errors"
William Wheatly	"To say nothing, answer nothing, and be nothing"

The life and soul of the party was Anna, who entertained the company with riddles which Albert later wrote into a little book for her:

Question:	When was B the first letter of the alphabet?
Answer:	In the time of Noah (no a).
Question:	Why is Desmoulin's Brewery like a Jew's coffee house?
Answer:	Because He-brews drink there.
Question:	Why is the Emperor of Russia's nose like the second letter in iniquity?
Answer:	Because it stands between two Is.
Question:	Where was Noah when the light went out?
Answer:	In the pitch dark.
Question:	What tree is a man like who pinches a Jew?
Answer:	A juniper (Jew-nipper).
Question:	Why, said one Jew to another, do people of quality

like venison?

Answer: Because they prefer what is deer to what is sheep.

The frequent reference to Jews cannot be interpreted as anti-Semitism. If anything it was the reverse. Lewis Way, at that time, was the greatest champion the Jews then had, and his lifelong efforts on their behalf had a most singular origin.

Jane Parmenter's home "À la Ronde" based on the basilica of San Vitale Ravenna ~ as it appeared to Lewis Way

Lewis on how to love Jews

A wealthy businessman, by name John Way, but no relation to Lewis* had decided to leave his considerable fortune to his only nephew. Before finally making his will he invited the young man to dinner. In the course of the evening he asked him for the loan of a corkscrew which the nephew, unluckily for him, promptly produced from his pocket.

The elder Way immediately decided that a young man who habitually carried a corkscrew around with him was not to be safely entrusted with a fortune, and looked around for another heir. Having no further relations to whom he could leave the money he decided that a namesake would be the next best thing. While walking through Lincoln's Inn he noticed the nameplate of Lewis Way, then a struggling young barrister on the verge of bankruptcy. Lewis was accordingly invited to dinner and passed the corkscrew test successfully. John Way was much impressed by the piety of the young man, who shortly afterwards found he had inherited a fortune of £300,000 with the proviso that the money should be used "to the Glory of God".

* John Way of Acton had acquired his fortune as the Agent of Lord Mansfield, from whom he also inherited a handsome annuity when that gentleman died in 1793.

Lewis took his responsibilities very seriously. He gave up the law, took Holy Orders, and prayed for guidance as to how the money should be best used. Not long afterwards, when riding between Exeter and Exmouth, he noticed a remarkable clump of oak trees known as 'Oaks À la Ronde'. On enquiry he was told, inaccurately as it turned out, that under the will of a certain Miss Jane Parmenter, a local crank and philanthropist, these oak trees were not to be cut down until the Jews had been restored to Palestine, then they were to be used to build ships to carry them. Suddenly it dawned on Lewis that here was the answer. From that moment he dedicated his life to the welfare of the Jews. His object, which developed into an obsession, was to restore them to Jerusalem and he must be recognised as one of the world's first Zionists.* He hoped, however, that on the way they would be converted to Christianity. One of his first acts was to give £10,000 to the newly founded London Society for Promoting Christianity amongst the Jews.

In 1805 he bought Stansted Park, an estate of 1,666 acres, and installed his young wife, Mary Drew, and his first two children. Mary came from an illustrious Devon family** and her father, a squire and clergyman, had opposed the match until Lewis came into his fortune. She was a good-looking, intelligent girl, and bore with fortitude the hardships that her husband's missionary zeal imposed on the family: his long absences, the financial strictures produced by the rapid disappearance of Mr John Way's fortune into the pockets of bogus disciples and indigent Jews, and finally the loss of their lovely home when Lewis handed it over to the Jewish Society for use as a Hebrew Training College for missionaries.

Warm-hearted, generous to a fault, and blinded by his mission, Lewis could not distinguish between men attracted to his high principles and those who just came for the cash. George Canning, William Wilberforce and others of the Clapham Sect, who were often invited to Stansted, rubbed shoulders with a motley band of parasites. On one unfortunate occasion he had sixteen young Jews in the house who had been duly shaved, baptised and welcomed into the fold, when suddenly a false rumour went round that their host had gone bankrupt. The next morning all the converts had decamped, taking with them every portable object they could lay hands on, even the books from the library and the Chapel, and the silver spoons. Some of them were afterwards caught, and one was condemned to transportation for having forged Lewis Way's signature. The episode caused Macaulay to write:

"Each, says the Proverb, has his taste. 'Tis true
Marsh loves a Controversy, Coates a play,
Bennet a felon, Lewis Way a Jew.
The Jew, the silver spoons of Lewis Way."

* Theodore Herzl is generally regarded as the founder of the Zionist Movement, 1897.

** The Grange, Broadhembury, near Honiton.

While the fashionable world made merry at his expense, Lewis suffered moments of shock and disillusionment, but his optimism quickly returned. Events in Europe after 1812 seemed to indicate an approaching apocalypse. For men like Lewis Way and his circle the overthrow of Napoleon and the new order established at the Congress of Vienna, seemed to inaugurate a new era of peace and justice. Was this not the promised millennium? Surely, in this new order, all the people of Europe would be redeemed from their oppressions, and the Jews rescued from the ghettoes, welcomed as equals, restored to their status as a nation and given the blessing and protection of the great powers.

Lewis and the Czar of Russia

All that was required was an influential patron, and the starry-eyed members of the Jewish Society were drawn irresistibly to that extraordinary personage who, in 1814, stepped on to the centre of the European stage. Czar Alexander I, un- vanquished by Napoleon in Moscow, having sent his armies rolling back the tide, now stood in Paris amid the victors - a tall, blond, imposing figure; an autocrat of millions, but known to have liberal sympathies, and to be a Christian who had dared to suggest at the meeting of the peacemakers in 1814 that all kings and their representatives should pledge themselves to a Christian brotherhood. Though statesmen scorned 'The Holy Alliance', men of faith saw in Alexander the person who could realise their dreams. It is typical of Lewis Way that he failed to see that behind the high sounding words was an impulsive, unstable man; that his liberalism was a passing whim, and his Christianity the result of his having fallen temporarily under the influence of a religious maniac, the Baroness Krüdener.

Nonetheless he was determined to see the Emperor of all the Russias and put before him his plan for the redemption of the world's Jews. Armed with a brief from the Jewish Society to investigate the condition of Jews in Central Europe; an introduction to the Czar from his uncle, Edward Gore, who had been undersecretary at the Foreign Office in 1814 and had met Alexander in Vienna; and a portrait of his four children in a red leather portfolio, he set off in 1817 with five companions, including Sultan Kattegarry an interpreter, Charles Maberley his secretary, Solomon a converted Jew who was to launch a mission in the Crimea, and, to wait on them, the servant John, 'The Duke of Puddledock'. In a carriage of his own design, Lewis and his little party set off across Europe. In Holland, Hanover and Prussia, Jewish ghettoes were visited, and contacts made with the Chief Rabbis. In Berlin Lewis was received by the Crown Prince, later King Frederick William IV. They had a long conversation and the Crown Prince, who was of a mystical temperament, was swept along by Lewis' euphoria and eloquence.

At Posen "full of Jews, a fine station for future operations", Lewis wrote to his wife "....we slept 5 in a small room in a Jewish inn, like this: Two beds and the rest on the floor

"The Rev.C. L.W.	Maberley Secretary	B.N. Solomon Deacon	Sultan Kattegarry Interpreter	Robert Cox,
Bed	floor	floor	floor	Bed"

He does not relate where poor John 'The Duke of Puddledock' slept!

The party took the coastal route, which involved nego-tiating the currische, a gravel spit 80 miles long, during which the wheels of the carriage on one side were in the Baltic most of the time. "It looks very tremendous on the map," wrote Drusilla to her father.

Back view of Revd L Way's Carriage in the Baltic - when passing the Curische Nehrung

They reached Riga on Dec. 2. "....the winter now being set in, wheels are no longer useful," wrote Lewis, "so we left the carriage and the Jew and Mr Cox at Riga, and Sultan, Maberley and I have passed two delightful days travelling faster than an English mail, in a sledge.... This is drawn by 3 horses abreast and they gallop as hard as they can, as far as from London to Windsor or Denham, stopping only for snaps. This is done by moonlight or starlight just as well as by daylight, of which there is now but little. The thermometer stands at about 20 degrees below freezing on the outside; at summer heat above 70 inside. When we come to an inn we are sure to find the temperature the same; as the fireplaces, here called ovens, are always hot, and you wake and get up in the same heat as you lie down on what is called a bench in England and a bed in Russia.

"I now sleep in my own blanket with the same clothes over me as I wear in the carriage. I have not yet had recourse to fur except one little animal, the skin of which I wear under my shirt as a warm friend; two of the legs go round my neck, and the other two are held as a stumager below; under this is a woollen waistcoat and over the shirt a leather waistcoat stuffed with wadding. It is surprising how completely the elements are brought into subjection! for after all, when the air is too cold to breathe it is brought through a pipe of fuming tobacco, and then it is better than summer.... I have not yet tasted tallow candle except in soup.... you see I live in a cradle and my chief food is rusks! We hope to reach our destination in St. Petersburg in two days."

But the Czar was in Moscow and the party sped on across the frozen wastes, this time inwardly warmed by a bundle of letters from home. Mrs Way had filled the page with snippets of daily life in beloved Stansted: daily drives in the park with Mrs Hodson; Mr Hodson's Sunday sermons; and the children's progress, they had started German. "It goes on pretty well," wrote Drusilla, "we like it better than at first. We read every evening. Mamma in the Bible, and Albert and I in a book of Dr. Boque's. Mamma is excepted from the grammar, but as we are to write letters for Papa and his Jews, we have begun it....

"Olivia is a sweet child and has names for us all. How does John ('The Duke of Puddledock') get on - does he like bear's fat and oil?"

Albert, then 12, was rather more outspoken about having to learn German. "It certainly is a very ugly language; there was a service in Chapel on Christmas Day. It has looked much better than these last Sundays and is not near so Viel Gluck und Segen zum Neuen Jahr Herr Vater!"

Anna, then 4½, added her scrawl:

"My dear Papa, how do you do? I have begun reading Mrs Bartauld's hymns and now I am reading another pretty book. I am a very naughty girl and promise every day to be better. I hope I really shall be before you come home. Everybody dislikes me. How is vain Don the Duke of Puddledock? Does it eat tallow candles? Anna Way."

"Moscow, Jan 1st. 1818.

"My dearest Mary,

".... It is performed," wrote Lewis Way with elation. "After 3 days and nights on a sledge between a white bear skin and a black bear skin, Ursa Major and Ursa Minor, we arrived at this interesting and extraordinary city on Monday...." It was only six years since the city burnt before the eyes of Napoleon and Lewis described it as "half rebuilt, half in ruins". However, a dwelling of unhewn fir planks was found for him "....built since the fire, all of wood, ceiling, walls and floor, no bricks, no plaster, no paper, one bed, and neither carpet nor curtain. Yet we are warmer than you with all your curtains and carpets and comforts, for if we have nothing else we have double windows and a stove in each room - it is a good **missionary barrack"**.

Maberley drew a sketch of it with a note underneath to the effect that: "This house is situated in the district of Moscow called Metreperoulochpreecheestinker."

Russia and the Russians had begun to penetrate the soul of Lewis Way. Referring to the baby his wife was expecting he wrote, "If there are 2 boys, one is to be Alexander and the other Basil, for those are the names of my good friends Popoff and Galitzin; if one boy, he must receive both names. If it should prove a female, she can be Catherine or Louisa (the latter after the sister of King Frederick Wilhelm III of Prussia, whom he had met in Berlin) whichever you prefer." It did prove female as it happened, and Mrs Way preferred Louisa.

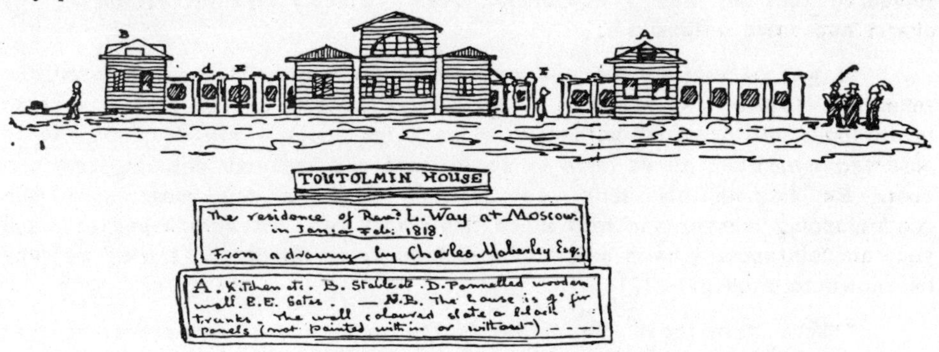

This house was situated in the district of Moscow call Metrepareoulochpreechestinker

"Jan. 3. 1818.

"Soon after six in the evening the courier came as appointed, who was to conduct me to the precise room where I was to wait for His Imperial Majesty. He preceded me in a sledge to the private door of the New Palace in the Kremlin and, on entering, he led me up a long set of stone stairs to the attic storey of the building. There he opened a door into a passage near 100 feet in length,at the end of which a servant opened another door on the side which led into a room with plain walls and plainly furnished, with a table covered with green cloth, candles, pen and ink etc.

"There I was left to my meditations for about 10 minutes when a page came in who spoke only Russian and retired at last without making me out. Next appeared an aide-de-camp who asked my name and desired me to write it, and he then wrote it on another paper. They spoke a few words to me in French, but while these preliminaries were passing yet another person appeared and hearing the word 'L'Empereur' I supposed His Majesty was coming. On expla-nation it seemed I was to follow this fresh person, which I did, through another passage and room full of pages and attendants who, being accustomed, I suppose, to see no other but (members of the) staff in those upper regions, stared at a man in a black coat as a portentous phenomenon. My conductor then opened a **large** door, which he immediately shut upon me and I found my feet were set in a large room in the presence of the first potentate on the face of the globe...."

Czar Alexander I was then 41: tall and dignified, with curling hair, a fresh boyish complexion and eager eyes. But, as if to complement his character, his appearance was singularly lacking in balance. The forehead was a little too broad, the mouth too small, the face too smooth, the hips too wide - almost feminine. Napoleon had once said, "It would be impossible to meet anyone more intelligent than the Emperor Alexander, but there is a piece missing and I have not been able to find out what it is." It was even rumoured that he was a eunuchoid. Lewis immediately fell victim to his charm and naive enthusiasm.

"I was perfectly calm and collected," he wrote. "When I entered the room His Majesty was standing at the fireplace near a large screen, dressed in an upper military coat without star, and high boots. I bowed as soon as he observed me, when he at once came forward and met me not far from the door. He immediately took me by the hand in the most easy and condescending manner and said in English 'Mr Way, I am very happy to make your acquaintance. I have heard of you from our friends and I wish we may be known to each other'.

"There were three long tables in the room and at the corner of that nearest the fire 2 candles and 3 chairs. The Emperor desired me to take one and sit close to him on one side at the angle, as if he would hear best on the right side.

"'I speak English a little,' said the Czar, 'and understand what I read in that language, but on subjects of such nature as those on which I converse with you I cannot express myself as I wish, and may sometimes use French....'" "Your Majesty speaks English very correctly" replied Lewis, "but I shall understand French, though not sufficiently accustomed to that language to speak it with propriety."

Lewis at once launched into his favourite theme and expressed the hope that all monarchs should jointly undertake to grant protection and equality to the Jews. Alexander was due to attend an international congress at Aix-la-Chapelle later that year, and Lewis suggested that he try to introduce a clause into the Protocol which was designed, among oither things, to admit France into the Quadruple Alliance. 'A difficult matter,' nodded the Czar, 'there are many clashing interests. But you may be assured that I will do all in my power to assist it. I consider your coming to Russia as a providential concurrence of circumstances: each must do his part; and in time, by the blessing of God, all will be achieved.' Already a new cause was taking shape in Alexander's mind which might further his image as an international arbiter, and was bound, by the same token, to sting Metternich, Castlereagh and the other pragmatists into more charges of 'sublime mysticism and claptrap'.

Lewis was ecstatic. "I shall never forget the sweet expression of his countenance as he spoke those words. He took my right hand in his left, and held me fast.... what most delighted me was the full conviction of the spirituality of his mind...." Too simple-minded and warm-hearted to take anybody at less than face value, he could not see the shadow of the Baroness Krüdener.

The two men were mutually attracted and spoke with fervour on a large range of topics: from Jews to Gentiles, the Holy Alliance, the Millennium - the Czar reaching again and again for his French Vulgate and reading relevant passages aloud with great vehemence. When he came to the 44th chapter of Isaiah: 'He is my shepherd, and shall perform all my pleasures, even saying to Jerusalem Thou shalt be built, and to the Temple, Thy foundations shall be laid....' he paused, and their eyes met, transfixed by the same thought. As Lewis went back through the bitter night to his 'missionary barrack' in Metreperouloch-preecheestinker, his mind seemed to be on fire, "....to hear the first sovereign upon Earth converse upon such subjects, with the zeal and energy of a missionary, the sagacity of a politician, the dignity of a monarch, and the simplicity of a private individual, is truly a Phenomenon in the present state of the world....He is exactly what Israel wants at present; and so God bless him abundantly".

On three subsequent occasions Lewis sat in solemn conclave with 'The First Sovereign on Earth' before setting out on his travels again. Four months and 967 miles later he was at Odessa on the Black Sea to establish Pastor Solomon among the Jewish community there, and on 18th May he was summoned to meet the Czar again, now at his summer residence at Simferapol in the Crimea.

"....the officer showed me into an anteroom delightfully perfumed by citron and lemon trees in full leaf and fruit. A servant then appeared who opened a folding door into His Majesty's private room. In the middle was a narrow travelling bed, without curtain or ornament; between the windows a dressing table, with razor, long scissors, bell, candle, etc., and on one side, dispatches, and the big Bible I had seen before in four volumes.

"His Majesty met me at the door, and took my hand just as he had done in Moscow and addressed me in English: 'Sit down here, and tell me where you have been and what you have seen'." The Czar poured out a lot about his having visited Jews in their homes, and how to discuss the nature of the Messiah with them, which again left Lewis speechless, "....it is impossible to describe the animation and affability of His Majesty's manner". The Czar begged him to stay and work among the Jews in Russia.

"I have a wife and family whom I want to see, but Pastor Solomon will stay." "**You** have begun, and **you must** go on," said the Czar, and at least extracted a promise from Lewis that he would attend the Congress of Aix-la-Chapelle where he could put his views before the crowned heads of Europe and their plenipotentiaries. At last the Emperor rose, pressed Lewis' hand and bade him goodnight. "I apologised for having stayed so long, by saying that I could not leave till he first gave the sign," wrote Lewis, "and he replied, 'Use no ceremony with me at any time - **we** are friends, and let me know how you go on'. I replied 'Dieu Benira Votre Majesté' and departed."

So, by stages, Lewis Way travelled to the scene of his greatest triumph, through Galicia, Silesia, Moravia, Prague, Vienna, Augsburg, Berne, Lausanne and Geneva, visiting synagogues, Jewish ghettoes and graveyards wherever he could. He eventually reached Paris by Dijon and Fontainebleau where ".... we saw the table on which he (Boney) signed his abdication in favour of the little man we saw in Baden; it is a small mahogany table on one leg, round, and about the size of a tea tray. There is a mark which it is said was made by the Imperial pen- knife which he threw down in a passion...." As for the 'little man' Lewis wrote, "On reaching Paris yesterday at 9 o'clock, I saw Louis XVIII in full cavalcade in his coach and eight; all very handsome and proper. The people pulled off their hats but made no noise. I saw the Austerlitz column on the top of which for 7 years stood the statue of Bonaparte, ten feet high, having cost **cinq mille cent douze livres,** but which was torn down in May 1814. It was replaced by a **fleur-de-lis** 3 feet high which supports a column of 18 feet, on which is placed a **drapeau blanc,** a monument which alike commemorates the bravery of the French and the moderation of the Allied Sovereigns. The Austrians would have destroyed it, being made of their own cannon, but Alexander said 'My troops shall keep it'. So it stands today and is become one of **his** monuments."

The Czar was still Lewis Way's sun and he was moving back into its golden orbit. Travelling via Magdeburg, Potsdam, Frankfurt, Cologne, Coblenz and Mainz, Lewis Way came at last to Aix-la-Chapelle, which was bursting to over-flowing as the allied sovereigns, their ministers, suites and splendid liveried equipages jostled for lodgings in the old cobbled streets; and the rabble that such an assembly attracts - singers, speculators, clairvoyants, supplicants and beggars - swarmed into every bistro and coffee house.

"As to balls, I have been to none: though dancing the Polonaise is walking round a room with a lady. Sunday is the great day for balls .... I was at Duke William's concert with all the monarchs, and last night at Lord Castlereagh's with whom I dine in half an hour today; and also the Emperor....

"....A few nights since I was at the Duke of Wellington's soirée, where I met all the sovereigns. Dear Alexander shook me by the paw like an old friend! and I drank the health of old Eton, with former Etonians, in champagne...."

On 22nd November, the last day of the Congress, Lewis was given the opportunity to put before the assembled potentates of Europe the Manifesto he and the Czar had drawn up for the emancipation of the world's Jews. The passionate speech he made, calling for toleration and Christian charity towards these oppressed people, made a profound impression, especially when, in the heat of the moment, he lapsed unknowingly into English.

"…. what I plead for on behalf of this distressed people, is civil and political freedom: an entrance into the great family of society. It is vain to ask the Jews to become Christian otherwise…. Un édit pouvait emener de cette assemblée des Souverains par lequel un pays serait enfante dans un jour, et une nation naitraît tout d'un coup…." There was a burst of applause and a clause to that end was inserted into the Protocol, and signed by the Emperor of Russia, the King of Prussia, Metternich, Richelieu, Castlereagh, Wellington, Hardenberg, Bernstorff, Nesselrode and Capodistrias.

"It is certain," he wrote later, that such an appeal has not been made for the poor Jews since the days of Mordecai and Esther."

At last he set out for home, after a final farewell to the Czar - they never met again - and in his pocket a gold snuff box presented to him by the assembled statesmen in recognition of his services, and inscribed with their names.

A final delay at Brussels was occasioned by "….the entire decrepitude of my carriage, which is fairly worn out in the service. One wheel is come off 3 times, 2 of the springs are down, and not a timber sound. I shall change or mend it as fast as possible, and fly to you by night and day." And so he came back to Stansted in time to spend Christmas with his delighted family - which now included baby Louisa.

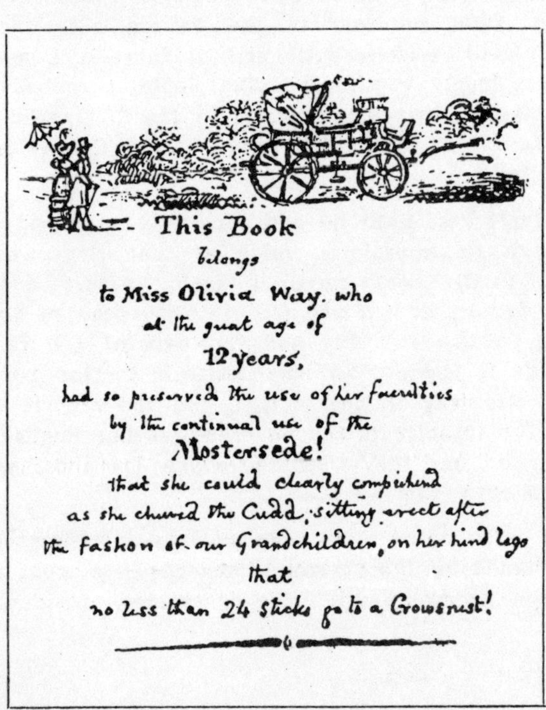

Living "whole centuries in a day": Drusilla in Rome

All that was in 1818. Now let us return to the winter of 1822 when Lewis Way and his family were at Nice. It was not long before other humanitarian causes took possession of his generous nature. On their arrival they found the place full of destitute Italian labourers who had been reduced to begging by a succession of frosts and droughts. The Sardinian government would do nothing for them, so it was left to the well-to-do English community to do what it could. Lady Olivia Sparrow and Lady Mandeville were doing their best by distributing food and money, and Lewis Way thought of a plan by which the men could be employed making a road along the seafront from the mouth of the Paillon to the Croix de Marber, which was then the quarter occupied by the English colony. The entire English community was mobilised into supporting the idea. Lewis Way, of course, bore the expense, for which the Niçois gratefully nicknamed him 'Louis d'Or'; and so was born the **Promenade des** Anglais. But Lewis didn't stay to see the project completed. The plight of the world's Jews again intervened. Already in Nice he had sought them out in their ghetto.

"....We had, last Sunday, the wonder of the Chief Rabbi attending the chapel," wrote Mrs Way to her mother, "when Lewis preached a most striking, excellent sermon. He (the Rabbi) does not speak English, but a Jew who does sat by him and showed him the reference to Scripture, explaining the appli- cation. He took Dilla to the synagogue where they fortunately met with a wedding. Dilla was put in the gallery with the bride and her attendants, all dressed in white satin and fit for a ball, and the chanson du mariage was most loudly vociferated. The Rabbi, perceiving Lewis, sent for him and placed him by his side, pointing to the 2nd psalm 'Sit thou on my right hand'. He was delighted with Dilla reading Hebrew and said she was 'belle comme la lune'."

Lewis couldn't rest until he had personally examined the possibility of returning the Jews to Jerusalem, which at that time was in the Turkish Empire, so the family was uprooted again. Albert and Drusilla would accompany their father; Aunt Kitty and Mr Nosworthy to Rome to indulge in some sightseeing; while Mrs Way and the rest of the family were to be wintered in a villa in Lucca. "My only desire is to find a cool place for the children," wrote Mrs Way to her mother, "as the reports of the heat here are formidable. The inhabitants say no creatures but English people and dogs **move** in the summer, and they sleep the whole day under every wall or tree which affords a shadow, and work all night."

Lewis and party sailed to Leghorn and reached Florence in March 1823. Drusilla was intrigued by the statues. "Yesterday we went to the Duomo or Cathedral, a large handsome pile, full of statues of saints. Over the high altar is an immense marble statue of the Bon Dieu (as they say) contemplating the figure of the dead Christ before it. This disgusted us much, particularly Papa...." Drusilla was even more disgusted by the Venus de Medici. "The Venus is just the one in the dressing room at Stansted, broken by the cat," she wrote to her mother, "Aunt Kitty may say what she will about the Venus, but it is not worth your coming to see. Indeed, no **lady** ought to look at or speak of either the Venus or Apollo Belvedere, in my opinion. She is most shamefacedly bold I think. As to the Venus, she looks just like what she is, and ought to be. **A naked woman thoroughly ashamed of herself! Perfect Nudity** I never saw before, and how ladies can stand **looking** and **staring** and **admiring** with **gentlemen** at it, I cannot conceive, and **I hope I never shall."**

Much more to her taste were the "....delicious drives out of town in the style of the parks in London and the Champs Elysees at Paris. We there saw the Grand Duke's carriage with his two sons". The Grand Duke of Tuscany was Ferdinand III of Hapsburg-Lorraine, a dotty old freak who died a year or two later. His son, Leopold II was a little more congenial, and was often to be seen bumbling about his vineyards in his gaiters and traditional straw hat of Tuscany. Of all the detested Austrian rulers of Italy at that time he was probably the most tolerant, in fact he was reprimanded by Metternich for allowing his secret police to be so ineffective.

Albert found Florence "....a most handsome city, clean, streets all flagged, myriads of palaces with the appearance of prisons - and has quite the guise of a capital." Lewis, of course, had his own affairs to attend to. "Our father and self," Albert continued, "went early to the Jewish quarter. Though they are separated in this part of the town, they enjoy many more privileges under the Tuscan government than elsewhere, and one of them is said to be richer than all the princes. The synagogue was a neat and pretty little building. The Rabbi was ill, but his son and his family received us cordially in the garret storey of a most miserable and filthy abode, and accepted books...." Then follows a long description of the galleries, with illustrations and plans.

"My dear Mother, Nous voila! At length we have attained to this mighty Capital," wrote Albert, in exultation, as the party arrived in Rome. "We entered the Compagna di Roma, a desolate flat, uncultivated to the very walls of Rome. The people are more ferocious and murky in their appearance, and everything looks wretched and barbarous.... Rome soon appeared, situated rather in a hollow, for the hills of Rome are those of moles.... it was about 5 when we arrived, and after passports and douane* we hunted in vain for lodging for between 2 and 3 hours, hotels full long ago.

* This was the territory of the Pope, who at that time ruled the whole of central Italy as a secular Prince.

"At last we got rooms, not over gay to be sure, but very passable and a most civil host and wife who waited on us most sedulously.

"We were in time for one ceremony on Friday in the Sistine Chapel, singing most beautiful. Dill went with the Carnarvons to Miserere, and at night a vast cross formed of lamps was suspended from the interior of the Dome of St. Peter's.... which was very fine, but what sort of religion!

"Saturday we witnessed the baptism of a Jew which is done every year...." Drusilla, meanwhile, was satisfying her curiosity about naked statues. In the Vatican, she says,

"I ran on to the room where the Apollo stands in solitary majesty, and gave it that examination which I **could not do** in company, and being the masterpiece of sculpture, I thought I should like to know what people were thinking of while talking of the Apollo.... It is truly a wonderful statue, and worthy of its character; but **fie** on those ladies who dare to look at and speak of it in the terms they do!"

"Dilla," wrote her father, "has been a very good interpreter. She is quite up to Quanto domandate? and Quanti cosi?" - which was facetious, of course, for she was quite fluent already.

"We live here whole centuries in a day," wrote Dilla to her mother. "I have been introduced to Cardinal Gonsalvi and the Pope and the Neapolitan Ambassador. At a ball we attended we saw 20 Cardinals" - who evidently did not think it beneath their dignity to attend such functions; in fact they were also seen at the card tables. "The Pope was dressed in the most dirty, snuffy, old flannel dressing gown imaginable. He was very courteous, but his appearance most abject." This was Pius VII, Chiamamonti, whom Napoleon had carried off to Fontainebleau and bullied into surrendering his temporal estates. Restored to Rome in 1815, he was now a frail old man, who showed the greatest partiality for English visitors, bestowing upon them an affectionate embrace instead of the customary toe-kissing. Indeed, English visitors were admitted when Italians were refused, so that the latter would sometimes plead 'Inglese' in order to be allowed a pass. Lewis presented His Holiness with his "Memoires sur L'Etat des Israélites", and drew his attention to the fact that 300 Jews were every Sunday compelled to listen to the preaching of a priest or monk at St. Angelo Pescari. "This is an old law revived," he wrote indignantly to his wife, "against these long-suffering people."

"The day before we left Rome we had the happiness and content of seeing His Holiness," wrote Dilla, "but were not near enough to kiss his toe. He was returning from his daily drive. All the people in the streets knelt as he passed. We followed him into his garden entrance to the palace and saw him descend, wrapped in scarlet, with an immense scarlet hat, into a scarlet chair, with a canopy over it, in which he was conveyed away."

Lewis and Albert, meanwhile, left Rome for Naples, having secured the services of Giave, a Greek, and brother of the Patriarch of Lebanon, as interpreter, for their journey to the Holy Land. "He is a Catholic, educated in propaganda, but quite a Protestant in reality," wrote Albert, "not esteeming miracles, saints, images, relics or the like, but says he must think for himself. He knows the Eastern tongues well but has no common language with us but Latin and Italian. In the former our father communicates easily, and myself in the latter. It is a great advantage to be obliged to speak it. We left the dear ladies at 8 on Thursday to the conduct of our Nos."

Drusilla had set her heart on accompanying her father and brother to the Holy Land, but the interpreter said that the monasteries, which were the only hotels in those parts, could not accommodate ladies. "We were all sorry to turn our backs on Rome without seeing Naples, but when Papa was leaving there were so many idle reports of robberies and banditti raised, merely to keep the English in Rome, that he did not like to take us further...." Just as well; the horses proved so weak and worn out that Lewis, Albert and the dragoman had to walk 7 miles up the hills, "....in despair that the carriage would follow...." Nor could they obtain accommodation and were obliged to spend the next two nights in lofts, in which they slept in their clothes.

"By the way, our Dad has had his bust taken in Rome," wrote Dilla to her mother, "but you will not see it, as it goes straight to Stansted. The likeness is perfectly ridiculous. In short, I never saw such a **second self.** I wish we had it with us during his **long, long** absence, it is really consolatory.

"I have writ this in great haste. Nos, being all in a fidget to go to the Gallery, as indeed I am.... Pray let the pianoforte be packed with care; love to all: farewell,

"Your loving Daughter,

"D. Way."

The Grand Duchy of Tuscany

Drusilla, Aunt Kitty and Nos made their way back to Florence by 'vettura', the best that Italy of that period could offer by way of public transport, before the railway, "....a most tedious but not unpleasant mode of travelling. We had the whole inside to ourselves, and without, a busy Austrian officer* and an English-man who were no annoyance to us. Our vetturino was very civil and attentive to us, which was a great comfort, our Nos being helpless as an infant.

"....our vetturino came to wake us every morning at 3 and 4, and hurrying into the vettura with all our roba. We went dawdling, on a foot's pace till 12 or 1, when the mules rested for 2 or 3 hours and we **breakfasted.** Then, setting out again, we went on at **waggon** rate till 7 when **dinners dreadful** and **beds beastly beyond all comparison** closed the day. This had been our mode of life for 6 days; and to find ourselves again once more in rooms which we can inhabit without disgust and with food we can eat without nausea, is truly luxurious.... Our journey has been most prosperous; our Nos very amusing and amiable...."

In Florence Drusilla sneaked another look at the Venus de Medici and related with relish that at the Hôtel de Suisse, where they stayed, "....wicked Queen Caroline passed 8 days with **her** Bergami, or 'Caro Barone' as the people there called him.** The children who followed us were full of histories of them, telling us how she **kissed** him etc. Her example has been duly followed since as every little **brat** of 10 years old and under has his **Amoroso.** It would have amused you to have heard the gallantries of the cicerone to me all the way. I rode Queen Caroline's ass and English saddle which I hope has not contaminated me."

Meanwhile, Mrs Way, with the four younger children, their nurse, 'the heavy' and Drusilla's harp and pianoforte, were loaded on to the steam packet at Nice. There were only two cabins and the children were packed into one with their nurse and Mrs Way was given, by common consent, the

* Italy was subject at this time to direct or indirect Austrian control, and Austrian troops were much in evidence following the Carbonarist risings in 1820-21.

** The estranged wife of George IV, she travelled on the continent, 1814-20, with an Italian courier. Their immoralities were exposed in the celebrated trial of the Queen in the House of Lords, 1820, when she returned to England to demand her rights on the accession of her husband. Proceedings were dropped against her in the face of much public support for her cause. She was barred from the Coronation, 1821, and died soon afterwards.

only sofa available in the other, which has "....benches with cushions all round, on which the other passengers reposed, among whom were a French lady, a curious old French man who announced that he had been Mayor of Nice under Bonaparte; a Persian count, and a Nizan perfumer; these stationed themselves in different ways for the night, altogether making a curious cabin scene, which alas was soon heightened by the introduction of as many basins and tin tubs, which were very needful as the wind being unfavourable we had a wretched sick party.... and the poor dear children too were wretched during the whole passage, which was much prolonged as the wind impeded our progress".

After twenty-four hours of misery they arrived at Genoa, but had to remain in the harbour and no one was allowed to land until they had been inspected by the health officer. "We were therefore obliged to make ourselves as comfortable as we could without undressing a second night."

The next morning at seven they were summoned on deck for the inspection and were then allowed to make for a hotel where they rested from Sunday to Wednesday, and then embarked for Leghorn. The wind was still contrary, and they were unable to leave harbour until Friday when, suffering acute discomfort, they were blown into the Gulf of Spezia and went aground in the mud. An entire day was spent in extricating the vessel and finally they reached Leghorn, which they found "a hot, dusty, disagreeable place, quite given up to trade, with scarcely a tree to be seen, and no walks by the sea or anywhere; bugs and mosquitoes abound, which sadly torment us....".

But the family, reunited with Drusilla, Aunt Kitty and Mr Nosworthy, soon recovered their spirits, and Mrs Way went on to relate matters close to her husband's heart.

"We visited the synagogue in Leghorn, which is one of the finest in Europe, and not less than 15,000 Jews reside in Leghorn. The Cathedral is small and poor; the English and Dutch cemeteries more interesting. We left on the 23rd and the same horses took us all the way to Lucca. We rested 3 hours at Pisa to see the handsome Cathedral, Baptistry, Leaning Tower and Campo Santo, a large, square burying-place with a handsome cloister all round, painted al fresco and full of monuments; and the ground within the cloister is filled 7 feet deep with earth from Jerusalem, which some pious devotee had in ship-loads from the Holy Land many centuries ago."

Anna collected some of the holy earth and the family clambered aboard 'the heavy' for the last part of the journey, seventeen miles along the valley of the Serchio, past broad meadows of corn, hemp, flax and lupins, and "rows of high poplars cut off so as to form a support for the most luxuriant, double, sweeping festoons of vines".

The Little Duchy of Lucca

The situation of the house they had taken at Bagni delle Villa was graphically described by Mrs Way to her mother.

"We are on the side of the mountains, so steep that a carriage cannot come to our house, and below us, close by, is the Palace of the Grand Duchess of Lucca* where she is expected in a few days, and then we shall have a band of music every evening before our house. This is considered the coolest part of Italy, the mountains being so high that we neither see the sun rise nor set, and lose it at 6 o'clock, and have not its full range before 8, which gives us a long, cool night, being so lengthened by the twilight.

"We have an Italian master. Drusilla seems very happy here, and sketches, draws, plays the harp and pianoforte etc., having made the attempt of going with her Father, and giving it up by his opinion, she is contented...."

The earnest Mr Whitby and Marianne joined them and conducted morning service, but Mrs Way hesitated to ask him to do a second one each day "as he is not strong and suffers from fatigue, therefore I read the servants a sermon in the afternoon".

The tranquil scene was transformed a few days later by the arrival of the Court and one of Mrs Way's most entertaining letters captures the intimate and homely character of one of the most minute of all the ancient princi-palities of Europe. "The Palace, being so very close that the children of the Royal Party talk with my children in their respective windows, and the grand suite and ceremony attending the Court, their guards and sentinels, numerous carriages and attendants, keep up an incessant bustle.

"The Duchess and King (her son) and Queen of Etruria appear very agreeable, extremely devout, attending 2 or 3 masses a day. They do not receive or visit strangers, or mix in any way, but attending the theatre, which is a private one belonging to a Russian Nobleman, said to be the richest subject in Europe, as I have heard from good authority, he has £1,000 **a Day.** He is the best friend of the gay people, having 2 balls, 2 plays and 2 grand dinners a week. We were invited but declined. The play is as full as possible and very gay. I should think 2/3rds of the summer birds are

* Lucca was an anomaly which had somehow survived the territorial up-heavals of 1797-1815. The Grand Duchess was the Spanish Maria Luiza of Bourbon-Parma, widow of Louis, King of Etruria, a kingdom created by Napoleon in 1801 out of the Grand Duchy of Tuscany. Maria Luiza was later ousted in favour of Eliza Buonaparte, Napoleon's sister and her Italian husband. When the Grand Duchy of Tuscany was re-established in 1814, Lucca was retained as a separate principality for Maria Luiza and her son, Carlo Ludovico.

English and the company appears genteel and good. The Evening Promenade is the pleasantest time, from 6 to 8.

"The Duchess has innumerable horses and carriages, and a landau with 6 horses and 3 others with 4 each, take her and her suite with a great train of attendants. We enter our carriage at the same time and place and it is no small amusement to us to bring up the rear in the old Stansted 'heavy' and you may imagine how pleased the children are with the gay scene."

Lewis in Lebanon

The journey to the Holy Land on which Lewis Way had set such high hopes was beset with frustration and disappointments. While waiting for their vessel 'Hebe' at Naples, he and Albert had time to visit Pompeii and Herculaneum, then little known to travellers. Albert, as usual, wrote detailed and illustrated accounts of both places to his mother which, he was advised, would arrive in Lucca sooner if sent via England!

They sailed via Malta. "We had all, I believe, figured this hot rock, as father calls it, to be high, cliffy and barren. Instead it appears flat, the shores rocky, devoid of trees, but few spots uncultivated. The first object that we beheld was 4 pirates swinging on their gibbets."

They landed at Valetta and made an excursion to St. Paul's Bay. "We traversed a most singular country, thickly peopled, and saw numerous churches which are handsomely built. There is little verdure, most of it being brown, and only here and there a carobeus fig. The corn grows short and seemed almost ripening, and indeed everything savours of the hot rock. The men are of a mahogany colour, but the womenfolk preserve their complexion by an extraordinary fashion for a hot climate - a black silk shawl thrown over the head which is the guise of all without variety, and the more respectable are entirely in black. Giave (the dragoman) says it is the fashion likewise in Egypt. All the community are shoeless except those who adopt the luxury of sandals." On reaching the bay the three travellers discussed the exact locality of the Apostle's shipwreck. "They show St. Paul's fountain at the spot where he was brought ashore and the church where he delivered his first discourse, which contains many tolerable old paintings of the event."

Their voyage proceeded uneventfully but on approaching the coast of Syria the party learned that the plague had broken out in Jerusalem and Alexandria. It was a bitter disappointment, but making the best of it they landed at Sidon, instead of Jaffa, and having an introduction to Lady Hester Stanhope, 'The Nun of Lebanon', they made their way to the mountain retreat she had made her home.

"The Daughter of the King of England"

This alarming and eccentric lady was the niece of Pitt, and as hostess at No.10 Downing Street, 1803-06, she had been at the very centre of politics in an age which radiated talent and wit. The experience had so widened her horizons that on the death of her uncle she found she could no longer tolerate the constricted life that an aristocratic maiden lady was obliged to lead, and she left the country, never to return. Europe was barred to her because of Napoleon, so she made for the Levant. After a scandalous love affair with Michael Bruce, son of a Scottish baronet and many years her junior (with whom she was briefly, in 1812, shipwrecked on the island of Rhodes) she cut herself off from her family and settled with a few faithful retainers in a half-ruined convent high up on the slopes of Mount Lebanon, a position which suited her imperious and autocratic spirit.

She adopted oriental dress and manners, and rapidly acquired immense power and influence over the local Arab community, among whom she travelled totally without fear. Even the bloodthirsty Prince of the Druses, on whose mountain she made her home, failed to daunt her, despite the fact that he had grasped his position by the torture and mutilation of scores of his relations. "Tell him he is a dog and a monster," she said to his emissary and he, together with the other pashas of the region, gave her a wide berth, believing her to be 'The Daughter of the King of England',

In the winter of 1813, accompanied by her lover, her doctor and an immense band of camp followers, she travelled across the Syrian deserts to the lost city of Palmyra. Civil war among the Bedouin tribes was endemic, but she took no armed escort and trusted totally to the goodwill of the local sheikhs, handsomely lubricated, it must be said, by large sums of money she had extricated from Michael Bruce's father by ingenious letters saying it was all for the good of his son's education! She wanted to be the first European woman to set foot in Palmyra and she had her glory. A huge throng of Bedouins, naked to the waist, greeted her, escorted her dancing and singing, down the processional way, and at the triumphal arch placed a wreath on her head. She already saw herself as a second Zenobia*. Some years before, when in England, a clairvoyant had predicted that she "would go to Jerusalem and be crowned 'Queen of the East'." The prophecy now seemed to be fulfilled, and a second followed later when Metta, an Arab mystic whom she had taken into her household as a doctor, produced a little book of prophecies in which it said that 'A European woman would come to the East, and live on Mount Lebanon, and, on the coming of the Mahdi he would ride into Jerusalem on a horse born saddled, and escorted by a woman'. As the orient gradually took possession of her mind, Lady Hester saw herself in the role. Were not all the religions of the Middle East saying the same thing? A second coming? A Messiah? A Mahdi? It was all one and the same, and the downfall of earthly princes which would precede this celestial Kingdom, was surely indicated by the Buonaparte system. The birth of a hollow backed foal to one of her Arab mares seemed to prove her theories to be true, and 'Luli' as it was called, was kept in a sacred stall, fed, watered and surrounded by blossoms, awaiting the Messiah to ride her saddle-less into Jerusalem. Lewis Way was about to find himself another soul mate, but Lady Hester could be an exacting hostess.

Her neurotic temperament and sharp tongue increased in proportion to the fading of her personal beauty and shrinking wealth - a process accelerated by the disappearance of Bruce, no doubt fed up with her eternal fussing over his health and his underlinen, and an attack of the plague which had nearly cost her her life. But her intellectual powers, moulded by some of the sharpest minds of the age, survived untarnished and, starved of society, she took an almost insane delight in haranguing her visitors and abusing her servants. She subjected those intrepid travellers who braved the journey up the steep and rocky mountain path, to the brilliance of her monologue for eight to ten hours without stopping; ranging from the iniquities of British politics (since, no doubt, she had ceased to have any influence on them); the uselessness of women (Pitt had once said that if she had been a man he would have given her the command of an army of 50,000!); and the vulgarity of the middle class, to the despicable habits of diplomats who used their position to make money (which did not endear her to the British Consuls at

* Zenobia, Queen of Palmyra, famed for her beauty, masculine energy and sensational powers of mind. She defied the Romans and occupied Egypt, but was defeated by the Emperor Aurelian in AD 272, and spent the rest of her life in honorable captivity

Beirut, Aleppo and elsewhere). She lectured one unfortunate gentleman for so many hours that he fainted from fatigue. On summoning her servants to his assistance she remarked coolly that he had been overcome listening to the state of disgrace to which his country was reduced by its ministers.

Abstemious in her habits and shunning all luxuries, she was totally oblivious to the comfort of her guests. She usually expected them to stand while, wearing a red fez, she lounged on a divan smoking a pipe from which sparks showered on to the counterpane and burnt holes in it, and servants, slaves and eunuchs were prostrated around her in attitudes of oriental servility. From time to time she grabbed at the convent bell which she rang with a violence which seemed to rock the whole building, a performance which spun her household into bursts of frenzied activity, accompanied by yelling from her Ladyship and a few well directed blows with a mace. "Scarcely a night passed without a disturbance," said her long-suffering doctor. For servants she preferred Syrians because, although they stole from her and were dirty, they were obsequious and required no definite hours for repose. She couldn't afford her retinue and the doctor constantly urged her to send them away for they were only a torment to her. "Yes, but my rank," was her characteristic answer.

Lewis seems to have had the usual reception. The building, surrounded by labyrinthian outhouses, was sordid inside and out, and stank of cats. The only furniture in the room into which he was shown was a rough sofa, a rush-bottomed chair and an unpainted deal table with no cloth. The only ornaments appeared to be medicine bottles, and a mass of dirty books and papers covered with dust.

Lady Hester esconced herself on the sofa and Lewis was granted the great privilege of the rush-bottomed chair. It was then 3 p.m. He was treated to the usual shafts of vituperative sarcasm, but for intellectual stamina and verbosity Lady Hester had met her match. Once the conversation turned to the Millennium the two found they had much in common and the interview went on until daybreak the next morning, when Lewis, with shattered nerves and aching limbs, was allowed to retire to an outhouse. With regard to the Second Coming, Lady Hester, and after that extraordinary session Lewis also, believed that they had a vital part to play. Lady Hester even gave Lewis an

Arab mare, one of the sacred breed, on which to ride into Jerusalem on the divinely appointed day. She named it 'Metwell' in honour of his visit, and in the meantime he was allowed to roam around the bare mountainside on it.

"Lady Hester provides all for me, like a mother, wife, sister and brother and is, I trust, placed here like a Deborah," he wrote to his wife. "She has given me her best Arabian mare and lends me all her other horses and servants as I want them, and as I am partaker of her temporal, I hope she will be made partaker of my spiritual benefits. She is altogether a wonderful woman, and her Kindness to me is extraordinary...."

Lewis was not the only one to benefit from Lady Hester's hospitality. In 1827 (three years later) when the great powers found themselves at war with Turkey over the Greek question, Mehemet Ali, Pasha of Egypt, invaded Lebanon, and thousands of terrified Europeans fled to Lady Hester's mountain retreat. She sheltered and fed them at her own expense, an episode the British Government conveniently forgot when, in 1837, they cancelled her pension on the grounds that she had not honoured her debts to local merchants and money-lenders. On that occasion she wrote a spirited letter to Queen Victoria, which was ignored:

"Djonn, Mount Lebanon.
"Feb. 12. 1838

"Madam,

"Your Majesty will allow me to say that few things are more disgraceful and inimical to loyalty than giving commands without examining all their different bearings, and casting without reason an aspersion upon the integrity of any branch of a family who had faithfully served their country and the house of Hanover.

"As no enquiries have been made of me what circumstances induced me to incur the debts alluded to, I deem it unnecessary to enter into any details upon the subject. I shall not allow the pension given by your Royal Grandfather to be stopped by force, but I shall resign it for the payment of my debts, and with it the name of English subject, and the slavery that is at present annexed to it, and, as your Majesty had given publicity to the business by your orders to Consular Agents, I surely cannot be blamed for following your Royal example.

"Hester Lucy Stanhope"

Less than a year later, abandoned by her servants and wracked by terrible coughing, she died alone in her mountain slum.

Ways & Means

Lewis Way's voyage back to Italy was destined to stretch his stamina to the very limits, and sometimes beyond. Already fatigued by the rigours of Mount Lebanon and disheartened by the failure of his mission to Jerusalem, their ship was then blown this way and that by contrary winds. The crew were illiterate Genoese, there was nothing to eat "but stale bread, common rice and the starved poultry of Syria", and no fellow travellers with whom to share their troubles. Albert, so keen on the outward journey, was now openly homesick.

"I long to see you, dearest Mother, sisterhood and relations to the furthest degree of consanguinity, at home or abroad, with excessive longings. I am your constant advocate, pleading that we may be incarcerated at Leghorn where we may look on one another and talk through a grille, and if any kind soul likes to join loving hands through the bars we shall be sure of a companion in prison, and medicament for our weariness.

"My father is much fatigued by the voyage, the tossings and shakings, but I hope he will be recovered by the sight of you all. Our abode in this moving jail has been a time affording no comfort but the prospect of termination. Plague, pestilence and the like evils we have been free from, but 'famine' has been our portion - evil are the shores of Canaan! We have had contrary winds all along, but some hours more calms than storms.

"NB: **Calms** are by no means **calm**, but are most horrible and untold tossings!"

They hoped to reach Valetta but offshore winds again frustrated them, and at last they reached Syracuse in Sicily. All the passengers from the east were subject to quarantine as the plague was still raging in Syria, and a further term of 'imprisonment' was only slightly mitigated by the change of diet and contact with other Europeans.

"They only who have shared their daily bread with maggots can know how to estimate a fresh and wholesome loaf, the sight and taste of which was marvellously grateful to our empty stomachs, but that which refreshed me most was the sound of an English voice and the tidings of modern Europe, which I collected from the English Consul, with whom I was only permitted to converse as outlandish animals are addressed at Exeter Change: through a strong fence and at a distance of several feet, for this is all the intercourse allowed to fresh-comers from Syria."

The vessel continued in due course to Leghorn where Lewis and Albert were again incarcerated in the lazaretto until the period of quarantine was over. Mrs Way and her two eldest daughters left the Court at Lucca and voluntarily joined her husband and son. To her mother:

"....Here we are safely arrived at one o'clock today. In the Lazaretto we have little to complain of as we are allowed to walk in the outer courts and fields, and to go out in the large boat belonging to the vessel which brought Lewis from Syria, in which, in fine weather, we had a pleasant row of 2 hours daily. However, the place got so full of all nations, sick people, etc. that we were heartily rejoiced to be set at liberty the 25th day and to rejoin the dear children."

The family, re-united at last, decided to return to Nice. Lewis couldn't stomach any more sea journeys and hoped to re-establish his health by riding his Arab horses. In case of bad weather a small carriage was engaged in which Drusilla and Aunt Kitty travelled. The rest of the family, the Whitbys, servants and 'the heavy' embarked on the brig 'Anitzia'. The story of how the ship was driven ashore in a gale; how the indefatigable Mrs Way had 'the heavy' disembarked and then proceeded to cross the Alps with four small children and no courier, is best told in her own words.

The litel girl going on board the Packet.

"Towards next evening (the 2nd of our voyage) a gale sprang up which increased violently and carried us within 30 miles of Nice, and we were cheered with the hope that we should be here by noon on Friday; but alas, a violent siroc wind arose and drove us back again and a wretched night we have of it: wind, rain, thunder, lightning, and I was afraid the children would be thrown out of their beds, as the tossing was so violent I could scarce keep my berth. Towards Friday afternoon the gale being little diminished and appearing to threaten another rough night, the Captain took refuge in a little bay where 10 other vessels in the same plight had anchored. Here he said we might stay probably 3 or 4 days as the siroc winds generally continued so long. The prospect was not agreeable as all had suffered so much, and a new cause of anxiety arose as the great anchor of the ship failed, and a smaller one was the only dependence, which in a little open bay was an anxious prospect with the threatening appearance of the weather. Some of the party were much alarmed (Mr

Whitby and Miss Wells) and most anxious to land. I consulted the Captain and he gave me his opinion that the winter was begun and we had better go by land, as even if the weather enabled him to sail towards Nice the next day, we should probably be driven back again, as the sea is so rough and the wind so variable in the Gulf of Genoa.

"I felt very unwilling to give up the attempt; however, we attempted to land for the night at Vedo where we found a wretched little inn which just accommodated us. The next day, the wind continuing the same, we landed the carriage and proceeded to travel by land - a most formidable and tedious journey.

"We spent Sunday quietly at Savona, and Monday Nov. 3rd set forth on our journey rather nervous at the undertaking before us, not having our courier, who I left to attend Lewis and the Ladies from Leghorn, and John ('The Duke of Puddledock'), Mr Whitby and Albert being our only other male attendants; but the dear little man after his travels is quite a host in himself and managed excellently.

"Savona is an extremely pretty town in a beautiful bay. On leaving it we passed through a most picturesque country along the winding of a river with beautiful rocks and woody mountains. The road at first good, but soon became extremely rough and hilly. We rested at noon at Millesimo, where, seeking an inn or house to eat our luncheon which we always carry for the children's dinner, seeing two neat young women in a clean house, we asked admittance, which was courteously granted, and ascending the stairs we were informed we were in the Palazzo of the Countess of Caretto who was from home.

"Speedily the table was laid with napkins, plate, fruit cakes, delicious wines etc. where we spread our viands and made our repast. We were waited on by the young women and a respectable man, apparently Major Domo.

"I mention this as an instance of foreign courtesy and difference from English manners. After our meal we again set forth and slept at Ceva; next day passed through a beautiful country, dined at Mondova, and slept at Coni or Cuneo with stupendous mountains covered with snow before us, which we were to pass, and were thrown into sad alarm for some hours by a report that they were impassable. However, on arrival at Coni we were rejoiced to hear that the diligence had arrived, and the road was yet good. Accordingly by Wednesday, we proceeded a short day's journey to set out early on Thursday for the tremendous passage of the Col di Tende, a most stupendous mountain, the passage of which took 7 hours, and in winter it is only possible on sledges, being generally 25 or 20 feet deep in snow. It is most wonderful how easy the ascent and descent of such mountains is made, though at first the road is most terrific, being a succession of angles with precipices at every turning, at least 100 in number.

"The weather and road were good, and thank God we passed it without any accident. We dined at Tende, a village at the foot of the mountains and hanging rocks out of which the road is hollowed, we arrived at the beautiful village of Chindola where we slept.

"Friday we again set out early, having two mountains of 4 hours each to pass, the first, Monte Briosa, tho' high, after the Col di Tende was nothing, and brought us to Sospello to dinner (having the same horses we were always obliged to rest at that time) after which we set out to cross Monte Briosa, the steepest and most terrific of all. We were 3 hours reaching the summit where we were a whole hour travelling in the clouds. The descent most steep and full of precipices, was rendered more terrific by rapidly approaching darkness as we were an hour too late; but we were mercifully preserved from any alarm or accident, and a friendly lanthorn met us at the foot of the mountain and lighted us to Scavina where we slept last night, and arrived here (Nice) safe at 1 o'clock today.

"Have we not cause of thankfulness, my dear Mother, to have passed such dangers by land and sea and to be brought to our journey's end in health and safety, the dear children all well and ourselves, except fatigue. Here we find a comfortable house taken for us by our friend Lacrois, and prepared for our reception."

In a subsequent letter she comments on the progress of Lewis, Drusilla and Aunt Kitty: "Lewis' journey on horseback was very beneficial to him. He travelled slowly, spent 2 days at Pisa, one at Lucca to see our summer abode, and 3 at Genoa where (meeting many friends) it was a very pleasant change, and they then proceeded by the road called the Corniche along the coast, 3 days of which is performed on mules, not possible in carriages. Lewis' beautiful Arabian carried him delightfully and Drusilla's Bedouin, though she had never carried a lady before, is so tractable and quiet that she mounted her without fear, and rode the chief part of the journey, and they arrived here quite safe and dear Lewis in much improved looks."

The original intention was not to stay abroad indefinitely but to return by slow stages to Stansted. But a new crisis was developing in the affairs of Lewis Way. In the first place his fortune had been so depleted by his travels and numerous acts of charity that the family simply couldn't afford it. Secondly, a serious disagreement broke out between him and the Jewish Society over doctrinal matters. Lewis had unshakeable views on the Second Advent and Millennium. Most of the Society held the traditional view that the Kingdom of Heaven would inaugurate a period of universal peace "in which the Lion would lie down with the Lamb.... etc," and objected to the apocalyptic vision which Lewis shared with many evangelicals of his day that "a general conflagration would accompany the Second Coming, in which **this** heaven and **this** earth would be dissolved by fire. Christ would then rule on earth for a thousand years, after which a final Judgement would take place and the Satanical army would be destroyed".

If Lewis had been prepared to keep this opinion to himself all would have been well, but he published it in a series of tracts called 'Basilicus'. His enemies petitioned the President of the Society that as these matters were 'primarily a matter of individual opinion, it would be more tactful to preach only the simple and essential facts of Christianity, and leave all intricate and controversial matters in abeyance'.

There could be no compromise. The Jewish Society even sent some of its representatives to Paris (whence Lewis had removed himself in the spring of 1824, presumably the better to conduct his defence), but they found him adamant. There could be only one outcome: Lewis, who had dedicated the best years of his life and the greater part of his fortune to the Society, resigned the vice-presidency. He made light of it, writing to the press: "There is an abundance of space in the present world for Abraham, Lot, Judah and Ephraim, Paul and Barnabas, if they disagree.... Go on, then, my friends in the way you judge most expedient. I will never trouble you by my further interference in the management of your concerns. I have enough to do if my life be spared, and as it was devoted to the cause of Israel before I belonged to your Society, it will be so when that connection has ceased....

"My heart, be assured, is still with you, and with your cause and Society. My **head** has perhaps outrun you or itself, but my conscience is free from ill. While you think you are better without Basilicus, he is content to be laid aside - prove him wrong, as you will, or find him right!" But privately he was heartbroken. "....of all my many, many trials, this is the greatest," he wrote. "My soul has been deeply wounded like that of my adored Saviour in the home of my friends."

"What do you think of his resignation?" wrote Drusilla to her brother, "though I need not ask because he said that Atty and Kit had approved of it. I confess that it was painful to me because it is so completely cutting all his former acquaintances and pursuits, and will bring such an imputation of fickleness in him from those who will not enter into his real reasons. I think his being so near home, he might have returned and consulted the Bishops and other friends before sending his conge to the Society."

This letter was written from the Hotel de Provence, Lyons, May 11 1824, to which the family had transferred on their way to join Father, Albert and Aunt Kitty in Paris. "We arrived here yesterday at 12," she continued, "having left Nice the Tuesday preceding.

"The road was bad between Avignon and Vienne, and the scenery more dull and uninteresting than ever. Notwithstanding rain and wind, heat and cold, and other maternal sources of anxiety, I maintained my station in the open carriage all the way and often thought of its former occupants on the same road. One day we had pouring rain, when we enclosed ourselves in the Hole, as Arminger was wont to designate the interior, and Miss Wells and the Ancient of Excessive Worth and equal bulk* were my co-partners in it; and the sulking Mr Haines and the self-sufficient Duke of Puddledock sulked on the box; the Family Heavy with Mother and the 4 within, and 2 maids without, preceding all the way, and the beloved Bergami habilled en courier**, riding on in the true guise of the Gentlemen of his Profession, to order horses, make bargains, quarrel with drivers and abuse innkeepers.

"The Heavy has borne jumbling wonderously, not to say miraculously, and I really think it must be insured against all misadventures. As we arrived at the Post-Houses, often times Anna's long neck was seen to project and the words 'Something's broken in the Heavy' were vociferated. Nevertheless it continues to rumble-tumble on in perfect security, regardless of inward and outward agitation.

"The children have, I believe, comported themselves as usual, with the exception of 'Length' (Anna, now 12) who has behaved herself with great reectitude and sagacity. I imagine her character will become quite

* Probably Betty, the cook.

** The family had evidently nicknamed their courier after the notorious courier and lover of Queen Caroline.

formed, now she looks forward to **settling in life**, for perhaps you do not know that she has formed an attachment for Distraction which partakes of the Nature of 'Your's to Death'. At least, so she professed when at Nice, but I have great fears of the effects of Time and Absence. Flowers, shells, stones, Jerusalem earth from Pisa, were interchanged with the most greyish superscriptions you can conceive:

for Mr willium grahAm

"Georgie (Georgiana, then aged 5) shows much more affinity to the Satanic than the Angelic order, I fear. The Second Day of Travel she told Mother she would do everything to 'unplease' her, a word which savours strongly of ye Great Enemy's Vocabulary and speaks volumes on ye depravity of Man!"

Means and Ways

So the family journeyed to Paris, where a piece of good fortune awaited them. An uncle of Mrs Way had died leaving her £25,000; there were also handsome legacies for Lewis and Drusilla. This more than solved their financial problems. They could have returned at once to Stansted and resumed the life style to which they were accustomed, but Lewis meanwhile had found another cause to champion. There was at this time no regular church for English residents in Paris. "There are," Lewis wrote, "at the lowest computation 1,500 residents and sojourners of our nation in this city. The Ambassador's Room, where service is performed, cannot hold 300. Servants and tradesmen never go there, and I am told a school of young ladies has been excluded for want of room...."

What he sought was a room capable of holding 1,000, licensed for worship according to the Anglican Church. He applied in vain to the French Prime Minister, de Villèle, who made evasive promises until he finally announced that if Louis XVIII granted such a request it would give great offence to the Roman Catholic population. The permission might only be obtained if the King of England were to write directly to the King of France to request him, as a personal favour, to allow the English to have a place of worship in Paris.

Lewis sent Dr. Marsh, an old friend, to Sir William Knighton, physician to the Prince Regent and now his private secretary, and through his influence a letter was written and permission was obtained. Lewis at once bought the Hôtel Marboeuf* in the Rue Chaillot, which leads from the Champs Élysées to the Place de Mars, and at his own expense transformed the large hall adjoining (which had formerly served as a café for the 'Jardins Marboeuf') into a chapel. He installed his family in the 'hôtel' and conducted services in person, Drusilla assisting as organist.

* Hôtel: the word in French has a wider meaning than in English. In this sense it means a large private town house.

The Chapel Marboeuf very quickly became the centre of the English community in Paris. Crowds of up to five hundred flocked to hear Lewis' sermons, and from all sides tributes poured in testifying to the eloquence of his address and the reverential manner in which services were conducted.

"I went this morning to hear Lewis Way preach," wrote Lady Granville, wife of the British Ambassador, to Lady Morpeth. "His sermons are extempore; he is evangelical and very striking and impressive. The English flock there. If anyone whispers he stops and says 'When Lady Such-and-such has done talking, I will proceed'. His sermon began today with a little warning to those delegated by their Sovereign to represent him to take heed of their conduct and conversation."

And in August 1824, some curious relations, attracted in large measure by the magnetism of Lewis Way and his diverting family, arrived in Paris.

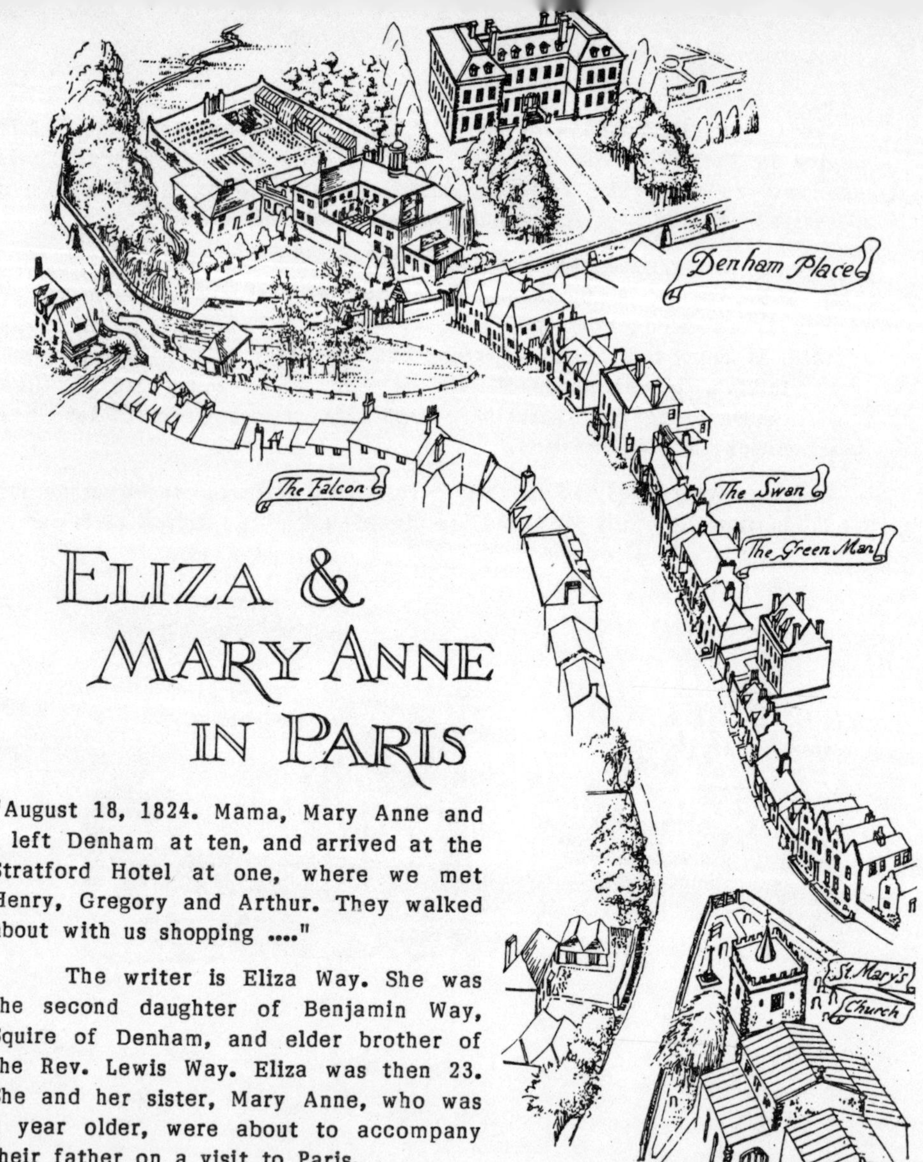

ELIZA & MARY ANNE IN PARIS

"August 18, 1824. Mama, Mary Anne and I left Denham at ten, and arrived at the Stratford Hotel at one, where we met Henry, Gregory and Arthur. They walked about with us shopping ...."

The writer is Eliza Way. She was the second daughter of Benjamin Way, Squire of Denham, and elder brother of the Rev. Lewis Way. Eliza was then 23. She and her sister, Mary Anne, who was a year older, were about to accompany their father on a visit to Paris.

Both sisters kept detailed diaries of the trip in clothbound exercise books: Eliza's in a neat and rounded hand was in marked contrast to the sloping, masculine scrawl of her elder sister. The two girls were devoted to each other but very different in character. Eliza was pretty, vivacious and high-spirited, and she overflowed with comical asides which kept her brothers and sisters in fits of laughter. Mary Anne was the bossy, managing type. She was more enterprising than Eliza and determined to squeeze every ounce of enjoyment from the trip. She was observant and practical and possessed of endless stamina. Unlike the children of Lewis Way, their country cousins from Denham were provincial and unsophisticated. The flow of words committed by the sisters to their floppy clothbound books is always lively and uninhibited and betrays all the prejudices of their age and class.

Their father, Benjamin Way, was a typical country squire. As the eldest son he had been required to do little more than inherit the handsome Queen Anne mansion at Denham and provide a home for a superfluity of maiden aunts; for Ways ran to large families and frequently outstripped the means to marry them off. Ben Way was of a retiring disposition and a country lover. Between 1808 and 1814 he kept a 'Naturalist's Diary' almost daily: but the three slim volumes in which it was written have disappeared and we only have a few extracts quoted in a letter by his great-granddaughter, Miss Constance Way, in 1930:

"Oct.5, 1808	Thermometer 78 in the sun. Gathering apples, a generally large crop.
Nov.1.	Planted 2 rows of willows from Stansted in garden.
Nov.18.	Killed 1st woodcock. Weighed $11\frac{3}{4}$ oz.
Nov.30.	Ye highest wind I ever remember. 7 elms thrown down in warren. Ye damage very great everywhere.
1809	Planted in Nursery from Scotland larch, spruce and Scotch, 1000 of each.
August	Carried Bailey Hill oats.
Jan.17. 1810	River frozen in 2 places.
Feb.22.	Mary safely delivered of a girl at 2 a.m.*
Apr.15.	A colt born. Black cart mare.
Apr.17.	7 chickens hatched.
May 13.	A fine calf today. Ye cob flies at the approach of anyone much to the annoyance of Mary Anne (she was then 11 years old)."

.... and so on, and so on; records of sowing, planting, harvests, births of birds, animals and children, totals of game killed, vermin caught, and fish caught from the river (1811 - 11 pike, 30 perch, 73 eels and 436 roach).

Eliza had omitted to mention in her journal of 1824 that 'Papa' would also travel with them to Paris. Mary Anne was more explicit: "Papa, Henry, Gregory and Arthur had gone up the day before. The two little boys went per coach to Rochester; we were to follow in a chaise. Mama and Henry returned to Denham. We left London at half-past two ...."

Henry Hugh was 17, Gregory 12 and Arthur 11. There were ten of them altogether, five boys and five girls. Their mother was born Mary Smyth of Stapleton, youngest child of Thomas Smyth and Jane Whitchurch.**

* Mary Louisa, their third daughter and sixth child.

** See the chapter 'Thomas of Stapleton', the Later Smyths of Ashton Court, 1741-1802.

The union of the Smyths and Ways was to rejuvenate the former and enrich the latter. Mary Smyth came to Denham in 1798 at the height of the invasion scare from France. Benjamin Way was then Lieutenant Colonel of the Buckinghamshire Militia. Through the stirring years of the Napoleonic wars, life passed uneventfully at Denham; the babies arrived at frequent intervals and every year Mary took them to visit her old mother at Stapleton. They always stayed at the same posting inns to rest and change the horses, with the same servants noticing year by year "how the little ladies and gentlemen had grown".*

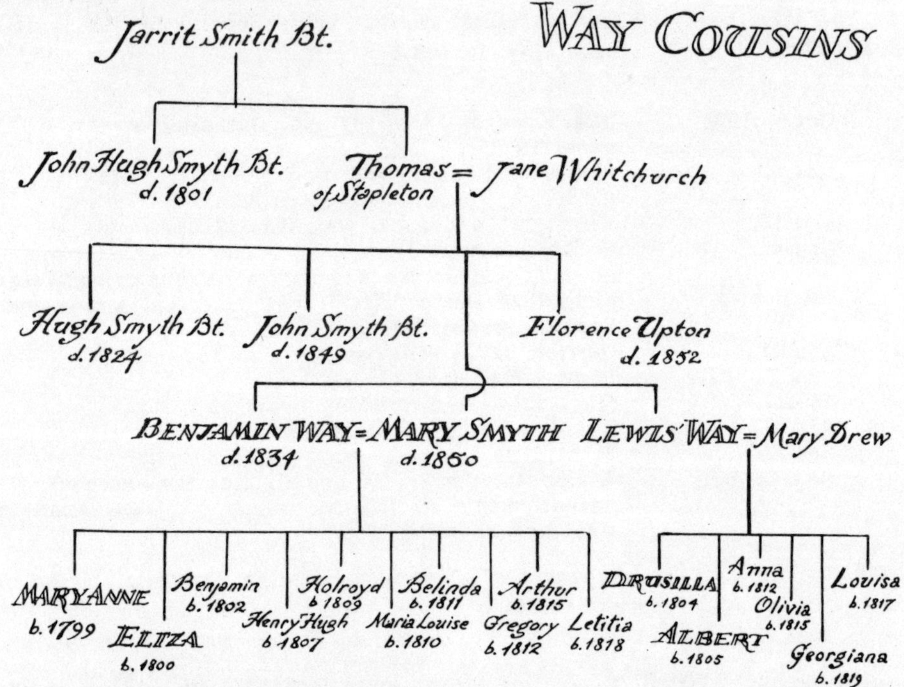

Mary Anne and Eliza dreaded these visits. Grandmother Whitchurch in old age was a martinet. She had brought up her own children strictly and so that the education of her granddaughters should not be interrupted during their visits to Stapleton, she had a music mistress engaged who was in the habit of holding locks of their hair in her hand and giving a sharp pull every time a wrong note was played. Far more awesome was Uncle John. John Smyth, Mary's elder brother and later Baronet, was a silent, sinister, misanthropic figure. He was heir to Heath House, Stapleton, and all but master of it. He had not been bad-looking as a young man, but became

* Diary of Florence Upton Cottrell-Dormer, daughter of Eliza Way.

increasingly hooknosed and hunched, so that some people mistook him for a Jew. He was a bachelor who disliked people in general and children in particular. For company he preferred a number of huge and ferocious dogs, and if the visiting nephews and nieces misbehaved he had them dangled out of the window, which excited the beasts to a frenzy of barking in the darkness below.

HEATH HOUSE

Occasionally Mary Way took her children over to Ashton Court, home of their uncle, the Baronet, Sir Hugh Smyth, and they stood in awe of the cavernous Long Gallery with its portraits of Smyths going back to the 16th Century, and the even more imposing stable wing that Uncle Hugh was building in a mock Elizabethan style on the same axis as the Long Gallery - a development that was to make Ashton Court the longest building in Somerset. Sir Hugh was in fact transforming Ashton Court into the ungainly pile we see today, quite different in feeling to the romantic intentions of Sir Hugh Repton.*

At the same time (c.1813) all the common land in Failand and Long Ashton was enclosed on the pretext that it had become a refuge for gipsies and other disreputable characters, and some of it was brought into the park and surrounded with a five mile wall. Part of this cut right across the public highway, which was obliged to make a wide sweep to the south of the house, which was thereafter screened from the vulgar gaze of the hoi polloi.

Mary Way was not on particularly good terms with her brother Hugh. In her eyes he had put himself beyond the pale of respectable folk by establishing a mistress in a house in Ashton Park and installing his son by her in Ashton Court, when his wife was still alive.

* pp.132-137: The Later Smyths of Ashton Court.

In spite of the vast sums expended during these years (1802-1812) Sir Hugh soon tired of Ashton Court and bought a house at Rockley, a little hamlet in a hollow in the Marlborough Downs where the hunting was better than in North Somerset. John Hugh, his bastard son, continued to reside at Ashton Court and in 1815 married Ann Provis, the Piggott heiress, bringing up at Ashton a crowd of little Smith-Piggotts. Although his mother, Elizabeth Howell, married his father on the death of his wife, Sir Hugh neglected to have John Hugh made legitimate, so there was no question of his inheriting the estate and title.

ROCKLEY HOUSE

Mary Anne and Eliza were rather fond of their Uncle Hugh. He was their naughty uncle. He had staring eyes, a wide mouth and a startled expression, and looked rather like a surprised frog. He used to drive them for hours on the Marlborough Downs, and being very fond of music he had a resident organist at Rockley called Miss Emmins. His practical jokes on poor Miss Emmins were such that the children could never forget. For example, she had a horror of stag beetles, so Sir Hugh had one made of black satin, which he continually made pop out of his waistcoat pocket, and so sent the musical lady shrieking away.

But to return to the visit to Paris of these young ladies with their Papa, in August 1824.

Their two younger brothers Gregory and Arthur were left in the care of Dr. Griffiths, evidently the principal of a Boys' Academy in Rochester and, writes Eliza: "We proceeded on about two miles when the carriage wheel was so musical we fortunately stopt, as they said if we had gone much further, it would have been on fire. We remained a quarter of an hour while they threw pails of water over it, and fresh greased it...."

Mary Anne's version: "The wheels of the carriage gave notice they would go no further without refreshment; we, to accommodate them, drove to a post house, and found the spokes in a most distressed state, the iron burning hot and the wood smelling strongly of fire - obliged to hold wet hay bands for a quarter of an hour before the grease could be applied. The girls and their father slept at the George, Sittingbourne that night. "Papa hearing it was the Canterbury race week," writes Mary Anne, "he dined, and we, in true old maidish style, were much refreshed by tea after which harmless beverage we retired to rest in a good old-fashioned bed."

Eliza: "19th August. The most **remarkable** thing I have yet to record is **Papa** was ready to start at 5."

Mary Anne: "We breakfasted at Canterbury and I fell in love with a dun-coloured pony with a mane and tail of flowing white silk."

At Dover the Captains of the different steam packets touted for passengers. Mary Anne: "The Boulogne Captain had just persuaded us to sail for that town, assuring us we would be there in 5 hours, when the Captain of the Spitfire said that he should not go till two, but even then would be in long before his rival, as the wind was set fair for Calais but not for Boulogne...."

To kill time: "....we walked all over the town enquiring for Miss Chabocceau at Miss Burgess's school in the High Street; no such school or street to be heard of.... as a last hope we enquired for Miss Burgess at the Post Office and found her in Town Wall Street; everything appeared very comfortable, table laid for 20 and Miss Chabocceau quite well and much pleased with our visit."

Eliza was more interested in recording the 'luncheon at the York Hotel' after which the party went aboard the 'Spitfire' which was not a bad name for a steam packet in 1824. They were an innovation; fast, but uncomfortable, especially if rolling caused a paddle wheel to rise out of the water, for the engine then raced and was followed by terrific vibration as the wheel hit the waves again. There was limited accommodation, dark and stuffy below, but the majority of the passengers, horses, carriages, etc., travelled on deck with no protection from the sea, or the funnel which showered soot and smoke.

Eliza: "....we had hardly room to move; some were obliged to stand, others to sit on the floor." Mary Anne: "....the deck so full, not a seat to be had: I suppose from 50 to 100 on board, several French and Italian, among the latter the opera dancers who went below immediately. Papa found, fortunately for us, one of his **particular friends,** Mr Hudson and his Lady...." who made room for Eliza and her father to sit down. Mary Anne remained standing and by all accounts thoroughly enjoyed the crossing.

"As soon as we were out of the harbour our vessel rose over the waves and cut through them majestically; waving of hands to the crowd on the pier.... basins beginning to be handed round to the motley company on deck. Papa sitting edgeways on one of the fixed seats, holding with his hands and looking most uncomfortable and could not enjoy the swift sailing vessel or even look at the grandeur of the waves; but he was not ill. Poor Eliza was sick enough and I was not a little astonished at finding it would be my happy fate to escape such a nuisance, which I owe chiefly to standing which prevented me feeling the motion of the vessel, and to Mr Hudson keeping me in conversation not really allowing me time to be ill."

Meanwhile, Eliza was discharging her luncheon at the York Hotel, and a lot more besides, into the Straits of Dover, with Mr Hudson hanging on to her: "....an uncommonly good-tempered, pleasant man," she wrote afterwards, "and was **exceedingly** kind in giving up his seat to me, and holding me from falling overboard, when **almost** dead with seasickness.

"There was such a swell on the water that immense waves burst over our heads several times, Mary Anne in high **spirits** the whole way; stood all the time holding the rope and laughing **incessantly** at our **miseries.** Almost everyone else on board was ill excepting **herself, Papa** and the **Hudsons,** that it was a horrid scene, though as long as ever I could enjoy it, I thought it **beautiful**; the sea was so **very rough,** one lady who was too faint to hold the rope was lashed to the deck. The Captain wanted me to be fastened also, but I declined, not **much** caring at the time whether I went **overboard or not**; indeed, I made up my mind **once on terra firma,** never to trust myself to the care of Neptune again, and I took leave of the White Cliffs of England as I thought for the last time; for never in my life had I been as ill before, but to my **great surprise** the instant the vessel arrived in the Harbour, I was quite well and able to enjoy the novelty of the scene.

"A poor Italian who understood no language but her own was even worse than I was. Mary Anne offered her a bottle of **Hartshorn,** which she, thinking it was a cordial, was just going to take off in a **draught,** when Mary Anne almost **bursting** with laughter, caught the bottle out of her hand, and brought her the **Brandy bottle** instead, but she seeing Mary Anne and Mr Hudson in **fits of laughter** at the mistake, suspected some **trick,** shook her head at both bottles."

The crossing took 2½ hours, not a bad record in 1824. Mary Anne, having been abroad before, glossed over the business of customs and the unwelcome attentions of rival hoteliers, but for Eliza it was a new experience and, as usual, she was quick to spot the ridiculous, "....there was quite a battle between the commissioners as to which (lodging) house we should go to, as Papa did not know from the name which he was at the time before, but said he should know as soon as he saw the Hotel. So a man from Tuillac's and one from Dessin's walked with us, each carrying part of the luggage and jabbering French as fast as possible, till we came to the Square, when Papa fixed upon Dessin's, and the other with true **politesse Française** wished us good morning and hoped we should honour **him** another time.

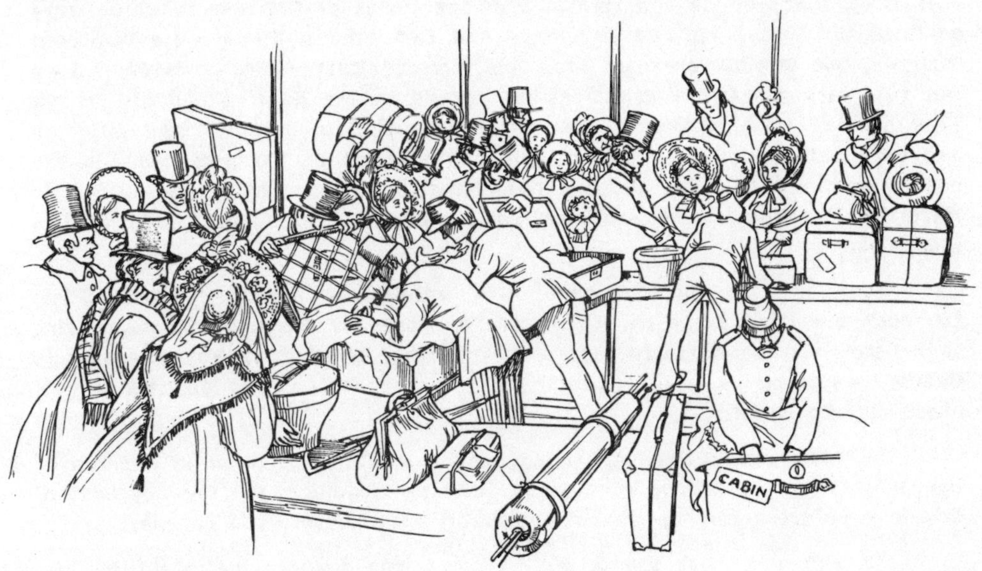

"Mary and I then returned to the vessel and went with the things to the Custom House. We were allowed to carry our writing desks without being searched, but Papa was very near to losing his snuff and some cotton stockings that were unmarked; and I had great difficulty in regaining a large red shawl which, tho' I assured them I had worn it nearly **2 years,** they were **positive** was a new one, and took it away to Monsieur le Commissaire, but Dessin's man got it back again by assuring them there was no fear of any smuggling as he had known the family **all his life.** They then proceeded to open the Band-box, not waiting to untie it, but cut the string in every direction with their **sabres....**

"Mr & Mrs Hudson came to the same Hotel and he came in the evening to pay us a visit, and was **amused** to find us **both** (particularly Sadly Badly) hard at work marking Papa's stockings (for fear of another Custom House Examination) instead of resting after our journey...." One suspects that

Mary Anne had organised this particular exercise, and Eliza had been pressed 'sadly badly' into doing her share.

20th August: Mary Anne: "We left Calais by nine, breakfasted at Boulogne - une déjeuner à la Fourchette - very bad, the fowls etc. so hard we could not cut them, and all the vegetables dressed in oil...." Eliza was even more disgusted: "....the vegetables all stewed in **Lamp Oil**, and at 3 francs a head."

The Ways travelled in a public conveyance called a 'diligence' which carried eighteen - six in the middle, three in the coupé ("....the three Miss Edwards had the coupé which is by far the **best** place," added Eliza, enviously), four outside and five in a compartment at the rear in which were confined Col. Way, his two daughters and two others. There were "....three windows, but terribly cramped for room," wrote Mary Anne; however, "....we had two very pleasant companions de voyage in Mr Keating and his friend. They seemed to have passed their life in travelling and the old gentleman was very enter-taining." Evidently the conversation of the passengers in the middle section could be heard through the partition. There was a "....Mr Watts, a Mr Cowper and a rather noisy party in the middle," added Eliza wistfully.

Soon after leaving Boulogne: "We were much alarmed," wrote Eliza, "to hear the Conducteur say there was a passenger **missing**, and on running back found him **comfortably** seated on the other coach that was returning to **Calais**; we found he was a **Scotchman**, but thought it rather an **Irish** way of proceeding to **Paris**!

"A little out of Boulogne we passed a magnificent pillar in memory of Buonaparte" - it had been erected in 1805 to commemorate the conquest of Britain - unfortunately the monument materialised before the conquest!

"It rained almost the whole day and was so hazy we could see but little of the country, but what we **did** see appeared very much like the Marlborough Downs; the road, observed the 'Irishman' was a very **triste** looking place."

There was a stop for supper at the Hôtel d'Angleterre, Abbeville: "....everything most excellent," observed Mary Anne, "and then back to our prison home again. Papa and the Gentlemen slept, but I could not close my eyes; indeed it was so strange a situation that I could not make myself at home." Eliza: "The journey to us seemed **endless**, as neither Mary nor I slept once all night, so by the time we arrived at Beauvais at 10 the next day we were completely tired; but breakfast soon revived us," and, "a little warm water, brushing etc," added Mary Anne. But 'lamp oil' again? Eliza: "It was difficult to say which was most sour, the **Rolls** or the **Wine**."

The sisters found the market place at Beauvais "a very pretty sight", the town "curiously built", the Cathedral "very handsome", but there was no time to visit "L'Interieure". Once again it is Eliza's sense of humour that saves these journals from the usual banalities. Soon after leaving Beauvais she records: "We were much amused by seeing the Conducteur and a French gentleman playing **cards**, as comfortably on the **outside** as possible, neither uphill nor down made any difference to them. Their game seemed a very gambling one as there was cutting and shuffling every minute."

As for the countryside, it was becoming prettier, but Eliza soon got fed up with the orchards. "Indeed, I never was so tired of **Apple & Pear** trees in all my life and think if the rest of the country is like the road from Calais to Paris, I cannot say much for La Belle France, as I think that the drive through Kent is **much** prettier than anything I have yet seen cette côté de l'eau.

"We were very much amused going through Noailles with some poor little children who talked very pretty English and danced a Quadrille, singing all the while, without either shoes or stockings, and almost ankle deep in mud.

"Soon after, a courier got up on the step behind; Papa had some chat with him, and a pinch of snuff, which he was very pleased with. He asked him to name the place; the man popped his head in at the window and said he was **then** in the **département des Oies** much to our amusement."*

The terminus of public conveyances travelling to Paris at that time was the yard of the Messagerie Royale. Practical Mary Anne tells us that the gates were locked and not opened till each party had their luggage unloaded for a further customs check, "....a rare scene of bustle, but all well ordered".

* Department of Geese - a pun on the name 'Oise'.

When all had been checked and found in order "....a commissaire called a coach and ourselves and trunks were soon settled. We drove in a gallop to the Hôtel Maurice, which was quite full. They recommended us to the Hôtel Prince Regent, where we found rooms looking onto the Marché St. Honoré, very small, and plenty of odours, but not of the most agreeable kind". The building still stands, a five-storeyed 18th century tenement at the corner of the Rue St. Honoré and the Marché St. Honoré. It is no longer a hotel; some of the windows are blocked up, and the ground floor is now a fashionable children's clothes shop. The Rue St. Honoré runs parallel to the Champs Élysées and is only a stone's throw from the Tuileries Gardens. The Marché, a side street, was still presumably in 1824 the scene of a vegetable market, hence the 'odeurs' that Mary Anne objected to.

Mary Anne professed herself much shocked by some of the French customs. "....it being a complete French hotel we were, of course, called in the morning by the Garçon, who also made the beds and waited on us without stockings and in shirt sleeves"; and the noise and smells coming up from the vegetable market below their windows obliged them to move to another room on the side of the hotel facing the main thoroughfare.

The liberties taken by the French hairdresser scandalised Mary Anne, especially "....his very cool questions and advice".

"Mademoiselle, quel âge avez-vous? Vingt-deux ans, n'est ce pas? Pourquoi ne vous mariez vous pas? Est que votre religion vous oblige de rester toujours fille?", and on telling him she never went to amusements on Sunday, he replied: "Bah, bah! Laissez de côté votre religion quand vous venez ici".

One of the main purposes of the visit to Paris was to hear Uncle Lewis preach at the Hotel Marboeuf. Eliza gives us a vivid description of their first visit.

"Sunday, 22 August. Mary and I went immediately after breakfast to Gaglimani's to enquire Uncle Lewis's address, and then went to the Hôtel Marboeuf près de Chaillot. The chapel is the most beautiful I ever saw;

you enter through a suite of magnificent rooms, the Chapel is furnished with blue velvet trimmed with silver lace and fringe, carpeted all over, and beautiful lamps. The pulpit is very handsome. There are two desks, one on each side, with blue and silver cushions etc., and at the back there is a slab of white marble with the words 'Go ye into all the World and preach the Gospel to every creature'."

Mary Anne's comment was typical "....impossible for anything to be more chaste and simple, but at the same time as handsome as it ought to be having cost, first and last, £20,000; everything in order, a servant at the door to show you in, pay your coach, etc."

The garden had once been a public garden and the drawing room of the Hotel a restaurant where "....the company had ices, coffee etc., and danced in the grand saloon adjoining" (Eliza). It worried Mary Anne's sense of propriety that the inscription over the portico of the Chapel 'To the only true God' had not quite obliterated the words 'Café Restaurant, Glacière etc.', and "....from the Chapel itself not having been consecrated by a Bishop it is, should any revolution take place, liable to be sold for a café again, which would be a profanation".

Eliza was Uncle Lewis' goddaughter, and she was curious to see if he recognised her. "We sat about a quarter of an hour before Uncle Lewis entered, looking uncommonly well. We rose as he passed, and were advancing to shake hands when a **low formal bow** convinced us he did not recollect us, and we resumed our seats. Two other clergymen were in the desks, who read the prayers and then retired to the vestry where Uncle Lewis joined them and all three entered from another door near the pulpit, from which he preached a most beautiful discourse extempore, on the worship of God." Mary Anne: "Drusilla played the organ and Anna accompanied it with her voice."

"After service we went into the vestry and remained some time when Mr Harrington came and told us if we were waiting to see Mr Way it would be **useless** as the vestry was so crowded the Sunday before he was unequal to such a fatigue again, and had retired to his apartment above; and a few minutes after he entered, saying as he held out a hand to each, he knew we were **cousins,** but from **whence** we came and who we were, he had not the **least idea.** He was much pleased to see us and took us up to his rooms. On the stairs we passed a fine looking old Arab dressed in the costume of his country, whom Uncle Lewis appointed to come again with his books at six. We sat with him about a quarter of an hour, saw pictures of the family etc., when he told us his reasons for remaining in France; that **dearly** as he loved Stansted, he could not return there while three thousand souls were staying here, who without him would not hear the word of God. Then turning to a picture of our Saviour he said that was enough for him; his every **hope, wish and desire** centred there, and that he should think himself unworthy of the blessing he enjoyed if he did not devote them to the service of Christ."

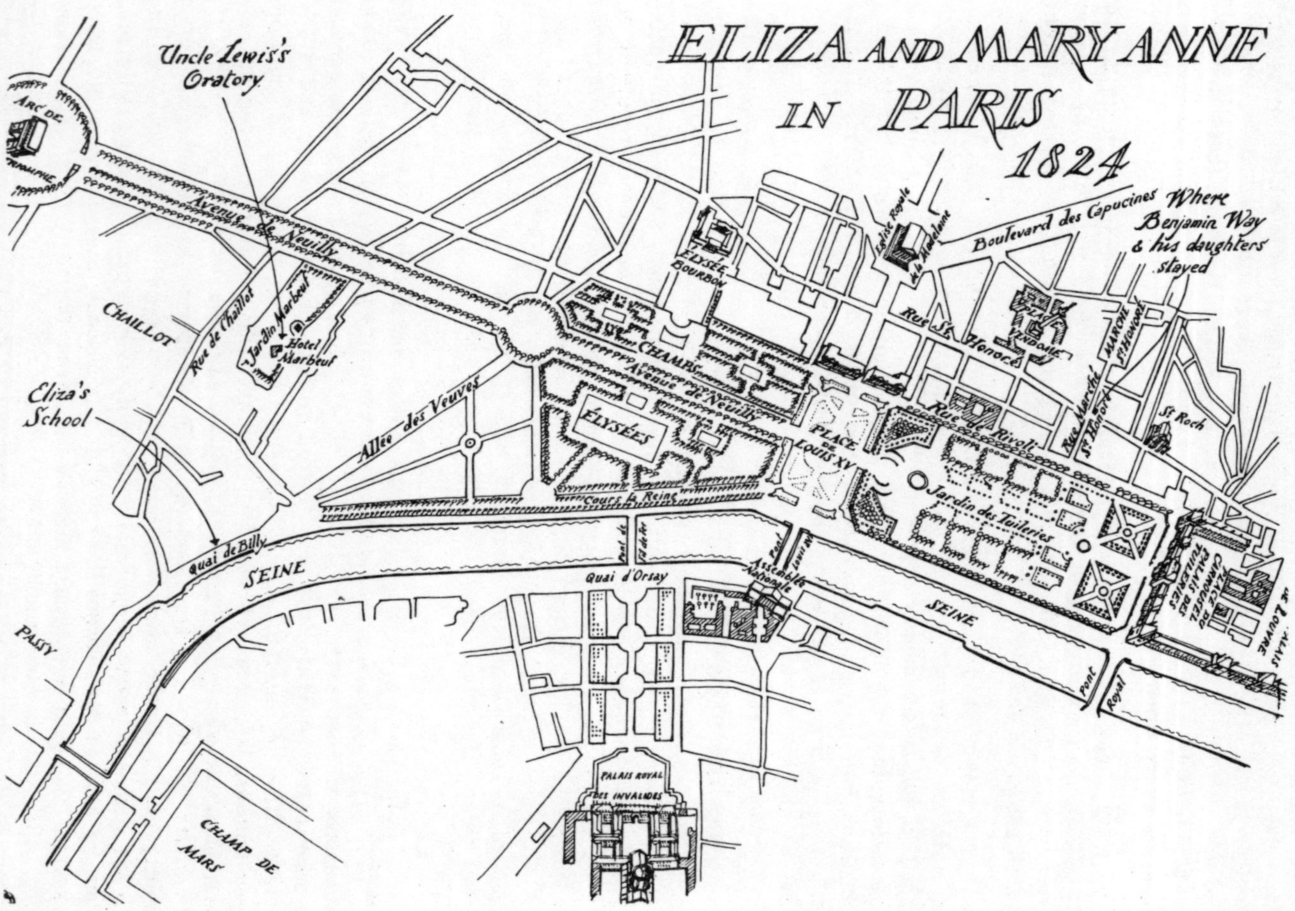
ELIZA AND MARY ANNE IN PARIS 1824
Uncle Lewis's Oratory
Boulevard des Capucines Where Benjamin Way & his daughters stayed
Eliza's School
CHAILLOT
Rue de Chaillot
Avenue de Neuilly
Jardin Marbeuf
Hotel Marbeuf
Allée des Veuves
ÉLYSÉE BOURBON
Eglise Royale de la Madeleine
CHAMPS
ÉLYSÉES
Cours la Reine
PLACE DE LOUIS XV
Rue St Honoré
PLACE VENDOME
MARCHÉ St HONORÉ
Rue Marché St Honoré
Rue de Rivoli
St Roch
Jardin des Tuileries
PLACE DU CARROUSEL
PALAIS DES TUILERIES
Quai de Billy
SEINE
SEINE
Quai d'Orsay
Assemblée Nationale
Pont Royal
PASSY
CHAMP DE MARS
PALAIS ROYAL DES INVALIDES

Mary Anne was less impressed with what he said than the way he said it, "....his manner was very hurried; told us to listen to him but not to speak; his head would not bear it". She also had the presence of mind to notice "....an octagon print of the Holy Family the same as hangs over the drawing room door at Denham and a dressing stand the same as father used; two pretty French doves, the hen sitting; and drawings by Drusilla and Albert of Sidon, Nice, etc".

Before parting Lewis gave Eliza, as his godchild, his blessing and a copy of his work 'Palingenesia' which he had composed on his way from Syria to Paris. On passing through the vestry they found Drusilla, Anna and Olivia "....but they were busy at dinner: we did not stay," said Eliza. "I should not have known any of them again," wrote Mary Anne, "particularly Anna who we left a beautiful baby, now grown taller than her sister, and a complete skeleton. Olivia is very fair and pretty."

Eliza: "We walked home as far as the Tuileries, but rain coming on we got into a fiacre. I was much surprised to see every shop open the same as in the week, and a full market before our windows. Papa took us to dine at Very's which was very full of French people all appearing to talk each faster and louder than the other, without anyone seeming to listen."

The next day Uncle Lewis, accompanied by Drusilla, paid Benjamin and his daughters a visit, riding "....the horse given to him by Lady Hester Stanhope" (Mary Anne). He invited them to join them for dinner at Miss Rowden's house in the Bois de Boulogne which, says Mary Anne "....stands high and close to the barrier, better situated than the Hôtel Marboeuf, which in winter must be damp".

Eliza had never met Uncle Lewis' family before: "I had much pleasure in being introduced to **Aunt** and **five cousins,** of whom I had heard so much, but **never** seen before," but Mary Anne found "Mrs Way much altered" and Louisa and Georgiana "very pretty; the latter had been very ill, but full of life and fun". Also of the party were a Mr Mason and a Mr Foote: "Mr Mason, a complete character, and told many good stories of his and his Lady's adventures".

The Fête of St. Louis

This was a great occasion in Catholic France, especially after the restoration of the Bourbon monarchy, and evidently anticipated with much excitement by the two young ladies from Denham:

"24 August - the theatres all open gratis, crowds trying to get in at each, but all of the lowest class...." wrote Mary Anne. "Walked in the Tuileries garden till 9. A grand concert on the Terrace and the Palace partially illuminated and looked very grand. The crowd great, the evening beautiful." Eliza: "Sat some time on the boulevards and then had Glace à la Biscuit at Tortoni's."

25 August. Mary Anne: "Breakfasted at Café Castiglione; saw the carriages going with the officers etc. full dressed for court. After breakfast, to the gardens; got into the Palace* as the wife of an officer." Eliza was more explicit: "Seeing an officer and his wife pass the gate, we went in with them, and **three** other ladies took the same advantage; the Soldier **smiled** as we passed and asked how many **more** were coming, saying he thought the officer had a very **numerous family.** We stood at the foot of the stairs, saw all the company ascend to the Drawing Room, the Duke of Orleans** and two pages, and all the officers in full uniform - the most magnificent coats I ever saw." Mary Anne: "The dresses of the Gentlemen of Honour, blue worked in gold; the officers, green and gold.... the two most at their ease were two country girls from Normandy (identified no doubt by their characteristic dress and coif) who had the entrée whilst many well dressed ladies were turned back." Eliza: "We afterwards went to the Champs Élysées where many thousand people were assembled; wine, rolls and sausages were thrown among them, which occasioned a fine scramble; there were games of every description going on. Theatres open gratis; horse racing etc; in short, it was a very gay scene." Mary Anne: "Back and dressed for dinner at Beauvilliers; found a note to invite us to **tea** and **turnout** at Marboeuf."

* The Palace of the Tuileries, adjoining the Louvre, was then the principal Royal Residence in Paris. It was burnt down during the regime of the Commune, 1871.

** Destined in 1830 to become King Louis Philippe.

Eliza: "But being in hopes of seeing the **Ladies** go to Court we went to the Tuileries Gardens instead, and saw a most magnificent illumination, and the finest fireworks I ever saw. Madame Saqui ascended in a blaze of them from an illuminated castle, composed entirely of fireworks." Mary Anne: "The Chamber of Commons* like a fairy palace; all the pillars illuminated and the order of St. Louis partout; a French Gentleman gave us half his chair and the fireworks were superb, but the mass of people beyond everything; the Place Louis 15 (now Place de la Concorde) you might have walked on their heads; I never saw such a multitude.

"The fête in the daytime resembled a large fair in England; round-abouts, swings, shooting at Targets etc; and the walk home through the crowds parti-cularly disagreeable to me - a rare mob and one I have no wish to encounter again at night.

"The King (Louis XVIII) in the course of the day was wheeled to the balcony and the cheering of the multitude very hearty, totally different to the greeting our King met at Ascot**," wrote Mary Anne. "But we missed seeing him," added Eliza.

A Visit to the Louvre

26 August: "Breakfasted at Tortoni's which was very full of company," wrote Eliza. "We did not chuse(sic) our table so well as usual."

Mary Anne was always more alive to the propriety of the occasion, "....but placed ourselves close to the larder - every sort of meat prepared for cooking - cutlets, kidneys, fowls, pigeons, veal, beef etc. all garnished with Parsley, crumbs of bread, etc; this en passant would not have been amiss, but in the salon with 15 or 20 breakfasting l'odeur of the undressed meat was rather too much; but all the French as they came in went there to choose their breakfast, which generally consisted of wine, melon, beef-steak etc. Both

* The National Assembly.
** George IV was then at the height of his unpopularity and could not appear in public without being jeered.

at dinner and breakfast they eat double what the English do - the leg of mutton sleeves very ugly, the hair dressed à la tricadore." The outlandish size of ladies sleeves was just too much for our provincial sisters, as was the strange fashion of tying one's hair in a tuft on the crown of the head, called in England 'Apollo's Knot'. However, Mary Anne consented to her father buying her a 'Leghorn hat', "now worn as they are imported without being cut," - an interesting comment on the rustic origin of the straw poke bonnet which became so much the rage in Victorian England - ".... the man had this year more orders from England than any year before," and she couldn't resist "4 pr. of silk stockings at 5 shillings per pr.". In England they would have been much dearer.

On their walk from the Boulevard des Italiens to the Porte St. Martin, Mary Anne had some more censorious remarks to make: "....building everywhere, but the way in which they carry large stones from the bottom to the top of the house is barbarous. A long ladder with a man on every five bars, the lowest hands the stone over his head to the one above him, and so on to the top - the labour must be immense, and certainly a disgusting sight...."

They took a fiacre to the Louvre, "....being the 2nd day of opening", to see an exhibition of modern artists, "....the same as our Somerset House except this is only shown once in two years," adds Mary Anne.

Eliza was ecstatic: "The most magnificent collection of pictures that can be imagined, tho' the crowd was too great to enjoy them. Amongst thousands of others we admired particularly a very interesting picture of the Death of the Duc de Berri*, the Duchess kneeling at the side, and the rest of the family standing round the bed, his daughter is on the bed, and he is just saying to her 'My child, may you be less **unfortunate** than the rest of your family'."

* Son of the Duc d'Artois (later Charles X) and heir to the throne, who was shot by a terrorist in 1821.

Mary Anne: "Dined at Very's and for the third day following, though at different places, met the same trio at the next table - an old Monsieur with the Order of St. Louis, a young wife, and a pallipon** of a boy, playing antics all the time," "whom," adds Eliza, "they made say a **very long grace,** and cross himself a great many times the first two days, but seeing us smile, no grace was said in public today."

The Theâtre Français

Benjamin Way was an admirer of the celebrated Talma, the hero of the French stage and much applauded for his role in the leading tragedies of his time. "We got very good places, next box but one to the stage, surrounded by our compatriots," wrote Mary Anne. Says Eliza: "Saw **Le Grand Talma** in Sylla which I should have enjoyed more had I read the play first. I could understand **him** perfectly, but the others spoke too fast for me." Mary Anne: "He was very good in the scene on the sofa, like our Richard, and last act where he refuses the purple and addresses the people from the tribune." Eliza especially liked the part where he said, 'Je suis pere, me dis-tu! Non, je suis dictateur'.

"The afterpiece 'La Pandore' was "very lively and pretty, all complimentary to the King, his bust brought forward and crowned with laurel, which was very much applauded". Mary Anne was scornful: "It was truly French and ridiculous enough in the last act bringing on to the stage a dirty plaster of Paris head of Louis which was crowned with laurel." The Grand Talma, apparently, got less applause.

"Talma was faintly called for after the play, but did not appear; the house much improved in appearance during the last 3 years, better lighted and well-decorated as no improper persons (the disgrace of our theatres) were admitted. All over by half past ten. Went in our morning dresses and much pleased with the spectacle."

The next day "Papa called on Talma", and in the evening they went to see him in the comedy 'L'Ecole des Veillards'. "Could only get three places at the back of the stagebox," wrote Mary Anne. "The French gentleman instantly insisted on our taking his chair, much to the annoyance of Madame, and insisted on our keeping it for the rest of the evening. Talma and Madame Mars a great treat, I like him as well in comedy as tragedy, but so altered by dress I should never have known him again. Mde. Mars looking younger and prettier than she did three years ago."

Sightseeing

28 August: "Eliza, being tired, stayed at home," wrote Mary Anne, who, indefatigable as always, set out with Papa to see the Marché des Fleurs. "Not near such a variety of flowers as I expected", and then breakfasted at the Jardin des Plantes. "The cutlets, wine etc. for 4 francs. Of course, the luxuries of table cloth etc. were wanting. Saw the animals, many quite new

* Perhaps she meant 'papillon' (butterfly).

both to Papa and myself. Were much amused by Auguste and his father. Took them for French but they were not. A soldier who had served 27 years, now retired on a pension of 400 francs to take care of the gardens, had been in Egypt with Boney, prisoner in England, and could speak five languages.

"To the Post Office and had a good letter from Mama." Meanwhile, Eliza was writing to her mother, but neither letter survives, and later "....went with Mary to St. Roche where many Catholics were counting their beads. The man placed at the door to sprinkle people with holy water was **sound asleep,** and one poor woman amused us very much as she muttered her prayers as fast as possible, counting her beads with one hand while she held out the other for money."

Sunday, 29 August. After attending morning service at the Chapel Marboeuf, where Lewis Way preached 'Wash and be clean', ("I can recollect the substance and heads of discourse perfectly," wrote Mary Anne, "but have tried in vain to arrange to write it down"), there was further chat with the family. "Mrs Lewis Way looked ill, overcome by the heat, but the children very pretty, particularly Olivia." There was other company recently arrived from England, including a "Mr Smith we had met at Marlborough, viz Rockley - he was in mourning for his wife". One wonders if this was John Smith-Piggott, Uncle Hugh's illegitimate son by Elizabeth Howell, but if Mary Anne had known this she was far too proper to mention it. Eliza: "He (Mr Smith) said he was going to Versailles to see the water-works, and as Papa wished to join the party he very good-temperedly gave up his place in the carriage and took his seat on the box in a most burning sun." Mary Anne: "It was the last day of the grand water-works which cost the Government 95 thousand francs every time they play." Eliza: "We declined going as we preferred hearing Uncle Lewis preach in the evening," but they were disappointed. Mary Anne: "After dinner Eliza and myself walked to the Hôtel Marboeuf and were half an hour too early, but Drusilla seeing us invited us into the pavilion where Uncle Lewis, Mrs Noel and Anna were taking refreshment. Mr Noel preached and Uncle Lewis read the prayers; the text 'Whom having not seen ye love, in whom though now ye see him not, yet believing ye rejoice with joy unspeakable and full of glory' - a remarkably slow reader." The waterworks at Versailles would have been more fun.

30 August. The sisters breakfasted at the Café de Paris, "....at present the fashionable house," wrote Mary Anne. "300 to 400 plates laid every day and rooms all handsomely furnished. Le beau monde crowd here as the bourgeoisie do to Very's." Eliza: "We then went to Gaglione's to read the English papers; Papa went to the opera which was so crowded he could not procure places for us. Mr Ludgate called soon after and invited us to spend the next day with him sightseeing."

The company that assembled at the Hotel Castiglione for the sightseeing trip consisted of Ben Way, his two daughters, Mr Ludgate, Mr

Smith-Piggott, Mr Hunter and "another gentleman". Mary Anne tells us that Mr Ludgate "....took a glass coach for the day" and they went first to the Grand Hotel opposite the Hotel Castiglione "now a building for the M. de Villèle", the Prime Minister.* Eliza: "The suite of apartments is magnificent and the walls of each room covered with the richest Lyons silk. The hall is of marble, and several of the rooms inlaid with different color'd wood; the ceiling white and gold." Mary Anne was more interested in the domestic arrangements, "Le boudoir de Madame quite a petit bijou - over their suite of apartments their married daughter has hers, and below, the servants".

Eliza: "We then went to the Bourse, which we mounted to the top of; the interior is made of cast iron, with a very curious sort of tile. We walked on the roof where the heat was so intense that the walls almost burnt your hand. There is a very handsome colonnade all round the building. The next sight was the immense elephant (that was a Lion indeed!). It was intended by Buonaparte to be made in bronze, and was to supply all Paris with water. You go up **stairs** inside one of the **legs,** the **stomach** is a good-sized room (though not large enough for a Quadrille). On the top is an observatory, and the water is to spout out from the trunk and from a fine Cascade all round.

* Prime Minister 1822-27. His ultra-royalist politics did much to provoke the Revolution of July 1830.

"From thence we went to l'église of St. Geneviève, the handsomest church I ever saw, with the altars beautifully decorated, with the best artificial flowers under glass cases, but what looked bad was about a dozen **farthing rushlights** burning at the side and the holy water they sprinkle you with so **dirty** I was glad the man was absent that we escaped.

"We then went to the Café St. Foix where we found lemonade and groseille a la glace very acceptable, having been the hottest day I ever felt.

Mr Ludgate had a ticket for the Tuileries so we went there, but when we arrived found it was dated for the following day, so the Gendarmes sent us back and we went to the Louvre where Mr Smith showed us a set of rooms Papa had never discovered before.

"They took us back to our hotel, where we dressed and then went to dine at the Café de Paris which was very full of company. On our return in the evening we found the Hudsons and Sir John and Lady Richardson had been to call on us; likewise an English gentleman whose **name** they could not recollect, but from the description and his having **'Un très grand nez'** we guessed to be John Upton.

The Uptons of Ingmire Hall

Christopher Wilson, Bishop of Bristol (1783-92) was instrumental in uniting the houses of Smyth and Upton. He came of a good Yorkshire family from Bradford, and was anxious to see his daughters marry well. In 1795 his eldest daughter Dorothy, a singularly ugly young lady, was married to John Upton of Ingmire Hall, Westmorland. At that time Ingmire Hall was an austere Jacobean mansion, built on to a pele tower of much earlier date. It is situated in the lovely Vale of Lune, about a mile from the sturdy little North Yorkshire market town of Sedbergh. All around the fells rise majestically, presenting an endless vista of bald, convex slopes and plunging wooded vales. A few miles down-stream where the Lune tumbles over huge rounded boulders in a ravine overhung with oaks and beeches, is the older Upton manor of Killington, a crumbling, Elizabethan farmhouse, ruined pele tower and tiny church, where John's sister, Mary, made a runaway marriage. Her lover was a Mr Moreland of Capplethwaite Hall, adjoining the Ingmire estate, who had fallen out with John Upton over shooting rights. Mary defied her brother, jumped out of a window on to a grassy bank at the back of the house, and ran off to join Mr Moreland. John never spoke to his sister again, and had the window in question partly bricked up so that "no Miss Upton might in future escape from it".

Bishop Wilson, meanwhile, had found an excellent match, so he thought, for his second daughter, Margaret. He was a close friend of Sir John Hugh Smyth of Ashton Court, and the childless baronet had selected Margaret as the intended bride for his nephew and heir, Hugh. This marriage was celebrated in 1798 and, as has been already related, was desperately unhappy, for Hugh's affections were firmly planted elsewhere.

In 1796 Dorothy Upton gave birth to a son, John 'Le grand nez', but died three years later. She was buried, like all Uptons before and since, in the Upton Chapel in Sedbergh Church.

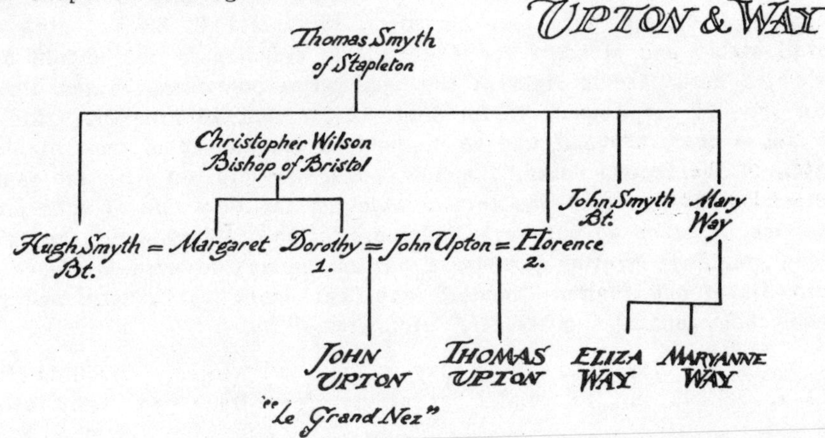

The Ashton Court connection had brought the Uptons into the Smyth circle which, at the turn of the century, had gravitated to the fashionable west of England spas of Clifton, Cheltenham and Bath. At Bath, in 1799, the recently bereaved John Upton was betrothed to Hugh Smyth's elder sister, Florence, whose hope of marriage was already being despaired of by her family. Florence journeyed north and in due course produced one son, Thomas Upton, born 1800. Florence did not take kindly to the north of England. Ingmire Hall was a depressing place in those days and the Moreland affair had cast a shadow over the neighbourhood. Florence must have looked forward to the rare visits of her sister, Mary Way of Denham with her lively brood, for then there were outings and picnics, and on one of these Mary carved her initials on a boulder below Killington bridge, a tradition followed by several generations of Uptons. John Upton, one suspects, did not take part in these frivolities and the picture that has come down to us is one of a dour, north country squire, who collected the rents in person at a bay window in the courtyard and then rode over the lonely moor to Kendal to bank them. By 1822 Hugh's excesses on the hunting field were undermining his health and he asked his brother, a more businesslike man, to look out for a villa for him on the south coast. Sea air was now considered the universal panacea for the ailments of the upper classes, and they were beginning to forsake the mineral waters for sea bathing at Weymouth, Brighton and Worthing.

"I was glad to find by my sister Upton's letter from Leamington that you was in good health," replied John, good-naturedly, from Cheltenham on the 27th August, 1822, "and was enjoying the Gaieties of Leamington. According to your wish in Mrs Upton's letter to me, I made every inquiry concerning the lodging houses at Worthing, and for two of the best lodging houses I will give you the terms.

"The first is Warwick House, belonging to Ld. Warwick, which contains 3 good sized sitting rooms, 5 best bedrooms, 6 servants rooms, with 2 water closets, 2 cellars, housekeeper's room, servants hall, kitchen etc., with six-stall stable and standing for 4 carriages, standing in the middle of a lawn about 2 acres and in sight of the sea. Terms per week, 16 gns. for June, 18 for July, 22 for August, 27 for Sept, 14 for Oct, 10 for Nov, 7 for Dec, and if for a year, £500...." and so on, and so on; and the rooms, stables, terms etc., of the second house, Summer Lodge, are laid out with the same deadly precision. The rest of the letter, which is the only one of John Smyth's to survive, is taken up with a tedious description of "long eared, heavy tongued, blue mouthed" hunting hounds, a passión he shared with Sir Hugh, and the prowess of one "called Thunder" who "has never lost a hare, and you could hear them running 4 miles off," etc., etc.

"Eliza Way joins me in love to you, and with my compliments to your Lady, believe me to remain ever, my dear Hugh, yr. truly affectionate Brother."

It is not known which house Hugh took, but in the autumn of 1823 he returned to Rockley claiming a cure, though his days were numbered.

"My Dear Sister Upton," he writes to Florence from Rockley (29 Nov. 1823). "Many thanks pray accept, my Dearest Sister, for your kind letter, and also for three very fine mongoose (sic) which pray remember me to your nephew, and thank him for. I find myself much better for the sea air, and since my return home to Rockley have enjoyed the fine air of the Wiltshire Downs. The weather has been very fine since the last storm, which destroyed many of my best trees at Rockley and has done me much damage....

"My brother came about a week ago to make some stay with me, and has been enjoying many good days of sport. Tell Mr Thos. Upton now is his Time to take a lesson of his Uncle in cashing hounds and hunting them.

"There is a lady that is come with her husband to live in Mr Smith's new House at Marlborough, who is a remarkable good horsewoman, and hunts often with me. She will set the Field. I never met with a better or bolder rider. She takes everything in her way. I saw her ride over some high Fence, very high hurdles. A Gentleman took a leap before her, and from breaking his stirrup he fell. She fell. I was just behind her, and had her horse moved when she was on the ground, must have stood on her. But by Good Luck she was not much hurt. Her nose bled very much. She got on her horse and rode out the Chase and has been out several times since. She gained the Brush with Mr Ward's Foxhounds on Saturday last, after a long run. She is a Devonshire lady of the name of Williams. A very stout, good-looking woman. Her husband, Mr Williams, has a house near Salisbury and has taken a House at Marlborough for three years to be near Mr Ward's and my Hounds. They both breakfasted with me the other morning, and I got her to weigh. She is about 12 stone and with her saddle must be nearly 14 stone. Nothing but the Huntsmen and a few of the best riders can live with her in the Field...."

Uncle Hugh's weakness for "stout, good-looking women", especially if they were good horsewomen, was a family joke.

"Should my nephew like to take a peep of his Uncle, mounted on one of the best Horses in the World, of which he has three, he cannot do better than make his appearance at Rockley. I shall be happy to see him, yourself, Mr Upton and Mr John Upton should you be inclined to make me a visit. I shall go to Bath sometime in January and should any bad weather set in at Xmas to prevent hunting, I shall go at that time.

"Mr & Mrs Gore* of Barrow Court are coming here on Tuesday next on their way into Surrey with Mr Hugh Gore. Mr Montague was coming but was prevented by his being about to enter the Life Guards in London.

* The Rev. Charles Gore, son of Edward Gore.

"I received a few days ago a very good letter from my sister Way that her son was better, that the Vapour Bath had been of much service to him. I shall hope to have a letter from you soon, with a good account of your own Health.

"I remain, my Dearest Sister Upton,

"Your affectionate Brother, Hugh Smyth.

"PS. I have just heard of a fine pot of char just arrived which I am much obliged to you and Mr Upton for."

Hugh died in January 1824 at the age of 53, just five months before his nieces Mary Anne and Eliza set out for Paris. The considerable Ashton Court estates passed to Hugh's brother, John, who was a confirmed bachelor. If his sisters Florence Upton and Mary Way outlived him, they were next in succession. It is more than likely, in view of what later occurred, that the sisters dangled their respective offspring in front of each other in the hope of consolidating the enormous legacy which would one day come their way. Hence the presence of 'Le grand nez' in Paris in September 1824. The situation was pregnant with possibilities. In actual fact, neither John Upton ('Le grand nez') nor his stepbrother Thomas were particularly prepossessing. John Upton was a solitary young man; virtuous, pious, but totally lacking any interest in estate matters. When his father died in 1832 from a chill, it was said contracted from riding over the moors in a rainstorm to bank his rent money in Kendal, John, who inherited the Ingmire estate* made it over to his stepbrother, and went off to live in rented rooms in Sidney Street, London. Here he lived all his life, only rarely returning to Westmorland. He was reported to be fabulously wealthy and amassed a prodigious collection of precious stones and telescopes, but took little interest in public life, except for being churchwarden for many years at St. George's, Hanover Square. As far as the fair sex was concerned he was possessed of a very big nose!

Thomas Upton was a fair, frail, sensitive youth, with transparent blue eyes and a delicate constitution. He was a diabetic, which may explain his mother's partiality for spas. As for Mary Anne and Eliza, the two most nubile cousins, we are already beginning to form quite an intimate picture of them. Now let us return to Paris, September 1824....

The arrival of 'Le grand nez' was a welcome relief to Mary Anne and Eliza. They were beginning to wilt under the strain of sightseeing, and the heat wave didn't help. The first to collapse was Papa, who took to his bed and medicines were sent for from Mr Roberts, an apothecary who had settled in Paris and was reputedly making a fortune from wealthy English clients. Then Mary Anne lost her voice, "very unwell," she wrote (4th September), "and not a little nervous as I fancied I had the same symptoms as in my first visit".

* His sister, Mary Moreland, was left £100, which may have been intended as a token of reconciliation.

In these circumstances it was comforting to have John Upton to keep them company in their rooms, exchanging family gossip and taking an occasional evening stroll in the Tuileries Gardens. Sometimes they ventured further afield: they did the pictures in the Palais de Luxembourg and went to the Gobelin factory of tapestries. "They were copying some very fine pictures in the Luxembourg and Louvre," wrote Eliza, "we saw the work in every stage: the ground work and very rough parts are done by very young boys to teach them the work." Mary Anne was impressed with the "very civil guide who took delight in telling you the subject of the pictures they were copying, would make you examine the work, and try'd to convince you that tapestry looked very well in all lights and that painting could only be seen to advantage in one light. They work in two ways: the upright looms and the horizontal, both I should think excessively fatiguing from the sameness of the work and the length of time it takes to finish even a moderate sized piece - the Duchess of Berri and her two children now just begun. It will take 3 years to finish...."

One day Eliza and John Upton ventured to the Place Vêndome "....to ascend the column Napoleon had constructed to commemorate his victories," but, she admits, "my courage **failed** after I had gone a few steps, as the stairs were **quite dark** and so narrow no one could pass".

At the Opera Comique they saw 'The Caliph of Baghdad', 'Felix ou L'enfant Trouvé' and 'A Night in the Forest', which they enjoyed, but at the Variétés "....a crowded house," wrote Mary Anne, "but not understanding the jokes and having bad places, we were bien ennuie before it was over. Cinderella, the three sisters according to our ideas horribly represented, two of them an immense size, and the pretty Cinderella's part was played by Pahir, who even in woman's dress, did not appear a day under 60 - quite a caricature." They dined that evening at Very's: "Mary Anne spied Mr Cowley just opposite, she jump't up to speak to him," wrote Eliza, "and he in his hurry overturned his soup, so **delighted** with the **Right** travellers to meet. Mr Cowley immediately joined our table, and is a very pleasant old man." Mr Cowley later accompanied them to the Jardin des Plantes, along with Mrs Way, Drusilla, Anna and Olivia. Also of the party was Fanny Strickland, an old family friend from

FANNY STRICKLAND

Cokethorpe Hall in Oxfordshire. Fanny was about Eliza's age and her family, like the Uptons, was destined to be united to the Ways.

In fact the circle of friends in Paris was widening all the time, mainly through their regular visits to the Chapel Marboeuf and Uncle Lewis who, of course, was known by and knew, everybody. As Drusilla wrote some years later, "I remember going to the Ambassador's reception at Paris; crowds of élite male and female. As we edged among them, I holding fast to the paternal arm, he nudged me and said 'Talleyrand!': and there he was, lame but with a head like Saul, above all the rest and a peculiar one."

Eliza: "Mr Cowley pressed us so much to see the Anatomical Museum that Fanny and I (much against our will) went in; have no doubt it is a very interesting sight to those who understand **Anatomy**, but we thought it most **disgusting**, and were glad to escape from it as soon as possible." Mary Anne was more explicit. "It must be curious to naturalists, surgeons, etc., but to us a most disgusting sight. Papa obliged to go out, as well as poor Miss Strickland who was really very ill. Eliza and myself both felt quite sick. NB. Never intend to make a second visit."

A distinguished, if eccentric, resident of Paris at that time was Sir William Sidney Smith. He was a vainglorious and bombastic extrovert, whose controversial naval career had drawn censure from his superiors, including Earl St. Vincent and Nelson, and was redeemed by his one great exploit - the bombardment of Acre in 1799, which had compelled Napoleon to abandon his army in Palestine.

Mary Anne, Eliza and their father met him at a dinner given by Uncle Lewis, who sent his carriage to collect them and the voluble old admiral, but let Eliza relate what happened:

"Sir William Sidney Smith is as gallant as ever to the ladies; was quite shocked to find us sitting with our backs to the horses, and Papa in front; insisted on the whole party changing places before he would enter the carriage. He was very entertaining the whole way, tho' sometimes told rather too long stories, of which he was always the hero! He said he was the first who introduced the fashion of wearing his own hair. He returned from abroad when those enormous wigs were worn, and went to call on the King (George III) at Windsor, who laughed very much at him and said he looked like a waiter. He told His Majesty that was quite right, for he came to wait upon him. The Princess Sophia rowed him very much for not wearing a queue, but he said she would never have an opportunity of knowing if he wore one or not, as she knew he was not allowed to turn his back upon her or any of her family.

"When we were preparing to return at night he begged to be allowed to put our shawls in the Jerusalem fashion, so as to form shawl, frill, veil, hood and long sleeves, by which means they were not only useful but ornamental. He arranged the drapery very prettily and seemed quite au fait with the subject. He said the English ladies wore theirs as if only intended to sweep the opera stairs."

Eliza goes to School

One of the purposes of the visit to Paris was to complete Eliza's education, and as this would take a year it was necessary to find her tutors in French, Italian, music etc., and a suitable pension at which to reside after Mary Anne and Papa had returned to England. Having been recommended to a Mme. Madeleine, Mrs Way took her two nieces and Fanny Strickland on a tour of inspection. The place seemed comfortable and respectable and the terms reasonable, and Madame suggested they might like to talk to the only English girl there, a Miss Jones "....to which we agreed," says Mary Anne. "Eliza and Miss Strickland went into the garden with the young lady .... Her first word was 'Do not name cards, as the three sisters enjoy a good game most evenings, and as for the priests interfering, instead of coming to confess (the girls) they join in the card party'." Eliza: "She then told us that the French was taught by an Irish woman, and as she did not like that she just crossed the street, whenever she was inclined, for a lesson from a French gentleman who lived opposite...." "....and as for getting out," added Mary Anne in a scandalised tone, "you can whenever you like.... no questions asked; and you have only to appoint anybody you like and you have permission to go out.... Whose pretty little girl is the one in black? Oh, she is English! Or rather was, for she has forgot all her English. Her mother resides in Paris, but seldom sees her. Indeed, she is quite a woman of the world!

"We made up our minds this was quite enough; equally bad to fall in with such a girl or with the school, even if the account were true. In one thing it was correct for she said 'Do not engage for the first room they show you, as that will be bad, and there is one disengaged much better', which proved to be correct...."

Two days later (14th Sept.) they had more luck at Mme. Vigogne, 14 Quai de Billy. Mary Anne reported "....the appearance of the young ladies, house etc. far superior to Mme. Madeleine, close to the Seine as you go to Passy; a good sized garden and two houses joined in one, allowing for the difference of comforts in a French school, thought this was quite as well conducted. Six or ten beds in each room, only for sleeping, each bedroom having its separate dressing room. Eliza chose a room to herself and arranged everything most comfortably. The terms 60 francs without masters; washing and French included."

So it was settled and a few days later Eliza moved in, though she continued to see a great deal of her family until they departed three weeks later.

Death of the King

Meanwhile, events of great consequence were taking place at the heart of the French nation. The first indication we get is on the 13th September, when the sisters went to a dressmaker, Madame Hypolite on the Boulevard des Capucins, "....an extremely pretty woman," says Mary Anne, "but she could not engage to make anything for us till the end of the week as her orders for mourning were very great, as half Paris believed the King to be dead. All the theatres and gardens shut up for 12 days."

Major Gore, whom they met in the Boulevard, told them that Louis XVIII had in fact died the day before, but the news had not been released. The next morning they found the Musée at the Jardin des Plantes shut. Mary Anne: "As we returned by the Tuileries, the Place Carousel was full of people waiting to enquire after the poor King, whose death they were expecting any minute. The scene was really quite awful, mais bien triste. When he received the sacrament they gave notice of it from the windows, and all the people of their own accord fell on their knees. I must say, if this was the feeling of the populace, that the shopkeepers seemed to be quite indifferent. On asking at the shops if anything had been heard of the state of his health, it was with a shrug of indifference: 'Oh, je crois qu'il est bien mort, mais on n'ose pas l'annoncer au public avant qu'ils ont fait leur arrangements'."

15th: Mary Anne: "The King sent for the children of the Duke de Berri and took leave of them."

16th: Mary Anne: "The first question to Baptiste was after the king. He died this morning at 4; has passed a most horrid night; was taken in agony at 9 and had struggled till four this morning. The Royal Family were with him to the last."

Dead he really was at last. The reason why the rumours had been circu-lating for three days was probably on account of the nature of his illness. Louis XVIII was a prodigiously fat gentleman. In fact George IV, when investing him with the Order of the Garter, had great difficulty in getting it round his leg which, he later admitted, was more like the waist of a child. He was afflicted with an unfortunate malady which may have been leprosy, for his valet, on peeling off his stockings was accustomed to find parts of the royal feet adhering inside. The royal physician later made a statement to the press which Mary Anne reported, to the effect that: "Louis dix-huit had, though in one, the constitution of two different persons, the upper part of his body being perfectly healthy and the lower, not only dead but mortified for several days before he died, which occasioned his struggle at the last".

The body was exposed to the public in the traditional manner and, as Louis XVIII was the last king of France to die in his bed, and still be king (all the others having been guillotined or chased into exile), there was an ugly rush to witness the spectacle.

"John Upton coming in at the moment," continued Mary Anne, "I persuaded him to accompany me to see him. Eliza went with us as far as the Place Carousel, but hearing somebody spit behind said she would go no further; indeed, she was quite in the right as the heat was very great and she would have fainted at the first squeeze.

"We entered the mob at 10. It only differs from an English mob in that there is no use, indeed you are not allowed, to press forward. As you join you must keep in your file. If you attempt to pass on the soldiers put you back in the last file à la queue de tout le monde. We stood stationary for half an hour, and then as those before us were let through the gate, gained about half a yard at a time, each time we got more crowded. At first it was not so bad as, curiously enough, I was next to the same lady who had passed us into the Tuileries on the day of poor Louis' fête. She was chatty and made the first hour pass pleasant enough, but her patience failing she went off. No siege in battle could well be worse than what we went through with no possibility of getting out. To prevent my arms being broke, I gave John one corner of my pocket handkerchief and held the other which, between whiles, amused the crowd who seemed only to be actuated by curiosity. 'Voici une chaine légère entre mari et femme; ce n'est pas en puit le couper quand on veut'.*

"I had not long to wait before there was proof of this, as in the next crush we were quite separated. We were all in a complete vapour bath and watched with impatience the opening of the grille - was once nearly crushed when pushed up against the railing. The soldiers on horseback are complete savages. Those on foot civil and helped us as far as they could. John got in first, and at last I was carried in by the mob - got leave to sit in a chair at the foot of the staircase before I went into the room. On telling the gens d'armes I had lost my party he allowed me to pass. On the first landing place I found poor John, looking more dead than alive from fatigue and fright of having lost me. We went through three large rooms left in the same state as the Royal Family had quitted them. Louis dix-huit was lying on a simple bed, the one on which he had breathed his last, with green curtains.

"I had never seen death (although I had made many attempts at Denham, but my courage had always failed me) but the sorrow I had felt before from hearing of his suffering was instantly dispelled by the sight of his face. I could never have imagined anything so beautiful, so placid and calm. Only had one expression and that of perfect resignation. He held a

* She is trying to say "Here is a light chain linking husband and wife, it cannot be cut at will".

silver crucifix in his hands, which were joined, and he really seemed to be pressing it. I hope never to forget the impression this scene made on me. He was much thinner than when I saw him three years before, but his features were very little altered - his hands so white I thought he had gloves on - was dressed in a rich French white silk, the shape that the children wear here, tied under his chin. On one side sat the priests chanting a Latin service for the repose of his soul; on the other, officers and gentlemen of the bedroom. Five tapers burning; shutters and windows open, that we had broad daylight; there could have been no deception. We passed through, only John and myself; he was much too hurried to see anything but just the profile of the King's face. We descended into the Tuileries, rare figures, faces vermilion and trembling from fatigue, but grateful to have escaped without broken arms. The only accident I saw was a poor woman who from a sudden jerk had bit through her lip. In spite of all this I am delighted that I persevered and I felt a secret delight I cannot describe. Came back, took some eau de Cologne; laid half an hour between the blankets, fresh dressed and felt quite comfortable.

"Whilst in the mob .... saw a Bourgeois; a suspected character upon being refused entrance drew a pistol from his pocket and shot the officer, who escaped but ran the man through the arm. He was secured and sent to the Watch House."

The Bourgeoisie were almost totally alienated from the restored Bourbons by 1825, and five years later drove them from the throne for good. The Bonapartists, of course, took no part in all this royalist emotion, and Eliza, after extricating herself from the mob, went with Uncle William to the Père Lachaise cemetery and, in the heat, sat in the shade of his tomb, where three Bonapartists joined them and gave them "....the particulars of Louis 18th's death, and their opinion of the family". One could have wished Eliza had been more explicit.

Meanwhile the mob was still sufficiently royalist to yell on the proclamation of Charles X, 'Le Roi est mort; mais le Roi vit encore' which upset Mary Anne: "It seemed as if poor Louis was to be forgot as soon as the breath was out of his body."

That evening the sisters went to Mrs Lewis Way's soirée at the Hôtel Mirabeau where "....we met Ld. Clonbrook and his daughters" and "Mr Kemp waltzed with his daughter so different from what would have been the case a few years before," remarked Mary Anne in her censorious manner. The 'waltz', of course, was a new and shocking dance from Vienna and was taking Europe by storm. Never before in a dance had the gentleman been permitted to take his partner round the waist. Fanny Strickland and Miss Dillon also waltzed with each other, but one doesn't yet hear of ladies waltzing with men other than their fathers or brothers.

Next morning Mr Cowley invited them all to breakfast at the Dover Hotel. "A capital breakfast of partridges, omelettes, strawberries, peaches, tea, coffee and sweetmeats," said Eliza, after which they went to look at Count Sameriva's private collection of pictures, but Mary Anne, admired more the sculpture, "....particularly the Madeleine reckoned to be Canova's chef d'oeuvre".

"How curious to have seen the Count d'Artois having entered Paris only a week before in a chariot and four with a guard of out-riders, and in a short space of time to have seen him enter as King," wrote Mary Anne. Charles X, brother of the late King, was a tall, florid, good-looking man. "A print of Charles the 10th already out," she had remarked on the 17th, but there was also a hint of his bigotry, and the morbid stranglehold of the church which was to become such a feature of the new regime, in the arrangements for the lying in state of Louis XVIII.

17th: "The King embalmed today."

18th: "The King lying in state today, the rooms all to be hung in black with fleurs de lys; the crowd very great although more English than French in mourning."

19th. "Walking home we most fortunately, seeing a crowd, stopped at the top of the Rue de Castiglione and saw the King, Charles 10th enter. (He lived at this time at St. Cloud.) Four carriages and eight, the servants' cocked hats in deep mourning; the harness purple velvet and black; 4 of the officers of the Chambre in the first carriage; then 8 greys with the King, Mme. La Dauphine and Mr Le Dauphin et Madame; the ladies, of course, in deep black with hoods; they all looked very much agitated, as it was a melancholy ceremony they were going to perform, that of throwing the holy water on the corpse of their brother. Mr Cowley said 'Chapeaux bas', but had he not called 'Hats off' I do not think it would have been done. A faint 'Huzza' which was perhaps owing to the situation of the Royal Family for, of course, the King could take no notice of the mob, and it would have been more delicate to have let him pass in silence."

In point of fact the new King was not popular, for he was known to be an arrogan and uncompromising supporter of the extreme right, and volatile Paris was swinging to the left. "The cheers as they passed were very faint," wrote Eliza. She continues:

20th: "Uncle William called for us at one and took us with Mrs Way, and Mr Hynde, to the Tuileries to see the lying in state; as we passed the gates at the Place Carousel several persons got on the carriage, but the Guards made them all dismount immediately. We waited about 10 minutes at the hall door, and then entered with the crowd, which was so great behind that they carried us on close to the soldiers who were standing with drawn bayonets to receive them. We ascended the grand staircase (at the bottom of which only three weeks before we had stood for two hours seeing the officers etc. go up to congratulate Louis on his fête), passed through the hall where all the Marshals are, and then through another room drapée en violette, and lighted by beautiful chandeliers, to the Apartment where his Majesty lay in state. A herald at arms, in a dress which was covered with gold, and a black velvet cap with about 12 ostrich plumes, sat on each side of the coffin, and two mutes at the foot; a great many of the nobility were in the room in full dress uniform. The coffin was covered with Cloth of Gold with the Crown at the top. At the foot there was a most superb velvet mantle, trimmed with ermine and covered with fleurs de lys. The tout ensemble had a most magnificent appearance (greatly superior to George the Third's at Windsor). The room was in a blaze of light, the walls covered with Cloth of Gold. In short, there was nothing funereal about it; the windows wide open, with the Venetian blinds drawn. It was curious to see all the English in deep mourning, and most of the French in colours."

21st: Mary Anne saw "7 or 8 regiments file into the Place Carousel and enter to see the lying in state. The National Guards were very entertaining, being a complete set of living caricatures." They dined, twelve of them, at the Café de Paris, but looking for a carriage in the boulevards to take them home, "we all separated accidentally and lost our party, Mr Cowley going off with Mrs Thackeray entertained us not a little".

22nd: A lady's maid came to offer her services, "....a very pleasant young woman, a German by birth, who spoke French well and wished much to come to England. She dressed Eliza's hair well". One wonders if this was in the ridiculous Apollo's knot then much in vogue; and thus decked out the sisters went with Mrs Way to see the Élysée Bourbon, "....but owing to the King's death they would not admit us; and so we went to the Hotel des Invalides," continued Eliza, "which is a noble Institution for wounded officers and soldiers; they receive their half-pay, and are taken care of for life, many of them to live to a great age. They have a beautiful library; a large Council Chamber where 12 Generals assemble once every month to settle the accounts, and it is adorned with full length pictures of several of their Chief Marshals ('all created by Bonaparte but have the head of Louis in their pictures' observed Mary Anne. 'The table for the Council very well arranged, even pincushions are furnished'). We went all over the house: Chapel, kitchen, dormitories, etc. Everything was in beautiful order and they all appeared very comfortable. We saw them at supper; they are allowed a bottle of wine a day each, the room set out like a college hall. Twelve men dine at each table, with one large dish in the middle. I admired the cleansing of their plates when they sat down, but not when I saw how they were made so, as I observed that each person as he finished, cleaned his plate by rubbing a piece of bread round it, and those who were very cleanly first applied the bread to their mouths, and then gave the plate a good scouring."

Mary Anne was more impressed with the kitchens: "....the coppers for the different potages of an immense size; a separate room for the vegetables etc., all nicely picked," and the "very handsome library; the officers allowed to take the books to their rooms, the soldiers to read in their room. We were not allowed to enter the tombe (where Napoleon was re-interred in 1840) as they were preparing the lit de mort for the Requiem tomorrow."

Eliza: "We afterwards went to St. Roche and remained there during the service for the repose of the Soul of the King", which service, continued Mary Anne, "....has been held in every church, beginning at Notre Dame: the middle aisle hung with black, on each end a large white cross worked on the black one; the same on the altar; the funeral bed, the hangings supported by wire from the ceiling, on the bed something resembling a coffin covered with a velvet pall worked in silver with death's heads etc. Large tapers all lighted and incense burning at each corner; the priests' dresses of velvet and silver; the body of the church filled with the military and the military band, large drums and kettle ditto all muffled....

"The service began at 11. The first beating of the drums made us, French and all, jump from our seats; it sounded as loud as cannon; the music and chanting very good, and the service lasted about an hour, when the host or holy wafer was carried round by the priest with a soldier at each side. The word was given 'a terre' and on their knees all went, with the exception of the English. One poor man, I pitied him greatly, for during the service he trembled exceedingly and seemed quite overcome, quite crouched on the ground, and looked as if he wished himself annihilated; very different from the soldiers, at least those of the band who were laughing. They all had to walk in procession and kiss a gold plate on which was the crucifix. The Duchess de (illegible) and two officers went round to make a collection for the poor; my surprise was great to find it contained only sous, very different to what it would have been in England."

The 24th was the day the old King was carried to St. Denis for burial. Mary Anne: "John Upton breakfasted with us, brought us the programme for the procession; we went with Eliza to Mr Way's. Papa and I took our chance in the Rue de la Paix, and saw the procession very well, military without end; the most singular part was the 400 poor carrying torches, in grey cloaks." "Many of them having a strong resemblance to the witches in Macbeth," added Eliza, who witnessed the procession from the Hôtel Mirabeau and listed the different bodies of the cavalcade as they passed:

" - the Gendarmerie of Paris
- Staff of the Royal Guards
- National Guards
- 3 battalions of Infantry of the Line
- 2 squadrons of Light Cavalry
- 60 men of the horse artillery of the Royal Guards, with a Battery
- 2 battalions of Infantry

- 6 funereal flags of the first 6 Legions of the National Guard
- A deputation of the pupils of the Military School of St. Cyr
- The Polytechnic School
- The Riding School
- Officers of all ranks on an unlimited congé
- The Ecclesiastics of Paris with lighted tapers
- The officers of the Legion of Honour, and of St. Louis, in coaches drawn by 8 horses
- 4 Knights of the Order of the Holy Ghost
- 4 Marshals of France
- 4 Peers of France
- The Household of the Duke of Bourbon, the Duke of Orleans the Dauphin, and the King's Household, all in coaches drawn by 8 horses
- The King's Bodyguard
- HRH the Dauphin, the Dukes of Orleans & Bourbon - the 8 horses with black velvet housings, trimmed with silver fringe, and covered with silver tears (the only tears visible that day!)
- Many pages, guards etc; a carriage with His Majesty's hearse borne by the Grand Almoner
- Heralds at Arms; a magnificent funeral car, richly gilt. The top formed by angels in gilt with hands joined; the King's velvet mantle was over the Coffin and quantities of Cloth of Gold drapery etc."

Eliza was obviously impressed though she thought it had "more the appearance of a Review than a Funeral". Mary Anne was much more scornful: "The funeral car was much too glittering", and as for the suite of 30 state carriages, "It was truly French and highly ridiculous; they very much resembled the Ascot Heath races as represented at Astley's* only much inferior. Coachmen, footmen, and liveries all of a piece - just like monkeys"; and "such a noise in the street that we did not hear the coups de canons as they passed the barriers as far as the Porte St. Denis".

Near to where they were standing was a box in which were the Duchess of Orleans** and her nine children. "The Duke and the officers bowed to her en passant, and some kissed their hands, which I think was rather indecorous. She is by no means handsome, tall and thin."

The Boulevards were crowded but Mary Anne says "....the mob did not appear to take the least interest in the spectacle more than curiosity, not one remark or regret did we hear" for the death of a king who had been restored to the throne in 1814 "in the baggage of the Allies". Enthusiasm for his successor was even less, but this may have been due partly to the weather, for it rained the next three days. "It came down in such torrents that the boys were out with wooden bridges on wheels to help you pass the gutter," wrote Mary Anne; fortunately "the woman in the passage De Lorne found my bonnet, after having lost it for more than a week".

* A famous circus in London.
** Marie Amelie, later Queen of France, 1830.

On the day after the funeral of Louis XVIII Eliza took up residence at Madame Vigogne's. "Found the house very dull without Eliza," wrote Mary Anne, but she soon found things to interest her.

On the 27th the new king made a formal entry into Paris, but "....it rained so very incessantly that we were obliged to wait at the Café de Paris to see the procession....the Master of the house very civil, gave me a good place in the window with his family.

101 guns fired as the King entered the Barrière de L'Étoile; on hearing them I mounted on my chair, which amused the party as they said it would be a good hour before the royal party arrived....the Duke of Bourbon was the first and many people mistook him for the King; he had a chaplet of white roses and lilies presented to him by mistake. The Regiment of Lancers very handsome; the Duke of Orleans, the Dauphin etc. He was cordially received, but looked as old as his father, who followed at some distance, surrounded by the Marshals. To me the applause seemed very faint, not more than 100 or so crying 'Vive le Roi' and then quiet again. Only one voice 'Vivent les Bourbons': no wearing of handkerchiefs or any real interest taken. The King bowed on each side and looked very cheerful and affable, but (had) no dignity and sat ill on his horse. Uncle Lewis rode by the side of the Royal carriage and was the best-mounted there. The cannon fired as the King entered and left Notre Dame, and as he entered the Tuileries. As soon as the procession had passed our window we waded through the mud to Mr Cowley at the Hôtel Donane....and were well warmed by a very good déjeuner à la fourchette."

Mary Anne had conceived a sneaking admiration for the new king and contrived to be at certain strategic points where it was known he would pass. Hearing the guns fire on the 27th, she hurried to the Tuileries Gardens and saw the king enter the Château by the Place Carousel, "....and for the first time that I heard hearty cheers; a French lady lent me an umbrella, and every cordon bleu and rouge that appeared at the window, the mob cried 'Vive le Roi' which was very amusing. Another woman came, quite glad to see me again. 'Aha, Mme, vous aimez beaucoup a voir nos Rois; j'ai entre dix minutes apres vous l'autre jour; voici ma petite' etc." (It is more probable that she said 'Je suis entre' but Mary Anne's French wasn't as good as her sister's.)

Mary Anne was not so fortunate at La Bagatelle in the Bois de Boulogne, where the royal children were expected. "We were not admitted and returned by water," but on the 30th she was on the Pont Royale to see the King, Dauphin and Duc d'Orleans return from a review in the Louvre. "When His Majesty came the applause was very great, quite in the English style. One woman presented a petition close to us; the King received it amid cries of 'Vive le Roi'; on his entering the King, hearing her cries of 'Sire, Sire', approached, took the petition and shook hands with the lady, which gracious act of condescension made the air resound with cries of 'Vive le Roi'.

"The Duc de Bordeaux was held up to the windows of the carriage, dressed en militaire....kissing his hands to the people and smiling. To make him popular the ordinance for the liberty of the Press was signed on his birthday...."

2nd October: "The lady who presented the petition yesterday had a private audience of the King today at the Palace of the Tuileries."

Meanwhile, Eliza, with three of the young ladies from Mme. Vigogne's school, walked to the Champs de Mars (now the site of the Eiffel Tower), "....where the King received the Garde National, Swiss Guards etc., about 20 thousand men; it was a most beautiful sight; the King rode close by where we stood several times, all the Princes with him; the Duchesses de Born & d'Angoulême followed in open carriages with the two children....the Duchess of Orleans with all her family after. The whole party were received with loud acclamations. The Duke of Bordeaux, who was only four years old, was in full uniform as Col. of the Swiss Guards; he seemed quite tired with saluting the soldiers as he passed down the lines, and had he been dressed otherwise would not have look't so much like a monkey, as he is a very nice little child.

"On returning to the Tuileries, the Duke of Orleans' carriage broke down; he jump't into a fiacre and told the man to drive him to the Tuileries, but as hackney coaches are not allowed to enter there he stopt at the Place Carousel; the Duke cried out 'Passer, passer - vite' and made him drive up to the door. When he got out the Duke gave him 10 francs."

At tea afterwards at Mademoiselle Auger's "....where we met some of the officers who had been on duty at the Champs to Mars", there was the usual exchange of gossip about the Royal Family.

"On his return to France (1814) the Compte d'Artois (now Charles X) went to call on Josephine; at the gates of Malmaison there sat a poor woman selling apples and pears. She offered him some en passant and he gave her a louis; she immediately cried out 'Vive Louis dix-huit; vive Bonaparte; vive le Compte d'Artois!' The King laughed very much and said 'C'est bien ma pauvre femme; il faut que tout le monde vive'!"

In the meantime Eliza was learning how Madame Vigogne's establishment was conducted. "Once a year the prizes are distributed here, and whoever has been the most amiable and obliging during all that time receives (by the unanimous votes of the whole school, servants and all) a very handsome WHITE SASH. It is put on by Mlle. Auger, the whole school being present, and is always worn on her birthday. She gives a Ball where every pupil subscribes 10 francs. Last year they gave her a very handsome salver that cost a thousand francs...."

Mme. Vigogne assured Mary Anne that "....she never had a more amiable young person in her house...." Eliza evidently had set her heart on that white sash if not the salver worth 1,000 francs.

"October 1st. Wrote my first exercise and was MUCH praised, mine having but 3 faults, and many French girls 15; they are more ignorant of their own language than anyone could imagine", wrote Eliza smugly; and for the next few days wrote her journal in French, which passages are a tedious display of vanity and lack her usual humour.

Eliza was evidently allowed out fairly often, but always with a chaperone, sometimes Mme. Vigogne herself, but usually two other young ladies of the establishment, who were senior and more experienced. We hear much of the "Misses Buckler & Newton". Frequent visits were made to the Chapel at Marboeuf and this was followed by "elegant drawing rooms" at Uncle Lewis', which were always thronged with English élite, and not a few French nobility as well. "Oct. 5th. The Duchesse de Reggis and her daughter called while we were at dinner; Stephanie ran into the refectoire and kissed us all; she appeared in high spirits; her mother was at the Duchesse de Berri's drawing room the day before; all the ladies wore long trains; the Duchesse d'Angoulême's was 7 yards in length...."*

* The Duchesse d'Angoulême was the daughter of Louis XVI and Marie Antoinette, one of the few Bourbons to have survived the French Revolution.

Farewells

The day was approaching for the return of Mary Anne and her father to England. There was the usual hassle over passports and there was an orgy of shopping, dining out and sightseeing, not to mention visits to the Opéra-Comique. "The second piece - La Neige, or Le Nouvel Eginard - an historical fact in the time of Charlemagne; the last scene with snow falling - exceedingly pretty," but Mary Anne's determination to sample, to the very last, the delights of French cuisine, met with disappointment.

"Dined with Mr Cowley and John (Upton) at the Café de Paris meaning to have dinner superb, and were properly punished for epicurean ideas by each dish worse than the former; the soup thin, the meat **too** high, partridges half done, and the omelettes smoking - in short, the only dinner dégoûtant que nous avons eu à Paris. Home, packed clothes, books, etc. Not in bed till 12. Woke at half past one. No more sleep that night."

It had been a hectic week of farewells and preparations for departure. On Monday she had been to the Messagerie Royal with her father to reserve places in the coach, and had dined "....at the Trois Frères Provenceaux - met quite a different sort of people; de vrais gourmands. Room, furniture etc. far inferior to Café de Paris but cheaper and better dinners; and a very good view of the Palais Royal as you see 3 sides of the Square; being all lighted up it looked like a fairy palace...."

Tuesday, and they went to say goodbye to the cousins at Marboeuf. "Saw Drusilla's pony, given by Lady Hester Stanhope; having heard so much about it was rather disappointed; the grey the servant was riding I admired much more...." (Metwell, the Arabian, by the way, returned to Stansted with the family in 1826 and was much ridden by Drusilla. 'What a lovely creature', a gentleman was heard to say. 'Does he mean you or the horse?' asked Lewis. But Drusilla rode her too hard and she fell and broke her knees, and that was the end of Lady Hester's famous mare.)

Mary Anne made a last visit to the Louvre: "Papa's copy of the Holy Family by Raphael appears to us to be larger than the original here; the date of this 1518." Wednesday, a farewell visit to Mme. Vigogne: "Papa paid Mme. Vigogne for the first Quarter. Madame gave me a packet for her daughter who keeps a French School in England, and promised to come and see us in the Spring."

Thursday, their last day: "Dear Eliza and myself breakfasted together. John Upton called with his letters for England; a wet morning. Eliza in very low spirits on account of our leaving Paris, but we begged her not to remain if she was not comfortable. She said she is as happy as it is possible to be at school, that Madame Vigogne was exceedingly kind, and that it was her desire to remain....took leave of Eliza in the Court of the Louvre."

"Returned en fiacre," wrote Eliza, "bien triste to the Pension", but she cheered up: "Miss Rowden arrived in the evening and brought me letters from England."

"Up at 5," wrote Mary Anne, the day of their departure. "Went to Papa's room to light my candle; found him awake but not inclined to rise."

Somehow all the trunks, bandboxes, a cage of partridges and another of canaries that Col. Way wanted to take home to Denham, were got to the Messagerie by eight, though "Papa had not time for breakfast" and John Upton helped to get them stowed. "On examining the partridges found them in a dreadful state of starvation and suffocation. One dead. Changed their cage and fed them - all present agreed they would be dead before our arrival at Calais."

True to her character, Mary Anne got herself a seat next to the most interesting looking traveller: "Charles Lloyd by name. 15 years Governor of a province or district in India, where he lived as a king and enjoyed his health and made his fortune. Lives in North Wales and enjoys fishing and shooting; by his own account excels in every field sport but cannot condescend to kill pheasants and partridges after shooting Tygers etc."

The carriage travelled on through the night "....by the same triste route that we came". A stop was made at Abbeville at 6 a.m. for "a cup of coffee, very refreshing. Mr Lloyd and I walked on for about a mile...." until the carriage caught them up. "Dined at Montreuil: viz a déjeuner à la fourchette: partridges, turkey, leg of mutton, cutlets, coffee etc., all at 2 fr. 10 c. par tête. Arrived at Calais by 10, and really, though very giddy, not much fatigued; warm water and fresh dressing a great comfort." This was at Quillac's "which is by far the most comfortable in Calais....4 of the poor partridges dead; six very strong; the canaries quite hearty".

Next day they sailed on the Spitfire, "....the same vessel that we came over in", a passage of 2½ hours; "....could have been very good, had it not been for the heavy rain and very cold wind....landed at half past one in our great cloaks that we might, had we been so inclined, have smuggled with perfect ease as many silk stockings as we liked; but were too cold to think of anything of the kind." They put up at the Ship "....where Mrs Smith, the respectable old landlady, was very glad to see us", but finding that none of the luggage could be collected from the custom house till four "....I borrowed stockings and shoes and dried the rest of the clothes on; and warmed myself by a glass of negus".

Mary Anne was full of indignation for the Customs Commissioner: "He was confused, and slow and not up to the business. In appearance much improved in dress but grave with an air of importance. My companion attributed this change for the worse to the Methodists, but on enquiring of Mrs Smith she said it was grief for the loss of his wife; and we pitied him.

Presently came in the master of the Inn, and he, I fear, let us into the real secret: that brandy was the cause of the man having lost his senses."

The next day: "Followed Papa to the Custom House, a rare scene of confusion - books etc. all thrown out without any compassion to them or the entreaties of their owners; trunks broken open, hinges taken off. Bandboxes knocked to pieces, quite barbarous; where, with a little patience all might be done in order....could not get away till 12."

At Canterbury and Rochester Mary Anne was delighted to meet old acquaintances. She gathered up the latest scandal and pretended to be shocked by it. "Whoever would have thought to have heard any scandal of that good tempered lady...." etc. etc. "The two dear boys G & A* dined with us, looking fat and well. In London by 11 and put up at the Bedford.

"A wet, foggy morning; the markets full of carrots, turnips, cabbages and green apples - very different from the Marché St. Honoré that we had just left well stocked with grapes of Fontainebleau, currants, strawberries, peaches, figs etc: not to forget the most beautiful nosegays of violets, whose perfume you could trace at a good distance.

"Called on Mme. Biron, Mme. Vigogne's daughter, with her parcel; a very pleasant woman who was, with her daughter, delighted to hear of her mother. She has opened a French School and appears to have everything very well arranged, and in good style. French servants and the lady does not speak English."

Then to Campden Street where her three youngest sisters, Maria (15), Belinda (14), and Laetitia (10) were at school. "Found the trio much surprised at seeing me, as they thought we had been home for some time; they were busily engaged in bringing in apples, handfuls, which all fell to the ground as we entered: 'Oh! Mary Anne, it is you!' They assured me Mama was at Denham and waiting Papa's return to come to spend a week in London."

But on reaching Denham they found all the party - Mama, Lady E. Bourke, Ben, the eldest brother (23), Miss Hamlet and Miss Thornton - had left the day before for Leamington to visit Uncle John Smyth, the new Baronet of Ashton, leaving Henry Hugh, the studious second brother (19) "....very comfortable in the library". "New carpets," she added, "and the exterior of the house much improved by iron railings."

"And thus ends our eight weeks of badandiere (sic)** but not of amusement, the recollection of the various scenes and persons will serve for entertainment for lat least as many months to come. Left Paris on Friday at

* Gregory and Arthur, her younger brothers, then aged 13 and 12.
** This 'French' word was evidently invented by Eliza.

10 and in London on Monday; had it not been for the Custom House could have been Sunday, making it only a journey of three days and one night."

So, on this banal and very typical note, Mary Anne passes out of these annals. There is a brief glimpse of her again, a year or two later, in a letter she wrote to Fanny Strickland, her erstwhile reluctant companion to the Anatomical Museum in Paris, on the occasion of the latter's marriage to Charles Cottrell-Dormer of Rousham, Oxfordshire.

"My dear Fanny,

"Being returned to the quiet of Denham, I must send you a few lines of congratulation to tell you how truly happy Papa and myself were to have had a glimpse of you on your bridal day and to beg your acceptance of the trifle which accompanies this as a 'gage d'amitié' and which would have been presented in person on the proper day, had I conceived the least idea of close contact - to have caught your eye and kissed your hand en passant was all I dreamt of, but on seeing the stoppage occasioned by the boys sending in for favours, I couldn't resist the impulse of stepping forward, and it was most kind and good-natured of you and Mr Cottrell to receive me as you did.

Uncle William and Mrs Way kindly called on us after the clergy and party had dispersed and gave us the particulars of the wedding dress etc; am glad to find you adopted the French fashion, the veil and wreath of orange flowers so much more simple and pretty than the English style of hat and bonnet. Friday I dined in Harley Street and had the pleasure of being introduced to Lady Cottrell and your two sisters. You may guess the bumper toast after dinner, and if any truth in old sayings you were in no want of rouge that evening as you, of course, were the chief topic of conversation, and all the party were warm in your praises, not excepting Mr Griffiths, of whom you appear to be a great favourite. Saturday, called in Clarges Street and was happy to find all your party quite well....they had all been at the Covent Garden ball the evening before - it must have been a great sight from the splendour of the dresses.... Hope, when you have unpacked and are sufficiently settled to have an idle moment, you will employ it by letting me hear from you and pray give my best comps. to Mr Cottrell, and with love and every good wish for many, many years of health and happiness in which Pa, Ma, Eliza and all our circle join,

"Am your affectionate friend,

"Mary Anne Way"

Mary Anne never married. She became another of the maiden aunts of Denham Place and died, aged 50, in 1850. Years later Fanny Strickland's son, Clement Cottrell-Dormer, married Eliza's daughter, Florence, but to see how all that came to pass we must now return to Eliza, where Mary Anne left her, at Madame Vigogne's establishment in Paris.

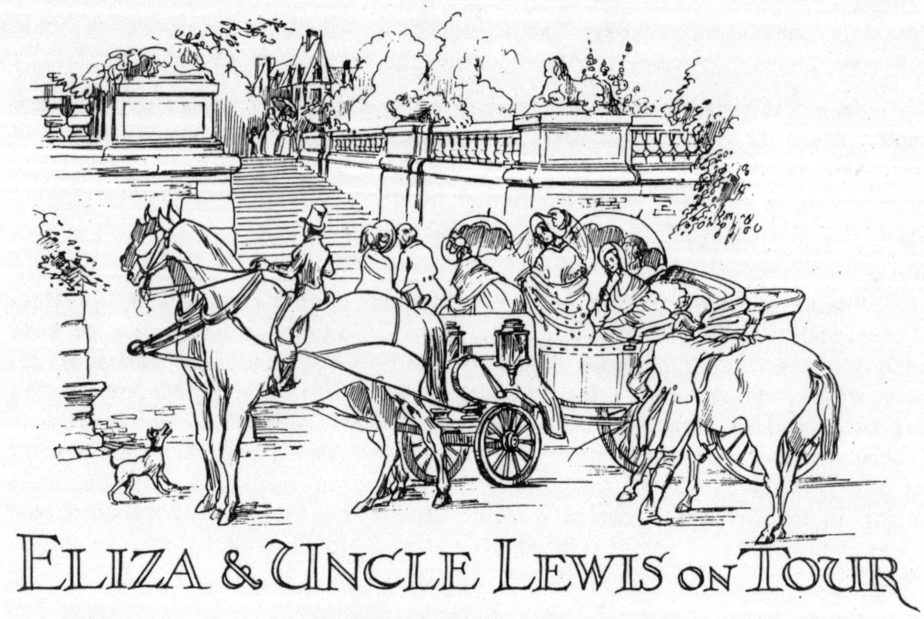

ELIZA & UNCLE LEWIS ON TOUR

The Young Ladies of the Pension

Eliza's journal is mostly concerned with social activities, but now and again there is a glimpse of the daily routine at Mme. Vigogne's establishment.

"12th Oct. Breakfast at ½ past 7

From	8 to 11	Writing and translating French with Mons. de Busne
	11 to 12	Italian with Signor Ribera
	12 to 1	Recreation
	1 to 2	Music with Madame Recout
	2 to 3	Writing and reading French with Mde. Jeunehomme
	3 to 4	Dinner
	4 to 5	Recreation
	5 to 8	Italian dialogue and reading with Mde. Buckler
	8	An excellent supper of milk, cheese and large tureens full of stewed prunes."

Then to tea at Mlle. Auger's. Here the young ladies relaxed and were treated to the sort of anecdotes which found their way into the commonplace books of the time. On the 22nd Eliza confided just such a story to her journal, this one related by Mme. Vigogne about the evening of the entrance of the allies into Paris.

"The first night the Duke de Berri landed he slept at Cherbourg, and was so hospitably received that when he departed in the morning he asked his host if there was anything he could do for him. He said he wished to be employed in some public office in Paris. The Duke sent for him soon after and appointed him Manager of the Opera House, where he immediately removed, taking his household goods with him, and it was a very singular coincidence that he (the Duke de Berri) died on the same bed which he slept in the first night he landed in France."

On other occasions Mlle. Auger read aloud to the girls from 'Le fils d'honneur'. "She reads beautifully," records Eliza.

Sunday evenings were reserved for special treats like amateur theatricals, although not always with success. October 7th Eliza relates: "The young ladies of the pension had learnt a play which they were going to act tonight, but unfortunately for them Madame La Baronne de Barbier called in the morning to see her daughter, Pauline, and was so angry with her for having sent her an ill-written letter the day before, that she forbad her acting. So Mlle. Auger would not allow the play to be performed which was a great disappointment to all as they had taken great pains with it."

Saints' days were very special occasions. These were holidays, but church and collections for the poor seem to have been obligatory, followed by écarté and chat. On the Fete of St. Esprit (14th Oct) Eliza wrote:

"Went to Church at Chaillot with Mlle Auger and all the young ladies, dressed in white, 46 in number. All the schools in France meet at their Parish Churches on this day, every year, to pray for the Divine Blessing on themselves and their teachers. The minister, a fine looking old man of 83, commenced the service with a very beautiful address to the Pensionats on their behaviour to their instructors, making a proper use of their time and improving the talents entrusted to them. They afterwards all joined in singing a hymn, and then concluded with a mass to the Virgin Mary. A lady who keeps a school in the Champs Élysées then went around to every one and collected money for the poor of the parish. It was a very pretty sight, the Church being entirely filled with children, all dressed in their best clothes, charity children and all. There was a boys school with 83...."

November brought a whole deluge of saints' days: "November 1st being the Fête des Toussaints - a whole holiday; 2nd Fetes de Morts - also a holiday, walked to Passy with Miss Ainsworth; 4th La Fete de St. Charles - a whole holiday.... In the evening Mlle. amused the children by shewing the magic lantern which was invented by Fersher, a Jesuit, in 1645. 25th - a whole holiday, being the Fête of St. Catherine, the girls acted the tragedy of Esther beautifully. They had the proper dresses from the theatre. Afterwards Quadrilles and waltzes till 12. We subscribe 3 frs. each for the supper, music etc; had a very pleasant evening."

Scarcely a day seems to have passed without an interesting visitor calling at the establishment. 13th Oct: "Mr & Mrs Lewis Way and Drusilla called. They went all over the house, chapel, refectory, dormitories etc., and approved of all very much. While they were in the parlour there were two English ladies sitting in the room talking to Mlle. Auger who, after they were gone, sent for me as they said they had a letter of introduction to Mr

Lewis Way. I told them they had been sitting with him for a quarter of an hour and directed them to Marboeuf."

Lewis, perhaps because of the departure of Ben and Mary Anne, was particularly attentive to Eliza's needs and not long after his visit she wrote, "Mrs L. Way called and brought me a silver cup from Uncle Lewis who had observed when in the refectoire that I was the only person without one...."

"While I was having my Italian lesson," wrote Eliza on 18th Nov. "....a young lady sent to say she wished to see me. I went into the parlour and found a stranger who informed me she was recommended to that pension by Mr Upton, and begged I would tell her all the particulars about it, which I did, and shewed her the rooms etc. She was much pleased with the arrangement of everything (is a Miss Smyth from Taunton), but Mlle. Auger not having a single-bedded room disengaged, she was not able to come, not liking the idea of a dortoir."

Eliza seems to have been much in demand as a liaison officer: "After dinner (29th Nov) a gentleman called to see Mlle. Auger. Pauline went for her and when she returned he said, 'N'est pas qu'il-y-a une Mlle. Way ici?' 'Oui, Monsieur, le-connaissez vous?' 'Non, mais je connais son père et son oncle.' I, who was sitting at the piano, then said (Malgré, Pauline's shakes of the head) 'Monsieur, je suis Mlle. Way.' 'Oh', he said, 'Do you speak English, for I want to make some enquiries about this school, and never shall be able to make them in French?' He then introduced himself as Mr Temple. He said Mrs Gore had promised to bring him there but that the Major was taken so ill she could not leave home, and that he was looking for a school for Miss Byng, Lord Torrington's niece, and had been highly recommended to this by Uncle William. I told him all particulars of the masters, house, etc., and he said his lady and daughter would call on Monday."

Into the Orbit of Lewis Way

At first Eliza took her studies very seriously and even declined invitations out. "Miss Ainsworth and I were walking in the court after dinner when who should arrive but Mrs Thackeray and her Daughters, to fetch Miss A. They were much surprised to see me and very kindly pressed me to join the dinner party, but not liking to detain them while I dressed, I declined. The musical examination was tonight, rather a formidable undertaking, before Mesdames Vigogne, Recout, Le Page and Auger...."

But more and more she was drawn into the circle of Lewis Way and his family, a temptation that was hard to resist, especially when Uncle Lewis sent his carriage to fetch her. By this time Lewis Way, at the height of his powers, with his dynamic sermons and magnetic personality was attracting interesting people from all walks of life, from princes to beggars. It is not surprising that when the Christmas holidays came Eliza accepted Uncle Lewis' invitation to a house he had taken for his family in the Bois de Boulogne.

She got on well with her cousins Drusilla and lanky Anna, and did not return to the pension in the New Year, except once or twice to pay her respects to Madame Vigogne and the other teachers. After this her journal becomes rather tedious and repetitive, recording the formal social round of engagements expected of one of her class. In the course of the next six months she met the entire English establishment in Paris, the composition of which, in those days, was tight and aristocratic. Among the names dropped into the leaves of her journal were the Earl & Countess of Strathallan, Lord & Lady Henry Cholmondely, the Marchioness of Arbercorn, Lady Mary Stanley, Lady William Bentinck (a distant relation), the Duke of Somerset, Lady Caroline Wortley, Sir Gordon & Lady Drummond (British Consul), Captain Craddock (attaché to the British Ambassador), Lady Charlotte Fitzgerald, Lord & Lady Sheffield, Lady Castle Stuart, and Mr Brown, the American Ambassador. There is an equally impressive list of French ladies and gentlemen who were frequent visitors at the receptions of the British Ambassador, and at the more informal gatherings at the home of Lewis Way. On these occasions Lewis was the perfect host; his generous and expansive nature and wide repertoire of funny stories, made him beloved of English and French alike. Eliza wrote that a very English plum pudding served at one of these gatherings prompted Mrs Way to record "...the difficulty they had at an Inn in the south of France to get one made, or even to make them understand what was wanted. Uncle Lewis asked for 'Un pouding de plomb'. They said 'C'est impossible Monsieur, il sera trop lourd.' He then said 'Un pouding de plume'. 'Oh, Monsieur, ce sera trop légèr'. At last when they made them understand they had a very different pudding to any they had ever seen before". (NB: Plomb = lead; plume = feather. 'Prune' was the word he wanted.)

Among the more celebrated of this charmed circle was Sir Thomas Lawrence. Eliza and Drusilla occasionally accompanied Uncle Lewis when he sat for his portrait, but it is not clear from the journal whether the painter was Lawrence or someone else. While staying at St. Germaine with Uncle Lewis and family, Eliza writes (20th Aug): "Lady Nelson, who was staying at the same hotel with Mr & Mrs Nesbit, sent to say if we had any service, she begged she might join it." A few days later Lady Nelson paid the Ways a formal visit, but Eliza has no witty observation to make about 'Dearest Fanny' whom Nelson had abandoned for Emma Hamilton.

Eliza was evidently more intrigued by the exotic and some of Lewis Way's more colourful guests were treated to exacting descriptions. One day a Persian Aga called at Marboeuf. "He was dressed with a rich Cashmere round his waist, a blue silk pelisse covered with flowers in gold, a black and white head dress; a most magnificent black beard, large expressive black eyes - a very animated, pleasing countenance. He talked French well, tho' not fluently and understands English; was introduced at our Court last year and likes England much better than France, as there he could go out without being observed, here he is always obliged to go in his closed carriage, his dress is taken so much notice of. After tea Drusilla and Mrs Yates sang duets, and Miss Ainsworth a very pretty Scotch song which delighted the Persian...."

April 20th: "Prince Kiraschin (chamberlain to the Emperor of Russia) came with 3 ladies to see the Temple" - undoubtedly an old acquaintance of Lewis Way from the time of his historic visit to Russia in 1817. More interesting to Eliza was Prince Leopold of Saxe-Coburg, who had married the Prince Regent's daughter, Charlotte, in 1816 and was left a widower a year later when she died in childbirth.

30th Nov: "Being the first day of the Fête at Longchamps, we promenaded en voiture up and down the Champs Élysées. It was a very gay scene. In the evening the Duchess of Somerset sent a note to say if Uncle Lewis would keep seats she and the Duke would accompany Prince Leopold to the Chapel on Sunday...." and on the day concerned "Prince Leopold came with the Duke and Duchess of Somerset and the Ladies St. Maur; they all partook of the sacrament. Prince Leopold gave 5 Louis; impossible to be more attentive than he was, quite a pattern to all. He afterwards came into the drawing-room, where he had his luncheon; and admired the Chapel etc. exceedingly." Prince Leopold later became the first King of Belgium (1830) and the much beloved uncle of Queen Victoria.

A very popular visitor was Captain Craddock "....who is one of the attachés à l'Ambassade de S. M. Britannique," writes Eliza. He had been in Syria two years before at the same time as Lewis Way and, like him, had interesting stories to tell about Lady Hester Stanhope.

"Lady H. dresses always like a Mameluke," quoted Eliza, "and makes her companion, Miss Williams, dress in the Turkish style, with her face always veiled. He (Capt. Craddock) says she is a complete tyrant in her house, is very fond of chickens, and feeds them herself of an evening, but before she shuts them up for the night poor Miss Williams has to wash all their feet and wipe them with muslin. Mr Wolf called to see her but she sent word 'had he been a learned Jew she would have admitted him with pleasure, but had no wish to see an Apostate who had abandoned a sublime tho' faulty religion for a shadow'. She and Mr Barker, the Consul at Aleppo, used to be great friends, till one day he received a note from her saying 'Sir, you are a Consul: now a Consul is nothing but an ambassador and an ambassador depends upon a King, but as I depend on neither, but stand alone, never desire to see you again'. He gave the note to Captain Craddock who has it in her own writing, but could never find out what offence he had committed."

Eliza was always wittiest in describing the French. One can almost picture the Marquis of Lally Tolendal "....who was delighted to hear of the Chapel; said he was 'for Liberty of de conscience all over de world', is a most agreeable, entertaining man, and very good looking, but much more like a John Bull in appearance than a Frogeater. Madame de Staël humorously remarked of him that he was the fattest and most feeling man she ever knew".

Lewis Way's reckless charity to anyone in distress, whatever their credentials, attracted the same kind of riffraff that had flocked to his doors in Stansted and Nice. Eliza: "At breakfast there was quite a levée of people: first a German; then a London tailor with his wife and two children; they had some breakfast and told us their history; afterwards another German who talked a little French, shrugged his shoulders and bowed just like a strolling player. He said he had a wife and two children. Uncle Lewis gave them all money and bread and thinking of other things said, while he put the roll into the man's hand: 'Présentez ceci à Madame, votre épouse, avec mes compliments'; the man bowed to the ground." The news got around, for next day at breakfast:

"A poet presented himself with an Elegy he had written on Louis dix-huit. Presently a descendant of Van Dyke arrived, and so like him that it was quite ridiculous. He stood about 2 hours. Then a French woman with a petition popt up at the window. Uncle Lewis gave a 5 franc piece to all in distress, let them be of what religion or country they may." One is relieved to learn that it was not only Lewis' pocket that was touched, and that at the Chapel Marboeuf there were frequent collections for the needy, and Eliza records on one occasion that a very handsome sum was raised for the poor English 'stranded' in Paris to help them return home.

Even the well-to-do English expatriate community had need of Lewis Way's benevolence from time to time.

One evening he received a note from a Miss Talbot saying "....she was requested by Miss Smith, an acquaintance of Mr Upton's, to write and beg he would call upon her between services, as she was dangerously ill". Eliza goes on to relate what happened:

"We dined, and then Uncle Lewis and I set off at 6 for the Faubourg Poissonnier (which is quite the other end of Paris). When we arrived I went up and saw her. At first her head seemed quite confused and she did not recollect ever having seen me before. The Nurse gave her a composing draught and she then said she would see Uncle Lewis and begged him to pray for her. He said he could not do that till he knew the state of her mind, and asked what were her hopes and expectations with regard to a future state. She said she had never committed any sins and that she hoped to be saved, as she had led a good life. He told her while her mind was in that state her prayers would be quite useless, and asked if she believed that Christ was the Son of God. Whom he came to save? and that if she trusted in her own righteousness what was the use of his coming into the world to save souls if she could work out her own salvation; that that was like the Catholic faith. They thought that by counting their beads and saying certain prayers so many times over, they would be saved. He conversed with her some time and then prayed with her. I was surprised to see the two Catholic nurses kneel down and continue kneeling during the whole prayer. We afterwards saw Madame Jenny (a completely superannuated old woman) and Lord Anson's daughter. The former said Miss Smith had brought all her illness on herself; that with a bad cold she would go to a Ball, and the Sunday following to the Oratoire, very thinly dressed; in short, said the old lady, she is a complete casse-tête. She arrived here alone and I believe she has not a single friend in France."

Lewis Way sent Mr Roberts, the English apothecary, to her but Eliza, calling to enquire a few days later "....could gain no tidings of her, his attendance having been dispensed with for a French doctor".

Eliza Enjoys Herself

Eliza was very correct in her attendance at the Chapel Marboeuf every Sunday, and records the texts of Uncle Lewis' sermons, which she followed with interest, though she once added wryly "Uncle Lewis preached for an hour and a half. He had forgotten his watch". She was much more intrigued by his extempore outbursts, especially when the young ladies whispered during the sermon. These she related verbatim, with evident relish.

"....I am astonished in this apparently enlightened congregation, so few among them join in either the prayers or the singing. Follow these people to their homes, you will find they have tongues there, ready enough to talk of the Amusements and Vanities of the World! Ah, and voices too, to sing profane songs, but here something seems to be wanting...." and much more in the same vein, with a good deal of underlining. After the hot-gospelling at the Chapel Marboeuf, Eliza found the services of the Catholic church an endless source of amusement and made frequent visits to various French places of worship. On Ash Wednesday she went to High Mass at St. Roche, the big baroque church in the Rue St. Honoré, very near to the Hotel Prince Regent, where "....the priest today touched every person's forehead with Ashes, saying to each, as they knelt and he made the sign of the Cross 'Ashes to Ashes, Dust to Dust....' etc".

On 5th March she went with Mlle. Auger, Mrs Yates, Miss Ainsworth, Evaline Hébrand and Eulalie St. Renne to the Église St. Nicholas to attend Pauline Barthelemi's wedding. "She was dresst in white satin, with a lace dress over, short sleeves and a bouquet of orange flowers in her hair, and a magnificent lace veil, pearl necklace, diamond cross and earrings. Her father handed her to the altar, M. Moreau handed her mother. The organ played till they were seated, each in a crimson velvet armchair facing the altar and a Prie Dieu before each, covered with crimson silk. The service commenced with a Sermon full of compliments to them and their parents, and advising them how to bring up their children. The rest of the service much the same as ours, except that the lady had only to say yes; and that when the husband put on the Ring, he gave her a piece of money which had been blessed by the Priest. There was likewise a Louis placed on 20 candles which were burning round the altar by way of offering. It concluded by the Bridesmen holding an embroidered piece of silk over their heads, and then kissing the gold plate. Her sister made a collection for the Poor as soon as the Sermon was ended, and there was a grand Ball in the evening for 300 people."

Thirsting for more such experiences, Eliza went on 13th February "....to the Oratoire, with Misses Ainsworth and Pearson; heard Mons. Marron preach, but he being very old and having lost some of his front teeth, I was not much edified". Much more diverting was the visit to the Chapel Royal for which Eliza was given tickets by Madame le Franc. "I went there at 3 with Miss Ainsworth; met Madame Le Roux in the hall, who sat with us; the King (Charles X) entered soon after with the Duke and Duchess d'Angoulême. We had a seat close to them. La Dauphine was in an evening dress, I thought her very handsome. A herald at arms stood on each side of them, dressed in White Satin, richly embroidered in gold, with Black velvet caps, covered with Ostrich Feathers, and several soldiers with drawn swords stood close to them. The music when they entered was beautiful. The Service commenced with a Sermon in the middle of which I was much amused by the Priest saying 'Sujets, mouchez vous', and he actually sat down and stopped for 5 minutes while all the noses joined in concert. It had the drollest effect imaginable. The Royal Party rose as soon as the Sermon was concluded, bowed to the company several times and then went up to the gallery for the prayers. The Chapel is very handsome, lighted with beautiful Chandeliers. The seats, altar, etc. were all covered with purple cloth on account of the mourning."

Easter, 1825 brought its own brand of ceremonials and Eliza and her friends sallied forth again to St. Roche: "....the Interior Chapel was almost dark, being lighted only by a few candles, which shed a most beautiful light on the figures round the tomb. The Sacrament was placed in the Coffin and is to remain there three days. The Service commenced by the Priests purifying every Altar in the Church by pouring over them wine and water, then washing them with Hysop and wiping them with a linen Cloth; after which the pious French flocked round them and covered them with Kisses as well as small images of our Saviour which were placed about the Church. Afterwards 12 poor men sat in a row and the Priests knelt down to each, with a tub of water and washed their feet. Another wiped them, tho' not effectually as I observed they all finished that operation with their pocket handkerchiefs. Then each poor man had a Roll given him, some wine and money; and there were bunches of violets placed on the table for each of the Priests who had assisted at the ceremony."

The next day they went to St. Eustace and "....saw a child baptised, who was only one day old. First of all they put Salt into his mouth, then the Priest spat on his finger and made the sign of the Cross on the child's forehead, then on the arm with a pencil; afterwards they put a piece of cotton dipped in oil into his mouth and then on the back of his neck. The service was said in Latin, as fast as possible, and concluded by the Priest holding a banner with a Cross embroidered on it in gold, over the Child's head, saying 'Au nom du Pere, du Fils et du St. Esprit'."

The second week in April 1825 was the climax of Eliza's sojourn at the Hotel Marboeuf. There occurred, in rapid succession, four events: the meetings of the Jews' Committee, the Bible Society, the Missionary Society and the Society for Promoting Christian Morals - all causes close to the heart of Lewis Way and in which he was the leading star. Though no longer president of the Jewish Society, Lewis continued to take a great interest in its affairs. Eliza writes:

8th: "The Jews Committee was held here this morning. Mons. Olivier opened the meeting with an extemporary prayer. Afterwards Uncle Lewis expounded the 10 first verses of the 31st of Jeremiah. I was astonished at the facility with which he did it in French without the least hesitation once. They all dined here, a party of 17. Mr Simeon, Mr Rankin, Mons. Olivier and his brother, Mr & Miss Harrington, 2 Bartolozzi's, Mr Royston, Mr Anderson, and Mons. St. Jullien - the author of 'L'essai sur l'emploi des Terms' - a most pleasing Octogenarian. The exact figure of Old Time, with a forelock as white as snow. The following Sunday, Lewis preached and £60 was raised for the Jewish Society.

13th: "Went with Uncle Lewis and Drusilla to the meeting of the Bible Society. Le Marquis de Jancour was President; Boissy d'Anglais sat next to him. We remained there only a short time; met Mons. St. Quentin who introduced me to his cara sposa. In the evening we went to the Countess of Grenaud's where we met Lady Newberg, Lady Rancliffe, Lady C. Fitzgerald, the two Lady Forbes, etc., and many French people. Staid there till 10, and then went to the Marquise d'Harcourt's soirée where we met the Earl and Countess of Strathallan, and a great many English and French grandees; amongst others Uncle Lewis recognised Count Como who bound books for him 20 years ago. He emigrated and employed himself in that manner during the

Revolution. Uncle Lewis and his party returned at 12; I staid and went home with the Campbells.

14th: "Went with Uncle Lewis to the Missionary Society meeting at the Oratoire and heard several good speakers, amongst others the Baron de Staël. We staid there till 6, met Mr Greathead; returned to dinner and then went to a Ball at Mlle. Auger's; took Miss Campbell with me; danced quadrilles till 12, then went home.

15th: "Went to the meeting of the Society for Promoting Christian Morals with Uncle Lewis and Drusilla. Heard several good speeches and to the Surprise of all present, a Quakeress, Miss Walker, addressed the assembly in English. Uncle Lewis was much pleased with her and invited her to dinner, but she declined as she sets off for America tomorrow."

At this point Uncle Lewis' stamina, stretched to the utmost by his multifarious activities, cracked under the strain. The almost obsessive zeal with which he pursued his vocation had frequently reduced him to nervous prostration, and to avoid a total breakdown his doctor prescribed a complete change. He accordingly went off with Drusilla for a week at Montmorency: "....was cupped at the Bain Chinoise", and on his return, largely to escape the hordes of well-wishers who called daily at Marboeuf, it was decided to make a prolonged visit to Tours. Eliza writes, May 2nd: "Uncle Lewis said he would set off towards Tours the next day and invited me to join the party, which I very gladly accepted."

May 3rd: "Miss Ainsworth called, her journey (home) being delayed till Wednesday and was much surprised to find my trunks packed and ourselves just setting off to Tours instead of to England." There was just time to make some hasty farewells. "I went to Papa's bookshop, where the old woman was delighted to see me. Off came the spectacles and with her hands raised above her head she exclaimed 'Quoi! Est la jeune Demoiselle de la Pension'."

Eliza broadens her horizons

The decision to visit Tours was dictated by the fact that Uncle George Way, a younger brother of Lewis and also a clergyman, had taken a house there for his family. His little boy, Georgie, had been sick with chickenpox and his wife, Susan, was expecting another child, so they had already proceeded thither, together with Aunt Susan's indispensable companion and nurse, Miss Dacre.

Uncle Lewis' party included Drusilla, Eliza, Dr. Bruno Bonnechose, an old family friend whom Eliza described as "a very interesting person, having lived with Lord Byron during his sojourn in Greece and attended him till his death", and two servants, Levi and Carlo.

On 3rd May they set out. "Drusilla and I went in the open carriage to Versailles, Uncle Lewis and Dr. Bruno on horseback. Drusilla and I walked in the gardens belonging to the Palace, which is the most beautiful I ever saw. We dined and slept there at L'hôtel du Réservoir, which is a nice house, but **swarming** with bugs." Nonetheless, they stayed two nights, and on the 5th set out for Orleans. "At Longuemont, where we dined, the hostess quite a character and famous for a cake she manufactures called Croquignole." The next night was spent at Arpagnon: "....the **best** inn is a very **Bad** one (Hôtel du Courier), though no bugs...." The party was evidently still scratching after their Versailles experience.

"A little beyond Etrechy Uncle Lewis stopt the carriage to show us a beautiful view which reminded him of a similar one near Mount Lebanon."

The party spent the next night at Angerville and continued the next day. Soon after passing Tours, "....a large windmill close to the road, which was going full sail, frightened the off horse so much that he reared and jumpt off the road, throwing himself about in all directions and then trying to lie down. As soon as they could hold him quiet an instant we jumpt out and I ran to the mill and begged the man to stop it when they led the horses by. Uncle Lewis then mounted the box and drove us a capital pace to Artenay.

"Hôtel Grand Bretagne is a very curious old fashioned house, the walls of each room covered with tapestry representing the battles of Alexander and Darius. Uncle Lewis sent the horses back to Paris and we went on with posters, he in the carriage with us, Dr. Bruno and Levi on the box, and Carlo following with Vendredi and Jeudi.

"We arrived at 6 at Orleans, found the town in a great bustle preparing for la Fête de la Pucelle* the next day. We drove to Les Trois Empereurs but, every room being engaged, went on to the Hôtel de France. Were shewn up there into a double bedded room (where the table was laid for three). Presently in came the Baron de Staël** and Duc de Broglie*** who were delighted to meet Uncle Lewis and wanted him to speak at a public meeting there tomorrow. The third gentleman (a friend of theirs) said three ladies, cousins of his, having heard much of Mr Way's preaching from the Baron de Staël and others, had set off that morning to Paris purposely to hear him.

"The doctor, (Bruno) told us that the Baron's mother (Mme. de Stael) was a great admirer of Lord Byron and often said she would exchange her renommée and all her talents to be even the **forsaken** Lady Byron, which amused Lord Byron exceedingly; who could not bear to read any of his works

* Commemoration of the raising of the siege of Orleans by Joan of Arc ('la Pucelle').

** Son of the celebrated intellectual Mme. de Stael.

*** Duc de Broglie, later Prime Minister, 1835, in the reign of Louis Philippe.

a second time, but was disgusted with them as soon as he had written them and never kept even one copy by him."

8th May, Orleans: "Uncle Lewis very unwell having had a very bad night." Nonetheless, the party visited the Calvinistic Church, "dreadful **loud** singing"; the Cathedral "very handsome"; and walked on the boulevards. "During Divine Service the procession passed: La Pucelle was represented by a boy dressed in Regimentals, sword etc. He entered the town at the head of a Regiment of soldiers, with the band playing and flags waving from every window in the streets thro' which it passed.... There is a beautiful figure in bronze of La Pucelle in the Square which on this day was crowned with white roses.

"In the evening we all went to the Cathedral Church and on our return to the inn found Prince Maximilian* just arrived. The soldiers mounted guard before the door and the Maire and Prefect went in full court dress to pay their respects."

9th May: "Being Rogation Week all the Catholic priests in the town walked in procession out into the fields to bless the crops. Prince Maximilian set off early with his suite for Paris, which prevented us going till late as no horses were to be had.

"Arrived at Blois at 5, dined, and then took a good walk. We had green peas and strawberries at dinner, which are already very plentiful here; and some excellent cream in small pots, which comes from St. Gervais where the pasture is very rich, about a league from here.

"Blois is the prettiest town I have yet seen in France; and the Inn a very nice one - Hôtel d'Angleterre.... in the livre des voyageurs here we found the names of Mons. Gregory and Madame Way."

12th May: "Uncle Lewis and Drusilla rode to Noyeux. Dr. Bruno gave me an Italian lesson and I began Tasso with him; afterwards I gave him an English one and he began Milton in the evening. Uncle Lewis and the Doctor read the Batimeas to us which amused me so much (at least the way of reading it) that when the Diligence arrived at 8 with Uncle George, and he was made to guess thro' the window who the party consisted of, he said he was certain Marianne Halifax was of the party."

13th May: "Drusilla, Doctor Bruno and I set off at 11 in the open carriage for Chambord. The 2 uncles went on horseback. We arrived there at 1. Uncle George delighted on the road with finding a boar's footmark in several places, which when we arrived we found they were hunting near the Chateau."

* Son of Ludwig I of Bavaria, later King Maximilian II, 1848-64.

Eliza goes on to relate the history of the Château, and some curious anecdotes about its occupants. "In one of the grande salons Molière acted the Bourgeois Gentilhomme before Louis XIV and his Court. In 1725 it became the asylum of Stanislas Lazinski, the unfortunate King of Poland. In 1748 Louis XV presented the Château to Marshal Saxe as a reward for his services, and he lived there in great splendour for 2 years. When he died his body was embalmed on a large marble table in his **dining room** (which we saw) and then conveyed to Strasbourg. When he was dying he said to his doctor, Mons. de Senac 'La vie n'est qu'un songe; le mien a été beau mais il est court'.*

In 1809 it again became a reward for military service by Napoleon's giving it to Marshal Berthier (Prince de Wagram) who only slept in it one night. At his death his widow sold it and it was bought by general subscription and presented to the Duc de Bordeaux.... François I (in a fit of jealousy) wrote on the window with a diamond: 'Souvent femme varie, Mal habil que s'y fie'.* They showed us the window but the pane has been taken out and is still shown at the Tuileries.

"The rooms were entirely unfurnished, and they say it would require a million of money to repair the house before any furniture was put in!" There follows a good deal else besides, mostly facts and figures about the rooms, towers, staircases etc. and, verbatim, a poem composed by Lewis Way that same evening, entitled:

"CHAMBORD

"Tenant of earth, and candidate for heav'n!
To whom such vast aspiring hopes are giv'n...."

and several pages in the same vein; a splendid piece of poetic virtuosity but, like all Lewis Way's literary outpourings, totally lacking in inspiration.

May 14. Eliza went with Dr. Bruno and Capt. Barnard to see the old Castle at Blois "....now used as Barracks. We saw the stairs where the Duc de Guise was killed, the chamber of Catherine de Medici and the observatory where she used to consult the stars and the astrologers. Also Henry III's rooms and the oubliette, which is a round hole in a dungeon. 20 feet from the top there is a wheel which tore the unfortunate victim to pieces and then he fell 80 feet lower, where a trap door opened with the weight of the fall and immediately closed upon him."

After a week in Blois the party proceeded to Amboise "....by the banks of the Loire the whole way", visited the Château "....belonging to the Duc d'Orleans. The man who showed it knew Uncle George well and told us

* "Life is only a dream; mine has been beautiful, but short."

he was 'un très bon chasseur; et le grand ennemi des sangliers'." Eliza states that the Château was formerly the residence of the Princess Lambelle who was guillotined during the Revolution. In point of fact she was wrong, for the Princess was torn to pieces by the mob in the September Massacre.

May 18. "Left Amboise about 11; about a mile from there is Chanteloue, a very fine old place formerly belonging to the Duc de Choiseul. It has lately been bought by the Bande Noire, who are demolishing it as fast as possible. There is a very handsome pagoda in the Park which stands at the centre of 8 avenues.

"Uncles Lewis and George rode a short way through the forest and met us at the Château of Chenonceaux which I believe is the only castle in France where the furniture etc. remains as it was in the time of François I. There is a Gallery (which reminded us of Ashton) 160 feet long, which contains many curious old pictures, Holbeins etc.... it stands on the Cher, large boats, barges etc. pass under the windows, being built on arches. The kitchen and other offices are between the Arches, very handy to the water where, by throwing the net, they catch very fine carp, etc.

"The pleasure grounds are very pretty. We had a very merry dinner at the little inn in the village, and the finest carp I ever saw. A drive of 20 miles after brought us to Tours where Mr George Way and Miss Dacre joined us at tea at the Hotel d'Angleterre."

The Dacre & The Doctor

The party found a house to let, a little way out of Tours at Beaulieu, and the next few weeks seem to have been spent in sightseeing, socialising with other members of the English community, and going for rides in the country.

May 28th. "Drusilla's birthday," wrote Eliza. "Uncle Lewis very unwell, kept to his bed all day." He continued to be ill all week and was subjected to the usual cuppings and bleedings then considered necessary, one doctor coming all the way from Paris for the purpose. He was, in fact, suffering from the nervous disorder which ultimately terminated his career and his life. Uncle George was also having problems.

4th June: Eliza writes: "Uncle George and his Lady arrived soon after breakfast and brought George and his French nurse to stay with us, Caroline having the scarlet fever." Two weeks later, Caroline was brought to join her brother at Beaulieu for Mrs George Way's confinement was imminent and her nurse, a woman from Ireland evidently, was in "sad distress" at parting with the child and "set up a regular Irish howl which was performed over the child till she was asleep".

The next day, inevitably, the party returned to Beaulieu to find "Georgy so covered with spots (quite up in large blisters) that they took him back to his parents to be under Dr. Conolly's care". Two days later Eliza joined them and next morning wrote, "Uncle George came to my room at 6 with the good news of his having another little boy". There was much toing and froing that day and, writes Eliza, "Miss Dacre had been so indefatigable.... that we amused ourselves with writing down all she had done which, for the benefit of all future attachées, I here transcribe:

"Labours of the Dacre
"June 23rd 1825

"Rises at 4½ past, uncalled, thinking she might be wanted - carries Georgy up to his bed without waking him - goes down and is in at the birth at 6, helps to dress the child - goes upstairs and dresses herself - descends and lays the table for breakfast - returns to see all going on well and carries the Nurse her breakfast and takes her own. Dresses Georgy - got breakfast and beat up eggs for 2 interlopers (probably Eliza herself and Uncle George) - brings down the Infant's Clothes and Cradle - went out shopping with me - arranged with washerwoman for Beaulieu, telling everybody in the Street that Madame was accouchée. Trimmed up the old Corbeille de Mariage to hold the Infant's clothes - fetch't a Large Currant Pie for luncheon - carried the Nurse some. Took Georgy up to bed - read Cowper's Letters at intervals - gave Georgy his dinner - made a pair of full sleeves for herself - then attended Mother and Child while Nurse dined - the shades of evening threw a veil over the mysteries of the Soirée, but this we learnt: 'that the Dacre n'est pas seulement une femme sage mais aussi une sage femme'."*

The Dacre was undoubtedly shown these lines, in fact she was the sort that rather enjoyed having her leg pulled. Presently the party concocted a romance between her and Dr. Bruno, the Sardinian bachelor friend of Uncle Lewis. It began in a playful manner at the christening of the child when Uncle Lewis, the godfather, and after whom the child was named, bought a large cake "and another," relates Eliza with much amusement, "in the shape of a Heart, which Dr. Bruno presented with great pleasure to Miss Dacre, telling her to take care how she cut it, as it was an emblem of his own. On our return home Uncle Lewis composed the following lines for Dr. Bruno to present to Miss Dacre the next time he saw her.

"To Miss Dacre, with a Cake in the shape of a Heart, presented with similar offerings on the Christening of Lewis Albert Martin Way, June 24, 1825.

"Dear Dacre! When this gift you see - A proper Christening cake -
Think tenderly on it and me or else my heart will break!

"Oh! do not cut it with a knife, for that may fatal prove,
To future husband, future wife, and sweetheart's tender love!

"Already we are one in name, St. Francis, hear my vow.
What holy man shall fan the flame, St. Bruno, be it thou

* 'Femme sage' - wise woman; 'sage femme' - midwife!

"No more I bow with suppliant knee before his marble shrine.
Renouncing all idolatry for Dacre, the divine!

"A protestant in heart I feel, for such my fair one's faith
A willing devotee I kneel to hear what Dacre saith.

"She will not sure reject my plea while trembling thus I stand.
But raise me from my bended knee with other heart in hand.

"Oh! may the Baker's subtle art another cake provide,
More precious than Sardinian heart, that of a British Bride.

"Thus joined in holy wedlock's band our hearts will never break
But little Brunos clap their hands o'er many a Christening cake!"

The next day at tea at Beaulieu, Dr. Bruno presented Miss Dacre with the verses and Eliza, now almost beside herself, wrote: "We were in anxious expectation all day for Uncle George's appearance, in hopes of having Miss Dacre's answer. At dinner I begged the Doctor to walk to Tours, or that lady would think him trop insouciant. He went, but finding company at tea, could only talk on indifferent subjects. He complained on his return that she took too long a time to consider and that it made him suffer 'trop de tourments', which surprised us not a little as we had treated it all as a joke, and had no idea he would take it so seriously."

June 29: "Uncle Lewis and Dilla went to have breakfast at Uncle George's. He asked Miss Dacre if she could recommend him a hair-dresser; she said **she** had often been Uncle George's and would be his with pleasure. So she pinned a sheet round him and commenced her operations. While doing it she said 'Pray when am I to have any **more** verses?', and when she had finished she went out and brought from her room a **matrimonial ladder** which

represented on one side Heartsease and Roses with 2 Doves at the top; and on the other side **Chains** with a Cat & Dog fighting at the bottom. He asked her how many steps she had taken on the ladder, saying he knew she had passed Admiration and he thought the present was Agitation. She said she was 'quite at the bottom and thought it best to remain there'.

"This he told Dr. Bruno on his return, who said he was glad it was settled as he had suffered much the last 3 days; still he appeared hurt at the refusal and when we were at dinner said to Uncle Lewis he should be much obliged if he would write another set of verses to turn it into ridicule, and make the whole appear a **badinage,** which he promised to do, and in the evening wrote the following, which were sent to Miss Dacre the next morning.

Impromptu
written by mutual request
on
the day of arrangement
June 29th
1825

"Shall I not have more verses? asks the fair,
Whose scissors circumscrib'd my grizzle hair;
Yes, surely - just as many as you please,
If you will only clip such Locks as these;
And spare these Tresses which luxuriant flow
Upon your tender Lover's youthful brow,
For that sharp instrument, like Clotho's shears
Will cut the thread which might prolong his years,
And that with many teeth, if such its fate,
(Its proper use to comb your husband's pate);
Might useful prove in various scenes of life,
When man feels half inclined to scratch his wife,
Wise to consult the monitory card
That puts all sorts of sweethearts on their guard.
Doves at the bottom of the Ladder; Two
With matrimonial fondness, bill and coo;
Then quarrel, end in fighting. What of that?
'Tis natural enough - to Dog and Cat.
Better no vows be made, than thus to break
T'heart it may be in shape; 'twill heartless prove
A Contract less substantial than a cake.
For cold as charity, connubial love -
Let disappointed Lovers seek redress
In single, undisturbed blessedness!
Nor care if maidens should regret their man
Who cut, instead of catch him when they can."

And that was the end of the affair. Or was it? The truth was that Eliza had developed a momentary crush on the Doctor and he, on the eve of his departure for Paris, had given her his journal in five exercise books, beginning with the time of his first meeting with Lord Byron, on condition they were never published in his lifetime. Eliza kept her word, but the journal, regrettably, has not survived. Uncle Lewis, as usual, rose to the occasion, and another effusion was penned into Eliza's diary:

"When Bruno quitted fair Beaulieu
He wept Eliza - wept for you,
And since he is so spruce and trim
Hast thou no tears to shed of him?
'Yes, that I have' Eliza said
Or saying, she had not betrayed
With sudden unsuspected sigh,
The listening moisture of her eye.
That eye which now must cease to gaze
On Tresses in disordered maze.
That once bewildered little Dacre
When B had half a mind to take her!
But wanting t'other half, remains
Entangled in Eliza's chains,
Who primly sits and sighs alone,
For Bruno lost and Bruno gone,
E'er decency could yet allow
The suit of a rejected Beau.
Thus between charms on either side
He lost the basket or the bride.
For men, like Donkeys, plight their troth
To twain at once, and lose them both!
But each retains its proper station
Determined by Predestination."

Albert and Drusilla, who accompanied the Doctor back to Paris, could not resist a little joke at Eliza's expense, and sent her a parcel containing a pair of the Doctor's stockings, signed by the Doctor himself. Uncle Lewis was enormously amused:

"In days of true Gallantry, Courage and Love
The Suitor of old sent the Damsel a Glove,
And won by the tender and touching offrande
The Fair in return would present him her hand.
But she he approaches in manner so shocking
And forwards his suit by the foot of a Stocking!
A touch sympathetic the Damsel will feel
A present to such Suitor the point of her heel.
In vain will you plead for your Bruno Bonnechose
By urging his claim with a pair of his Hose.
What 'Agrément en petit' are his pretty toes
His Shoes and they only can fully disclose!
When on such a footing with cotton and leather
Are found in sweet harmony joined together.

They only can prove how Superior their Love
To that less refin'd of the Hand and the Glove!"

Drusilla and Eliza, it should be stated, were the best of friends, and Uncle & Aunt Whitby, who had arrived in town from Nice, settled a "....much disputed point of precedence between them". Writes Aunt Kitty:

"The daughter of the 2nd brother, when under her own roof, must of course take the head in everything - whether at the head of her own Table, or in her drawing room. And now for the decision between the Precedence of the Second Daughter of the Eldest Son when not at home, or the Eldest Daughter of the Second Son. Oh! How nice it is! Why it is so nice that whenever possible they must go 'arm in arm' - but when it be not, Miss Eliza Way must take the office of Chaperone and go before Miss Drusilla Way, inasmuch as the Children of the First House, bearing the  must take the precedence of the Children of the Second House bearing the  from the Throne to the Cottage, where happily all such distinctions are at an end."

Eliza getting very French

On the 29th May all the party at Beaulieu had heard cannons firing at four in the morning in celebration of the coronation of Charles X. Had they been present they would have witnessed the extraordinary spectacle of the King, prostrated on cushions, while the ecclesiastics injected him with holy oil through apertures in his clothing. It was another ominous symbol of the triumph of Divine Right over the nameless horrors that had usurped the throne since the Revolution. The Roman Catholic Church was once again in the ascendant, and France for the time being acquiesced. At the Cathedral of Tours (24th July) the whole congregation, with the exception of the English visitors, fell on their knees when the Archbishop and Bishop of Brie passed, for which "the beadle scolded us soundly," wrote Eliza.

The Bonapartists remained aloof. "General Enoff spent the morning with us," wrote Eliza. "He is a great Bonapartist; expects that the Son will make a great stir before 10 years are over and that many Statues will soon be erected to the Father." The General was nearly right in his prediction. The son, the Prince of Rome, and known to the Bonapartists as Napoleon II, was to die in Vienna in 1832, a prisoner of Metternich; but the nephew, ultimately Napoleon III, launched the first of his coups d'état in 1836.

Meanwhile, the 'Napoleonic Legend' was being manufactured by the Bonapartists. "Though only 10 years of age," related the General, "Napoleon steered the vessel which brought himself and family for the first time to France." Paoli, his godfather, said, "Place him in France.... he will do well; Corsica is too confined a sphere for a boy of his intellect." "General Enoff," said Eliza, "had fought with the Emperor in many battles and speaks of him in a manner little short of Adoration. He believes that tho' his body is dead (which curiously enough he remarked is buried within a few degrees of the exact centre of the World), his spirit will return again in the presence of antichrist foretold in Daniel."

It was the sort of argument that appealed to Uncle Lewis, and it is a relief that he didn't, on this occasion, wax lyrical on the subject. He saved his talents for the Château of Chinon which they all visited on the 12th August. "....a magnificent ruin," remarked Eliza. "It stands on a very high hill and reminded us of Windsor." She dutifully recorded episodes of its stirring history, a lot of it inaccurately, and the party then set off for Fontevrault, but "the road through the forest was so very bad that I got out and walked. Met 2 women who shewed me a pretty little Chapel at the end of the Forest. They said that a statue of the Virgin had been found on that spot and the Priest had it placed in the Church of St. Étienne, which was done 'several times' as it always returned to the place where it was found, on which account the Chapel was built.

"The old Abbey of Fontevrault is at present a Maison de Force; fifteen hundred prisoners are confined there and several large manufactories carried on. In the Chapel within the Abbey we saw the figures cut in stone of Henry, Eleanor and of Richard Coeur de Lion and Jean of Navarre."

At Azay-Le-Rideau they were unable to visit the Château because its owner, M. Le Biencour, had only arrived from Paris the day before, so in the heat they sat on the church steps at the foot of a wayside cross.

After three months at Tours, Uncle Lewis and Eliza began their return journey to Paris. There were farewells to Uncle George Way, the children and the Dacre, which were somewhat prolonged when they discovered they had left Uncle Lewis' trunk behind.

Eliza recorded the curiosities along the route with her usual naive charm: "....about a mile from the road in the forest of Château Rynault, a rich farmer, nearly 200 years ago, was murdered by his brother, and what is very curious, the mark still remains in the ground where the man lay; and it appears (like the ground on which Babylon stood) to have been cursed by the Almighty, as it has been barren ever since, not even a herb or blade of grass growing there, nor even a weed...."

After Chartres, ("the most beautiful cathedral I ever saw ... the painted glass windows magnificent"), they continued to Maintenon and "....went immediately to see Madame de Maintenon's château, which is very handsome and contains a fine Gallery of pictures. There is a beautiful, though shocking, one of Madame de Montespan in which she is represented as the Virgin, her eldest son (the Duc de Maine) as St. John with a lamb; and the other as the Infant Jesus sitting on her lap. We saw the Chapel (which is bien petite) in which Louis Quatorze privately married Madame de Maintenon - it remains exactly in the state it was then."

Soon after St. Cyr "....a magnificent looking place.... we met a French carriage coming the road we were going. The postillion begged we would change horses, which was agreed to (they happened to be all four greys), and our boy had no sooner undone the harness than he began to put the same horses to the carriage again - the other laught at him for being so stupid when he said 'Comment est-ce possible de les connâitre; ils sont tous les quatre - blanc'."

And so to Versailles and St. Germain-en-Laye, where a large crowd of friends and relations, including Mrs Way, Louisa and Georgiana, awaited them at the Hôtel d'Étrangers. "Albert and I searched all over the town for a furnished house; saw at least 30 but not one large enough for so numerous a party, so in the evening we divided company: Uncle Lewis and Albert remaining there, and we all went to the Hôtel d'Angleterre."

The next few days were spent riding in the Bois de Boulogne, visiting Versailles, society dinners, and no doubt catching up on the news after such a long absence from Paris. Not all of it was good. "Received a letter from Mary Anne with a bad account of dear Mama's eye," wrote Eliza on the 30th September. This seemed to suggest a return to England. She had been in France now for over a year. The last month was spent at Marboeuf and the time passed quickly enough, scarcely a day passing without making or receiving visits and of course there were shopping expeditions in preparation for the return home. It had been arranged that Eliza should travel with Mr Tyner and his daughter. She says nothing about parting with Uncle Lewis and family. Perhaps by now she was homesick, and the remaining part of her journal is a dutiful record of names and dates and lacks her usual sparkle. The party left Paris on 7th October: "There were 8 other gentlemen of the party; we had 6 horses all the way and very often 8". They dined at Beauvais and continued through the night and "saw the comet very plain about 2 in the morning" - an interesting reference to Halley's comet, which was not to reappear until 1912.

They found Boulogne "....swarming with English, the Ladies with their long ringlets and little bonnets I did not admire after the Parisians". At Calais they put up at Maurice's Hotel and the last morning was spent visiting the Protestant Chapel. "It was half filled and those a sad looking set. We felt quite ashamed of our compatriots." They walked on the pier until dinner time and "saw Dover Castle quite plain without a glass". The last meal in France was rendered memorable by "....two women who played and sang some pretty French airs at dessert, and afterwards a man who whistled uncommonly well and imitated different kinds of birds, amused us very much".

There was the usual touting for passengers and after first inspecting the 'Lord Melville' where "....everything was certainly well arranged", Eliza and the Tyners opted for the 'Duc de Bordeaux' packet. They sailed at "20 minutes before 7 the next morning, the wind quite against us, and at the end of 2 hours we had the pleasure of finding ourselves close to Boulogne. They then hoisted sails which, at the end of 4 hours more, brought us to the coast off Deal. To describe how the company amused themselves all this time would be, as I think Washington Irving observed, to conjugate the verb:

"I was sick, Thou wast sick, He was sick, We were sick...etc. etc.

"At last, a few minutes before 2, we got to Dover, but as the Vessel could not enter the harbour, all were obliged to get out into little Boats and be rowed in. I did not taste a single thing till we got to the Union Hotel at 3, when I was just sufficiently alive to creep from the boat to the inn; but do not think I suffered half so much as last Summer when we went on board immediately after a good luncheon."

In London Eliza called on her small sisters, who were "not a little surprised to see me, as they had not heard I was coming". She "....saw Papa for a few minutes before I set off, and arrived at Denham at 7 and found dear Mama and all the party looking uncommonly well, and so ends my Tour which, however tedious in details, was in reality most delightful." And there she thankfully laid down her pen.

OSTEND Packet in a SQUALL

GETTING UNDER WAY

"Thomas Upton of the parish of Sedbergh in the County of Westmorland, a bachelor and Eliza Way of this parish, a spinster, were married in this church by licence on the 16th day of July 1829 by me, William Way, Rector of Denham in the presence of Benjamin Way, Mary Way, Holroyd Fitzwilliam Way, Mary Anne, Louisa, Belinda and Laetitia Way."

William Way was another of Eliza's uncles, also a clergyman. One would like to think that all the relations were there on such a propitious occasion; certainly the two proud mothers who had done all the hatching - sisters Mary Way and Florence Upton; perhaps also Uncle Lewis, the bride's godfather; Uncle John Smyth, the bachelor Baronet of Ashton Court whose vast wealth must one day pass to this happy pair; and it would not be surprising if some of the old friends of the Paris days were also in attendance: John 'Big Nose' Upton, the Dacre and Dr. Bruno, Fanny Strickland and Drusilla Way.

It was the first marriage of the ten children of the squire of Denham and it is not difficult to imagine Denham Place that day: the great Queen Anne house and park, festively decorated for the occasion; the reunion of Ways from far and near; the enormous coal scuttle bonnets and leg-of-mutton sleeves; stovepipe hats; and the procession of carriages down the village street, lined with tenants and well-wishers.

Old Sir John Smyth, so unapproachable in other respects, was sufficiently interested in his young nephew and niece to grant them, on their marriage, the old Manor of Wraxall, only four miles from Ashton on the Clevedon road. It had once been the home of their Gorges ancestors. In the

1650s it had been largely rebuilt by Colonel Samuel Gorges* and had been bought by Sir John Hugh Smyth in 1800.

Thomas Upton was a young man of taste and sensitivity. He refashioned Wraxall Court, and threw out side wings with wide oval bays from which, framed in oak and beech, was a far view of the gentle Vale of Clevedon and the sea. Tom's father, the squire of Ingmire, died in 1832 from a chill contracted after riding over the moors in the rain to bank his rent money in Kendal. Florence Upton then took up residence at Laura Place, Bath, and when Benjamin Way died in 1834 Eliza's mother also moved back into the west country to live with her brother the Baronet, in Ashton Court and Heath House by turns.

Eliza had four children, the first three born in Bath**, evidently regarded as the proper place for confinements: Thomas born 1830, Fanny 1832, John Henry Greville 1834***, and Florence 1838. Nearby, in Clifton, Eliza's young cousin Georgiana was completing her education and in due course she and her sisters, 'Lanky' Anna, Olivia and Louisa made excellent marriages into titled families.****

Albert became a celebrated antiquarian and founder of the Royal Archaeological Institute in 1844. Lewis Way gave up the Marboeuf Chapel for health reasons and retired to Leamington Spa, where he died in 1840. His widow preserved her wit, intelligence and good looks for a good many years. Drusilla, who had turned down two offers of marriage to be her father's companion, remained unmarried and lived to a great age, the brilliance of her conversation charming all who came within her circle.

John 'Le Grand Nez' Upton inherited Ingmire on the death of his father, but he showed no interest in the place and about 1837 his stepbrother Thomas and family gave up Wraxall Court and returned to Ingmire, where their youngest child, Florence, was born. There, Thomas showed the same energy and imagination which had transformed Wraxall. A new drawing room and study were thrown out on the garden side of the old, austere 17th Century wing; baronial embellishments were added in the form of battlements

* See 'The Earlier Smyths of Ashton Court', page 161.

** No. 12 Green Park Place.

*** Named after his godfather, General Upton of Levens Hall.

**** Anna, m.1848, John Ashford Wise of Clapton Hall, Newcastle, Co. Stafford, MP for the Potteries.
Olivia, m.1845, Rev. Charles Kennaway of Chipping Campden, son of Sir John Kennaway, Bt.
Louisa, m.1854, Rev. Henry Clarence Pigon, Rector of Wyke Regis, Dorset, son of Sir Montague Cholmeley, Bt.

and mock towers. What had been quite a modest house now assumed the proportions of a castle and presented a romantic outline against the steeply rising fells. Here Eliza's brood spent an enchanted childhood.*

"When I was a very little child," wrote Florence, the youngest, "I remember the dining room at Ingmire being painted and papered. The workmen who did the ceiling were foreigners, I think, and used to tell my brother and me to fetch them flowers from the garden to copy, blue and pink....

"In those days at Ingmire, as a child, we always drove to church on Sunday and sat in a pew in the chancel under Sir John Otway's tomb, with a high screen on one side, and on two others curtains through the chinks of which one often caught sight of one of the 80 or 100 boys of the Grammar School who sat on the other side. During one of my sister's long illnesses, the Bishop at confirmation ordered the curtains to be taken down so that she might see, and they were never replaced, so the boys could look as they chose at the occupants of the long pew. The servants always went, and the maids sat where the vestry now is; and once, when a new cook dressed with unnecessary smartness came out of church, she found pinned to one of her garments by one of the schoolboys 'In want of a lover', or words to that effect. For a long time cousin Caroline Way used to find little notes on her seat from an enamoured schoolboy called Dunn."

"About that time there was an outbreak of typhus fever in Sedbergh," wrote Florence, "and my mother used to anoint the noses of Caroline and myself with 'Thieves Vinegar' which was supposed to keep off infection, every Sunday morning. It was certainly effective in this instance, and with our noses stinging with the stuff we went to church all the same."

Caroline lived with the Uptons and there were other regular visitors who came and went.

"Every year, about August," writes Florence, "there arrived a Mr Thomas Lister Parker on a visit. He appeared to us very old and his visit was, I should think, a kind of inheritance, for he could not have given pleasure. On arrival he made straight for the kitchen to enquire what was for dinner, and to suggest, perhaps, another sauce.

"He had owned a fine place in Lancashire, Browsholme, but gave up all for a few months vanity, and for the pleasure of representing an English gentleman 'en voyage' at the command of some Empress of Russia. He travelled to the capital of that country, with three carriages for himself, his

* The arms of Thomas Upton and Eliza Way which were carved above the main door at Ingmire, and are now at Lilymere, appear on the spine of the paperback edition of this volume.

secretary and retinue, and remained happily the rest of his life next door to a pauper. He always, at Ingmire, occupied the study bedroom called then, as a matter of course, 'Mr Parker's Room'. At last he got to walking about on two sticks, and my mother had a pet workman (Lupton by name) who worked wonderfully, but to move from one place to another was obliged to support his rheumatic back on two sticks. When Mr Parker on his sticks passed Lupton for the first time on his, he was much displeased and said 'I never saw that man about the place before'."

Thomas and Eliza Upton lived in some style and had a full complement of servants, but they were loving parents. "I remember going in to dessert, in those days dinners were much earlier, and he (father) used to cut for myself and my brother what we called 'apple candles' as they were pieces of apple cut square with almonds stuck in, and lighted. This may have been a means of getting rid of us quietly, for we were quite pleased to say goodnight and march upstairs with our tiny torches.

"I also remember playing as a small child in the garrets as they were then.... and being specially told not to go near a glass skylight which lighted what was then the housemaid's closet. I naturally ventured there and one poor little leg went crashing through the glass and had to be dragged out again streaming with blood. I only wonder that I did not bleed to death but old Sisson carried me to the nursery where Anne Williams (afterwards Anne Sisson) tended me with the help of Mr Brydges. It was reported that when he was strapping up my wound I held a rose to his nose! My father and mother were leaving home next day, but they sent me back a toy from Lancaster, and on his return father caused a funny little carriage to be made for my use, and in this I was propelled about till I could walk again."

The childhood of the young Uptons was relatively uneventful, but one event seems to have been memorable. About 1842, when Greville was six, the Dowager Queen Adelaide came to the hotel at Kirkby Lonsdale to inspect the Clergy Daughters' School at Castleton. "The very day she arrived some char were caught in the river and my father sent them over for the Queen's dinner. In honour of her visit the hotel has always since been called 'The Royal'."

The Upton children were carted around the country to visit relatives, often making use of the novelty of having the family travelling carriage lashed to a truck on one of the new railways, and accomplishing the whole journey inside. In the summer they went for the annual sea bathing visit to Blackpool; and every year they visited the two grandmothers, Florence Upton and Mary Way. Old Mrs Upton then lived at Laura Place, Pulteney Street, Bath.

"She was a small, alarming-looking old lady, in a high-pointed cap. She had some old servants and I was as much afraid of them as I was of her...."; and then they went to see Grandmother Way who lived at Ashton

Court with her brother, Great Uncle John. This the children also disliked. While their parents were downstairs at dinner with the old people, and the nurse taking her supper with the servants, they "....had a dreary time of it until taken down to the drawing room to see my elders have tea, and what we called 'milk cakes'".

There were endless Way uncles and aunts to visit. While on one of these visits, Greville's sister Fanny developed measles, and while staying at the Clifton Down Hotel Mrs Upton also caught it. "The landlady," said Florence, "was much annoyed by the visits of my Great Aunt Anne who would come to the window and shout out 'How are the measles going on?', causing any visitor who heard it to leave the next day."

"One day my mother and I went to see John Way,* who was at school at Exmouth. A large, fat, fair good boy, so good that to my astonishment he, after being taken to a confectioners, sternly refused an enormous cake offered to him by my mother - such gifts not being allowed."

From Upton to Smyth

How young Greville Upton came into the Smyth inheritance is the old story of the failure of male heirs in the senior branch. Sir John Hugh Smyth, Baronet, died in 1801, childless. His two nephews, Sir Hugh and Sir John, who succeeded to the title, both died without legitimate heirs (1825 and 1849), and the Smyth empire passed to Greville's grandmother, Florence Upton, then eighty-three years of age. The premature deaths of Greville's father in 1843, and his eldest brother Thomas in 1849, brought him into direct line of succession.

Greville was only seven years old when his father died. Florence said: "I remember going to his bedside on the 7th December 1843 to receive a little tea set and tray for my 6th birthday present, and very soon after that, I think, he met with an accident and died on 23rd December, and I remember objecting to black stockings because the maids wore them! .... I also have an indistinct recollection of asking if I might go down and see the coffin in the dining room on the morning of the funeral, and if my mother intended to marry again! Also of seeing the farmers riding up to follow the procession to Sedbergh Church.... I believe it was ten days before he was buried because Mr Platt, the vicar, objected to him being laid in the chancel. My Mother, of course, would not give in, and my father was placed near his father."

On the death of their father, the Upton children were sent away to school. Greville went to Dr. Mayo's Academy at Cheam, near Epsom, and then to Eton. His elder brother, Thomas, was sent to Grandmother Upton in Bath, and there he was thoroughly spoiled. The old woman doted on him and gave

* Eldest son of Henry Hugh Way, vicar of Henbury, near Bristol.

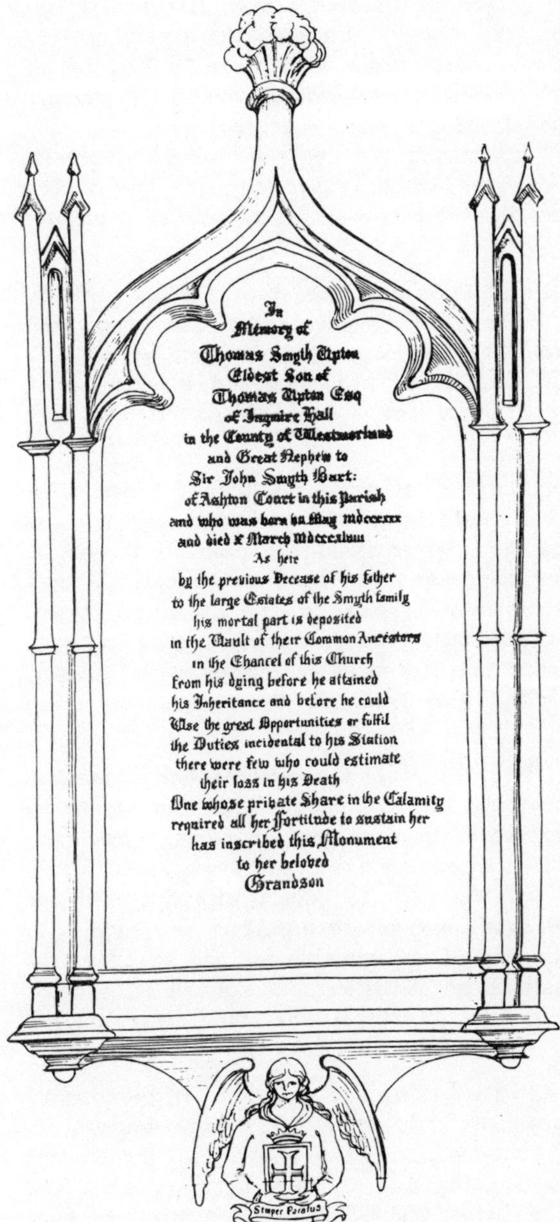

free rein to his licentious nature. He was not without talents; he wrote poems with facility and even published a little book called 'The Last of the Vampires'.* But his grandmother could deny him nothing; he once paid fifteen guineas for a seat to hear Jenny Lind, and his passion for horses led to a serious fall which damaged his spine. It was drink that finished him off. During his last months he was in a constant state of intoxication. Old Mrs Upton sent him to Cheltenham and paid for the best surgeons of the day to attend him, but it was of no avail and he died in a state of delirium tremens in 1848, aged eighteen.

"I remember his funeral taking place in Ashton Church," recalled Florence. "I went as a child of 10, in a carriage from Ashton to Bristol where we joined the procession, and went at a foot's pace to Ashton Church. I remember nothing of the funeral. I suppose I did not dare look up, for the only things that particularly struck me were the beautiful shining boots worn by Mr Gore-Langton of Newton Park, a distant relative who always appeared at family gatherings."

* This may have been inspired by the grave of the vampire in front of the church porch at Dent, Yorkshire.

This was the notorious William Henry Gore-Langton, grandson of the radical MP for Somerset, who had consistently supported the left wing issues of the day: Catholic Emancipation, the Reform Bill, and the Repeal of the Corn Laws. William's elopement two years before with the only daughter of the ultra-Tory Duke of Buckingham who was, furthermore, a diehard protectionist, was one of the scandals of the age. The fact that the Duke had discovered the elopement and interrupted the ceremony at St. George's, Hanover Square, and dragged away the bride, added to the drama. The incident and its happy sequel a few weeks later was the subject of a popular street ballad.

Greville's two sisters went to a private school at Clifton, Bristol, called Alva House. It was run by a Miss Saunders who had once been governess to the Johnstons of Alva. "She always wore black satin gowns with white lace in front and a lot of little pearl brooches, and a white cap," wrote Florence. "She had a very wrinkled and wizened face, but was very kind and clever...."

Florence was sent there at the age of seven, in place of her elder sister who should have gone, but had developed whooping cough. Miss Saunders insisted that the fee for the quarter should be paid all the same, "....so a brilliant idea occurred to my mother - she sent me instead. When I got to Clifton I said 'Oh Mamma, something keeps on jumping here!' It was my poor little heart! There was one mite younger than I, Lucy Walbank Chedders, afterwards Lady Auckland. She was only 6. I cried when I went, and I cried when I came away the following June, my sister taking my place after the summer holidays."

Florence later returned to Alva House and completed her education. "We were taught a little of everything and a great deal of the Bible. An unfortunate clergyman, not always the same one, used to come periodically to tea, having this meal with 23 girls and several governesses, and would afterwards expound a chapter to us. We were too much with books in our hands; in the summer when we all went out before breakfast, we took it in turn to sit on a little stool behind one of the governesses and say dates as hard as we could. How our digestions or our governesses stood it, I don't know. Then we read the Bible before our breakfast was taken away and the maids came in to prayers.

"A dear old Mr Brown, a born naturalist, and a shoemaker the rest of the week, used to come on Mondays and show us objects in the microscope, and tell us interesting things of botany etc. That I liked. A Mr Hodges taught music, and the girls pretended to be dreadfully afraid of him. The German master, Herr Koch, was a little, black-eyed man. I loved to hear him read poetry, though I did not understand a word, but neither he nor Mr Hodges ever taught me."

Florence left the school in 1849 when Miss Saunders retired at the age of eighty. For a while her nieces tried to keep the school going, but without success. Fanny's experience at Alva House was less fortunate. At the age of fourteen she fell downstairs on the back of her head. After that she suffered terrible headaches. Many physicians were consulted but nothing succeeded in curing her, and she became a chronic invalid. She grew to dread noise of any kind, the slamming of a door, the report of a gun, etc., and when the railway came to Sedbergh the din of the navvies was too much for her. She had a chalet built in Westmorland, above Lake Lilymere and ultimately died, unmarried, in 1878, aged forty-four.

Grev and Flo

The tragedies that overwhelmed their father, elder brother and sister threw Greville and Florence together. Throughout their lives they were completely devoted to each other. Their education had developed along separate, but parallel, lines and their interests coincided at many points. Their enterprising Way uncles exposed them to new experience and stirred their curiosity. In 1851 they were taken to the Great Exhibition, "A grand sight," wrote thirteen year old Florence. One wishes she had said more on this occasion.

Their first excursion abroad in 1847 with Uncle Arthur Way "....who had been a great deal in Australia," introduced them to Germany, Switzerland and Paris. "There was £5 over at the end of the trip, and Mr Capes (a friend of Uncle Arthur) promised to spend it for me in Paris. For years I expected results - they never came."

Grev and Flo remained insatiable travellers all their lives. Their love of good company, their interest in the exotic and the unknown, their urge to investigate, to classify and record, have left us Florence's fascinating journals and Greville's enormous botanical and zoological collection, now the nucleus of the Natural History Section of the Bristol City Museum.

Between 1848 and 1852 death carried off most of the superannuated members of the family. In 1849 Sir John Smyth, the old Baronet, died; in 1850 Grandmother Way; in 1851 Aunt Mary Anne Way, snd in 1852 Grandmother Upton-Smyth. These were the days of the grotesque and macabre funeral processions, with their mutes and mourners and black plumed caparisoned horses. The order of the procession for Grandmother Way from Crofton House, Clifton, where she died, to Henbury Church, still survives. At the head of the column were the undertakers and assistants, with four mutes in a chariot and four. Then came two clergymen with two footmen in a coach and four; and then the hearse drawn by six horses and accompanied by ten bearers, two abreast. Then came Greville's mother with his numerous Way uncles and aunts, four to a coach with two footmen up behind, and four caparisoned horses out in front. Altogether five magnificent equipages followed by the private carriage of the dead woman herself, her sister Mrs Upton-Smyth of Ashton Court and, of course, Captain Gore-Langton with his polished boots.

"....for some years we must have been a source of income to the various shops where mourning was sold," wrote Florence in her journal.

The most significant of these deaths was that of the other grandmother, Mrs Upton-Smyth, two years later. This made Greville, then aged sixteen, the owner of Ashton Court, Heath House, the furniture, paintings and wine cellar, and an estate worth £25,000 a year in rents and mining royalties. It was an empire which had few equals in the west of England, but almost at once two bogeys appeared which threatened to deprive him of it. The first was Charles Hardcastle Abbott, and the second was Tom Provis.

It was found that Grandmother Upton-Smyth, after making the usual legacies - her wearing apparel to her maid Harriet Short, and £20 to most of her relations, including, of course, Mr Gore-Langton - had left the residue to her steward and executor, Mr Abbott. This consisted of a very healthy bank account which, over the years, she had permitted Mr Abbott to handle. Eliza, aided by her brothers, immediately challenged the validity of the will, and her solicitors brought a case on behalf of her children, who were minors, against Mr Abbott,

accusing him of extracting the will from the old woman when she was not in her right mind.

The case really hinged on the contention of Eliza's counsel that her mother-in-law was dotty and suffered from delusions. For nine days in 1854 witnesses were called to testify to the exact state of Mrs Upton-Smyth's mind in 1848 when the will was made. There seemed no doubt that in her later years she often behaved very oddly. Florence recalled that when she stayed with her grandmother in Bath "....she used to give money to a black man out of the window, and I used to pretend I saw him, to annoy her, and make her hurry to the window for nothing". Eliza's counsel now produced a catalogue of extra-ordinary stories to prove that the old lady was an imbecile.

1. The first was the evidence of a certain Dr. Wallis: "In the year 1846, I think the month of May, I was sent for by a special message, desiring me to go to her as soon as I could. I found her in a lodging house at Hampton Terrace, near Bristol, where she was to be near her grandson who was at school at Redland, distant about a quarter of a mile across Miller's Nursery Ground, under the care of the Rev. Mr Knight. I had observed previously that her mind had been failing; I cannot specify any particular time; it was apparently the effect of age. At the time now deposed of (1846) I found her in a state of complete delusion regarding her grandson. On my going in she took me to a back window of the drawing room and, pointing to a window in a house adjoining the Turnpike House, she told me that there was a creature of Sims's, that she had seen her appearing at that window, that Sims had placed her there to inveigle her boy, as she called her grandson, and get him to marry her, and he would be ruined. I endeavoured to quiet her excitement and told her that I would go to the house, and enquire who it was and learn all about it, and come back to inform her...." He enquired at the house and found that there was no woman there, at least no young woman at all. "I could not doubt her alarming state of delusion was so entire that, had she been a young person, and active, I should have caused her to be put under restraint."

The defence pointed out that Sims was a man who had been a valet, later butler, in the family at the time of the late Sir John Smyth, and that he had acquired an undue influence over him; and the whole family thought he was a very dangerous man. Even Mrs Upton-Smyth described him as a 'Jesuit' - a word she used for anyone she didn't trust. The charge that she was suffering from a delusion in this matter was finally demolished when the defence revealed that a similar plot had been aimed at another young man in the neighbourhood by the name of Upforth, and that it was quite natural for the old woman to think that it was her own grandson, to whom she was almost possessively attached, who was the object of such designs. However in Dr. Wallis' defence it must be said that the old lady refused to believe that it could be any other than her grandson, even when the Rev. Mr Knight was called and said that when the young man was questioned he denied any knowledge of the affair.

2. The next witness was Greville's Uncle Henry Hugh Way, vicar of Henbury, who said that he visited the old lady some months after the death of her grandson at her house in Gay Street, Bath. "She made," he said, "some very odd remarks. She said she had been up to heaven. She was quite sure that her grandson was happy, for she had seen him in heaven sitting on a haycock. She did not say that it was either a dream or a vision, but spoke of it as a fact. I asked no explanation but thought it strange, and the remarks of an old woman getting into her dotage. That is all that I remember of it." When cross-examined, the Rev. Henry Hugh had to admit that they had been talking of a dream a little earlier, and that at no time did he consider her to be insane.

3. Another of the Way uncles then came forward and said that Mrs Upton-Smyth must have been insane because she had declared that Lord Teignmouth, whom she had formerly allowed to "drive through the Park at Ashton with his Lady, when they thought proper, and go into the garden and cut what flowers they thought proper" should not be permitted to do so because he had murdered her dear friend the Rev. Mr Forsyth. Mrs Forsyth was called to the witness box and explained that her husband had been a minister of low church principles, and was much admired by Mrs Upton-Smyth who was of the same religious complexion. He had been in bad health, being a consumptive, and had been to Madeira for his health. Shortly after his return he was urged by Lord Teignmouth, who was also a low churchman, to attend a Bible Meeting in Exeter Hall, where he was overcome with the heat of the room, and the excitement of the occasion, spat blood, and died. Mrs Upton-Smyth, out of consideration for Mrs Forsyth, who continued to visit her at Ashton, did not wish to cause her any additional distress by seeing Lord Teignmouth driving through the Park, and withdrew the permission. The words she had used to Mrs Forsyth on this occasion were "Oh, My Dear. He murdered your husband!" or some such language which, of course, was meant metaphorically. But it could not be denied by the defence that "this Lady was in the habit of expressing herself strongly", and this had led to the misunderstanding.

4. Dr. Fox, the celebrated surgeon, and founder of the Brislington Lunatic Asylum, attended Mrs Upton-Smyth in 1846 for typhus fever, and visited her several times later. He stated that she had spoken in an excited and irrational manner about the Papists and Jesuits, and especially the Puseyites whom she described as Roman Catholics. The arrival of Cardinal Wiseman in the country in 1851 had much alarmed the old lady and, like other staunch Protestants, she believed that a Roman Catholic insurrection was about to take place. On that occasion she informed Dr. Fox that, "The

Roman Catholics had established emissaries in Ashton Park, and that one of her relations had fired twice at them that morning".

The defence called Mrs Prior (Greville's aunt, Louisa Way, who married Colonel Prior of the Indian Army) and she explained what had happened. "My husband, Mr Prior, had been out rabbit shooting. We had been talking about priests and Jesuits. Mrs Upton-Smyth was fond of speaking about them and expressed herself so strongly that we told her there were two Jesuits in the grounds. 'Do go and shoot them,' said Mrs Upton-Smyth. Then Mr Prior went and fired off his gun twice - that is, I presume he drew out the shot and fired off the double-barrelled powder as most people do when they come back from rabbit shooting. He came back and said he had killed two priests. I have no doubt she was as aware that there were not two dead priests lying there as we were."

5. Evidence of her insanity was also produced to the effect that she was always repeating the story of two curates at Stapleton fighting in the churchyard, and one had a black eye. This turned out to be an exaggerated version of a discussion in Stapleton churchyard between local farmers about high and low church principles which had become rather heated, and blows were exchanged.

In fact the investigation revealed that the old lady was perfectly sane, certainly at the time of writing her will in 1848. Lady Anna Gore-Langton met her in Bath the day afterwards and found her punctual and lucid, and the lady's diary was produced as proof. In Mr Abbott's defence it was said that he had given long and devoted service to Mrs Upton-Smyth and to her brother, Sir John Smyth, before that. Before inheriting the estate Mrs Upton-Smyth was a lady of only very modest income; nor could she, in view of her advanced age, have been expected to live long enough to come into the property. Mr Abbott was totally exonerated; but the judge decided that as Eliza Upton was a widow and might have been expected to do her utmost to ensure a fair settlement for her children, she should only pay £200 costs, but Mr Abbott "....was allowed to keep his ill-gotten gains," added Florence.

The Way

Eliza could not alone have handled the Upton - Abbott case and all the other problems that showered upon her on inheriting the Ashton estates. From the very start she secured the capable services of her younger brother, Arthur Way. He had been a good deal in Australia for, as a younger son, his prospects in England were meagre and the gold rush of 1849-51 had exercised a powerful attraction. He gained considerable experience as a magistrate in the colony of New South Wales, but little gold, so he returned home and married money instead. The lady was Harriet Butterworth, known to all as 'Hebe', and Arthur set up as a country gentleman in Cheltenham Spa, where he became master of the Gloucestershire foxhounds.

Eliza prevailed on Arthur to become steward of Ashton Court and guardian to her son Greville until he came of age. Arthur had little experience of estate management, but the Day Book he kept from 1852 to 1857 shows that he applied himself to his new responsibilities with vigour, tact and resolution.

"Sir," he wrote, in a circular to all the tenants on 6th September 1852, "We are directed to inform you that Mrs Upton, as the guardian of her son John Henry Greville Smyth (a minor) who has succeeded to the late Mrs Smyth of Ashton Court in the possession of the family estates, has approved her brother, Arthur Edwin Way Esq., now at Ashton Court, to take the management of the property, receipt of Rents etc. You will therefore be pleased to communicate with Mr Way on all matters relating to the premises in your occupation."

His first audit on 14th September at the Coach & Horses (now the Smyth Arms) was a shock. "The rent days appear to be very badly managed and no kind of rule maintained, only 60 tenants out of 240 having put in an appearance. This must be reformed forthwith."

The attendance of the Gloucestershire tenants was not much better. He studied the returns of the Westerleigh Colliery, of which the Smyths, along with Lord Middleton and Mr Colston, were part owners. They were not encouraging:

"1849	£8,000
1850	£7,600
1851	£5,600
1852	£3,200"

Arthur wrote in his Day Book: "During the last 15 months a sum exceeding £3,000 has been expended in overworks; the 4 pits now in work are capable of producing 100,000 tons per annum, which at profit estimated at two shillings per ton will yield a total of £10,000 per annum to be divided by the proprietors." By the end of 1852 the balance in favour of the owners was down to £1,927. "I thought this a very small profit on a concern capable of yielding £10,000 p.a. and am convinced of the necessity of extensive reforms in the management. Mr Dyke, traffic manager of the Midland Railway Co., which supplies our trucks, stated that other companies were doing more with 40 trucks than the Coalpit Heath Co. with 120 trucks!"

Why was the company doing so badly? He called a meeting of the proprietors and managers at his solicitor's office in Bristol. "There appeared to be much ill-feeling between Mr Hewitt and Mr Browne the traffic manager, the latter having been appointed by Mr Tugwell (Mr Colston's agent) as a sort of check on Hewitt and his father, who is manager of the works." It seemed that both the Hewitts and Mr Browne were holding back trucks for their favourite customers and complaints of discrimination and favouritism were heard from several coal merchants.

In fact, wherever Arthur Way looked he was confronted with neglect and gross mismanagement. Squatters were encroaching on Bedminster Down in full view of the south front of Ashton Court and John Hall, a member of the tribe of Halls of Bedminster Down, was quarrying stone with impunity.

"Gave orders to the Chief Constable of Bedminster to stop John Hall and others from quarrying and committing trespass on Bedminster Down." There were even trespassers in Ashton Park for Mrs Upton-Smyth had granted, in her old age, so many people the right to use it that the public came and went at leisure. "Issued written instructions to the different head keepers and to Thomas Woodruff, park keeper, for maintaining the privacy of Ashton Park," he wrote. Woodruff was notoriously lax and inefficient and clearly resented Arthur Way's exacting regime after the slackness of old Mrs Upton-Smyth. Arthur told Woodruff "....not to fire off Guns in future in the Park, without my notice" and, a little later: "Gave Woodruff notice that he would be suspended if he did not obey my orders."

Sept. 1852: "Went to Tickenham Court. Drainage and other matters connected with the Estate. On returning saw 3 men get over Ashton Park wall. Gave chase and they escaped. One, a notorious sheep-stealer, has been put in gaol for former offences."

Woodruff seems to have improved a little, but in 1854 Arthur wrote: "Discharged Woodruff, park keeper, on account of his not having any game in the park; he was very impertinent, telling me 'To go to the Devil and Shake Myself'. Fry, Head Gardener, took on the Park Keeper's job and Francis Waite engaged at 18/- a week."

Mr Reith, the head gardener, was dangerously ill and died on 27th September 1852, of 'apoplexy of the lungs' and there was difficulty in finding a home for his widow, for they had inhabited the Town Gatehouse.* Ambrose, the shepherd, had four sheep poisoned because he neglected to see the gates fastened into the plantation. Mr Llewellyn, the butler, and his wife, lady's maid to old Mrs Upton-Smyth, felt very much put out by the new order and resigned. R. Dunning replaced Llewellyn at fifty guineas per annum.

6th Jan. 1853: "Dismissed Charles Brewer, the footman, for having absented himself without leave, for impertinence, and for drunkenness on Saturdays. He had not one word to say in defence and I did not pay him his month's wages."

What enormously added to Arthur's difficulties was that the family could not accept Mr Abbott, the previous steward, as Mrs Upton-Smyth's executor while the case against him was being prepared, and the interminable problems of disposing of the old lady's personal effects, carriages, plants etc., not to mention the handing over of the keys and finding the right locks

* Now in the grounds of Ashton Park School.

for them in the infinite recesses of Ashton Court. All had to be done through Mr Abbott's solicitor. With a great deal of tact on both sides the transition was accomplished and Arthur admits in his Day Book that "Mr Abbott behaved at all times with perfect propriety".

It was not so easy to deal with trespassers.

18th Sept. 1852: "Mr Jellat, the Chief Constable of Bedminster, called and informed me that John Hall, Oldfield and other notorious characters were still continuing to quarry on Bedminster Down in defiance of my notice. Directed him to summon the parties on the next offence." The same warning was given to illegal turf cutters on the Down: "....two of them previously convicted for Highway Robbery, and another for passing counterfeit coin". The offences continued and in November Arthur Way, acting on behalf of the Lord of the Manor of Bedminster and Mr Gore-Langton of Newton Park* prosecuted the offenders. The case came before the magistrates in February 1853: "....the four trespassers were fined for damages each: 7/- each for costs and 14 days imprisonment". The case was reported in the press and this, among other things, did much to impress upon the minds of the poor of Bedminster and elsewhere that the new masters of Ashton Court were not to be trifled with.

Arthur Way could also be ruthless with refractory tenants.

13th June 1858: "Started at 7 a.m. on horseback and found Mr James Broad and 5 workmen engaged in erecting a wall on the land occupied by Joseph Nurse on this estate. I warned them to desist and threatened them with instant prosecution. Broad, who appeared to be head man, said his orders were to continue in spite of anybody." The next day Arthur Way, with two constables, his farm manager and a gang of twenty farm labourers, assailed Mr Broad and again ordered him to cease building the wall. "On his refusal I ordered my men instantly to destroy it, which they did. I then sent for posts and nails and instructed Goscombe where to erect the fence. I thought it best," he added, "to overawe all resistance, which a small fence could only have provoked. Farmer French, who brought his men to assist me, told me that Broad had said to him yesterday 'he should like to see the inside of a jail for a bit'."

Tenants and farmers were hounded for their arrears of rent and attendance at the next audit improved. During the lean years of the 40s the Ashton Court stewards, in common with other landlords, had allowed a 10% abatement.

* Greville Upton inherited two-thirds of the Manor and Colonel Gore-Langton one-third.

In June 1853 Arthur Way was writing: "The tenants paid up well and in consequence of the general improvement in prices, we lowered the 10% allowance to 5%." In November he gave notice to discontinue abatements altogether. On the 28th November 1854 he was writing triumphantly: "The farmers paid the Rent up without **one farthing** of arrears; the times are very favourable to them" - and a year later: "We gave the Tenants notice that their Lady Day Rents would be raised 5%."

This was the last golden age of British agriculture, but Arthur Way was conscious of the fragile state of food prices and was determined to extract the maximum profit from other sources of revenue. At the Westerleigh Colliery thirty more coal trucks were secured and contractors made to supply large coal on a regular basis. "Wages of colliers were raised 1d per ton, in consequence of the same being done in the neighbouring collieries." The continued bickering between Mr Hewitt and Mr Browne, the agent of Mr Tugwell, brought a sharp retort from Arthur Way. "Wrote a letter to Mr Browne to insist on his amending his language to the Messrs Hewitts," and letters were written to the other part-owners begging them to have greater confidence in Mr Hewitt junior, his father being in a "decrepit state".

"I want to see unity of actions, and when I do see it, I expect to see a great increase in the sale of coals, and I look upon the interests of the Lords as one and the same, and I would rather see Mr Hewitt mismanage the collieries for one year and replace him by a more efficient agent if he is not found to give satisfaction, than witness the bickering that has existed during the past years."

On 16th November 1853 at an audit of the Coalpit Heath account at the White Lion, Bristol: "We commenced at noon and did not conclude our discussions until 2 a.m. the next morning. I ultimately succeeded in obtaining the discharge of Mr Bruce and Gilbert (two superintendents) and getting Mr Hewitt appointed as manager for 12 months on trial. Various complaints were made to show that Mr Hewitt had favoured his Brothers, the coal dealers, but all failed, and I must say that Mr Hewitt rose considerably in my opinion for the straight forward, manly manner in which he confronted his accusers."

Mr Hewitt proposed a new railroad between Frog Lane Pit and the New Engine Pit, which was already connected to the Midland Railway, to facilitate the distribution of coals. Arthur Way instructed Mr Townsend, the Smyth agent for collieries, to submit plans and on 17th April 1854 persuaded the other part-owners to accept the idea. "Mr Townsend was instructed to enquire into the cost of a new weighbridge capable of sustaining a locomotive engine, and to communicate with Mr Hewitt about the cost of rails."

At the next meeting, 13th June, Mr Townsend produced maps and plans and "explained them in detail .... it appeared the line could be completed for £4,000".

"Excavating and fencing the line	£ 700
Drains through cutting	80
Ballasting the line	352
Rails	1,482 @ £9.5.0. per ton
600 feet of timber	750
Fencing	440
Completing ditto.	180
	£3,984"

Even before the railway was completed, Arthur Way was writing (29th Dec. 1853): "Last week's return of coals from Coalpit Heath 2,673 tons, is the greatest amount ever sent in one week from Coalpit Heath. This is to me very satisfactory after the anxious time I have had in endeavouring to improve Coalpit Heath affairs."

The other Smyth coalpits were also flourishing.
3rd May 1853: "Saw Mr Bennett, Manager of the Bedminster Coal Coy. and received from him £403 for purchase of coal worked at Bedminster on this Estate from July 15 to December 24, 1852, and £12.5.4. for rent of land to Sept. 29, 1852." The Ashton Vale Company ran its workings under Smyth land, for which it paid one shilling royalty per ton and a rent of £200 per annum for coal and £30 for iron. Other collieries, for example the Dudley Pit, Gloucestershire, and the Malago Pit, Bedminster, which were suspected of doing the same, were accused of trespass, warned off or made to pay the same rate.

Arthur Way drove hard bargains. The manager of the Redlington Colliery* (Radstock) sought permission to mine coal under Smyth land at Foxcote. Arthur proposed one eighth of the returns as royalty and minimum rent of £200-£300. The manager suggested one tenth, but no minimum rent. Arthur declined.

At Pucklechurch he suspected the manager of falsifying returns: "....they have already worked 346 tons from Mr Smyth's estate which, at a shilling per ton royalty, gives Mr Smyth only £3.19.8½ return". The problem of determining the exact amount of royalty and wayleave (transporting coal over or under somebody else's land) were almost insuperable and Arthur Way was shrewd enough to realise that all kinds of encroachment and trespass went undetected and that colliery companies had to be milked to ensure that the estate got its due.

Coal was not the only mineral asset of the Ashton Court Estate. The relentless demands of industry had attracted numbers of speculators to the outcrops of iron ore on Ashton Hill.

* This could be another name (or spelling) for Writhlington.

31st Jan. 1853: "Walked on Ashton Hill and inspected the various foremen digging for iron ore there and brought away some specimens to send to the Government Geological Institute in London to be analysed."

20th Aug. 1853: "Had an important interview at Mr Palmer's office with Mr Owen of Bilston, Staffs., and Mr Wilkes of Wolverhampton, about iron ore on Ashton Hill. They propose to work there on a gigantic scale and offer 1/- per ton royalty - to be considered immediately."

Arthur summoned his mining agent, Mr Dodd, and the next week they walked over the hills concerned and examined the different outcrops of ore: "....his estimate of the Royalty that the estate should receive is 1/4d per ton. I think this too much but have no experience except my own calculation to guide me."

During the next few months similar overtures were received from other ironmasters in Wolverhampton, Newport, and one from Mr Trevithick of Yatton, offering up to twelve shillings a ton royalty. Finally, in March 1855, a contract was signed with Captain Dolphin, "son-in-law of Wm. Crawshay Esq., the Great Ironmaster in Wales", to work the iron ore at one shilling and sixpence per ton. A month later (21st April) "....walked to the iron ore diggings which are commencing well".

The Ashton Court estate account books for the 1850s have not survived, so it is difficult to assess how much of the gross profits came from mines. The first complete record is for 1872, some sixteen years after Arthur Way became steward, and it is interesting to note that out of £44,360 raised on property, £17,110 came from mines, the second highest source of income after land rents, and after the slump in agriculture in the 1880s the most reliable.

After eighteen months of shaking up the Smyth establishment, Arthur Way had cause to be satisfied. The staff and tenants, accustomed to the easy-going regime of Charles Abbott, jibbed at being dragooned by an outsider, but Arthur Way kept up the pressure and they began to respond. Goscombe, the forester, was instructed to establish a new plantation of pines; Ambrose, the shepherd, to build up his stock of Southdown sheep; waterlogged farms were drained; new walls built; the deer herd improved; strawberry beds revived; greenhouses refurbished; sheep stealers and poachers tracked down and prosecuted; new horses and carriages bought; outhouses cleared out, and the ice house restocked. Arthur Way was everywhere: paying wages to staff; inspecting the carpenter's and blacksmith's shops ("....gave the blacksmith and carpenter each a book to enter all work done each week for my perusal."); upbraiding tenants for the slovenly state of their farms; revaluing others which were affected by subsidence or the neglect of previous landlords; listening to complaints of tenants like Mrs Lucas who, on leaving her house "pressed for an allowance of £10 for her ornamental mantelpiece to be considered"; scrutinising the Poor Rate and striking out "several demands which I did not consider to belong to the estate, though heretofore paid by Mr Abbott"; repairing holes in the chancel roofs at Long Ashton and Stapleton, for which the Smyths were responsible; discussing the rebuilding of St. John's, Bedminster with Mr Eland, the incumbent, and promising material support; providing winter coal to the Long Ashton poor from the Bedminster Colliery, to be doled out by Mr Blackburn, the vicar; exchanging sharp words with the Bishop of Bristol who requested the Smyths to give up their right to dispose of pews in Stapleton Church; writing to the local press about sheep stealers, and to the Bishop of Bristol, or anyone who threatened to prevent the Smyths of the third creation coming into their own.

On the last day of 1854, Arthur Way confided to his Day Book: "On the whole I have every reason to be satisfied with the progress that has been made in the arrangement of affairs this year."

From his first taking on the duties of steward, Arthur Way moved into Ashton Court and brought Hebe and his little boy, Gregory, from Cheltenham, sending them home for the winter. Not for some months did Eliza and family take up residence and Arthur Way's Day Book is full of references to the voluminous correspondence that passed between him and his sister. Once, Arthur travelled up to Ingmire to put Eliza fully in the picture and to explain money matters to her, for she had little idea about business and various advances from the estate had to be made to her to cover immediate expenses.

26 August 1852: "Went from Ashton Court to Ingmire Hall, leaving the former at 7 a.m. and arrived at the station at Kendal at 4.45 p.m." - not bad for the early days of railway travel. "Ingmire: weather very hot. Fanny a great invalid; Greville Smyth and Florence Upton looking well." Arthur was very particular about referring to his nephew as Greville Smyth for he had taken the initiative in securing that same month the Queen's licence for Greville to change his name. A few weeks later the actual document arrived:

"A morocco case emblazoned with the letters VR in six places upon it, containing the Royal licence and the Queen's sign manual for my nephew Greville Upton to take the name Smyth only." The baronetcy followed in 1859.

Certain arrangements had to be made at Ashton before Greville and family could move in. Old Mrs Upton-Smyth had taken exception to many of her ancestors and had their portraits removed. Arthur and the estate carpenter put them back in the places where they had hung at the time of Sir John Smyth's death in 1849. Ann Price was appointed head housemaid and, judging from the mops Arthur was required to get for her, there was a thorough flushing and cleansing of the old house.

It was not an easy move for Eliza and her family. The children had grown up at Ingmire and loved it. All his life Greville regretted the fact that, had his elder brother not died, Ingmire and not Ashton would have been his home.

Fanny's tantrums complicated matters. She didn't want to be moved. Eliza begged Arthur to find her a good doctor. Arthur sent them Dr. Shaw of Cheltenham, whose first reports seemed hopeful, and in 1853 the family moved south in slow stages - first to Manchester, then to Cheltenham, but Fanny could be induced to go no further and there the family lodged for some months, hoping for an improvement in her condition. Occasionally Greville rode over to Ashton with John Upton, 'Big Nose', to view his vast inheritance and to hunt rabbits in the park with Uncle Arthur.

Perhaps the delay was providential, for in September 1852 Arthur Way was confronted with the most perplexing ordeal of his whole stewardship - the arrival of an imposter.

SMYTH V: SMYTH

An Unwelcome Visitor

"Received this morning a letter* from a person signing himself Henry Brown .... forbidding me, on behalf of Sir Richard Smyth, who calls himself son and heir of Sir Hugh Smyth, from receiving rents of the tenantry, or acting as agent of the Estate," wrote Arthur Way, indignantly, on 10th September 1852, "....also announcing the fact of Sir Richard Smyth having taken legal possession of Heath House, Stapleton.

"I sent immediately a message to Stapleton and found that a person calling himself Sir Richard Smyth with another had attempted last evening to take possession of Heath House, where they had been turned out by Joseph Turvey, the bailiff of Stapleton."

* "Bristol, Sept. 8th 1852

"Sir, I am directed by Thomas Rodham Esq., of Wellington, the deputed Steward of Sir Richard Smyth, Bart. of Ashton Court, Sommersett, to advise you that after this notice you do not interfere in any way directly or indirectly, with the tenants or property of the said Barony, and I am also directed to forbid the destruction of the Deer in the Park, and to request that you will consider yourself from this date a trespasser upon the property of Ashton Court, and you are also advised that Sir Richard Smyth has this day in person taken possession of Heath House at Stapleton, and that in future your visits to that house, or the lands thereof, will be considered a trespass,

"Your most obedient Servant,

"Henry Brown

"For Thomas Rodham Esq."

Mr Turvey, an ancient retainer who had been in service with the Smyths for over half a century, was most eloquent on the subject. Two suspicious looking characters, he told Arthur Way, (one presumably a solicitor, Mr Rodham), having requested to see the house, were admitted, and on being shown the portrait of Sir Hugh Smyth, the other prostrated himself before the picture exclaiming: "Oh! My father; my beloved Father" and then announced himself as Sir Richard Smyth, the lawful owner of the estates. "Upon which," continued the honest Joseph, "unable to restrain myself I exclaimed 'Now I tell ye what it is; I've known the family man and boy this fifty year and I never se'ed the likes of ye among 'em, and if you don't just clear out, I'll kick ye out, and that's all about it'."

Arthur Way continues: "Went to Mr Palmer's (the Smyth solicitor) and had consultations. We proceeded to Mr Mirehouse's with Mr Latchford, the magistrate's clerk. I stated the case to Mr Mirehouse who declined to grant a summons as no breach of the peace had been committed. On my return to Ashton Court the soi-disant Sir Richard Smyth and his attorney, Thomas Rodham of Wellington, Somerset, were at the door. I saw them in the housekeeper's room. The lawyer introduced himself as the Solicitor of Sir Richard Smyth, his companion, stating him to be the lawful owner of the Ashton Court Estates. I heard patiently their statement, claiming the whole estates of Ashton Court, Stapleton, the mansions thereon and the properties devised by Sir Hugh Smyth. I asked them if they had anything further to state, to which Sir Richard replied, 'No Sir, except that I wish you to discharge the household as my own servants are coming here, and I request you will hand me the keys of the mansion; but you need not hurry Sir, I will allow you two hours to take your departure'."

Arthur Way asked if Sir Richard meant by this remark that he wished him to "pack up my own portmanteau and leave the premises to you?"

The lawyer replied: "That is exactly what we want."

Mr Way: "Mr Rodham, have you anything more to say?"

Mr Rodham: "Not a word more Sir. I have stated fully Sir Richard's case and I trust you will throw no impediments in the way of his regaining his family estates."

Arthur Way placed his watch on the table and said: "Now then, I must request your attention to what I say. You have come here in the face of the day to perpetrate a robbery of no ordinary kind. In a case so monstrous, I can make no distinction between solicitor and client. You must both leave the house within the minute or be prepared to take the consequences."

Sir Richard and his solicitor broke into loud expostulations. The minute elapsed and Arthur touched the bell. The menservants rushed in from the passage "....and forcibly ejected them, carrying them off by the arms and legs and unceremoniously dumping them in the drive, Sir Richard complimenting me with the epithet 'scoundrel' etc. Thus ended this extraordinary interview". Next day he sent Eliza a full account of what had happened.

The existence of this gentleman had been known to the Uptons and Ways for some time. He first appeared on the scene in 1848 and soon after set up house with his family at St. Vincent's Priory, Clifton, a pretentious mock Gothic folly opposite the Grand Spa Hotel. A contemporary account poked fun at the "would-be baronet .... supported by the funds of his dupes, living in style". It was amusing to see him and his wife make their exit from church on a Sunday, to observe the bowings and scrapings to 'Sir Richard and Lady Smyth', followed in the Roger de Coverley style by a well-dressed lackey carrying the family Bible and other accessories of devotion. In October 1852 he created some annoyance to the Upton family by masquerading as 'Sir Richard Smyth of Ashton Court, Somerset', which description appeared on printed leaflets advertising a lecture on Shakespeare he was supposed to have given at Newbury, Berkshire. Arthur Way: "Query - Should he not be pulled up as an Imposter?"

In February 1853, Arthur was outraged to learn that "....the false Baronet, Sir Richard Smyth, had issued notices to the Tenants of this Estate not to pay any rents except to **his** lawyer and agent, Mr Catlin, of Ely Place, Holborn.* Went to Mr Palmer and consulted with him and Mr Wansey what steps to take".

Mr Palmer went at once to London "to take the opinion of eminent Counsel upon the proper steps to be pursued", and the following week 200 circulars were sent to the tenants "to counteract Sir Richard Smyth's circular". By this time Sir Richard was busily enticing them with extravagant promises of reducing the rent, reviving the Bower Ashton pleasure gardens, throwing open the Park to the public and even building a suspension bridge at Rownham; and a crowd of sycophants, toadies and tradesmen gathered round in hopes of patronage, to the embarrassment and consternation of the Uptons and Ways. "He promised good berths to many" ran a contemporary account, "and one man was to have £2,000 a year and be land steward, and he actually sold his butter shop in London in full expectation of getting it". 'Sir Richard' borrowed money from everybody and, of course, promised a bonus for his loans.

He was now bombarding the whole Smyth clan, reiterating his claim: to the Rev. Henry Hugh Way at Henbury; to Captain Gore-Langton and to John Hugh Smith-Piggott. These letters Arthur Way gathered up and took to his solicitor for scrutiny. The pressure was building up. On 30th May 1853 Arthur Way writes:

* We hear no more of Mr Rodham after his undignified exit from Ashton Court. Perhaps he had no wish to share further in Sir Richard's adventures.

"Various rumours about Sir Richard Smyth, all confirming the opinion that an attack will be made shortly to get possession of Ashton Court.

"June 3 .... found reports at Ashton so rife of an intended attack on Ashton Court I thought it my duty in the absence of a full household of servants, to consult with Mr Palmer on the subject; went to his office and saw there Captain Fisher, Superintendent of the Bristol Police, and Inspector Webb; the rumour at that time in Bristol was that a row had already taken place at Ashton Court. It was agreed that Inspector Webb should send me tomorrow to Ashton 2 men thoroughly acquainted with police duties, and that I should establish immediate communication with the Bristol Police in case of the man calling himself Sir Richard Smyth bringing a mob to attack Ashton.

"June 4 .... had all the men mustered at Ashton Court, loaded the guns with swanshot and had the garden pikes brought into the House and dispersed them ready for use. Captain Fisher sent over John Collard and Nicholas Paramore Hole to act as policemen, and I agreed to pay them 5/- a day, finding themselves, and they are to be on duty from 8 a.m. to 8 p.m. for as many days as I may require them. I allotted different stations to all the men on the place in case of attack and made all necessary arrangements."

Two days passed without incident and on the 6th Arthur felt confident enough to go to the Ascot Races, leaving Goscombe, Woodruff and two policemen in charge of the house. The rumoured attack never materialised, but other mischief was in the making.

"11 June. Mr Catlin served me a Writ of Ejectment for Heath House, Stapleton and 30 acres of land more or less, on behalf of Sir Richard Smyth, Bart. v. John Henry Greville Smyth, a minor."

Sir Richard was now hellbent on making good his claims. In July he secured the services of the legal profession and assembled both witnesses and, it appeared, incontestable evidence to substantiate his claims. Arthur Way appointed a private detective, Mr Field, to watch Mr Catlin's office, to investigate the credibility of these claims, and to unravel Sir Richard's story. In August 1853 Richard Smyth brought a case against Greville Smyth, and Arthur Way, acting for his nephew, besought Sir Frederick Thesiger, an eminent lawyer,* to defend his rights. The case opened on 8th August 1853 at the Gloucestershire Assizes, amid considerable excitement.

* Lord Chelmsford, the celebrated and successful Victorian barrister who specialised in cases relating to the aristocracy.

Richard Smyth or Tom Provis?

Sir Richard's story, as recounted by his attorney, Mr Bovill, on the first day of the trial was, on the face of it, wholly credible. The fact that a claimant could challenge the ownership to such a prodigious estate indicates something rotten in the state of Smyth. The rot was laid at the door of Greville's great uncle, Sir Hugh Smyth, Bart. who died in 1825.

Back in 1796 when Hugh was twenty-four and heir to his uncle, Sir John Hugh, it was claimed by Sir Richard that he had made a secret marriage in Ireland to Jane Vandenburg*, who, on giving birth to him, her only child, died. The Vandenburg family Bible was produced with a record of the marriage and the names of witnesses, and a miniature of the lady was passed round the court. Greville, who attended the proceedings with his mother, was seen to scrutinise the portrait attentively, comparing it with the 56-year-old gentleman with a sallow complexion and iron grey hair, parted in the middle, who stood in the witness box claiming to be her son.

It all looked more than likely. Great Uncle Hugh had been an embarrassment to the family on account of his extra-marital adventures. Four years before his alleged marriage to Jane Vandenburg he had fathered a bastard child by Elizabeth Howell, whom he had wanted to marry, but whom he was obliged to set aside in favour of Margaret Wilson, daughter of the Bishop of Bristol, a bride chosen for him by his uncle, of whom he had great expectations. Though Sir Hugh later married Elizabeth Howell (1820) on the death of Margaret Wilson, the natural son, John Hugh, was never legitimised, through an oversight, and could not inherit the Smyth estates. This John Hugh married in 1815 an heiress, Ann Provis, who in 1827 inherited the Piggott estates from her uncle. The father of this Ann Provis was a William Provis of Shepton Mallet; and here was a sinister connection, or was it just coincidence, that young Richard Smyth was entrusted to one, John Provis of Warminster on the death of his mother.

Sir Frederick Thesiger, acting for Greville Smyth, was determined to prove that Sir Richard was, in fact, the son of John Provis. Though proved

* At Carrageen House, County Macsherry, County Cork, home of the Bandon family to whom, claimed Sir Richard, the Vandenburgs were related.

wrong on many genealogical points, it is strange that Sir Richard should have steadfastly maintained that John Provis was the brother of Ann, for it materially damaged his case. It would have served his cause better if he had been less honest on this point for the defence was able to make much of the so-called Provis plot to grab the Smyth empire. All other authorities maintained that Ann Provis was an only child. How else could she have been an heiress?

Actually there is a great deal of mystery surrounding Ann Provis. Her parents, Ann Piggott and William Provis, made a disastrous marriage in 1776. Ann Piggott was a social beauty, lived in the Royal Crescent, Bath, and was painted by Gainsborough, as were her brothers John and Wadham Piggott. Her husband was totally antipathetic to the social round and returned to his estates in Shepton Mallet. Their child, Ann, was disowned by her mother until 1808, and she was brought up by her bachelor uncle, the Rev. Wadham Piggott*, who left her the Piggott property in 1823, some seven years after her marriage to the illegitimate son of Sir Hugh.

If indeed John Provis of Warminster was her brother then he would certainly have felt disappointed of the Piggott estate. Could his son not have contrived to pass himself off as a Smyth and make a bid for the other estate, which was infinitely larger and currently beset with a chronic shortage of male heirs?

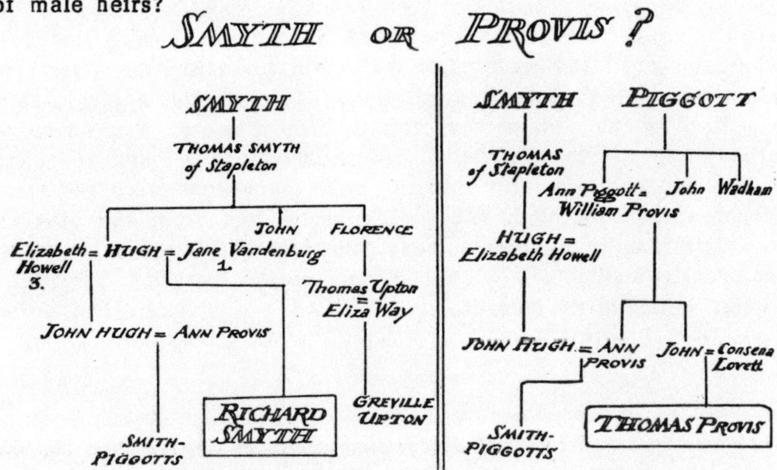

* Vicar of Weston-super-Mare. He lived at 'The Grove', Weston.

To get back to Sir Richard's story. The validity of his claim depended on satisfactory answers to a number of vital questions. Why, if he was the legitimate son of Sir Hugh, was he brought up in obscurity and not publicly recognised by his father? The answer: In deference to his uncle's wishes, Sir Hugh had married Margaret Wilson in 1798 and was bound to keep Jane Vandenburg and her child a secret, added to which, Sir Richard maintained, his father detested children and couldn't bear the sight of them.

Why was he sent to John Provis, a builder and carpenter in Warminster if, as was stated, his mother was so well connected in Ireland? Answer: In 1798, a few months after the marriage, the Earl of Bandon's castle was destroyed in the Irish Rebellion. Jane Vandenburg fled with some of her family to the home of her relations in England, the Marchioness of Bath at Longleat. The house was then being structurally altered following the death of the Marquis and Jane, now well advanced in pregnancy, was sent to the home of John Provis, one of the builders engaged in the operation*, a natural arrangement considering that John Provis had taken as his second wife Consena Lovett, the personal maid and old friend of Jane Vandenburg.

A letter was read in court, alleged to have been written by Hugh Smyth from Stapleton in February 1797:

"Dear Jane, The bearer is my old nurse Lydia Reed, in whom I have my confidence as to her skill and attention to you. Dr. Seguin will attend to you. I will endeavour to be over tomorrow and bring my mother with me. Till then, God bless you, and that you may have a safe delivery is the prayer of your affectionate husband, Hugh Smyth."

A Somerset magistrate and parson, the Rev. G. T. Seymour, testified to the letter being in Hugh's handwriting.

A most Audacious Child

According to Sir Richard, Lydia Reed of Nailsea, having just lost a child, suckled him until she gave birth to a son some months after, and then he was handed over to John Provis' niece, Mary Provis, a girl of sixteen, who was still living and whom the plaintiff was prepared to produce in court to identify him. He then recalled his childhood in a manner that was both ingenious and charming. He told the court he always wore red morocco shoes to denote his noble birth and to distinguish him from the other children in John Provis' family. "I was a most audacious child, not so much wickedly as mischievously inclined." "That I can easily believe," said Sir Frederick Thesiger, sarcastically (laughter).

* If these are the structural alterations made by Wyatt then the dates don't fit. These were undertaken in 1808, but that is not to say that other works were not carried out at an earlier date.

"I was termed the little gentleman of the place and pulled the people's shutters down and so on. I remember the Proclamation of Peace," (this was the Treaty of Amiens, 1802, which brought the end of the war against revolutionary France), "and to celebrate the event triumphal arches were put up across the streets in Warminster. On the occasion in question I procured a knife and slyly cut the rope that bound the whole, when down it fell, an old woman caught me up and saved my life. Replacing me on my feet, like a croaking raven she cried out 'Od rot thee, boy, thou'st be an unfortunate man, but an old woman will save thee at last'."

This anecdote, and those that follow, come from a little book written by Sir Richard from prison after he had lost the case, entitled 'The Victim of Fatality, or the Claimant of Ashton Court: A Romantic Tale of the Nineteenth Century'. It is a remarkable document in which facts have been interlarded with a good deal of fiction, and must be treated with considerable caution.

"The market house at that time stood in the centre of the town and in it, hanging against the walls, long poles with large hooks at the end of each. One market day I got up on one of these, and having but one hand to use (the other had been badly lacerated at birth and for many years was useless) I pressed too much on one side so that down went the end, and up went the hook on which I had slidden, and there I hung dangling by my clothes. I was fortunately unhurt and a man took me down, saying 'Ah, little Two-shoes, (a nickname I was known by, because I wore red morocco shoes) nothing will kill thee'.

"I remember once being caught by an old woman whom I had annoyed beyond measure. She watched for me on the opposite side of the road and caught me safe enough. She was just about to inflict a posterior flagellation when I cried out 'Mam!' (the name I gave my nurse). The old woman was softened in a moment. I had touched the proper spring and her anger was gone. She said, 'Poor child, I had forgot thou hast no mother. There, get thee gone. I won't beat thee.' I never annoyed her again, but as ever I could would run in and give her a kiss.

"My master trick was rather a novel one for a child. Opposite our house was a common bakehouse, frequented on certain days by all the gossips of the place, who, after putting in their cakes, would leisurely lounge against the troughs, and then away went all respect for everyone but themselves. On this especial day the shop was more than usually filled and my nurse had gone there and left me outside. Obtaining a long piece of cord I so completely with my left hand tied together the handle of the door and the shutter that no power but a knife could undo it.

"The cakes done, the bread put in, and the gossip over, the old and young wanted their tea (for scandal is proverbially dry work) but how to get out? There lay the quandary, no one being near. There was a raised bank opposite whereon I mounted to enjoy the fun. Such bawling and squalling and threatening and striving to get out was past all bearing. My nurse, at length, got out of the window guessing truly who had done the mischief, and cutting the fastening with a knife liberated the imprisoned party."

Strivings for Identity

Sir Richard said he believed that the reason why he was not disciplined as other children would have been for those pranks was because his guardians knew he was of noble birth. Among his earliest memories were two ladies who used to visit him at Warminster. He later discovered who they were: Caroline Bernard, the Countess of Bandon, and Isabella Thynne, the Dowager Marchioness of Bath. It was they, he claimed, who stood sponsors at his baptism, and from time to time he was invited to No. 1 Royal Crescent, Bath, where the Bernards had settled after the Irish Rebellion, and to the country seat of the Baths at Longleat.

Witnesses were called to identify the signatures of Caroline Bernard and Isabella Thynne in the Vandenburg family Bible. At least two of them testified to the authenticity of Isabella Thynne's signature but it was remarked by the defendants that one of them had spent some time in a workhouse and his collusion had been probably bought by the plaintiff. The defence, from the start, suspected that the Bible, or signatures, or both, were phoney* and they were ultimately proved right on this point.

From these ladies, Sir Richard said he had been given to believe he was the son of Sir Hugh; and occasionally they took him to visit his mother's grave in Warminster. It was still there, asserted Sir Richard, in a brick vault; but the Bishop, to whom he had applied, had refused to allow him to have it opened in order to find any identifying evidence, and his mother's name which he had once read in the burial register had subsequently, unaccountably, been erased.

Recalling his visits to No. 1 Royal Crescent, Sir Richard wrote: "I remember a little incident that occurred whilst there. The Countess of Bandon, a Boyle, after whose favourite and only brother Richard I was named, and who died young the year I was born, had brought with her from Ireland a large mastiff dog. It was very fond of me. I played with it, but never teased it. One day a number of ladies who had just come from the public rooms filled the drawing room. I took my ribbon from my neck, put it round the dog's neck, mounted its back, and up we went in gallant style into the room. The dog enjoyed the fun, and the Countess of Bandon roared with laughter, for it reminded her of an event that occurred to her in Ireland, when she flew on her pony across a rapid stream and nobody dared to follow."

* 15.5.1853: Arthur Way: "Mr Palmer has rec'd a letter from Oakhill, near Mendip, saying Mr Catlin had been there to examine the registers and asked the Rector to examine an old Bible with a magnifying glass to try to read the name of 'Thynne'!"

Of Longleat, where he said he spent his school holidays, he relates a singular incident. "....Over the door rested, in my day, a large coat of arms on a shield supported by stags, as large as life .... A servant unexpectedly came to announce a week's holiday, on account, I suppose, of the Peace of Amiens" (no, it couldn't have been, for he was only four in 1802), "and in the excitement of exuberant joy, up went my book" (a Latin grammar his tutor always expected him to carry), "and it lodged behind the shield, and it is still there, if not destroyed by the damp and time. It had my name and that of my father in it. I wrote to the present Marquis about it, but my enemies had been there before me and poisoned his mind, so that he paid no attention. I would rather have that book now than ten thousand pounds."

If there is any truth in this then it would suggest that Sir Hugh took an interest in his son's education. Certainly Mr Grace*, Sir Hugh's butler, arrived from time to time to superintend his schooling. "Good Heavens! I see him now: a great coarse, potbellied, unwieldy man, wholly deficient however in the Grace of God. They said he was my father's butler, but who my father was I did not enquire."

When about four years of age "Mr Grace took me to Mr Saunders' school at Beckhampton, and there I saw my brother John." His half-brother, to be more exact, was four years older, and they cordially detested each other at first sight. "We did not meet kindly," said Sir Richard. "He was older, but I was prouder and I never should have loved him, for he repelled my nature."

Little Dick of Lower Court

"I was not long at Beckhampton, for Grace took me away to Lower Court, Long Ashton, then inhabited by Mrs Hall." Sir Richard was very particular in his description of this place and its occupants. It was the nearest he ever came to Ashton Court and the inheritance he claimed, and if indeed he had never been there he got the story from somebody who evidently knew it very well. (18.2.1853. Arthur Way wrote in his Day Book, "Saw W. Wilde about Sir R. Smyth; a man of the name of Hall, now 66 years old, denies there was ever a boy named Richard Smyth brought up there".)

The Lower Court, or more properly the Manor of Ashton Phelips, is an ancient house a mile or so south west of Ashton Court, and from the 16th Century was part of the Smyth estate. It had been the home of Elizabeth Smyth, widow of the first Sir Hugh and her second husband, the celebrated coloniser, Ferdinando Gorges**, but it passed out of the family when it went as part of Arabella Smyth's portion, on her marriage to Edward Gore. In the 1790s Sir John Hugh Smyth's bailiff, Mr Hall, lived there and sometime after 1824 it was bought back by Sir John Smyth.

* This Grace was the grandfather of Dr W. G. Grace, the famous cricketer.
** See 'The Earlier Smyths of Ashton Court'.

The house, described by Sir Richard in 1853, recalling his stay there fifty years before, is recognisably the same house today, and the part it played in the annals of the Smyth family is not insignificant.

"It was a very large and grand structure for the period in which it was erected, but at the time referred to little remained beyond an eastern wing of the dwelling apartment in which was a large room, wainscotted, with the edges of the panels gilt. In a small closet in this room I used to sleep and many a prank have I played in the old and ancient place.

"There was, running along the front entrance to the Court, at the bottom of the field, a river, or rather a stream of water, one portion of which had been deepened for the convenience of washing sheep." A new housing estate (1980) now sprawls across the field, but the stream is still there. "Across the stream by the deep part ran one plank, but opposite the gate, or entrance, ran 2 or 3 planks forming a rude bridge." One day in 1802, Sir John Hugh sent for his bailiff, but he never arrived. "His termagant wife, who was a complete virago, had that evening so tantalised the poor fellow that he was glad to escape. He accordingly hurried out of the house, took the narrow plank and, it being dark, he fell in, and was found dead the next morning." This tragedy, which occurred a year or two before Sir Richard came to the Lower Court, was said to have hastened the death of old Sir John Hugh, and Mrs Hall was never the same woman again.

The episode was related to young Richard, so he said, by an old retainer who lived on the estate, called Philips, "....a fine, portly and jovial man, full of fun and anecdote, and one of the best fellows that ever breathed.... aving been born and brought up in the family he was well versed in its history....I went every day, if the weather suited, from Lower Court, through the lower grounds up to the back of the Church, through the Churchyard, down across the public field, down the road past the Coach & Horses Inn and Lodge, in at the left, and up to the house occupied by Philips. He lived in the house on the right, just as you enter the gates of the steward's house." At that date this was the principal entrance to Ashton Court, later blocked when Sir John extended and walled the park in the 1840s.

"Philips took a particular fancy to me, because I was never tired of listening to his tales. By him, too, I was plentifully supplied with fruit; and an old man now living used to bring it to Mrs Hall's for me. My whole resource of amusement thus rested on the narrations of Philips, and having heard them I would return home and ponder them well. There was one tale he told me of a most horrifying nature connected with an infant said to be of royal blood, whose beautiful coffin is to be seen in the vaults...."

Sir Richard had some curious things to say about the 14th Century chapel of Ashton Phelips, which is still standing, though overshadowed by the enormous concrete piers of the Long Ashton bypass.

"At the south end of the building stood the chapel, which was entire, being 22 feet long and 10 feet wide. The altar was of stone, and when I was there it stood in its pristine state, except that instead of its sacred viands and glittering vases it was then loaded with rubbish, dust and cobwebs" (it still is, 1983), "but above all with stones flung there in sport, by myself, from the garden. During my short stay there it was my thoughtless habit to throw every stone I could find upon the altar and when I went to visit Philips I crammed my pockets with stones for that purpose. Thus I inconsiderately insulted my God by the indignity offered to that altar once and for ever made sacred to Him, and dearly have I paid the penalty. What have I been gathering all my life but stones?*

"The pulpit stood on the left side" (now gone), "and in the south wall was a niche, a receptacle for holy water. There was a small bell" (also gone), "in the arcade over the entrance, but it has long been silent."

The large empty cider barrels stored there were ideal places where the wilful Richard could hide from the enraged Mrs Hall, and they no doubt suggested other possibilities to his fertile mind.

"I had a tub converted into a pigeon house for me, which was fixed to a pole, and raised up in the right-hand corner of the old chapel, at the altar end, in the centre of which a large peg had been fastened and is there still. Pieces of wood had been fastened at different distances on the pole, up which I one day climbed, and having only my left hand to use, I pulled the pole on one side, and down it fell, but was caught by the peg and I was thus again saved."

It was during these years at Lower Court that young Richard first caught sight of the man he believed to be his father. "He had a fair and open countenance, wore his hair, which was very short, thrown back from his forehead, and in after life he wore his neckcloth very large, and quite over his chin, a practice, it was claimed, adopted to conceal a weal on his neck which reached from ear to ear" - another of those peculiar birthmarks that his 'son' alleged ran in the family. According to Sir Richard, Hugh Smyth, Bart. was a man of few words, mildly eccentric, quick-tempered, and possessed of a strong aversion to children.

* Sir Richard made his little book almost unreadable by bestowing on every incident, however trivial, some pious or sentimental significance, designed to further his cause or excite compassion for his fate.

Sir Hugh Smyth & his son John Hugh.

"I remember once, when at Lower Court, then about six years of age, and my brother about 10 or 11, my father, who was a great hunter and excessively fond of dogs, more so than of his children, going one morning to join the hounds and having to pass the farm on his way to Dundry. My brother John was following on a small pony when the animal, from my brother's attempting to strike me with a whip as I held the gate to let my father pass, and letting it go before he (John) had passed, trod upon one of the dogs.

My father, urged to it no doubt by the dastardly blow directed at me, turned in a rage upon my brother, and horse-whipped him, so severely that it caused me to shudder, and although he always had a kind word for me, yet after this event I was always literally afraid of him."

Sometimes "My father would pat me on the head and say 'Good boy! Good boy! Oh, how like his mother!' He never, as far as I can recollect, called me son, but once. On account of some mischievous act I had been reported to him, when he shook his whip at me and said, 'That does not become you, my son'.

"When Mrs Hall had to go to Bristol she would leave me at the preparatory school opposite the church, kept by two sisters who used to take me backwards and forwards. I was known as Little Dick Smyth, or Master Dick. I used also occasionally to go to Stapleton, to a Miss Whitchurch." (A relation, presumably, of his father, whose mother had been a Whitchurch of Stapleton before her marriage.)

In later years Sir Richard made a return visit to Long Ashton and after enquiring at the Angel Inn "....was directed to old Vincent, a stonemason, who had been a gamekeeper to my father. I found the old man and said to him, 'I am come on the part of the new claimant, Sir Richard, to ask you a question'. 'Ah!' said he, 'I thought so. I heard enough about that business from old Grace.' 'Well then, Sir Richard says he was at Lower Court when a little boy, in Mrs Hall's time, and he declares that the dwelling house was on the right-hand as you go in.' The old man jumped up in a moment and exclaimed, 'Does Sir Richard say so?' 'He does, and swears it.' 'Then by G-- he is Sir Hugh's son, for no mortal but he and I know that fact. I was then serving my time as a mason, and helped to alter and build up the present house on the left for Mrs Smith, who succeeded Mrs Hall.' The old man is still living...." - but he was not called to the trial.

"The Promethean Spark"

The time at Lower Court came to an end when Grace removed him to a private school in Brislington, conducted by a Mr Hill. "It occurred thus," went on Sir Richard, "Mr Provis had a son of about 10 or 12 years old who, when I left, ran away also after me, and came to Bristol, to Mr Grace. His father came after him and I suppose placed him with Mr Hill."

Brislington was a pleasant village, situated between Bristol and Bath, and much esteemed by the city gentlemen, many of whom had splendid country houses there. "Whilst at Brislington, I always dined on Sunday either at Justice Ireland's or Colonel Gore's. I knew old Dr. Fox and was present when the foundation stone of the madhouse was laid (1804). The present Capt. Gore-Langton was my companion there. It was whilst at Hill's school that my poor hand broke in fighting with a boy called George Fowler, and in a dreadful state it was. It hung at my breast for 20 years of no use whatsoever to me.

"My holidays were spent at Stapleton (at his grandmother's home) and the gardener at Heath House would take me in the evening into Bristol, to the George Inn, Narrow Wine Street, a house famous for beer called 'Old Tom', and at that time kept by Mrs Charles Besset, who afterwards removed to the Swan. The gardener would at night drink deeply from 'Old Tom', and in the morning put me inside the London coach that started from the Bush Tavern, at that time the head inn in Bristol, but no more. The coach left early and would put me down at the White Hart at Brislington.

"I often visited the French prison at Stapleton, and this gave me an interest in France and Frenchmen. I have since seen them under every variety of circumstance and can truly say I neither love nor hate them.

"From Hill's school I was removed to Warminster Grammar School under Dr. Griffiths, with Mr Lewis as tutor. Here I was contemporary with the late Dr. Arnold. He was my school fellow, bedfellow and constant companion, but I may say here that he was a most indefatigable student. For myself I never in my life learnt a lesson in the ordinary way, which will in some measure account for my erroneous spelling. I would here say that I am one of those who have learnt all they know, as it were, intuitively.

"Whilst at Dr. Griffiths' I never by any chance went to the house of Mr Provis. I ever kept myself entire. Being a proud boy, too much like my family, I could not mix with those below me. My holidays I spent at Longleat and Marston. My companions were the sons of the Marquis of Bath, and Lord Cork, and such other young gentry as happened to be there.

"I well remember once going to Harrow School, and walking into the churchyard I encountered young Byron, stretched at his full length upon a tombstone, enjoying in silent contemplation worlds of dreamy fancy, engendered by one of the most splendid scenes in nature spread out before him. His imaginative eye was all on fire .... like me he was the child of destiny and fate, and he so far sympathised with me that he noticed me in his 'Childe Harold'. Those who are familiar with the poem will catch the Promethean Spark and instantly recognise the allusion. I spent the whole afternoon with him and his opinions respecting Napoleon were in harmony with my own.

"After I went to Warminster I never saw my father, Sir Hugh, nor anyone from Ashton Court but Grace. Two ladies came to see me, one I think was my grandmother (Jane Whitchurch); the other Mrs Fitzherbert, the lady who then gave me the invitation to Wycombe Abbey. I often went to Bath to visit my Aunt Florence in Gay Street. Since I have seen Mrs Upton I feel confident that it was her, the haughty bearing of the two being so similar and complete."

Left-handed Wykhamist

"From Warminster I was sent to Winchester College. I was a commoner under Dr. Goddard. Mr Gable was second, and Mr Williams was third master. Dr. Huntingford, afterwards Bishop of Hereford, was Warden. Mr Urquhart, private tutor; Bowers, the writing master. This Bowers had a son who was hump-backed and was called Cracknel.*

"Mr Le Croix, the present pastry-cook of the College, was then the boy that served the commoners, when shut into the College. He remembers me and he has known me all his life. I knew Dr. Bedford well, the blind master of Twyford School. The organist of the Cathedral and College Chapel was also blind.

"In my day we had the holiday and the remedy. On a holiday it was over the hills to Twyford and St. Cross, and away as far even as Southampton; but on a remedy we couldn't go out of bounds, being called in twice a day, unless our fags could answer for us. I was for a time, a fag, and did wonders for I could imitate any boy's voice. Boys of the higher forms had each one his fag, and many a con I have had and given. It is out of practice now; mammas have put a stop to all that. It was, however, a very foolish stop - that same Soft Motherapason stop. It was the only method by which the imbecility of mother-spoilt boys could be remedied, and by its suppression the development of energy and hardihood has been savagely impeded.

* There is no record at Winchester College of a Smyth or Provis being a commoner during these years. It is possible that 'Sir Richard' gleaned this information from Dr. Arnold whom he claims to have known and who studied at Warminster and Winchester about the same time. 0

"The officers in the school were the prefects, bible-clerks and sterius (sic). Dr. Goddard never flogged the boys, but at the gable's end. I once heard the reason. However, he never flogged me, my hand saved me. The floggings were inflicted chiefly for defective exercises and, as I could not write, so accordingly I escaped the tasks; nevertheless I was frequently called upon to correct the exercises of other boys. Poor lads! I often pity boys sent to public schools, when deficient in a priori knowledge. In such cases all is left to the master and the birch.

"Those who were at Winchester in those days will remember the small brush-handle with four birch twigs left in around it. There was a fellow who provided those twigs, but we boys could never discover who he was. The forms crossed and were joined together, and our boxes placed therein; so that we could walk up and down the whole length of the school. I shall be called to mind (by the many Wykhamists who will read this) by my poor hand hanging at my breast and my sonorous voice in singing; especially the song of 'Dulce Domum' which never failed to charm a Wykhamist. What glorious fun we enjoyed! We formed a little world, and I can but think that the public schools of olden days were, after all, the best.

"My holidays from Winchester I spent in Grosvenor Street, London, with the Marchioness of Bath, except when I visited elsewhere, which was often the case, boys frequently inviting each other."

Windfalls

At the close of the year 1810, when Sir Richard was thirteen years of age, Dr. Goddard resigned his mastership of Winchester College. Sir Richard was told that his bills had not been paid for eighteen months and that he must speak to Lady Bath on the subject. Mr Grace failed to appear and Sir Richard believed that he had deliberately withheld the money, much of which was found in his room when he died; and that he had later reported to Sir Hugh that his son was dead. Sir Hugh was ailing and it probably suited him at that point to forget about him. He was transferred to Dr. Richard's school on the other side of Winchester for a further eighteen months. He was no longer invited to Grosvenor Street and was obliged to spend his holidays at Bowers', the writing master.

At last, when fifteen or sixteen years old, Sir Richard said he found the courage to demand an interview with the Marchioness of Bath. He pressed her for information about his mother. Although "she spoke of her with the deepest emotion .... she said as little upon the subject as she possibly could". She mentioned no names, but said that she was well connected and related distantly to herself. If he was desperate for further details she could obtain them from the Bernards who were her nearest relations. She then, claimed Sir Richard, produced the Bishop's warrant for his mother's private marriage, which he later lost, from which it was inferred at the trial that it had never existed.*

Lady Bath then gave him a considerable sum of money, £1,400 to £1,500, which she said had been left by his mother and which had appreciated over the years. The last part of the interview turned out to have been invented by Sir Richard when he realised he had not sufficient evidence to back his claim. Lady Bath then told him that her steward, a Mr Davies of Warminster, had some personal belongings of his mother, among them an oil painting of his father, a miniature of herself, her rings and jewellery, and her Bible. Finally she gave him an obituary ring from her finger which, he claimed, had his mother's name, dates of marriage and death engraved on it.

Sowing Wild Oats

Sir Richard chose to gloss over the next fourteen years of his life. He explained the next eighteen months by stating that he had fallen ill with the smallpox and was slowly nursed back to health at the home of a Dr. Williams in Parliament Street, Westminster. This was to conceal the fact that while employed as an assistant master in a private academy in Bath he had stolen a gelding belonging to a Colonel Gladden of Keynsham. Such an offence carried the death penalty at that time but, in view of his youth, he was then only fifteen, his punishment was commuted to eighteen months imprisonment which was spent in Ilchester Gaol. When this was disclosed at the trial, and Sir Richard was made to expose in court the marks of the King's Evil on his neck and right hand, the same marks which had been noted at the time of his imprisonment, it created a sensation and did much to establish the belief that he must be an imposter.

What further damaged his case was that, at his second trial for perjury and forgery, a former pupil of his was produced and identified him as 'Mr Provis'. Sir Richard was enraged by this, and retorted vehemently that the man was a liar and had evidently been bribed to give this information.

The next twelve years, he went on, were spent abroad. It was 1814 and the allies were closing in on Paris. Suddenly the wider world seemed to beckon. "Oh, that I had then decided upon going home! I might have done so but I called in at Grosvenor Street and learnt that the Marchioness had gone

* 21.1.1853: Arthur Way wrote in his Day Book: "Returned to Ashton from Cheltenham; found that Mr Catlin on behalf of Sir R.Smyth had sent a circular to various parish clerks offering a reward of £15 to anyone who would produce a marriage certificate of Hugh Smyth Esq. to Jane Boyle, Jane Bernard or Jane Gookin between the years 1795 & 1797, there being abundant evidence that the marriage took place, to establish a claim to considerable estates."

LEWIS WAY

MRS. LEWIS WAY
"Bombie"

DRUSILLA, ALBERT
ANNA & OLIVIA WAY

COL. BENJAMIN WAY

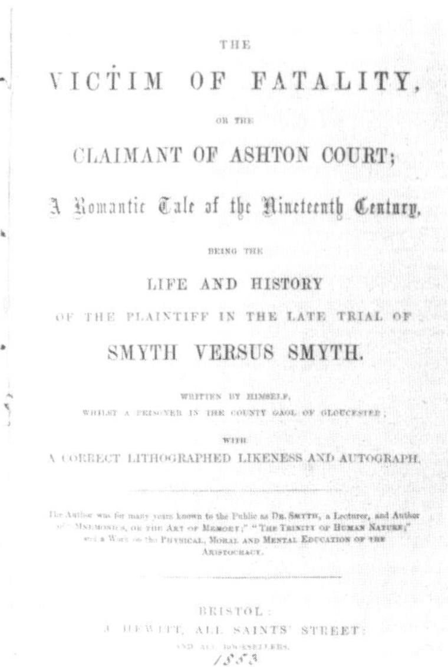

THE

VICTIM OF FATALITY,

OR THE

CLAIMANT OF ASHTON COURT;

A Romantic Tale of the Nineteenth Century,

BEING THE

LIFE AND HISTORY

OF THE PLAINTIFF IN THE LATE TRIAL OF

SMYTH VERSUS SMYTH.

WRITTEN BY HIMSELF,
WHILST A PRISONER IN THE COUNTY GAOL OF GLOUCESTER;

WITH

A CORRECT LITHOGRAPHED LIKENESS AND AUTOGRAPH.

The Author was for many years known to the Public as DR. SMYTH, a Lecturer, and Author of "MNEMONICS, OR THE ART OF MEMORY;" "THE TRINITY OF HUMAN NATURE;" and a Work on the PHYSICAL, MORAL AND MENTAL EDUCATION OF THE ARISTOCRACY.

BRISTOL:
J. HEWITT, ALL SAINTS' STREET;
AND ALL BOOKSELLERS.
1853

"SIR RICHARD SMYTH" (Thomas Provis) AND HIS BOOK

THOMAS UPTON

THOMAS UPTON Jun.
died aged 18.

Geo O. Edwards

GEORGE OLDHAM EDWARDS

EMILY WAY

GREVILLE UPTON
Aged 18

ELIZA UPTON

FLORENCE UPTON

FANNY UPTON

CLEMENT COTTRELL DORMER

SIR GREVILLE SMYTH Bt.

to Longleat. In strolling down the Strand I met with an old playmate called Knox, usually designated Lord Knox, the son of Lord Renferline. He was going on the continent to join his family and asked me where I was for. I replied, 'Home to Dad, for the first time in my life since I was a little fellow.' On finding how matters stood with me and above all the discovery that I had the needful (the all-pervading passport any whither and any how) he proposed and I assented and off we started together.

"Well, we next day started for the continent, posting it all the way to Dover, which occupied two days, for we did not travel, as we do now, at the rate of 50 mph. Besides we took our time, a stop both requisite and politic, in as much as it magnified our importance. Our fame preceded us, and all along our route it was bruted that we were two young noblemen travelling for the purpose of perfecting our education. You may be sure we paid for it; that is to say, I did, for I shrewdly suspect that my Lord Knox made me pay dearly for his patronage. Well, I will say this for him, he watched over me like a brother, and considering how helpless I was, that was something. Yet I had sometimes to watch over him, for occasionally he took trop de vin."

Sir Richard's narrative is liberally sprinkled with French idioms, not all grammatically correct, which were added for effect, for much was made at his trial of his misuse of language, but it is all evidence of some twelve years spent on the Continent. The events he records do not, however, have the same ring of authenticity as the earlier and later passages of his story. For example, he tells of the return of Napoleon from Elba when "we were all made prisoners" and the race to Brussels where "I was at the famous ball given to the sovereigns of Europe prior to the Battle of Waterloo". His description of the latter is full of extravagant and fanciful observations, scarcely worth repeating, eg: "At the Ball I stood opposite the great bay window in the centre of the hall, where the ill-fated Duke of Brunswick stood the whole evening. He did not join in the revelry but stood, evidently absorbed in the deepest thought .... on the alarm being given 'To arms, to arms', the trumpet clearly sounded, the drums rang in rattling mockery to the fiddlers' sound, all for a moment stood silent as the dead; panic struck. The men hurried to learn the truth; the ladies fainted with affright, and all was wild confusion .... I had with difficulty advanced to the side of the Duke in time to hear him say 'This is my death knell'. Surely some of those who were present that night will remember the flaxen, curly-headed youth with his right hand in a blue morocco case at his breast, looking like the shadow of a wounded officer?"

All this looks like a rather clumsy attempt to create an alibi for an incident that the defence made much of at his trial:

Sir Frederick: "Did you not marry Mary Ann Whittick at St. Michael's, Bath, at a quarter to nine, on Sunday 9th October 1814 in the name of Thomas William Provis?"

Sir Richard: "No. My wife's maiden name is Ashton and I have no past wife"

Sir Frederick: "Was not Mary Ann Heath (nee Provis) then aged 12, present?"

Sir Richard: "No."

Sir Frederick: "Did you not, 20 years ago, meet Mary Ann Heath, when she said, 'Tom, how are you?'"

Sir Richard: "No."

At his second trial Mrs Heath swore under oath that Sir Richard was her brother, Thomas William Provis, and that he had been married in her presence to Miss Mary Ann Whittick in Bath, and a Bible was produced in which was an entry of his marriage to Miss Whittick in his own handwriting. Sir Richard was incensed with this attempt to identify him with T. W. Provis. In the first place he, Sir Richard, was only sixteen in 1814, though his enemies would have it that he was older. This T. W. Provis, he said, was a tailor, then a sailor, who died at sea "who at Bath married a woman who must be now 80 years of age. His son lies buried at Plymouth. I have obtained a certificate, signed by the clergyman and sworn by the mayor that his son, had he lived till now, would have been 57 years of age".*

Sir Richard, in his account of the hardships he had suffered at the hands of his enemies, was generally fair and charitable, but for Mrs Heath he had nothing but scorn. "The person who would, were it possible, make me her brother, is an ugly, unpleasant, uneducated, snuff-taking, carroty-headed woman, looking old enough to be my mother, yet born years after me .... Besides as she was a Catholic, the distance was still greater than perhaps it might have been."

In the cross-examination Sir Frederick asked Sir Richard if it were true that he had taken two of Mrs Heath's children to place out in the world, but not to educate. He replied he had "but in Kindness, and was treated with downright ingratitude - but that it would all come out...." "It is coming out now, very fast," said Sir Frederick, sarcastically. At his trial Sir Richard was never given the chance to state his version of Mrs Heath's perfidy. In his little book he said that the last time he had seen Mrs Heath (apart from collecting the portrait) was when she was twenty years of age "....and under circumstances of a painful nature". What could this mean? Perhaps he was too chivalrous to enlarge.

Mrs Heath, he said, had explained to him later why she had claimed him as a brother. "It appears that two detective officers from London went to her house at night, dragged her out of bed, and told her that I was in great trouble about a certain affair; that I had declared her to be my sister,

* Something wrong here. If he was 57 in 1854 he would have been born seventeen years before his parents' marriage, unless of course he was born out of wedlock, or by a former wife of his father.

and that if she would sign a paper to that effect it would extricate and save me. She, thinking it to be really so and anxious to serve me, did as desired, and was caught in the snare thus carefully laid.

"When this happened I was at Frome and, hearing of it, drove over next day for the purpose of undeceiving her. No art can depict her consternation when I appeared. She honestly told me what she had done and saw distinctly that she had committed herself. She afterwards came to my house in Clifton, but I was not at home at the time. She solemnly promised to rectify the mistake, but yet almost immediately after she joined issue with my enemies. I am credibly informed that her perfidy was rewarded with a gift of £15.

"Now contrast my bearing with all this. Think of my education - sufficiently evidenced by this work and the other works I have published. Remember the number of years I have been engaged in public teaching. Then contrast me in look, in manner, in voice and every feature with the daughter of old Provis, and let her persuade twelve honest, independent, unprejudiced men that we are the progeny of the same parent - if she can."

As for the Bible he is supposed to have signed on his marriage to Miss Whittick, he does not mention it save to say that his enemies had considerable funds at their disposal and that money had been subtly used to thwart the course of justice. The public press at the time of the trial revelled in the story that Mary Ann Whittick had been a servant of the family of Sir John Smyth in 1814, and that through her he had come to know much about the family history, and in the 1830s a woman answering to the name of Mrs Provis had been a housekeeper at Ashton Court. But at the trial the defence failed to produce her, or one fact about her.

There remains a mystery about the alleged first wife of Sir Richard. That he had married previously is assumed from a letter he wrote to Mrs Florence Upton, c.1850, when he said, "I have a second wife with a young family from 4 to 8 years". Sir Frederick took him up on this and Sir Richard's explanation was both lame and unconvincing.

Sir Frederick: "What do you mean by this?"

Sir Richard: "I could not have meant that."

Sir Frederick: "What did you mean by it? It could not have been a second-hand wife" (laughter).

Sir Richard: "I must have meant some other word. I cannot say what it was.... it might have been 'young' wife...."

Dr. Smyth

After the Battle of Waterloo, said Sir Richard, he did not return to France but travelled in the Low Countries and Germany, and developed an interest in education. He claimed to have met Dr. Bell and Mr Lancaster who were then travelling on the Continent to disseminate their ideas on popular education, but that he disagreed fundamentally with their system. "That was to give all the instruction to as many children as could be gotten together into one room, to make as much noise as their system was so well calculated to produce; and for their children to obtain, under all these disadvantages, as much knowledge as two or three hundred boys could get out of one man, wretchedly educated and more miserably paid."

Dr. Smyth, as he was later to style himself, developed his own theories, that education of "the higher orders of society" required more attention than the lower "in order to draw out all the latent virtues which, without such help, would never make their appearance at all".

"No pains should be spared....no money begrudged....no saving of fortune to starve the intellect....for if those who rule, govern and lead are ignorant, of what benefit can a partial and defective education of the poor be to them." He reflected the opinion of many of the gentry of his time in denigrating the education of the 'lower classes'. "It only makes them ambitious and takes from them the boast of an Englishman, the proud distinction of dependence on their own labour."

His theories, so he claimed, later appeared in a published work entitled 'Physical, Moral and Mental Education of the Aristocracy', "....to which I have 1,400 autographed subscribers".

Not being able to write well himself, through his defective hand, he was interested in systems of committing facts to memory. He had derived some help from Grey's 'Tecnica Memoriae' and in the Low Countries he learned from one Baron Von Feineigle, "an ingenious system of remembering dates and amounts of figures called mnemonics". On his return to England in 1826 he lectured on the Baron's system "in almost every school in the country" and wrote two further works called 'Mnemonics, or the Art of Memory' and 'The Trinity of Human Nature'.

For the next twelve years he made a living from the talents of a child actor, Harry, the natural son, so he believed, of the Duke of Marlborough by the daughter of the gatekeeper at Blenheim Palace. "The child's mother, having become impoverished, had forsaken the boy." The vicar of Woodstock, Dr. Blair*, introduced the child to him one day at dinner.

"He was then 3 years of age, well-shaped, with sparkling black eyes, a pretty and knowing face, but having the voice and actions of a man; indeed, a perfect man in miniature. I instantly fancied the boy and undertook the charge of his future life. The worthy doctor....gave the boy five pounds to clothe him; I took him to Oxford with me in my gig, and proud and pleased he was. I went to my lodging and the landlady, at my request, got him com-

* There is no Dr. Blair among the list of incumbents displayed in Woodstock Church.

fortably and suitably clothed. From that moment he both looked and acted the part of a perfect gentleman....I had the boy 12 years and from the first day to the last he never disobeyed me."

Dr. Smyth taught him some passages from Richard III and he took to reciting and acting with such expression that the idea occurred to Dr. Smyth of forming a group of juvenile actors with Harry in the leading roles.

The chapter in Dr. Smyth's book describing their adventures as they toured the country playing to select audiences and in public theatres, reads like a passage lifted from a Dickens novel. Perhaps it was, or perhaps Dickens who was a journalist in the 1850s and would certainly have heard of this 'cause célèbre', and may even have read 'Victim of Fatality', lifted passages into his novels.* And like Dickens, Dr. Smyth also performed before the Queen, though it was before her accession. "We chanced to be at Kensington. The Duchess of Kent and her daughter, our present gracious Queen, were at the Palace. With an introduction from Dr. Butler of Harrow to Col. Conroy, we obtained the honour of performance before the royal party. Surely when Her Majesty reads this memorial she will remember me, for she assured me she should retain a pleasing remembrance of my discourse on that occasion." He spoke, so he said, on the 'Art of Oratory', and the child actors gave a demonstration.

"Perhaps it will be as well here to mention a little incident that occurred on the following morning. About 12 o'clock, I and the boys had gone to the Palace to receive the gratuity for our services, and were inspecting the greenhouse at the back of the Palace. Her Majesty was there, about to mount her horse for a ride, when she caught sight of the boys, but in beckoning them towards her she lost her hold and would have fallen had it not been for my timely aid. She thanked me most graciously and said, 'Ah, Doctor, you can aid in all circumstances'. Her Majesty could not then have been more than 12 years of age, if indeed so much."

Of the fate of poor Harry, that too has a Dickensian flavour. "We were at Gosport, at Dr. Burney's, and the officers of the guard-ship being present they invited all the boys on board, and goodbye to all acting. How strange that all clever lads have a penchant for the sea. Well, nothing would do but that I must apprentice them, and apprentice them I did. Fred is now an officer on the coastguard service in China. Poor Harry, after serving his time to a merchant in Liverpool, married his master's daughter, in three days after he went to sea, captain of a vessel, caught the smallpox and in 15 days after leaving land he was committed to the deep."

* In point of fact, 'Nicholas Nickleby', which deals with a troupe of juvenile actors, was written in 1838; but in 'Great Expectations', written in 1860, it is interesting that the convict Magwitch, adopted the assumed name 'Provis'

The 'Poor Harry' episode was almost certainly an invention to cover up another embarrassing chapter in his career. The Bristol Mercury & Gazette published on 20th August 1853, after the conclusion of the trial, the story of a Dr.Smyth or Smith who came to Cork in 1824 or 1825 and proposed to establish a collegiate school on the Feineiglian system. Respectable schoolmasters were induced to join him and a suitable building was fitted up and a number of boys paraded the streets in caps and gowns. Then this Dr. Smythor Smith disappeared again, leaving many debts unpaid. The "name, mnemonics and knavery" added the writer, wittily, "fit those of the plaintiff".

Spectre from the Past

Sir Richard admitted he gave little thought to his chances of coming into the Smyth property until 1849. He had heard that his father had died in 1824, two years before his return to England, and assumed that his half-brother, John Hugh Smith-Piggott, was now owner of Ashton Court. His public appearances as lecturer and orator were reduced, he said, owing to "....the schools having stopped all extras" and the "....rapacity of managers" had made his theatrical performances unprofitable. The idea, he stated quite openly, of forwarding his claims came to him suddenly, as a result of a chance meeting with Mr Smith, an accountant, of Field House, Stapleton.

"....going from Gloucester to Bristol by way of Thornbury, I called on Mr Helston at Alveston Academy, whom I had known for years; he did not very cordially receive me and I felt it severely.

"About 4 miles this side of Bristol the road turns down to the left-hand to Heath House, Stapleton, then the residence, I supposed, of my brother. At the commencement of this road I saw a respectable looking man, who was evidently vulgo vocato, in a 'brown study'. Reading my countenance (which is often an index to the mind) he respectfully addressed me, and said, 'What is the matter, Sir? You look vexed'. 'Aye,' said I, 'I am vexed; everyone is becoming selfish and unnatural'.

"'You say true, Sir,' was the rejoinder. I then enquired if the road did not lead to Heath House, the residence of Sir John Smyth. He said it did. The thought entered my mind to call on my brother, but I had no appetite for the feast, and the most trifling thing would turn me. I then said, 'Well, how is Sir John?'

'Oh, very well'.
'Married?'
'No, nor likely to be now; he is too old.'
'Why so?'
'He is much afflicted.'
'I am sorry to hear that. He cannot be so very old; he is my brother, and though my elder he cannot be so very old.'

the butler "....now living at No. 5. Castle Street, Liverpool, having been unaccountably sacked a week after the event" and he added that his master came home in a dreadful state and had to be completely changed before dinner. When Sims asked him what had occurred he said he had seen a person at the Court who had upset him. When pressed to say who, he refused, but remarked 'Oh, you will know tomorrow. Oh, he is a true man. Get me down my book. I did all I could but must do more. I must part with all I have.'

"He went to bed, first taking a little medicine, and ordering his carriage for early next morning, which was Saturday, but when his servant went as usual to call him he was dead in bed, half hanging out, as if he had been trying to reach something....

"Mr Sims declared to me in the presence of my landlord, Mr Nash, of No. 1 Queen's Square, Bloomsbury, that he gave his master his usual pill on going to bed, but that in the morning there stood on his bidet a vessel that had contained some liquid which he appeared to have drunk. Sims went downstairs and, during his absence, the vessel was removed." Sims told Sir Richard that Mrs Way then accused him of stealing a note that had been given to him by Sir John, and within a week he was discharged. "A most unusual thing .... and without any acknowledgement of his services."

Mrs Way then moved into a house in Clifton, leaving no money either at Heath House or Ashton Court, and having drawn out all the money from the bank so that Mr Abbott had to find the means to bring Mrs Upton from Bath. Sir Richard naively suggested that she was leaving the way clear for him, but it was much more likely that she was making off with as much as she could before her sister arrived. They were, according to Sir Richard, not on good terms, Florence always having taken sides with Hugh against John and Mary. As Mrs Upton was eighty and her only son was dead it was only a matter of time before the property descended to her grandchildren who were also Mrs Way's grandchildren (Thomas Upton having married his cousin, Eliza Way).

Mary Way

It is evident that Sir Richard's visit had triggered off a crisis in the House of Smyth. Sir John had died of shock, or from the onslaught of Mrs

Way, or of the effects of both, and the inference about the 'vessel of liquid', repeated by Sims, is that something was administered by his sister to help him on his way, before he made a will bypassing the Uptons and the Ways.

Confrontation II: Florence Upton

Sir Richard said that he was so crestfallen by his disappointments in 1849 that he took no further steps for some months to pursue his claims. His Aunt Mary Way died in 1850 before he got round to visiting her. Not that "....she would even have listened to me; in all probability she would have served me as did her discourteous son," (Arthur Way). But Florence, now in possession "....was my father's favourite, and would be sure to have taken my part". It was really the chronic shortage of funds which drove him on. In 1852 he called on Mr Elwell of Weston-super-Mare whom he hoped would employ him. He knew of Sir Richard's claims but he "could not engage me, and he rather reprehended me for not seeking for that which was my own. I felt so nettled that I turned without speaking and, with my son Joseph, took the first train and all but flew to Ashton Court. We reached it about 12 o'clock and immediately saw the butler, Mr Llewellyn, and his present wife, the lady's maid. They assured me I would not be allowed to see Mrs Upton, my aunt, for Mr Abbott had strictly forbidden them to let anyone see her. They moreover informed me that Mrs Upton had given every authority to Mr Abbott and he took responsibility entirely on himself."

Mr Llewellyn, however, invited Sir Richard in, and gave him dinner. He "....took me along the passage towards the servants' hall and the housekeeper's room. I hesitated to go into my own hall to dine with the servants and I walked into the other room. The butler saw in a moment that I was no stranger and apologised to me, not intending any insult."

Sir Richard was not able to see Mr Abbott that day, but the next day was at his house by 10 o'clock in the morning. "He was prepared for me, not as if he expected a stranger, but one he had long looked for. He opened the door himself and said 'Well, Sir, what do you want?' I gave my name as Dr. Smyth. I was dressed as a gentleman, and my appearance and name should have commanded respect and civility, instead of which he held the door half open and said, 'I am much engaged. Cannot you write?'

"'No, Sir,' I replied, 'my business is of importance and I must and will speak with you.' His sister then said something to him, and he forthwith desired me to walk in. I accordingly went into the parlour, wherein stood in the centre a large, long dining table. He ensconced himself the other side and was evidently afraid of me. He looked the picture of death and trembled exceedingly.

'Eh! What, Sir, your brother!" More likely your father, for I can see there is something of the Smyth about you.'

'Well Sir, I am the son of the late Sir Hugh Smyth, and the present Sir John is my elder brother.' The man stared.

'What then, Sir, you have been abroad. I now remember hearing the old gardener at Heath House declare that there was a son abroad, and that he used to take you to school. And so, Sir, you are that son. Then, Sir, allow me to set you right. Do you know Mr John Smith-Piggott of Weston-super-Mare?'

'I have heard of him, but do not know him.'

'Well, Sir, that is your brother; and your father was divorced from his first wife and John was illegitimate, and the Sir John so-called is your Uncle, your father's brother, and of course an usurper....'"

Sir Richard decided at that point to take the bull by the horns and stake all on a personal confrontation with his relations. The interviews he sought and obtained between 1849 and 1853 with his alleged uncle, Sir John, his aunts Mrs Way and Mrs Upton, his half-brother John Hugh Smith-Piggott, and their nearest relation, Mr William Gore-Langton, evidently caused alarm and consternation. As no one came forward to contradict the substance of these extraordinary interviews, either at the trial or later, we have to accept them at face value, making allowance, of course, for the literary embellishments with which Sir Richard liked to embroider his history.

Confrontation I: Sir John Smyth, Bart.

On the 18th May 1849, following the advice of Mr Penton, a Bristol undertaker and family friend of the Smyths, to whom he had been referred by the Stapleton accountant, Sir Richard made his first visit to Ashton Court.

"I arrived at the Court just as Sir John and his sister Mary (Mrs Way) were about to enter (they had, by chance, moved thither from Heath House that day). I requested to speak to him. Somehow Mrs Way knew me in a moment or Smith, the Stapleton accountant might have told her (to curry favour). She said 'You cannot speak to Sir John, man, he is not well; you can write or speak to Mr Abbott.' 'Madam,' I replied, 'you will excuse me, but my business is with Sir John and not with you. Sir John, have I your permission for an interview?'

"He gave such a look as only conscious guilt could give. He threw his sister from him, took my arm, and we retired into what appeared to be a half-library and dining room. We sat down together, facing each other.

"My uncle was rather a short man, not over stout, with a short bull-neck and, as I thought, covered with hair, but his back was to the light and I could not distinctly see. He had a florid complexion and looked a very Jew. He had a lame arm, and as he suffered from some peculiar complaint, his

In the summer of 1829, Rosina Sharples, the Bristol painter, went to Ashton Court to "....paint a sketch of Sir John Smith's carriage and four horses" - presumably for her famous painting 'The Bristol Races'. She writes in her journal: "Sir John was very polite and Mrs Way and her accomplished daughters particularly kind. Invited every day to lunch, partridges, pineapples, hothouse grapes and other luxuries".

The two ladies in the carriage are probably Mrs Way and Mrs Upton.

effluvia was highly offensive." Sir Richard stated elsewhere in his narrative that "this unpleasant complaint made him unfit for society, and in some measure prevented his marriage".

"The first words he uttered were 'Well, Sir. Where have you been all these years? I thought you dead and never expected to have seen you'. I ought to have replied 'What have you been doing all these years never to have enquired for me?' but merely said 'Do you know me, dear Uncle?'

"Whether it was the tone of voice, or the manner, I cannot tell, but he sprang almost out of his chair and said 'Know you! Yes, among a thousand'. He fell back, evidently disappointed and violently agitated, so much so I feared he would faint, and I be obliged to call in the servant.

"'Uncle, be calm,' I said. 'I am not come here today to deprive you of the title or the estates. You cannot live long, whilst you do enjoy it in peace. Provide for me and my family and treat me as your son, and secure me hereafter.'

"'God bless you, you are indeed the son of my beloved brother,' replied Sir John." He then told his nephew how unhappy he had been; no one seemed to care for anything but his death, to get the property. Even his beloved sister Mary had changed since he made his will. "He said this with a highly sarcastic smile which I did not like; he seemed revengeful and unforgiving.

"I imagined several times I heard a movement of someone listening, and mentioned it to Sir John. 'Tut, tut, nonsense,' he said." Mrs Way could be supposed to be more than curious about Sir Richard's intrusion. She had been widowed, and left with ten children and no means to support them, and relied on her brother for what Sir Richard would have called 'the needful'. As the younger sister she would not inherit the estate, and the will Sir John referred to left all to Florence Upton. Sir Richard had a notion that the will was made in his favour should he ever turn up to claim the estates, and in the agitated discussion that took place Sir John probably gave him this impression, and also that his father's will of 1814 said much the same, with the exception of providing John Hugh Smith-Piggott with a small annuity, and making Sir John simply a trustee until such time as Sir Richard turned up. The 'effluvia' was thus not the only reason for Sir John's remaining a bachelor. He was bound to hand over his estates to his nephew. The mysterious appearance of the two subsequent wills of Sir Hugh of 1822 and 1823 at the time of the trial reiterated these arrangements and deprived John Hugh Smith-Piggott of his annuity. Sir John "....did not, nor would not touch upon my brother; indeed he seemed to have a mortal aversion to him, and advised me not to go near him."

At the close of the conversation it was agreed that Sir Richard would bring his family from Chester, where they were living in obscurity, and live at Ashton Court while Sir John would go to Heath House. To assist with expenses ("It was not expected that I would allow them to come there but in first rate style among 40 servants") Sir John gave his nephew a £50 note which he changed at Miles' Bank, Corn Street, Bristol.* Sir John promised to see his solicitors the next morning to make all the necessary arrangements, Sir Richard took the 5 o'clock train to Gloucester and next day reached Chester.

The previous Saturday, Sir Richard claimed, he had been offered a post at Rugby by Dr. Arnold, his former schoolfriend. "'Dr. Smyth,' he said, 'your wandering life cannot be profitable and now that you have a family it must be unpleasant. Will you come here to Rugby? I will give you £70 per annum, make what you can of the boys and you can take a home and boarders the same as the other masters'. But nothing was settled in writing and the following Sunday Dr. Arnold, apparently in perfect health, collapsed with a heart attack and died at the age of 42."**

A far greater shock was in store for Sir Richard. He sold off his affairs in Chester, clad his family suitably for coming into their inheritance, and set off for Ashton Court. He arrived at Bristol twelve days after he left and called on Mr Penton on his way from the station to the White Hart Inn to take the omnibus. "I said, 'You see, Mr Penton, I am come to be amongst you'. He looked at me and said 'My dear Sir, be calm. You are too late. Your Uncle is dead and buried!' I looked at him with amazement, scarcely able to say '....and without acknowledging me?'. 'Yes. He was found dead in bed the morning after you were there.' Who can describe my disappointment, my utter helplessness at this moment? I said nothing but went back to the station and left for Cheltenham by the 5 o'clock train, and was very ill there in consequence, as the Rev. Mr Close can testify."

Sir Richard later learnt from Sir John's servant, the woman who looked after Heath House, that on that Friday her master, after leaving Ashton Court, went to Mr Braham, the optician in Bristol, and purchased a pair of spectacles. Mr Braham verified the fact that Sir John and his sister did call and that Sir John did purchase a pair, but had no money to pay for them. His sister said, 'What have you done with your money?' to which Sir John replied, 'Never mind. Mr Braham will trust me.' He then came home and quarrelled seriously with Mrs Way. Sir Richard also sought out Mr Sims,

* Arthur Way wrote, 27.12.1852: "When at Miles' Bank in Bristol learnt that the soi-disant Sir Richard Smyth had been there to trace out a £50 note of that Bank which, he said, Sir John Smyth gave him in 1849. The cashier told him they never issued £50 notes!"

** So much for mnemonics. Dr Arnold died in June 1842, seven years earlier! It seems extraordinary that Sir Richard should have timed these occurrences consecutively when there was such a wide gap between them. Perhaps it suited his theme 'victim of fatality' to run these two misfortunes together.

the butler "....now living at No. 5. Castle Street, Liverpool, having been unaccountably sacked a week after the event" and he added that his master came home in a dreadful state and had to be completely changed before dinner. When Sims asked him what had occurred he said he had seen a person at the Court who had upset him. When pressed to say who, he refused, but remarked 'Oh, you will know tomorrow. Oh, he is a true man. Get me down my book. I did all I could but must do more. I must part with all I have.'

"He went to bed, first taking a little medicine, and ordering his carriage for early next morning, which was Saturday, but when his servant went as usual to call him he was dead in bed, half hanging out, as if he had been trying to reach something....

"Mr Sims declared to me in the presence of my landlord, Mr Nash, of No. 1 Queen's Square, Bloomsbury, that he gave his master his usual pill on going to bed, but that in the morning there stood on his bidet a vessel that had contained some liquid which he appeared to have drunk. Sims went downstairs and, during his absence, the vessel was removed." Sims told Sir Richard that Mrs Way then accused him of stealing a note that had been given to him by Sir John, and within a week he was discharged. "A most unusual thing .... and without any acknowledgement of his services."

Mrs Way then moved into a house in Clifton, leaving no money either at Heath House or Ashton Court, and having drawn out all the money from the bank so that Mr Abbott had to find the means to bring Mrs Upton from Bath. Sir Richard naively suggested that she was leaving the way clear for him, but it was much more likely that she was making off with as much as she could before her sister arrived. They were, according to Sir Richard, not on good terms, Florence always having taken sides with Hugh against John and Mary. As Mrs Upton was eighty and her only son was dead it was only a matter of time before the property descended to her grandchildren who were also Mrs Way's grandchildren (Thomas Upton having married his cousin, Eliza Way).

Mary Way

It is evident that Sir Richard's visit had triggered off a crisis in the House of Smyth. Sir John had died of shock, or from the onslaught of Mrs

Way, or of the effects of both, and the inference about the 'vessel of liquid', repeated by Sims, is that something was administered by his sister to help him on his way, before he made a will bypassing the Uptons and the Ways.

Confrontation II: Florence Upton

Sir Richard said that he was so crestfallen by his disappointments in 1849 that he took no further steps for some months to pursue his claims. His Aunt Mary Way died in 1850 before he got round to visiting her. Not that "....she would even have listened to me; in all probability she would have served me as did her discourteous son," (Arthur Way). But Florence, now in possession "....was my father's favourite, and would be sure to have taken my part". It was really the chronic shortage of funds which drove him on. In 1852 he called on Mr Elwell of Weston-super-Mare whom he hoped would employ him. He knew of Sir Richard's claims but he "could not engage me, and he rather reprehended me for not seeking for that which was my own. I felt so nettled that I turned without speaking and, with my son Joseph, took the first train and all but flew to Ashton Court. We reached it about 12 o'clock and immediately saw the butler, Mr Llewellyn, and his present wife, the lady's maid. They assured me I would not be allowed to see Mrs Upton, my aunt, for Mr Abbott had strictly forbidden them to let anyone see her. They moreover informed me that Mrs Upton had given every authority to Mr Abbott and he took responsibility entirely on himself."

Mr Llewellyn, however, invited Sir Richard in, and gave him dinner. He "....took me along the passage towards the servants' hall and the housekeeper's room. I hesitated to go into my own hall to dine with the servants and I walked into the other room. The butler saw in a moment that I was no stranger and apologised to me, not intending any insult."

Sir Richard was not able to see Mr Abbott that day, but the next day was at his house by 10 o'clock in the morning. "He was prepared for me, not as if he expected a stranger, but one he had long looked for. He opened the door himself and said 'Well, Sir, what do you want?' I gave my name as Dr. Smyth. I was dressed as a gentleman, and my appearance and name should have commanded respect and civility, instead of which he held the door half open and said, 'I am much engaged. Cannot you write?'

"'No, Sir,' I replied, 'my business is of importance and I must and will speak with you.' His sister then said something to him, and he forthwith desired me to walk in. I accordingly went into the parlour, wherein stood in the centre a large, long dining table. He ensconced himself the other side and was evidently afraid of me. He looked the picture of death and trembled exceedingly.

"I then told him who I was, but I had scarcely finished when he began, 'Oh, it could not be! It never was! It was an improbable story'. It was lucky for him and fortunate for me that the table stood between us, for so exasperating was his behaviour that I felt strongly disposed to do that for which I should afterwards have been sorry. I could do nothing with him, but I am thoroughly convinced that he knows me, let him say what he will do to the contrary. So satisfied am I on this point that I believe the time is not far distant when he will confess all.

"I have only one thing to regret. Why did I respect my Aunt's infirmities to my own injury? Why did I not respect myself and go up to Ashton Court and see my Aunt? I did go up the next day with that intent, but when I got as far as the small gate my mind changed, and on return I met Abbott who seemed to have just come off a journey."

Sir Richard then tried writing to Abbott and he replied, "....that he would not give consent to give a letter from me to my Aunt, and that he would hold no further communication with me".

"Now why all this? He must have been conscious that I was either an imposter or a true man. If an imposter my Aunt would have said, 'Oh, nonsense man. I know you not; my brother had no son but John Piggott'. But Mr Abbott knew better. He must have heard my Aunt speak of me. I then wrote to my Aunt and to Abbott, and told him that if no notice was taken of my letters, that I would instantly throw my case into Chancery. This brought a letter from Mrs Upton's solicitors, Messrs Osborne & Ward, threatening to take any action they thought proper to adopt. They imagined this would quiet me as they knew I had no means to command. But would they have been prepared to spend so much money if they, for a moment, thought me an imposter?"

Confrontation III: John Hugh Smith-Piggott

John Hugh Smith-Piggott, the cultured, public-spirited squire of Weston, had by this time fathered ten children, enlarged Brockley Hall, and stocked it with one of the finest collections of paintings in the west country. He was a Fellow of the Society of Antiquaries, commissioned the first drawings of Somerset churches by Buckler, and spent much of his time improving the vast property that came to him on his marriage. He rebuilt Grove House, supplied it with statues from the Strawberry Hill sale, planted Weston Woods, and established the coastal toll road from Birnbeck to Kew Stoke. He was a JP, High Sheriff of Somerset in 1828, and played a vital role in the town's growth as a holiday resort.

He was at Grove House when his stepbrother called to see him. "At first he treated me as Abbott had done. He had been up to Abbott at his request the day before I went down, and did not return till 4 o'clock. He would not go into the house, and our interview took place in the garden. My son and the gardener were present....I so greatly resemble my brother John that the gatekeeper at Weston could scarcely believe but that it was his master coming as I went down the road, and from his great resemblance of me, my son Joseph singled him out from 50 gentlemen on his return from Abbott's.

"I reminded my brother of the incident, some 50 years ago, when our father horse-whipped him. 'What a memory you have,' said John Hugh. 'Write your life, Sir, write your life!' He tested me much and questioned me closely. He remarked on the similarity between my voice and my father's, especially when I spoke hastily or passionately. He could not deny anything I advanced and was satisfied with my story, '....but,' said he, 'you have come here without a single document. Go and do what you can to get some memorial, some evidence, and you will be protected'.

"But this was said only to get rid of me, for certainly he trembled for his annuity of £1,500. For this reason," added Sir Richard, "he urged me not to see my Aunt on any account, and he was bitterly disappointed when, at her funeral, he found that all had been given to Abbott."

Brother Smith-Piggott was right about the lack of documentary evidence and Sir Richard turned his hand to manufacturing some. First he invented Jane Vandenburg; or perhaps it would be better to say he procured some old relics one of which, a family Bible, had once been the property of the Vandenburgs. It was ingenious to place her in Ireland. In the land of rebellions and famines it was neither possible nor desirable to check credentials. In the Christmas of 1852 Sir Richard and his solicitor, Mr Catlin, went to Ireland to "....establish facts about his mother's marriage" and much was made of the success of his mission. He had pitched upon this family for Jane's background because they were related to the Smyths of Headborough, County Wexford, and according to a very phoney-looking pedigree which Sir Richard inserted at the end of 'Victim of Fatality' the Headborough Smyths were related to Sir Jarrit Smyth, Bart. The fact that Jarrit was a Smith not a Smyth is beside the point. Obviously the temptation to prove his inheritance to the Smyth estates which came from his mother and father was too great. Hot on his heels, Arthur Way went to Ireland (6.7.1853) "....to trace out the conspiracy of Catlin and Sir Rd. Smyth re these estates. Went to Court Macsherry where the alleged marriage of Sir Hugh is said to have taken place and returned after a most satisfactory investigation, bringing with me conclusive proof of the fraud attempted".

On arriving at Bandon, County Cork, Arthur Way found that Sir Richard and Mr Catlin had paid ten visits to that place. It appeared that Sir Richard had been received at Castle Bernard by the Earl of Bandon, and at other houses, as an honoured guest, his story being that "an illegitimate heir had got possession of his vast estates", but that his proofs were so clear he had hardly expected opposition. Arthur spent a fortnight in the locality, examining a large number of witnesses, many of whom had been subpoenaed by Mr Catlin to give evidence at Gloucester. At Balinadee Arthur found that the incumbent, a Mr Bennett, in return for a promise of the first of "....his many family livings becoming vacant, none of which were under £600 per annum," had provided Sir Richard with two specimens of the signature of the Rev. Verney Lovett who, Sir Richard alleged, had married his parents in 1796.

The need for objects with which to identify his mother explains that part of Sir Richard's story concerning his visit to Lady Bath in 1812, and the tracking down of objects was related with convincing detail. How Lady Bath's agent, Mr Davis, had died, and Jane's "possessions" had gone to Mr Provis; how Sir Richard had gone to the old man and demanded them; how there was a row and Sir Richard had called him a 'rogue' and Provis struck him with a stick; how he later regretted his action and "....led me upstairs and from his bureau produced my mother's jewels, a miniature of herself, and her Bible", and how the picture of his father had been believed in the old man's dotage to be "the likeness of his eldest son who died at sea", and how he had recovered the painting from the home of Provis' daughter, Mrs Heath, at Mere, Wiltshire.

All lies, lies, as the defence quite easily discovered. The manufacture of evidence with which to support his claims irreparably damaged his chances.

Confrontation IV: Captain William Gore-Langton

Captain Gore-Langton was the grandson of Edward Gore, the cousin of Sir Richard's great uncle, Sir John Hugh Smyth. He cannot be supposed to be a very near relation but he was an old family friend and a trustee of the estate.

"I went to the house and rang the bell. 'Is Mr Langton at home?' 'Yes, Sir.' 'Then say that Dr. Smyth would speak to him.'

"The servant who appeared was the butler and I heard either Mrs Langton or Miss Langton, I have yet to learn which, say to him, 'Oh, send him away. He shall not see Mr Langton'. The man replied, 'Oh Ma'am, I can't; he is a perfect gentleman and won't take my no for an answer; besides he has seen master.' 'Well then, send him to him'.

"The man came out and desired I would go down the field to his master. 'No, friend. Let your master come here to me. I will wait for him'. 'But you must,' said the man, 'he won't stir till he sees you'. Then down he came, and in a very pompous manner addressed me with, 'Well, Sir. who are you? Where do you come from?' (Very gentlemanly, I must confess, for it was uttered with an intent to look thunder and lightning.)

"To this I coolly replied, 'You will pardon my intrusion. I came to you supposing you to be a gentleman, and I come from a place where I learnt that civility is due to every man, be his station in life what it may'. 'Well, well then. What do you want with me?'

"I said, 'Understanding you are a trustee under the will of the late John Smyth Esq., of the Ashton Court property, I am here to say that I am the only legitimate son of the late Sir Hugh Smyth, Bart.' Upon this he fell into a most violent passion, which gave me an opportunity of saying, 'Sir, passion and violent actions can never convince you or me. Let us quietly reason together, and you will alter your opinion'.

"'Well, well,' said he, 'let us hear.' I then told him all I could at that time remember, especially about him taking me to Dr. Fox's madhouse (when at school in Brislington). This he could not deny, and he seemed to have a vivid recollection of it, so that I soon brought him to reason. One important question I put to him, namely, 'Now, Sir,' said I, 'you knew my father all his life: supposing then I prove myself his son, what then?'

"'Then by G--, Sir, you are an honest one. Your father would never have had a bastard, I'll swear to that. And more Sir. If you will get into my carriage and let me drive you to my solicitors, Messrs Palmer, and if you prove yourself the son, you shall have the property, but on no account go to law.' I defy Mr Langton to deny one word of this statement."

The fact that Captain Gore-Langton supported the defendants at the trial was, said Sir Richard, "....an act of consummate duplicity; yet because of his high-toned vindication of my father's honour, I freely forgive him".

Confrontation V: Mrs Eliza Upton and her family

We now come to Sir Richard's celebrated visit to Ashton Court in the spring of 1853 with his solicitor, Mr Catlin, to demand possession, and his ignominious expulsion by the servants, assembled en masse Sir Richard claimed, by Arthur Way for the purpose. Sir Richard was very particular about one servant by the name of Wild, whom he had first noticed on his visit to his uncle in 1849, and whom he had heard his uncle address by name. In the unseemly scuffle at the front door, said Sir Richard, I pointed to that man and instantly pronounced his name. He said 'Why, how should you know me?' 'Oh,' I said, 'I know you better than you think I do, for this is not the first time that I have seen you.'

"These words so powerfully operated on the man that shortly afterwards, when Arthur Way called in the servants to turn me and my solicitor out of the house, and when they used me very ill, Wild caught me in his arms and carried me out, and by so doing no doubt saved my life, for otherwise I must have fallen over and broken my neck. He also cried 'Shame!' and let him do what he may, he will ever stand excused in my mind."

The Trial: 8th-9th-10th August 1853

"The question at issue," began Mr Bovill (acting in the absence of Sir Richard's attorneys, Sir Fitzroy Kelly and Mr Keating), "is whether the plaintiff is entitled, not only to a small estate called Heath House and the adjoining Park at Stapleton in this County, but also to a small estate at Elmington in the parish of Henbury and Compton, near Bristol, and to other large estates in Somersetshire and Wiltshire belonging to the late Sir Hugh Smyth and to Sir John Smyth, late of Ashton Court, near Bristol. The rentals of these estates amount to upwards of £20,000 a year...." He then related in outline Sir Richard's extraordinary story, which was in every respect identical to that related in his 'Romantic Tale of the 19th Century' published the following year.

"The real point for us to determine is whether the plaintiff's father, Sir Hugh Smyth, was married, as was alleged, in 1796, whether the plaintiff was born in 1797, and whether he was the son of the late Sir Hugh. The defendants have said they will undertake to prove the deeds of 1822 and 1823 to be forgeries. We defy them to the proof. There are five assignees to one and six to the other, and if they are forged all the signatures must be forged."

The two wills of Sir Hugh, which had somehow mysteriously appeared among the papers of Sir Richard's old nurse, Lydia Reed, were then produced. After relating the dates and circumstances of the birth of his son, Sir Hugh had apparently written:

"From the circumstances of a family nature, this boy was brought up in private, and through the **rascallity** of my butler, Grace, under whose especial charge my son was, he left England clandestinely in the year 1813, and I had been assured by Grace that my son had died abroad, but at the death of Grace I became possessed of doubts of my son's demise. Now under the impression that my son had died I made a will in the year 1814. That will I now abrogate, annul and sett asside, by this last will and testament, and by the document do acknowledge Richard Hugh Smyth my legitimate son and heir."

Sir Richard had said that when his father discovered Grace's deception his body, on his death, was put out of the house. Elizabeth Grace, the butler's widow, now a schoolmistress in the parochial school at Long Ashton, was called, and vehemently denied that this had happened. She also said that her husband had only taken up service with Sir Hugh in 1802 and could not have been given care of a child of his born in 1797.

"Sir Frederick Thesiger: How do you spell 'set aside'?

Plaintiff: S-e-t-t a-s-i-d-e.

Sir Frederick: These words are so spelt 4 times in your letter.

Plaintiff: I spelt them with two t's and two s's from a learned commentator. I have authority for so spelling. I prefer spelling aside 'asside'.

Sir Frederick: I see in your letters to Mrs Upton and Mrs Way you say you made rapid studies in your education. How do you spell 'rapid'? Will you just spell it to us?

Plaintiff: No, I won't (laughter).
The Judge: You mustd spell it. It is a proper question.
Plaintiff: If I must, I must. I spell it R-A-P Rap, P-I-D, pid - RAPPID (shouts of laughter).
Sir Frederick: And that is right, is it?
Plaintiff: Yes, Sir. I say there are dictionaries in which the word is spelt in that manner.
Sir Frederick: No doubt edited by yourself."

Letters were produced, written by Sir Richard to Mr Gore-Langton, Mr Abbott, and Lady Caroline Thynne, and mention was made of repeated instances of the wrong doubling of consonants in the middle of words, such as 'holliday' and 'rascallity'. Sir Richard was ruffled and responded aggressively, rebuking his examiners for their lack of education. Turning on Arthur Way who was questioning him in his second trial, he asked if he knew the derivation of the word 'holliday'. Mr Way refused to answer, whereupon Sir Richard said that the word was derived from the holly branch, by the Catholics, and that therefore it was impossible a scholar could spell it otherwise.

"Sir Frederick: Do you ever spell the word 'raskel'?
Plaintiff: I never do. (The letter was shown to him.) I see that I certainly did write it here.
Sir Frederick: That was a slip of the pen, I suppose, or was it written with a bad pen?
Plaintiff: Yes, like your slip of the tongue. If you would only look at your grammar as much as my spelling, it would do you good. You speak as bad grammar as anyone in Court. You said repeatedly 'I have got'. Now, I appeal to any grammarian, if that is good grammar (laughter).
Sir Frederick: When I want a lesson from you, I will ask you."

The defence then produced notices which Sir Richard had issued to the tenants in Somersetshire, directing them to pay their rents to him and signed by him 'Henry Brown, for Mr Rodham'. Mr Rodham was called and denied the authority and Sir Richard at last admitted they had been written in a feigned hand to imitate Mr Rodham's.

The Bible, portrait of Sir Hugh, jewellery and obituary ring on which it was claimed was inscribed 'In memory of Jane, wife of Hugh Smyth Esq., married May 1796, died February 1797', were then passed up for examination.

"Sir Frederick: Where is that ring?
Plaintiff: In the box.
Sir Frederick: Find it, Sir."

Sir Richard then took up a case from which he produced a ring-box, but on opening it, no ring was to be seen.

"Sir Frederick: There was not a word said about this ring in the opening.
Plaintiff: It was in that box.
Sir Frederick: When did you see it last?
Plaintiff: I do not remember. It was taken with the other jewels to Ireland.
Sir Frederick: Did you see it in Ireland?
Plaintiff: Yes.
Sir Frederick: Was that the last time you saw it?
Plaintiff: I have seen it since, I believe, in London.
Sir Frederick: Where in London?
Plaintiff: In my attorney's office. I cannot exactly say when, but I have not seen it for some considerable time."

It was beginning to look as if the ring had never existed and the lady it mourned was becoming less tangible. When questioned about his mother Sir Richard's answers were tame and unconvincing.

"Yes, I went to Warminster in the beginning of the year. I saw an entry of the burial in the register when I first went. When I went the second time the entry was erased. The clergyman showed me the register. I will swear that there was an entry of the date of February 1797 of the burial of Jane Smyth, aged 16. I went to another village to enquire and on my return the entry was erased and another name substituted. The second time I went with my Attorney and the book was left to us both for an hour together, no one else being present."

Sir Richard said she had been buried in a brick vault in the churchyard, and that he had sought the permission of the Bishop of Salisbury to have it opened, but the Bishop had flatly refused.

On the second day Sir Frederick changed his tack.

"Sir Frederick: Is it not true that you have formerly represented yourself as Thomas Provis, or Thomas William Provis?
Plaintiff: No.
Sir Frederick: Have you at any time called John Provis your father?
Plaintiff: Never.
Sir Frederick: Have you ever been called by him his son?
Plaintiff: No.
Sir Frederick: Did you ever make an inventory of John Provis' goods?
Plaintiff: Never."

An inventory was handed up to the witness and he was asked if it was in his handwriting.

"Plaintiff: I cannot swear to it. I think it is in John Provis' handwriting."

On being pressed he admitted that he had helped the old gentleman with his books, and that it might be in his (the witness') handwriting. Sir

Frederick then drew attention to an entry in the inventory 'Picture of Provis' son, John', a sailor who was later lost at sea.

"Plaintiff: He used to call that painting his son.
Sir Frederick: Is it not the same painting that now has written on the back 'Hugh Smyth Esq. son of Thomas Smyth Esq. of Stapleton, Gloucestershire, 1796'?
Plaintiff: Yes, it is the same painting as the one in the inventory called 'Picture of Provis' son, John', but it is not the same one spoken of in my letters to Mrs Upton, Mrs Smyth and Mr Gore-Langton as the portrait of my father."

Sir Frederick then read the letters in which it was stated that this was the picture and there were two erasures on the back of it. Sir Richard then admitted that this was the picture referred to in the inventory and there was no other of Sir Hugh. He then requested that all the other witnesses who had anything to say on the picture should leave the court, which after some discussion was acceded to. The picture was then produced: it was an oil painting of about 20 inches by 30 inches, of a young man of about twenty years of age, sitting in an armchair covered in red leather, with a book in his hand, dressed in a blue coat with bright buttons, a white waistcoat, and a white cravat with a gold brooch set with a stone. He explained that the writing on the back was not in the same condition now as it was at first, as he had put an acid on and had brought it out. It was tartaric acid he used. He had applied it lightly and it merely took off the dirt. That was why he had asked all the witnesses to be taken out of court, because he knew they would swear they had never seen the inscription.

"I am not sure if it was tartaric acid or soda," he continued. "Tartaric acid, if applied in strong solution, would destroy the writing. This was my first experiment. I knew of it from my reading - as you ought to," he added, impertinently.

"Sir Frederick: Aye. But I do not want to bring out writings.
Plaintiff: But you bring out other things, and with considerable acidity. The acid was found in the back kitchen. Most people had soda and potash in their houses.
Sir Frederick: They are not acids.
Plaintiff: They are pulverised minerals."

Sir Frederick opened the third day with taking apart the two wills of 1822 and 1823. Sir Hugh's signature appeared very shaky in the first one, but in a steady hand in the second which, Sir Richard said, must be explained by the fact that in 1822 he was seriously ill. Sir Hugh's doctor, Dr. Morris of Marlborough, said that Sir Hugh was a sick man, or believed himself to be, imagining himself at death's door one day and out hunting the next. The second signature he felt fairly certain was genuine.

With the wills was a covering letter by Sir Hugh, desiring the wills to remain in the custody of "....my old nurse, Lydia Reed, and whome, no doubt, my son will be sure to seek".

"Sir Frederick: How do you spell whom?
Plaintiff: W-H-O-M-E. I could find you dictionaries in which it is so spelt".

Arthur Way had written three months before the trial (6.5.1853): "A great report of Sir Richard and his lawyers hawking a will of Sir Hugh Smyth about. The clerk at Messrs Miles told me they had been there to verify signatures." On 20th June he, Mr Palmer, Charles Abbott* and others went up to Mr Catlin's office in Ely Place, Holborn, "....to inspect the alleged will of Sir Hugh Smyth, made 2.7.22, which we unanimously decided to be a **Gross Forgery**".

Both wills were witnessed by James Abbott, his steward, William Edwards, his coachman, and William Dobson, a messenger boy. Much of the first day of the trial was spent by Sir Frederick Thesiger's attorneys requiring witnesses to verify the signatures. Mr Way and party were dismayed when John Lewis, butler of Sir John Smyth, and Mr Chadwick, a solicitor who had known James Abbott forty-four years and had seen him write frequently, believed that the signatures were authentic, though John Ayres, Sir Hugh's groom at Rockley, could not swear to it. William Edwards' signature was verified by his brothers Charles and Henry, and Mrs Charles Edwards, and William's daughter Eliza, and Ann Dobson, sister of William, swore to his handwriting; but his widow, Honor (he had died in 1852 aged 32) insisted that he never spelt his name with two b's, but "....she didn't know what he was before her marriage, but afterwards he was very steady....." which drew whispers from the court, and when Richard Brech, coach proprietor's clerk at Marlborough, blurted out "I seen him (William Edwards) many times, that be not his writing on the deeds", there was an explosion of laughter. It was left to Sir Frederick on the third day to demolish the wills.

Sir John Smyth

"Sir Frederick: Do you know a man named Crane?
Plaintiff: No."

* It is interesting to note that Charles Abbott, son of James, both former stewards at Ashton, should have testified against the plaintiff, considering that the case Upton v. Abbott was at that stage not resolved, and is a tribute to Arthur Way's tact.

At the second trial, Crane was produced. He said he had called at St. Vincent's Priory and was shown the wills by Sir Richard who, he said, told him he would be "set up in business for life" if he wrote a letter to the effect that a man called Coward brought them to his lodging and later died in an asylum, but he couldn't remember where. Crane said he could not do it. "Come. Can't you two do it?" (Another man, Mattick, was present.) "I have told you what to say". Crane then went downstairs and wrote the letter which he gave to Sir Richard. At that time, said Crane, there were no seals on the wills. Sir Richard said he had two seals made by Moring of London in March 1853 from the tracing of a letter he had obtained from Joseph Reed on 17th March, some time after the wills came into his possession. This was not corroborated by Moring in person, who said it was December 1852 and, as the wrapping paper of the wills was proved to have been the same as that in which the seals had been delivered, Sir Frederick imputed that the seals were obtained first, and with them Sir Richard had concocted the wills.

Sir Richard Thesiger

Sir Richard said, "My wife opened the seals and this explains how the wrapping paper went astray." A letter was then produced from Sir Richard with a seal dated December 1852.

"Sir Frederick: How did you seal a letter dated 13th March with a seal made from a document you did not see until the 17th?

Plaintiff: I must have received the seal before the 13th.

Sir Frederick: How could you have received the seal before receiving receiving the document?

Plaintiff: I cannot tell."

In his book Sir Richard said the seals had evidently been used by his enemies to forge this letter, for at Moring's they had inadvertently been 'lost' and were discovered later in the water closet, and Sir Richard had paid a sovereign for their return.

"Sir Frederick: Why on the seal is the motto 'Qui Capit Capitur' written 'Qui Capit Capitor'?

Plaintiff: The tracing had smudged and the seal from which it was made broke. So the 'u' looks like an 'o'."

Sir Frederick then showed that in the wills of 1822 and 1823 it was spelt 'capitor' as also in the letter of 1798 from Sir Hugh to his pretended wife. At the second trial it was reported that the process of engraving seals was different in 1823 and this would have been apparent. Also the parchment was proved to be of more recent origin and the ink of modern manufacture.

Under the relentless cross-examination which exposed Sir Richard's forgery of the wills, Sir Richard had answered with spirit and even flippancy, but on his exposure he seemed cowed and crestfallen and asked to be allowed to retire.

"Sir Frederick: That cannot be...."

At that moment a message was handed up to him. Sir Frederick read it, and then turned to the Judge. "My Lord, I have just had a telegraphic message from London of the greatest importance. 'Did you, on the 18th of January last,' he continued, now addressing himself to the plaintiff, 'apply to a person at 361 Oxford Street to engrave a ring with the Bandon crest, and a brooch with the words Jane Gookin?'*

Plaintiff: 'I did, Sir'."

The excitement caused by this extraordinary admission was intense. The tension had been building up and this sensational revelation completely dumbfounded the Counsels for prosecution and defence. Sir Frederick collapsed in his chair, unable to continue, or even repeat the question. Mr Bovill seemed overcome with emotion. It later transpired that Mr Robert Cox, a jeweller, of No. 361 Oxford Street, had been casually reading a report of the proceedings of the first day's trial in the 'Times' when he recalled that on 5th January 1853 a gentleman had come to his shop and said he was trustee of some children and had lost some jewels which had been entrusted to his charge. As the jewels were now being asked for he was anxious to acquire some others. As the children had never seen the originals new ones would do just as well. He also asked for a miniature which he said he wanted to pass off as that of the mother of the children. He selected two brooches on one of which he requested the name 'Jane Gookin' to be en-

* Sir Richard maintained that his grandmother's maiden name was Gookin.

graved, a signet ring on which the Bandon crest must be engraved, a wedding ring, and a mourning ring on which he requested the words 'Jane, wife of Sir Hugh Smyth, m.1796, d.1797'.

The true identity of the lovely young person in the miniature has never been established, and it is intriguing to learn how Sir Richard concocted the name Jane Vandenburg. Next door to Mr Moring, the seal engraver, was a bookseller who later came forward and said that he had bought a Bible from a Mr Vandenburg, who later testified that this was so and that the Bible had belonged to his father John S. Vandenburg whose name was written inside the front cover. The bookseller then sold it to Sir Richard.

In the awful silence which followed the plaintiff's confession, the Judge asked Mr Alexander to repeat the question, for Sir Frederick was still at a loss for words. The ring and brooch were then produced and admitted by the plaintiff to be the ones referred to.

"Sir Frederick, recovering his equilibrium: After this exhibition, I cannot spare you." He then confronted Sir Richard with his prison record for horse-stealing in 1811, which he denied vehemently.

"Sir Frederick: Have you got the marks of the King's Evil on your neck, and also on your right hand?" Sir Richard hesitated, and at last bared his neck and hand, and the marks were visible. He had always maintained that these were the indelible marks of identity in the Smyth family. (On his second trial he turned his back on the court and jury and revealed an enormous pigtail, two feet long, which up to that moment had been kept concealed under his coat. This, he announced, with solemn deliberation, was irrefutable proof of his aristocratic birth, adding that "he was born with it," and that his son "was born with one six inches long".)

The excitement in the court reached a new pitch. The Judge then asked Mr Bovill if he intended to proceed.

"Mr Bovill: I must say that the progress of this case has been the most painful I ever knew. At this moment I can scarcely speak owing to the emotion I see prevail in every part of the court at this appalling exhibition.... from the great importance of this case, and the extraordinary interest attached to it, we have felt that we could not consistently with our duty interpose during the cross-examination which has taken place. We felt it our duty not to make a single remark till the cross-examination should draw to a close. After this most appalling exhibition and this exposure so unparalleled in a court of justice, which has come upon us all by surprise, it would be impossible for us to appear further in a case of this description...."

The plaintiff was then taken into custody on a charge of perjury and forgery and at the next Assizes in Gloucester, April 1854, he was found guilty and sentenced to twenty years transportation.

Arthur Way, who had shouldered the whole burden of bringing the imposter to justice, had little doubt about the outcome. His chief concern was the expense. "Estimate of the expenses of the defendants on this Trial at £6,000!" he wrote on 31st July 1853. "A monstrous case, that an estate should be liable to be put to such expense to defend itself in a suit having no foundation whatsoever."

Nonetheless he was relieved when "....the wretch was fully committed for forgery and perjury" (11th August) and next day: "Returned to Ashton Court, delighted to have shaken off the imposter claiming the estate of my nephew and I met with congratulations from everyone I met in Bristol.... went to Ingmire for the grouse shooting...."

"Reflections on the manner in which I have been treated"

How did Sir Richard view the outcome? In the little book he wrote in prison, seven months later, he devotes Chapter X to 'My Trial & Imprisonment'.

"The first day went off well enough; all the documents were proved, my mother's marriage and my own baptism were duly admitted....etc. etc. On the second day I was examined as to my story. But it was folly to expect that a man like me, of naturally retired habits and possessed of the most delicate sensibility, could speak of himself with as much fulness as he could write. Nor did I like the manner of my solicitor. He appeared to me to take no interest in the issue of the case.

"Then began my friend, my very learned friend, Sir Frederick Thesiger, to cross-examine me - contrary to the rule laid down in the Act of Parliament. I had no right to have been examined at all - it was out of all rule...." He had evidently expected that he, Sir Richard Smyth, was going to do the cross-examining. He then goes on to vilify the legal profession, especially the Judge, who did not call all his seventy witnesses, particularly his old nurse and Lydia Reed who was still living and would have sworn to his true identity, and who heard all the defendant's witnesses before any of his. He deplored the presence of "....the Sheriff's officer and detective man from London - a most scandalous affair in a Court of Justice", and heaped opprobrium on his own Counsel for permitting him to be insulted without raising a single protest. He admits he made mistakes "....but they were not wilful - such that any man may make after 9 hours cross-examination the first day and 5 the next...."

"Indeed, I was left naked to my enemies who," he said, meaning Arthur Way and Co., "by their influence and a free dispensation of cash, had obtained the principal seats." Then comes a little pious hypocrisy: "Never shall I forget the looks of my enemies when the Judge set my mother's miniature before them. Too beautiful for them, they could not and did not despise it. No, I will do them the justice to say that they looked upon it with sad and sorrowful countenances, more kindly than I could have expected. Well, in consideration of those kind looks I freely forgive their faults. Young

Upton also, as I thought, looked first at it and then at me to trace the resemblance. Oh, it is too like. Let them restore it to me, or death may be the result. I would advise them not to injure or abuse it in any way." They did not restore it, nor did they abuse it. It was placed among all the other Smyth miniatures where it still remains.*

There follows a great deal of self-pity: "My cause was lost. I was hurried to gaol, cut off from friends, and deprived of the society of my dear wife and children (bless them all!). My character has been traduced, but thank God I can vindicate that. I am....deprived of the comforts of home, debarred the embrace of one's loved ones, those who cling around the heart with consuming fire...." and much else besides; especially about the solace of a good woman.

"Only think of the refined cruelty of putting a man like me into a cage, as you would a wild beast. How can my children ever think of me with respect? I remember my children on one occasion noticing the cruelty of confining the animals at the Zoological Gardens, to which I replied that as it was their nature to be wild, so it was necessary that they should be confined, whereupon my son said 'Dear Papa, how would you like to be so confined?' Ah me! How soon his artless words were verified! and in these degrading circumstances I am obliged to see my family...."

His final chapters are entitled 'Reflections on the manner in which I have been treated', 'Recapitulation' and 'The Conclusion', each one headed by apt quotations from Virgil, Socrates and Shakespeare - they are a final vindication of his rights. He reiterates the failure of his enemies to prove he was a bastard: "....it is true they attempted to prevail on several prostitutes to claim me as one of their offspring, but they were too honest", and he returns again to the perfidy of the old woman who claimed to be his sister, the recognition and evident guilt of all the members of the Smyth family when he pressed his claim upon them, and especially his extraordinary interview with his 'Uncle John' who was found dead the next morning in equivocal circumstances.

He ends with an impassioned appeal to the English public who "with all their faults, are never backward to acknowledge their errors, when convinced by fair and legitimate means". The concluding chapter contains a remarkable treatise on the reactions of the French, the Spaniards and the Germans to a case of slander, but the English: "I fear we have degenerated; for the inhabitants of our own enlightened country, the most Christian-like in the world, who send out their missionaries to all parts of the world to teach charity and goodwill to all beings - a nation which, above all others, should

* Now at Rousham House, Oxon., the property of T. Cottrell-Dormer Esq., grandson of Greville's sister, Florence.

exemplify the divine attribute of mercy - a people set up as a bright example of morality to all mankind - are debased by the most contemptible and uncharitable propensity".

He ends on a humorous note: "I believe it was Socrates who had a vituperative, stormy-tongued wife. He was himself a man of few words. If she scolded inside the house, he sat outside, under the window, with his book. One day she was in a more than ordinary rage, and hurrying upstairs she from the window tipped--------. Socrates quietly cleansed himself and, looking up, calmly said 'Well, thank the Gods, the storm is over and the sun will shine'. Let me hope that the storms of ill-report will soon cease, and that the sun of universal charity will so shine on your minds that, despite all you have heard to the contrary, you shall be brought to believe that I am a man 'more sinned against than sinning'."

His final words have a frankness and clarity which is almost endearing. "Let me, finally, say that I owe my degradation in public opinion more to thoughtlessness than to wilfulness; and my hope is that editors and others will now address me in something like the following strain:

"'Well, friend Smyth, we have done thee wrong, but now convinced of our error, we will do all we can to restore thee to reputation and honour!'

"But should I here again be doomed to disappointment, I beg distinctly and emphatically to declare that neither editors nor others will ever be able to make me other than their true well-wisher, or less than the world's friend and

SIR RICHARD HUGH SMYTH, BARONET."

The little book appeared, late in 1853 devoid, it should be said, of all the idiosyncratic spelling which had been detected in his other effusions, and graced with a handsome, signed lithograph of the author in academic robes, and a note 'The Reader is requested to observe that the portrait of the Author was taken when he was about 40 years of age, and then extensively engaged in public teaching'.

On the 24th May 1855 Arthur Way wrote in his Day Book:

"Received intelligence of the Death of Thomas Provis, alias Sir Richard Hugh Smyth, the late claimant of the Ashton Court Estates and the suit Smyth v. Smyth, in Dartmoor Gaol."

Much was made later in the century of his wife having been in service at Ashton Court in the time of Sir Hugh and his brother John, through whom it was believed the claimant had derived his knowledge of the family. Although the documents and heirlooms had been found to be forgeries, it has never been actually disproved that Richard Smyth, or Tom Provis, was the son of Sir Hugh, by a lady unknown.

The forged wills, the Bible, heirlooms, the miniature of Jane Vandenburg, and even the enormous pigtail of the pretender, were displayed for many years in a glass case at Ashton Court; reminders of one of the most bizarre episodes in all the annals of the Smyth family.

THE YOUNG BARONET

"26 December 1853. Gave orders to have all the rooms got ready for Mrs Upton," wrote Arthur Way. On New Year's Day, 1854, Greville's seventeenth birthday, with his mother Eliza and his sisters, Fanny and Florence, he took up residence at Ashton Court. "New Year set in with severe frost and deep snow." It was the beginning of a new era. In November 1853, Uncle Arthur had consulted the fellows of Christ Church and Magdalen College, Oxford, about a tutor for his nephew. In due course Mr Sandford was appointed, and in December 1853 Arthur took Greville to Oxford and had him enrolled as a Gentleman Commoner at Christ Church. "We then proceeded to Worcester College where he was matriculated by Dr. Cotton, the Vice Chancellor. A Gentleman commoner," he added grandly, "pays double fees to a commoner. Mr Smyth paid £53, a commoner entering Christ Church the same day paid £26."

"20 January 1854. Dear Greville with his tutor Mr Sandford went to Christ Church, Oxford today to keep his first term," wrote Arthur in his Day Book. He allowed Greville, to start with, £500 pocket money a year.

We don't hear much of Greville's university days. He never took a degree but he soon made himself at home among the other Gentlemen Commoners - the clique of landed gentry and their sons who controlled half the wealth and most of the politics of England at that time; but one gets the impression that it was not so much studies, or politics, or money that forged links between Greville and his college friends - many to last a lifetime - but the chase and other pursuits of the idle rich.

"26 May. Mr Smyth and a young Oxonian, Mr Harding, came to Ashton from Oxford to shoot rooks," wrote Arthur Way, rather testily, "when he should have been at his studies.

The long vacation was approaching and Arthur went to Oxford on the 26th June to arrange for Greville and Mr Sandford to spend a month in Switzerland. "Took the Foreign Office passports, a route of 1-30 days and £100 Bank of England notes on the account of Mrs Upton."

War

The Grand Tour was still very much part of a young man's education, but the troubled state of Europe in 1854 rather limited the scope. In April, Britain, France and Turkey declared war on Russia. On 26th April Arthur had written, "This day was kept as a day of General Humiliation throughout the Kingdom to pray for success in our war with Russia, and subscriptions were made in all churches for the widows and orphans of our soldiers and sailors." The reverberations of the Crimean War sent ripples into the stately homes of mid-Victorian England. On the 4th October Arthur wrote, "False report of the Fall of Sevastapol," and on the 20th Greville returned to Oxford.

That Christmas, their first at Ashton Court, Greville brought quite a crowd of Oxford cronies home. Arthur wrote, "December 15. I shot with Mr Smyth and party of Oxford friends at Barrow Wood. Bag: 19 pheasants, 9 hares, 9 woodcock..."

Greville's younger sister, Florence, a lively, good-looking girl, much enjoyed the company and was in great demand. "He hardly ever returned" (from Oxford)" alone," she wrote in her journal. "Mr Dyke, Mr Kennedy, Mr Mark John Stewart, Mr Herbert Hanney, Mr Lysley, Sir Charles Mordaunt* and his brother John - all these were constantly coming and going, and some

* Sir Charles Mordaunt, later MP for South Warwickshire. His divorce in 1869 caused a frightful scandal because his wife denied that he was father of their child and named, among others, HRH the Prince of Wales. It was generally believed that Lady Mordaunt had gone out of her mind, a condition induced by the premature birth of her child, who was afflicted with blindness; but the Prince's letters to the lady were produced and he had to appear in court - a circumstance which gave a regrettable and lasting impression of the Prince's infidelities.

" I very much disliked dancing Sir Roger de Coverley with the footman...."

of them were very pleasant. My brother was very fond of dancing, and as there was a deficiency of partners the servants used to be summoned to join the mazy dance to the sound of the great organ, then in the hall, and played by an organist from Bristol. I very much disliked dancing Sir Roger de Coverley with the footman...."

The old house, so long the residence of recluses or elderly or celibate persons, now resounded with youthful merriment - perhaps not heard since Sir John Smyth's eight children had romped through its halls in the first years of the 18th Century. The Way cousins were, as usual, much in evidence, and amateur theatricals were all the rage:

"We played Cinderella in the Long Gallery. Greville was the Beast and had to ask Cousin Izzie,* 'Beauty, will you marry me?' 'No, Beast, no!' I was one of the cruel sisters and finished my part saying:

'Your Royal Highness, 'tis an imposition
This is a girl of very low condition.
She is our servant, though her foot is small
But never in her life was at a Ball!'

It went off very well, and amused us at any rate...."**

It was a little less amusing for the British troops that Christmas, exposed to the Russian winter on the heights before Sevastopol. From his windswept, waterlogged tent, Private James Collard wrote on the 27th November to his parents at 5 Somerset Terrace, Bedminster - the overgrown industrial village whose unsightly collieries were plainly visible from the windows of Ashton Court, and the source of much of the Smyth wealth:

"Dear Father & Mother,

"I received your welcome letter of September 10 and was happy to hear that you was in the enjoyment of Good Health and I am happy to say this leaves me in at this time. Thank God for it, -dear Parents, I have underwent a great deal of hardship since I last wrote to you on the first of September last. We left Turkey and since that time we have never had our clothes off, constantly under arms day and night.

* Isabella Way, daughter of the Rev. Henry Hugh Way, vicar of Henbury, and sister of Emily.

** Florence, whose journal was written in retrospect, seems to have confused 'Cinderella' with 'Beauty and the Beast'.

"I suppose you have heard of the Battle of Alma on the 20th of September. We earned our laurels most dearly, but also most gallantly, but we have had two other hard fought battles since that time - the first after we came to the Hill in front of Sevastopol and preparations were made to besiege the place and many a slight skirmish we had to take up our position - all of which we gained with very little loss - so that on the 17th of Oct. the siege commenced - and my Dear Parents, at the first opening of our Guns and the Cannon it was awfully Grand - you have heard the heavens open in claps of thunder at home and it is nothing to the tremendous thunder of two Armys in fierce combat with each other - we carried on the warfare until the 20 when they thought to have put us off the hill that our Brigade occupied. There was about 10 thousand of them and for one hour fifty men of our Regiment kept them at bay until we were reinforced by the rest of our Regiment and some few others that came to our aid when we repulsed them with great slaughter into Sebastapol with about 4 thousand slain we had about 120 killed and as many more wounded...." (James Collard was here referring to the Battle of Balaclava, rendered famous by the Charge of the Light Brigade) "....that kept them quiet until the morning of the 5th Nov. when they being reinforced from the interior of the country they came out about 50,000 at half past five in the morning we came from our entrenching party when we got the word to stand to your arms then the fight commenced and we fought until 4 in the afternoon at which time they had to retire with the loss of more men than we had in the field." (This was the Battle of Inkerman, sometimes called the 'Soldiers' Battle', for in the thick mist the officers were unable to direct operations or give orders, so it was left to individual regiments to fight it out.) "....I have neither the time nor space or I would give you an awful picture of the Battlefield after it was all over - so I must pass that and say that in the next, if I am so lucky as to escape, I shall have many curious stories to tell you when I get home again, and if I should fall, all I have to request is that you apply for my small ledger and all the credit that is due to me. I know not how much it may be - and the medal which I have Dearly earned and keep it for my sake, but I hope to be wearing it myself at home with you, and laughing at the things which now seem no laughing Matter and now I conclude and believe me to remain, Ever your Affectionate Son till Death,

"James Collard: 30 Regiment, S Company, No. 3284."

The happy house party at Ashton Court was not totally oblivious to the futile courage and suffering of the British troops in the Crimea.

"Jan. 1st. 1855. The New Year set in with very mild weather," wrote Uncle Arthur, "but with sad accounts of our army before Sevastopol, which stronghold to my calculation cannot be expected to fall to the allied powers before the middle or end of May...."

"Jan. 19th. The Christmas party at Ashton Court broke up and Greville returned with his tutor to keep his Oxford terms."

February was bitterly cold, both in Russia and in Long Ashton. "16th. Excessive hard frost. The thermometer at midnight 17 degrees below freezing point," and 'General Fevrier' whom the Czar had boasted would be his chief ally in defeating the British and French turned traitor and gave him a fatal chill.

"Mar.3. The Emperor Nicholas of Russia died yesterday at St. Petersburg. It was known in London the same day at 2 o'clock. Henry Phelps came as Gardener to Ashton Court at 16/- a week. Shot rabbits with Fitz - killed 56...."

One feels that Uncle Arthur was more astonished with the speed of the news from Russia (by electric telegraph) than its substance. The Czar was laid to rest and hopes were entertained that the new Emperor, Alexander II, would be more disposed to listen to allied proposals for peace; but at Ashton, three weeks later, an event occurred which filled everyone with revulsion and horror.

Frightful Violation of the Smyth Family Vault

Florence: "A dreadful person called 'Bristol Joey' broke into the family vault in Ashton Church and most horrible and gruesome details were rumoured of the havoc he made there...." The Illustrated London News on 21st April interrupted its columns of small print and splendid metal engravings of the Crimean War to relate what happened:

"April 21. A painful sensation has been caused in Bristol by the sacrilegious violation of the vault in which for several centuries have reposed the remains of the Smyth family of Ashton Court, situated about three miles from that city. It appears that there must have been at least seven or eight persons engaged in it; and from the artistic manner in which the vault was laid open, it is equally plain that some stonemasons were engaged to conduct operations. The object of the plunderers is pretty well known. Owing to some family differences, the aunt of the late Sir John (d.1849) and Sir Hugh Smyth (d.1825) resided by herself.* She was of somewhat eccentric habits, and it was currently reported at the time of her funeral that a quantity of jewels were interred with her and that, the body having been embalmed, the heart was placed within the coffin, enclosed in a silver box, and that the breastplate, handles etc. of the coffin were of pure silver."

The Bristol Times of 21st April reported the precise manner in which the vault was broken open: "They first paid a visit to a small house in the neighbourhood of the Church in which the Sexton kept his tools. The door of this which was locked, must have been opened with a false key, as no mark of force having been used was apparent on its surface. From the tool house they took a hand spike and 2 strong iron crooks and then proceeded to a small side entrance to the chancel of the Church, carefully locking the door of the tool house after them. They must have been provided with a skeleton key for the Chancel door also, as there was no visible sign of a forcible entry on either that or the other door. Having entered the Church the robbers next proceeded to the North end of the Communion, the first step of which borders the entrance.

* Elizabeth Woolnough, widow of Sir John Hugh Smyth, who died 1801. See 'The Later Smyths of Ashton Court, 1741-1802. She moved to Clift House on the death of her husband, and died in 1825.

The Grand Tour

Why, everyone asked, could not Greville have delayed his departure for three days in order to be at his cousin's wedding? In the light of what was still a closely guarded secret, it was not surprising. It was too painful. In any case their paths would cross on the Continent, for George and Emily had also decided to make for the Riviera.

On the 14th February, St. Valentine's Day, Florence and her mother set out with Gandolfi the courier, and Spurway the lady's maid. Of the three parties travelling south during that extraordinarily fateful tour, we shall follow Florence, for she is the only one to have left a detailed account of what happened. Eliza, remembering her own girlhood jaunts on the Continent in the 1820s, prevailed upon Florence to keep a daily journal of events. Florence was seventeen and her journal is banal in the extreme - only enlivened by the irrepressible good humour of her mother.

"Mamma and I left Claridges Hotel, arrived at Folkestone at 2 and went immediately on board the steamer," began Florence. "A very rough passage and were both very ill and glad when we arrived at Boulogne at 5 - the novelty of the scene and the dresses took away the illness at once" - the Normandy coif was still much in evidence.

It was certainly Mamma's idea to go and have a look at the military camp two miles from Boulogne. The Emperor Napoleon had 50,000 men, many of them Crimean veterans, encamped on the cliffs, and ladies in all their finery, both there and in English camps, saw nothing indecorous in promenading down the lines to see men at their ablutions or polishing their

"The steps leading down to the vault are covered with a large stone, with a ring in its centre, fixed in place with cement. The removal of this was apparently too great a task for the strength of the burglars, and they therefore actually shifted the first step leading to the Communion from its place, breaking it in two in doing so, and thus succeeded in obtaining an entry into the vault. The coffin of the Dowager Lady Smyth being doubtlessly the one they desired to ransack, they proceeded to pull about the various coffins of the members of the Smyth family in search of it. That of Mrs Florence Smyth was dragged completely from its place and placed in a north-south direction; that of Sir John (Hugh) Smyth, buried in 1802, was turned on its side, and the breastplate torn off the coffin of a son of the former Sir Hugh Smyth*. At last the robbers arrived at the coffin of Mrs Jane Smyth, widow of Thomas, buried in 1818, and concluding it to be the one which contained the wished for booty, they forced it open, but probably to their great disgust found it to contain nothing but the fleshless bones of its former occupant. The way in which the coffin they were in search of (and which there seems no reason to doubt really does contain the supposed valuables) was preserved from discovery almost deserved to be called miraculous. A plank used for lowering the coffins into the vault had been left there. This the robbers appear to have found in their way and therefore moved it on one side, hiding by doing so the very coffin they so ardently wished to discover."

Arthur Way had an official advertisement posted in Bristol:

"SACRILEGE: £50 REWARD

"Whereas some evil disposed persons did last night sacrilegiously break open the vault of the Smyth family in the chancel of the parish church at Long Ashton, the undersigned will pay the above reward for such information as shall lead to the conviction of the offender."

'Bristol Joey' was eventually apprehended and given a long prison sentence, along with three of his gang, two of them Bedminster men.

"30 April. The Emperor Napoleon shot at....," wrote Arthur Way. The Glorious War he had promised his people was not yielding sufficient glory.

On the 3rd May, Mary Collard, who had waited in vain for further news of her son before Sevastopol, wrote to "The Right Honourable the Secretary at War, War Office, London":

"Honoured Gentlemen,

"I beg leave to inform you that my son James Collard entered the army in, I think 1850, and I received a letter from him last year and since

* Mr John Hugh Smith-Piggott, d.1853.

that time I have written several letters to him but have not received any answer. Therefore will feel greatly obliged in your being so kind as to give me some information respecting him as soon as possible and in so doing you will greatly oblige your Humble Servant,

"Mary Collard, 5 Somerset Terrace,
"Bedminster, Bristol."

In due course she received a questionnaire from the War Office, which is a model of the sort of red tape and crassness for which those 'Honoured Gentlemen' then, and subsequently, were notorious.

"What is the name of the man?	'James Collard' his mother wrote.
"Where was he born and in about what year?	In the parish of Spaxton, March 18, 1830
"Was he born in wedlock?	Yes
"When did he first enlist, the date to be given as near as you can?	I think it was in the year 1849 or 1850
"Where did he first enlist?	Bristol
"Into what Regiment?	30
"In what Regiment was he serving when you last heard of him?	30 Regiment
"What is his Regimental Number?	3284
"State the date of his letter or the last date on which he is known to have been serving with his Regiment?	Nov. 27. 1854
"Where was he last heard of?	On the heights, near Sevastopol
"Send his last letter if you have received any and have returned the letter received from this office.	Have sent his last letter Nov.27. 1854
"If he is supposed to be dead, state the date of his decease.	I hope he is still alive
"State the degree of your relationship and what is the know cause of your enquiry.	He is my son and I desire to know how and where he is, if please."

In the margin of the copy Mary kept for herself she wrote: "I hope that the Great God who ordereth all things and sure will soon put a stop to War and bloodshed and cause His Face to shine upon us and Give us Peace". But peace was still a long way off.

"23 June. Received news of our dreadful losses at the Redan and Malakoff," wrote Arthur Way. The forts guarding Sevastopol had fallen, the city was captured, its arsenals and docks blown up. The war objective had been realised, but still Mary Collard had no news of her son.

"July 18. My wife entertained above 100 of the village children to strawberries and tea, with Games on the lawn afterwards," wrote Arthur - the summer was approaching and the heroes of the war were returning.

"The Queen this day decorated the Crimean Soldiers," wrote Arthur, and a little later (25th July), "Lord Raglan's funeral cortege passed through Bristol to Badminton; all shops closed (attended) procession." Raglan was the British Commander in Chief and he had died of exhaustion at the battlefront - but .no news of James Collard. The Uptons, Greville and his college friends went to Ingmire for the summer. Before their departure Arthur wrote, rather pompously, "Saw Mrs Upton at the Court. It was agreed that I should apply to the Court of Chancery for an additional £500 for Greville, his present allowance of £600 not meeting his expenses at college, etc...."

He then packed his bags, bid farewell to Hebe and went to Paris and Germany "....with Mr Hamilton, for a vacational tour. Returned to Ashton Lodge, Sept. 14. A very pleasant excursion throughout."

Though Mary Collard was not to know it, James had been wounded in the taking of Sevastopol. In July he was shipped across the Black Sea in one of the foetid hospital transports and was delivered to the General Hospital at Scutari in Turkey. It was fortunate for him that he arrived at this appalling place six months after Florence Nightingale, for a semblance of order was emerging from the chaos she had found there.

Still the troops were being sent out. Florence, on holiday with her mother in Scotland, wrote on Oct. 29: "We repaired to the Station (Aberdeen) which we found full of the 79th Highlanders going to the Crimea; and tender Adieux numerous!"

"Nov. 1st. I sent Greville Smyth a cheque for £84 to pay for a new hunter," wrote Uncle Arthur.

"Nov. 14. Went with the vicar of Henbury to Stradley on family business." The vicar of Henbury was his brother, Henry Hugh.

"Nov. 16. Returned to Ashton Lodge with Mrs Lewis and her maid." Mrs Lewis was his youngest sister, Laetitia. Florence liked her Aunt Laetitia. "She had an old husband, much older than herself, about 20 years." She used to stay with her aunt at Brunswick Square, Brighton, and go riding over the Sussex Downs "....with Fanny, her daughter, and the riding master. Long rides which I rather enjoyed".

"At Christmas 1855 the family gathered again at Ashton Court; the Mordaunts, Mr Stewart, Mr Llewellyn and others made up the house party.

"17 December. Shot with Greville and friends at Cook's Wood; we killed 71 pheasants, 1 woodcock, 157 rabbits, 229 head," wrote Uncle Arthur.

"Jan. 2. 1856. A large Dinner Party in the new Dining Room at Ashton Court to commemorate Greville's birthday. This day next year he will attain his majority."

As for James Collard: that month he was discharged from the General Hospital, Scutari, and one hopes his mother was informed of his recovery, though she had to wait another two years before she saw him again. After a spell of duty at Gibraltar, working as a hospital orderly - a job usually undertaken by wounded or disabled men who were unfit for other duties - he was posted to Dublin with his regiment in September 1857. On the 29th March, 1858 he was discharged from the army. The census returns for No. 5 Somerset Terrace, Bedminster, 1861, tell us that James Collard 'discharged Crimean soldier, partly disabled from wounds' aged 30, was a lodger, sharing what must have been very cramped quarters with three other families - a total of eleven persons of whom six were children. There is no mention of Mary, and in 1871 her husband was designated 'widower'.

Love

"What we most enjoyed," wrote Florence, recalling those days, "Greville welcomed a Mrs Stone, a lovely woman like a great white swan." Already tongues were wagging, but she was married to a Captain of the Papal Guard. "He and I used to talk Pickwick together," added Florence.

Greville's disposition for married women did not augur well for the future. Perhaps it was because of Mrs Stone that, early in 1856, after the declaration of peace with Russia, there was much talk of the whole family going on the Grand Tour. Greville would not return to Oxford, but would be entrusted to a travelling tutor, a red-headed Oxonian called Thomas Jeans, whose father lived abroad for 'reasons of economy', with property in Tours and Catania (Sicily).

Thomas Jeans

Richard Orlebar*, one of Greville's Christ Church friends, who had graduated the previous year, would accompany them. Six months on the Continent would round off his education before taking up his responsibilities as country gentleman and public figure.

Eliza and Florence, with an Italian courier, Gandolfi, and a lady's maid, Spurway, would follow at a more leisurely pace, joining up with them at Nice and in Rome. "Fanny was to remain at Ashton with a succession of people, one at a time, to stay with her," wrote Florence, who was wildly excited, for it was her first trip to the Continent since 1847, when she was nine. Greville, Jeans and Orlebar left on 2nd February. Three days later, on 5th February, a family wedding of some significance took place at Henbury. "Attended the marriage of my niece Emily Way to Mr George Edwards of Henbury," wrote Uncle Arthur. "Ten bridesmaids, and all went off with gaiety and spirit."

"I was one of the bridesmaids," wrote Florence who, in those days, was full of admiration for Emily. "She had most beautiful hair and a lovely complexion." It was the occasion of a formidable gathering of Ways. Many of them had taken up residence in the locality after old Mary Way* gave up Denham on the death of her husband and came to Ashton Court to live with her brother John Smyth, the old Baronet. When the property passed to her grandson, Greville, in 1852, uncles and aunts moved in with a vengeance. Henry Hugh, his wife and eight children came to Henbury vicarage, (he was the first of three generations of Ways to hold the living). Great Aunt Ann Way, of whom they had expectations, lived with them. Arthur Way, as agent, gave up his home in Cheltenham and, with Hebe and little Gregory, moved to Ashton Lodge. Colonel Prior and Aunt Louisa (Way) and their eight children came to Brislington House, and later Sydney Place, Bath, and Edward Sampson with Aunt Belinda, "....a stately lady who always was rather stiff and imposing and dressed in fine garments", came to Henbury Manor; and the Fitzways (Uncle Holroyd and family) lived in Bath. "A goodly circle of relations - all within a carriage drive of Ashton," wrote Florence, "who could and did drop in daily."

She and Greville had known Emily Way from childhood. It had been said, when her father Henry Hugh took a rather elderly bride, Susannah Daniel, that there would of course be no children, for she was well past the child-bearing age, but the gossips were confounded for Susannah produced in

* Of Hinwick House, Bedfordshire, he was remotely related. An ancestor of his had married Diana Astry, sister of Elizabeth, wife of Sir John Smyth (d.1726). (See 'The Earlier Smyths of Ashton Court'.)

** Born Mary Smyth of Stapleton. (d.1850).

rapid succession four sons and four daughters - the last born when their mother was 54. She went feeble-minded in the process, but all her children were remarkably good-looking and talented. Emily was the eldest and the prettiest. She had an alabaster complexion, her eyes were like sapphires and her hair like spun gold. There exist in one of the Way scrapbooks some watercolours by Emily. One of them dated 1849, when she was thirteen, is a lively conversation piece, showing a family wedding taking place in Henbury Church. Her father, in the voluminous clerical robes of the time, is officiating and Emily ('Emmie'), Isabella ('Izzie'), Maria ('Murdy') and Alice ('Taff'), in pretty flounced dresses and poke bonnets are evidently bridesmaids.

Why Emily, aged twenty, married George Edwards, who was more than twice her age, was a lively topic of conversation at the time. The 'Bristol Mirror' reported that "The Settlement made by the bridegroom was worthy of a 'King of Crowns and Sovereigns'." He was a banker, a partner in the firm of Baillie, Ames and Co., of The Old Bank, Corn Street, Bristol, and enormously rich. He was the owner of Redland Court*, a splendid Palladian mansion within walking distance of Henbury. Emily, lame as a result of a childhood ailment, was not likely to get another chance.

"The village of Henbury was quite a fluster of rejoicing on the occasion," wrote our reporter from the 'Bristol Mirror' whose excruciating effusion is worthy of more than a passing quote. "Mine Host of the Salutation Inn hung out a line of flags which, stretching across the road, waved as if in welcome to the crowd of persons who came to witness the ceremony. A triumphal arch was erected in the Vicarage Lane, another near the residence of Edward Sampson Esq., and another at the east entrance to the Church.

"Groups of people were met at every turn and town-built equipages, in all the glory of emblazoned panels, literally splashed through the brook which crosses the road, and rolled by the village stocks, contrasting oddly with that ancient institution, the white favours which streamed from some of the horses heads distinguishing the wedding guests from the crowd. The doors of the Church were surrounded by something like a real crush and we fear that it is not often a congregation is so eager to get in.

"As the morning advanced, the sunshine bathed the Church with yellow light, and a gentle breeze with the flag, hoisted on its low, square tower, now and then unrolling the loyal inscription it bears: 'Church and Queen'.

* This house later became the first building of Redland High School for Girls.

"The body of the interior of the Church was filled with company displaying all the lights and shades of dress: indeed it was surprising where so many well-dressed persons had come from. The seats abutting on the centre aisle along which the bridal procession would, of course, pass were much coveted, while some ladies - presuming perhaps on their right to lecture if not preach - boldly took possession of the reading desk and the pulpit stairs.

"About 11 o'clock the bridesmaids fluttered into the Church, pretty butterflies, not yet fascinated by the flame. They were Miss Way, Miss Maria Way and Miss Alice Way, sisters of the bride; Miss Osborne, Miss Mary Osborne and Miss Georgie Osborne, nieces of the bridegroom; Miss Florence Upton, Miss M. Way, Miss Lewis and Miss Prior, cousins of the bride. Before their arrival the company had been gossiping about the match, and to tell the truth the reporters might have learnt a good deal of private history, but though they are the most inquisitive about business they are the least curious of mortals on matters which do not concern them. But now all attention was concentrated on the bridesmaids, as they formed a charming group near the altar, each 'fair as Helen, fair as she of Cytherea'.

"The bridesmaids wore white tarlatan dresses, the skirts edged with blue, light blue mantles, and white straw archery hats, the curl at the sides being very 'piquant' with a white feather tipped with blue where it dropped within the relief of the shoulder. We overheard one exclamation 'How fantastic', but we are bound to add generally the 'tout ensemble' was pronounced charming and picturesque. Yet the bridesmaids were outdone for a moment by the shining raiment of one of the clergymen as he stood at the altar in his robes, the sun's rays streaming through one of the painted windows, clothing him in all the colours of light, and it is impossible to imagine anything more classic and beautiful." (Evidently one of the bride's cousins, the Rev. H. Daniel, or the Rev. Charles Hill, who performed the ceremony.)

The bridal procession entered soon after 11 o'clock by the north door. There was a rustling and hushed silence as everyone strained to catch a glimpse. Our reporter again: "The bride wore a white silk dress, the flounces richly embroidered. The headdress was formed by an elegant lace veil and the bride's beautiful hair, which hung loosely round her face, was intertwined with orange blossoms. As she proceeded two of her sisters strewed flowers in her path, a touch of true poetry, which was evidently felt by the company."

After the service the bells crashed out in a joyous peal as George and Emily left the Church. Seated in a superbly appointed open carriage, drawn by four grey horses, they swept round the village to the vicarage gates and the bride, recorded our reporter: "....rewarded the cordial salutations of the villagers by a bright smile and a joyous wave of the hand".

As "the happy couple set off in a handsome travelling carriage en route for Paris", forty Ways sat down to a "bumper dejeuner" at the vicarage; 150 village school children were regaled with plum cake, music and the "wonders of the magic lantern", and the clerks of Bristol Old Bank were treated to "a sumptuous dinner at the Queen's Hotel, Clifton" at the expense of their bountiful boss.

Departure of George & Emily Edwards, courier & lady's maid to the Continent.

equipment. This extraordinary curiosity could be pardoned as patriotism. Anyway the soldiers liked it - well, most of them.

"We left the carriage and began walking about," wrote Florence, "which piece of forwardness was very soon stopped by two soldiers, and we were turning back much disappointed when a kind little Capitaine looked out of his window and told the men we had his orders and might go where we pleased. So we inspected the camp at our leisure...."

Contemporary lithographs of the camp reveal trim rows of lath and plaster huts with tiled roofs, which Florence described as "nice little mud houses", though nothing was said about the splendid shakos and cherry red pantaloons of the French soldiers.

Of the train journey to Paris Florence had only one observation: "We had but one companion - a solitary, slow, middle-aged, red-haired man, who said he had felt the crossing very much yesterday and had not been 'himself' since.... We dined at Amiens - the country is particularly ugly and uninteresting all the way...." Her mother had said much the same in 1824.

They stayed at 13 Rue des Champs Elysees and paraded round the Tuileries gardens, ".... amongst nurses and children innumerable....", and then Eliza took Florence to see the Hotel Marboeuf where she had stayed with Uncle Lewis thirty-one years before: "....but all was altered except one old cedar tree; it is now called the Hotel Geradin and belongs to the Empress' mother".

On the 18th February they travelled to Marseilles via Lyons, by the same route as that taken by Florence Nightingale and her nurses a little more than twelve months before. They broke the journey at Lyons to see the silk manufacturers, but Gandolfi, not feeling equal to the challenge, recommended a "laquais de place to take care of us; therefore he departed to procure the services of this functionary and we put on our things and, going down, found on the stairs a man of heavy and corpulent appearance. This was our guide. He walked first and we followed, and he took us straight before the windows of M. Marix, Frères, whose window contained the most lovely and impassable* silk dresses. Of course we entered this delightful shop and stayed there about two hours, and chose some pretty dresses, not thinking of the care and trouble unmade silks would be to us at every douane...."

"Wed. Feb 20. Woke in the morning by a dear voice, telling me to look out of the window. I did so and found the market place beneath a mass of huge straw hats covering the heads of numbers of females come in from the country to buy and sell. We went to see the very dirty Cathedral,

* What Florence meant was that it was impossible to pass the window without stopping.

and then Gandolfi" (undoubtedly handsomely tipped by the laquais de place) "took us a long stupid walk where we went yesterday", with Spurway no doubt a step or two deferentially behind, to carry the parcels.

They continued to Marseilles, remarking on the woods of olives and almonds in full blossom and got into conversation with "....a Miss Mills, who is travelling with her father, mother and aunt", but on arriving at the Hotel Bristol found that the Mills had taken all the best rooms "....and the man flew into an awful passion because we would not take the few stuffy, close ones he had left". But they found the Hotel Orient "guarded by soldiers inside and out, and were told the Pasha (representative of the Sultan of Turkey) was there on his way to Paris for the Conference (summoned to conclude the Crimean War) but he was going in an hour and we should have his rooms - an unenviable prospect seeing how filled they were with tobacco smoke; so we declined them and were very comfortable a storey higher".

At Marseilles they did a lot of climbing about in the heat which necessitated, at 7 a.m. the next day, a visit to the bonnet woman "....who, poor soul, had to get up and be teased in her nightcap". After breakfast the bonnets having arrived, "....mine highly satisfactory, Mamma's just the contrary, we walked to the Diligence Office", by which mode of conveyance they intended to make the next twenty-four hours of the journey to Cannes. Drawn by six horses, which were frequently changed at inns, the vehicle hurtled along the tortuous coast road.

"We soon passed the Mills, looking most disconsolate, and waiting for horses", having chosen evidently to proceed by private rather than public transport.

"The night was lovely and we made ourselves as comfortable as circumstances would allow, but I could not sleep. though Mamma did.... and we went galloping on through what seemed a great forest, occasionally getting glimpses of distant white mountains looking pink in the moonlight."

After a breakfast of coffee and oranges at Cannes, they pressed on to the Italian border, then to the River Var, ".......where we were obliged to stop and passports were examined. One side of the bridge was a French flag, the other a Sardinian. Here also was the horrid douane, all our luggage was hauled down and examined; it was rather amusing to see all the open boxes and portmanteaux containing our fellow passengers' treasures...."

And so they came to Nice and the Promenade des Anglais ......

which great-uncle Lewis had done so much to put on the map in the 1820s; and like Uncle Lewis and his circle the next generation were beginning to make it their rendezvous, but now there was the Victoria Hotel - "A beautiful, large house, close to the sea".

"We found that Greville, Mr Jeans, Mr Orlebar, the Edwards and Miss Osborne (George Edwards' niece and Emily's lifelong friend) were all staying there, but at church, so we had plenty of time to re-arrange our toilets after our long journey....

"About one Greville came in, very glad to see us, as we were to see him, looking remarkably well." At twenty, freshly down from Oxford, Greville was strikingly handsome. He was tall and fair, with beetling eyebrows and bushy hair and beard - the personification of Victorian manliness. "Soon afterwards Emily came in. She had been married rather more than a fortnight and looked pale...." They all went out driving.

What Florence's journal does not relate, but which must have become painfully evident to the family soon afterwards, was that during that honeymoon tour Emily and Greville conceived a helpless passion for each other. Their mutual attraction had begun some time before and the marriage to George Edwards was a terrible mistake. For Emily the outlook was bleak indeed. Married to a respectable banker, and a vicar's daughter into the bargain, the love affair remained a closely guarded secret for years. Meanwhile, the Grand Tour proceeded according to plan, though the emotion charged atmosphere was occasionally detected by the shrewd Eliza Upton. Whose idea was it, for example, to all go up on to the roof that night and see the view by moonlight? A Mr Singleton was pressed into joining the party "....who Emily introduced me to," wrote Florence irritably: the dissembling had already begun. "Unfortunately there was no moon, so we might have been spared toiling up so many stairs." Anyway, George Edwards whisked away Emily and Miss Osborne early next morning to Genoa "....in Mr Edwards' old carriage," wrote Florence disparagingly.

Gandolfi & Spurway

Meanwhile, Mr Jeans had found two most superior equipages for Florence and her mother. "We all went together to inspect them. One was a perfectly comfortable travelling carriage, with a bed, reading lamp and every convenience; it belonged to the Prince de Joinville,* but being very dark green and lined with the same colour, resembled rather a mourning coach. The other was very light, clean, airy, and large, so we decided that should be ours."

Greville was anxious to be off to Genoa and he, Mr Jeans and Mr Orlebar left, to the mortification of Florence who, that evening at the table d'hote, found herself ".....between Mamma and a chair, but as Mamma sat by Mrs Mills and talked the whole time to her, I found it rather dull, not to say slow", and she added fiendishly, "Going upstairs after this lively meal, met Mr Singleton; he looked wretched having lost his fair friend (Emily) and eaten no dinner, he asked me if we had a good one. I said 'No'."

The waspish mood persisted the next day: "The first news was that old Mr Mills had fallen out of bed and broken many things, but not himself." That day they left Nice: "Very giddy road the whole way; frightful precipices down to the sea on one side, and high rocks on the other. Mamma holding me by both hands, dear thing, and scolding me for laughing, saying it was tempting providence...."

* One of the sons of ex-King Louis Phillippe of France.

At the Hotel Vittoria, Mentone: "....found Greville's name in the arrival book," with a note of approbation from Mr Jeans "....for the Hotel de Turin looked more imposing". Florence was developing a curiosity about the Roman Catholics, like her mother in 1825. In their next little adventure it is difficult to know whether mother or daughter was more inquisitive. "While walking in Mentone before dinner," writes Florence, "we saw an interesting-looking Capuchin friar promenading under a lovely cool, green grove of olives. Determined to examine him more closely we clambered up many steep steps - Mamma a-panting, stopped half-way up to express her hope that the monk might be worth looking at. To our great disappointment, on reaching the grove the object of our curiosity turned and fled! - but, as we ascertained in onc glance, he was old and very ugly...."

As they continued their journey the next day, Florence read to her mother extracts from Murry's Guide Book. "Here (near the Castle of Andoro) a papal nuncio was murdered, and the curse pronounced in consequence of the misdeed is the cause of the decay and desolation of the surrounding territory....

"From Alassio - a daughter of Otho the Great, who fled to the forest with her betrothed, Aleramo, where they lived after the fashion of Lord Richard and Alice Brand, but who they were I can't say," adds Florence peevishly. It was a pity Mr Murry had not been more explicit. "At Alassio we intended to sleep. The hotel is a splendid old house, formerly a palace, immense rooms and numbers of them, but brick and stone floors, and fearfully cold, so we determined to dine and go on to the next inviting place...." They set off again in the dark and, stopping at one place to change horses, "....we heard a loud and curious noise, and found it came from a pond full of frogs kept for eating". Indeed, it was all getting very exotic: palm trees, colour-washed stuccoed houses, inflated pigskins containing wine, hangding up outside the houses, the local women wearing white and coloured veils. Mr Murry again, "Cogoletto - said to be the birthplace of Columbus, though that Gentleman when asked the question, told his friends he was born in Genoa - he ought to have known!" adds Florence.

At the Hotel d'Italia ("formed out of the Fieschi and Grimaldi palaces"), Genoa, there was another reunion. "In the middle of dinner in came dear Greville, and then Mr Jeans", and there was much to chat about, how to cheat the customs officers of the many Italian states through which they had to pass, out of the duty on the Lyons silks (perhaps they all took a length), and about Emily who was not well. No wonder. "Our rooms, 3 storeys high, have such a view of the port," gloats Florence, "while the Edwards, who are down much lower, can see nothing as a long colonnade in front hides the view."

Next day the three young men set off at eight; Emily, George and Miss Osborne at eleven, and Florence and her mother lingered another two days to do some sightseeing. "Mamma and I took a long walk, preceded by Gandolfi (in his livery and wig) and followed by Spurway (in bonnet and shawl). First we went through the curious high and narrow streets to the Palazzo Serra, which has recently been splendidly fitted up by a bachelor member of the family, etc. etc., and to the Cathedral where the people were very busy saying their prayers and staring at us all the time." Genoese filigree bracelets and collars were bought at Fieschi's Convent School and "....we went over the winter Palace of the King, which is very splendid". The King of Sardinia was the blustering Victor Emmanuel, destined four years later (1860) to become the first King of a united Italy. Florence does not relate whether he was in residence, but other royalty were. "We passed Marie-Amelie, ex-queen of the French this afternoon*, walking with the

* Wife of King Louis Philippe, 1836-48. Eliza evidently recognised her, having seen her several times in Paris, 1824-5, when she was the Duchess of Orleans.

Duchess de Nemours (her daughter-in-law) and some gentlemen, and followed by a richly gilt sedan chair."

After a visit to the bank, "Mr Gibbs, the Banker; he and Mamma **would** talk in French", the carriage rolled on again to Spezia. "Very good hotel, if people **would not** eat garlic." It was getting hotter. "The women wear funny little round hats at the very top of their heads. Spurway bought one; they are made of coarse straw and trimmed with red ribbon or braid." It is comforting to note that poor Spurway, whose first name we shall never know, had the opportunity and the means to treat herself occasionally. "A boy wanted me to buy one, Mamma pointed to the hat on my head, and he went away quite convinced that I could not require another."

At the Modena border they bribed the customs officer with three francs and none of their boxes was opened. "In Massa we saw two very handsome officers in blue uniforms. Mamma thought one had a perfectly lovely face ....we passed some great blocks of white marble coming from Carrara, drawn by lovely large, grey Tuscan oxen," as was done in the days of Michelangelo.

At the border of Tuscany the customs officer was intimidating and demanded to open the boxes. Bribes were no use here, but Eliza had other tricks up her sleeve. The first box opened revealed Florence's new bonnet from Marseilles, but Eliza feigned astonishment and released a stream of nonsense about the hat on Florenc's head, evidently in broken Italian. Florence: "I did not see the joke at all and got rather cross, but he was amused and kindly investigated no further, shut up the boxes and we drove on."

Greville and party and the Edwards had not fared so well at the frontier, for not all the personal belongings exposed for inspection were gathered up. Mr Jeans' pocket looking glass and a handkerchief belonging to Miss Osborne were left behind and handed to Florence as they passed through.

Greville was in bed when they got to Pisa "....but Mr Jeans came in and made himself agreeable". Florence's raptures next day over the Leaning Tower "....9 feet out of the perpendicular", the Baptistry and the Campo Santo where "....after the burial of a body nothing is left but the bones after 24 hours", recall those of her cousins, Drusilla and 'Lanky Anna' back in 1822.

In the Baptistry, "....our guide lifted up his beautiful voice and chanted a few notes and the echo came down through the immense dome, like the voices of angels answering. It was **lovely.** Many times he did it, and still we begged him to go on; I could have sat there for a week with pleasure."

There was, in 1856, a newly constructed railway connection to Florence, but the very idea of unprotected females - English at that - travelling alone, was too much for the Italian guard. At every station he poked his head in at the window and "....asked what he could do for us. At the third station Mamma got up and said, 'Niente, grazie'!"

Florence in Florence: 7th March. Hotel Grande-Bretagne. Greville in much excitement, brought Florence a letter he had just received from their cousin John - Emily's brother - who, like his father, was going into the Church, and in which he mentioned a possible or probable match between Minnie (their cousin, Uncle Fitz's daughter) and a certain fat, bandy-legged, elderly man. "I should hope they both knew better!" retorted Florence.

The Ways seemed to have had an irresistible attraction for each other, and the number of matches between first cousins during the next two generations was legion.* Two other first cousins, Greville and Emily, that day almost gave old George Edwards the slip. When they went riding with Richard Orlebar and Miss Osborne, George, "....not being a horseman, contented himself with the English paper at the Reading Room, but insisted on Pianizza, their courier, going with them". Pianizza was evidently not much of a horseman either and "....was constantly run away with...."

Florence was at the Uffizi making lists of Great Masters to put in her journal and later "....drove to the Convent of Santa Maria Novella, whose dear old monks spend their lives making bad scents and excellent liqueurs...." Mamma, that evening "....rep.airs to the Edwards' room and played Whist".

There was talk next day of the journey to Siena. "Our friends," relates Florence, "are all going tomorrow by the 7 a.m. train. There is only one other at 5 p.m. Mamma asked if they breakfasted first, going so early. Mr Orlebar said, 'Oh no. We only have a coffee and eggs; we shall not breakfast till we get to Siena at 11'." Mr Edwards said he intended to be punctual so went to bed at eight, preparatory to getting up at six.

Monday, 10th. "Greville, Mr Jeans and Mr Orlebar went at 7.0, the Edwards still au lit. Their carriage went by train and they foolishly went Vetturino and will not get to Siena till 10 tonight...." Maybe they didn's fancy Italian railways, or perhaps Mr Edwards had other reasons for missing the train.

Florence and her mother stayed another two days examining the treasures and beggars of Tuscany. She trotted out the usual effusions about the Great Masters; her skirmishes with the 'lazeroni' were much more entertaining. Walking in the Cascine: "Four beggars came to us and were

* John Hugh did not, in fact, marry Minnie. But Winnie soon found another first cousin to her liking, Nowell Fitz Upton Sampson Way.

clamorous and unpleasant; no one was near and we didn't like them at all, but Mamma wisely pretended to recognise a carriage we saw coming in the distance, and the beggars instantly trotted off, to our great satisfaction." The flower women were equally demanding. One of them, with lilies of the valley and camellias, even "....rushes up to the Grand Duke whenever she sees him and gives him a bouquet". Two years later that same Grand Duke (Leopold III) was chased into exile by a surge of Italian patriots, beggars and flower girls, and Tuscany merged for ever into the new Kingdom of Italy.

Bad hotels and worse weather cut short the visit to Siena, and the next night was spent in an albergo built by the Tuscan government in a mean mountain village called Radicopani. "It was like a Barrack," wrote Florence. "We had one bedroom in which to sleep and eat our wretched dinner. We were thankful to go to bed at half past eight." It is not related where Gandolfi and Spurway passed the night. "The waiter is a dreadful looking man, the proprietor of one eye.... the inn is built on what was once volcanic ground and great rocks of lava lie about outside."

At 10 a.m. the next day they crossed the border into "...the dominions of the Pope". The customs officer was bribed with a dollar, but the roads thereafter deteriorated sharply. "Wished the Pope would mend his ways, which are shocking!" observed Florence. It was customary for North European visitors to make irreverent remarks about His Holiness in those days, and about his territories which straddled the whole of central Italy. Almost at once there were problems. One of the horses of their vetturino reared so badly he had to be cut loose, and then flung himself down in the mud. "Mamma declared she would not go on if that horse went too. The Post-master, a little man with a red and white beard, went into a fearful passion and said that nothing would induce him to change it." Eventually the animal was scraped clean with a knife and was sufficiently pacified to continue. Then, at another post, Gandolfi picked a quarrel with one of the postboys who complained that the coin with which he had been paid was bad money. In no time fists were flying, until the ladies remonstrated and Gandolfi was called to heel.

At last they came in sight of Rome, whose walls and gates were still much in evidence. They rumbled in through the Porta del Populo and caught sight of George and Emily's courier, Pianizza. He called out that all the rooms in the Hotel European were full, and so Gandolfi went off in search of another, and "....after sitting an immense time in the carriage" he eventually returned and escorted them to the Hotel des Iles Britanniques. Greville and party were at the Hotel d'Allemagne. It is no accident that the hotels had French names. To all intents and purposes Rome was a French town after Louis Napoleon had sent a French army to restore Pius IX to his throne in 1849, and kept him there in the face of a rising tide of Italian nationalism. The French presence made itself felt the next day. "Woke at six by a French Regiment exercising under the window. 25th de la ligne. 6,000 French troops are now in Rome, to keep poor old Pius on his throne."

Florence and her mother had not yet stumbled on Greville's guilty secret, but somebody else had, though they mistook the object of his passion. Writing from Nice some acquaintances called the Ballies had sent to Minnie Way saying that 'Greville was engaged to Miss Osborne.' Perhaps Greville, while dancing attendance on Emily, had laboured to give that impression. At any rate, Eliza and her daughter were alerted and resolved to be vigilant. Visiting the Edwards at the Hotel de Londres, "We found Miss Osborne in the drawing room alone. We asked if any of our trio had been there and she said Mr Smyth had for a few minutes. Now we looked at her as she said this but she was perfectly innocent and unconscious that the Ballies certainly know more than she does...." Emily, at any rate, was behaving with perfect circumspection.

"In the afternoon," wrote Florence, on their second day in Rome, "the Edwards' carriage rolled under the archway. I went down to them with my locks blowing about in the wind. They brought us tickets for tomorrow and with them was an odd looking person, introduced to me as Mr Edwards' brother, Mr Alfred Edwards. He lived abroad and was peculiar-looking, with dark hair and expressive eyes and always wore a white hat...." Mr Alfred tried his charm and expressive eyes on Florence but she soon wearied of his fawning attentions and in the later pages of her narrative he gets a bad notice. The tickets which they brought were for admission to St. Peter's on Palm Sunday, an event eagerly sought by the English fraternity.

"Sunday, 16th March. Had to get up at six; dressed, black with veils on our heads of the same sombre hue. We started at eight for St. Peter's, found the two tribunes with raised seats on either side and managed to get seats on the right hand one. Two men were in each to place more than 300 ladies. One man in purple garments we pitied deeply - a nice, bright little man, pulled in all directions by excited females asking him questions, he seemed to enjoy being made so much of. Our other protector was dressed in dress of olden time - a doublet of dark cloth with the neatest and whitest of ruffs round his neck, gold chains and a ruby and diamond cross on his breast. The tribune was soon quite full and one of the parti-coloured Swiss guards stood at the entrance to prevent anyone else coming in. The Church was lined with French soldiers from the Great Door to the Pontifical Chapel.

"At 9.30 the Pope was carried in, seated on a chair, preceded by the Cardinals in violet. I thought the poor old gentleman must be quite giddy with such a sea of heads under him. Two ladies stood on the benches in front of us, hiding our view. We complained to our faithful little man in purple. He only laughed and said, 'Montez-donc'. So many of us also stood on the benches and were probably in our turn wished at Jericho by others too stiff or too lazy to get up too.

"Pio then dismounted from his chair and, walking up the steps, sat down on his own cosy throne, and all the Cardinals came and bowed to him and kissed his hand, which took a long time. Then hundreds of palms were brought and Pio must have been tired of taking them, blessing them and passing them on. Then, mounting in his chair, he was carried off again and I was by then quite a 'gone coon'. Mamma and I departed and crushing through the crowd, found Pianizza, who we followed to the door; but alas, all the doors were locked and myriads of soldiers said when the Pope had gone round the church we should be let loose. At last the doors were opened and we again breathed that inestimable blessing - fresh air! Pianizza found us a carriage and we returned home; heard cannons booming from St. Angelo. When Gandolfi came up he said the French minister had received a telegram in St. Peter's announcing the birth of the Prince Imperial.* Pio Nono, of course, was invited to stand Godfather and that evening there were grand illuminations at the French Embassy."

Florence, like her mother in Paris in 1824-5, was developing quite a thirst for the grand occasions of the Roman Church, although her Protestant scruples would not allow her to admit it.

"Wednesday, March 19th. We went again to St. Peter's where they said the Pope was coming to pray before the tomb of the saint. Three hours did we wait, and still the Pope came not and, what is more, had not the slightest intention of coming, being very comfortable in the Sistine Chapel blessing candles and listening to the Miserere.

"Thursday, 20th. To St. Peter's again with Mr Jeans and Greville. Stood outside to see the Pope give the benediction from a window. Then upstairs to see the pilgrims have their dinner attended by Pio, who before had washed their feet...."

The next day was Good Friday, but there was some confusion at the English Church about the time of the service. "We arrived in the Litany; Greville at the epistle; and others at the sermon.... the Edwards were not there, having forgotten all about it. Being reminded, they went to St. Peter's! Miss Osborne forgot her veil; a kind monk obligingly volunteered to lend her some black lace and did so."

That evening Richard Orlebar carried on so much about seeing the Colosseum by moonlight that they went off to visit it, "....the moon having, of course, retreated hopelessly behind clouds," added Florence, unromantically, but they found there George Edwards and his brother in his white hat, but no Emily.

* Only son of Napoleon III and the Empress Eugenie.

Greville Smyth & Richard Orlebar in Rome

Easter Saturday, while Eliza and Florence went sightseeing (Villa Borghese, where "....I fell desperately in love with Bernini's exquisite statue of David taking aim with his sling stone"), Greville, Richard and Captain Stavely went riding in the Campagna where they met Pio Nono out airing, escorted by a troop of the Guardia Nobile who made them dismount, "....while His Holiness passed"; he put up two fat fingers to bless them.

Easter Sunday. Florence wanted another look at the fat fingers and drove off early with Mamma to St. Peter's. "The tribunes were crammed; we had to stand for an age till a kind old lady made her daughter go up higher and so Mamma got room to sit. This good example induced a young lady by me to stand, and give me her seat for a long time. So we managed very well - often standing on the seats. The Pope came in at half past nine, and then High Mass which lasted till 11, and then he had the sacrament which (I believe) was first tasted to prevent Pio being poisoned. Then all had to kneel down: I was watching, perched on a seat, but the chamberlain looked so awfully cross, and made such faces at me, I got down.... Then came that splendid burst of silver trumpets which cannot be forgotten.

"We then, with many others, attempted to get to the door, a mob of pickpockets outside made a rush when we began to come out, and we were fearfully squeezed and pushed and Mamma had her pocket picked...."

They dined on hard lamb that evening "....probably killed yesterday. The Pope also had lamb for dinner; he blessed it on Feb 13, it had been fattened up since and killed yesterday for his Easter Sunday's dinner."

Florence's curiosity about such matters extended to holy places. She scampered down the dark narrow steps to see St. Peter's prison, "...but Mamma gave up at the second flight and returned to the light of day. I descended bravely," she went on, "and found that dismal and unhappy hole filled with about 20 French soldiers who appeared to take the deepest interest in the iron bars St. Peter was tied to, and the well which sprang up miraculously for him to baptise his jailers...."

The Scala Santa was also visited, "....which amused us extremely.... the stairs are said to have been brought from the house of Pontius Pilate; they consist of 28 steps, only allowed to be ascended by the penitents on their knees.... 9 years indulgence is granted for each step. A great many old men were scrambling up them on their knees, saying a prayer for each step; one beggar who began last beat them all, to our great amusement." She was even more intrigued to hear from Spurway that evening that "....she and some ladies' maids have actually been scrambling up the Scala Santa on their knees - giggling all the way!"

Gandolfi was also stirring things up: a group of Russian visitors to the Quirinale stepped back deferentially when the British arrived - the Crimean War was not yet officially concluded - but the Italian, in Florence's words, "....**cuttingly** remarked aloud in French 'The English have given the Russians cause to speak bitterly of them', which produced no little indignation from the Russians".

On Tuesday, 25th, the Edwards' crowd set off for Naples, and Greville and Co., who had been their devoted companions, were left high and dry. Eliza gathered up 'the trio' as Florence called them, and there were some outings: to the Quirinale gardens, "....certainly Pio has nothing to complain of," writes Florence, caustically, and to the Rome races. "....started for the Cechino at 10, arriving there much too early. The Downs just like Brighton, only the Sabine hills in the distance and the Apennines covered with snow. The company was quite Ascot-like: beautifully dressed, the princes and princesses came out strong. Nearly all the horses had English names. I won a pair of gloves; poor dear 'Bobby' fell at the first fence and 'Fox' at the next."

Attempts to visit the Palace of the Caesars were less successful, "....the man refused to admit us because the nuns and monks were having a picnic, or what Gandolfi calls a Bacchanal!" Two subsequent visits were met by the same refusal and for the same reason, to the intense disgust of the English ladies and secret amusement of Gandolfi, who evidently rather enjoyed shocking them. When the time came to continue the journey to Naples, it was the ladies' turn to laugh at his expense.

"Poor Gandolfi is in great trouble about his passport, which they will not give him because there is some refugee of the same name going about, who ought to be taken up. Three times the poor old man has been after it...."

At last the passports were ready and on 4th April our intrepid travellers were moving south again. At Albano, where they spent a night, "We had to walk down a **filthy** street, and up **filthy** steps with 50 **very** dirty children clawing one...." The next day they crossed the border and spent the night at Gaeta and were mystified to read in the visitors book at the Hotel Villa Cicerone the names of the Edwards, under which someone had pencilled in a message, evidently intended for Greville: "How's the young hussar?"

At the Hotel Vittoria, Naples, Eliza and Florence, after bursting unannounced into three drawing rooms on three floors, eventually found Emily and Miss Osborne, but Greville was not with them, only the peculiar Mr Alfred, who bored them stiff with his pompous mannerisms.

Eliza soon had 'the trio' brought to heel, and the five of them set out one fine morning in an open carriage to view the ruins of Herculaneum, but the rain came on and they went to look over the King's palace at Portici instead. The king was the notorious Ferdinand II, nicknamed 'Bomba' from his habit of shelling his unruly subjects into submission. The state of his political prisons, where Italian patriots spent years chained to common criminals, was well known to the English public at this time, owing to the revelations of Mr Gladstone who, in 1850, had a holiday in Italy for the sake of his daughter's health. The publication of his famous 'Letters to Lord Aberdeen' in which Ferdinand's regime was described as "the negation of God erected into a system of Government", evidently did not deter upper class English visitors to his territories. Of the lonely road through the Pontine Marshes, which had a fearful reputation for highway robbery, Florence said, "....most people are terribly afraid of brigands and try to keep 2 or 3 carriages together and only travel in broad daylight, but we saw none and went on in the dark...."

One thing to be thankful for in the Kingdom of Naples was the absence of beggars. "They were all locked up that the King might be able to say and remark to the Grand Duke of Tuscany, who was on a visit, that he had not a beggar in his dominions."

Mr & Mrs Gladstone, whom the Uptons had bumped into in the Villa Borghese, Rome, would probably have exploded with moral indignation on that as well, but Florence's journal has nothing to say on that extraordinary gentleman and his wife.

Herculaneum was done in due course, as was Pompeii and Vesuvius. Fire had been seen spurting out one evening by Mr Jeans, and they had all sallied forth (Mamma excepted) and climbed on a wall to get a better look; but it wasn't much, and next day they resolved to take a closer look.

On the 13th April two carriages set out: the Edwards and party in one; Eliza, Florence and 'the trio' in the other. At the Hermitage the ladies went in, as Florence puts it, "....in search of a room to arrange our dresses for the Donkey part of the expedition. We entered a room and found there the recluse himself; he understood neither French nor English.

In despair Mamma asked him 'Avete una Donna?'* which shocked him so much that he roused himself and indignantly pointed out the head of the stairs and the way down, evidently considering our behaviour neither proper nor pretty."

Eventually a room was found and the necessary adjustments made to their nether garments and, leaving Mamma, they set off over lava-strewn slopes for another mile and a half. At the foot of the cone they dismounted and were hoisted onto chairs, each carried by three men, "....all quarrelling and talking in their own language". The steep ascent over the ashes was too much for George Edwards who became giddy and demanded to be taken back.

The chair-bearers wouldn't hear of it as they were afraid they wouldn't be paid; but Florence managed to set their fears at rest, and old George, so thankful to be on his feet again "....that he distributed the contents of his brandy bottle between them far too freely...."

"We reached the top in about an hour," relates Florence. "Greville had walked up and we found him at the edge of the crater, enveloped in sulphurous smoke. Oh! What a fearful place it was to look down - awful rumblings and rattlings were going on beneath and the smell of the sulphur stifling...."

At this point Emily refused to go any further and, with Mr Alfred in his white hat, withdrew to a more sheltered spot. "Greville, Miss Osborne, Mr Orlebar and I were the only adventurous ones, and we went on to another horrible crater with a precipice on both sides...."

* "Is there a woman here?" - presumably to assist the ladies arrange their dresses.

So, back to the Hermitage - Florence falling off her donkey on the way down "....and had to be picked up! No damage done" - where Gandolfi had prepared "some exquisite lemonade". George Edwards, having no doubt replenished his brandy bottle, drove his party back to Rome while Eliza, Florence and "the two boys" went on to Sorrento and Amalfi, leaving Mr Jeans to inspect Vesuvius at a safe distance through his spyglass. They found him,on their return to Naples, in his usual state of suspended animation: "....in the evening," wrote Florence, "went out to inspect Vesuvius, Mr Jeans having promised us an eruption....but that mountain in a perfectly quiet and dark mood, we returned and went to bed".

They set off for Rome the next day for another round of sightseeing. Being St. Mark's Day (25th April) our tourists caught a glimpse of "....the holy relics, among them the Pope's cap, St. Mark's skull and bones in a glass case, also St. Bridget's and the hair shirt worn by that lady...." The Palace of the Caesars was visited and "....wonderful to say, there was no Bacchanal". At the table d'hote, Florence and her mother made the acquaintance of Mlle. Schimmelpeninck-Vanderoye, a Dutch lady, and a fat American captain who, "with his officers, always sits opposite us", and who evidently dared their chief to present Florence with a rose and rose bud, carefully pinned with paper. "'Please will you take this rose,' he drawled with a bland smile, the other officers **smirking** opposite; I felt such a fool!" wrote Florence.

They left Rome early next morning and, drawn by five horses and two grey Tuscan oxen, climbed high into the hills. Florence jumped down to gather flowers and was charmed by the peasants, celebrating a fiesta by bowling great cheeses along the road. At Perugia George Edwards fell out with his courier, Pianizza, who was left there and had to struggle on alone to Florence in a farm cart. In Florence, Greville was all for dragging his mother and sister off to see the monastery of Vallombrosa but they, having already requested to see the cloister of Santa Maria Novella to look at the frescos, "....the monks replied that if we did so, being women, the cloisters would have to be anointed with oil and swept, and have incense burnt in them.... we really had had enough of monasteries and monks".

They bumped again into the Mills family, last seen at Nice, and Eliza did her best to interest Greville in Miss Mills, "....but," wrote his sister, "instead of admiring her he audaciously compared her to a red apple".

Mr Alfred proposed a good walk to Fiesole, but Eliza and Florence declined and went to the Uffizi instead, for it was their last day and an early start was projected next morning. "Mr Alfred says he shall come and see us start at 6 - **very** unlikely!" wrote Florence. Tuesday, 6th: "Called at the frightful hour of half past four! Started at 6 precisely, no sign of the faithless Mr Alfred!" They didn't see him again until Venice, when he came to the foot of the stairs of the hotel where they were staying, "....he never goes any nearer", said Florence meaningfully. "He said he had really come to see us off at Florence, but we went so punctually at 6 that he had only seen the departing carriage."

The journey over the Apennines, now accomplished in an hour or two by train, in 1856 took twelve hours. The carriage climbed tediously into the clouds "....the ground covered with brilliant snow, the warm valleys below a pleasant change," wrote Florence.

They spent two nights in Bologna. "The Palace of the Archbishop is very handsome.... from the garden of which is a lovely view of Bologna, on whose sausages we had breakfasted...." Then off again to Ferrara and the frontier of the Austrian Empire. At that time this vast Germanic institution flooded over the Alps and embraced most of North Italy, including Milan and Venice. The Austrian authorities were nervous, for their Italian subjects were seething with discontent and periodically erupted into wild revolution. "The passports were examined so often.... we had to wait a long time for the officer had just gone to his dinner and said he could not sign it until the completion of that meal at two o'clock. Brave Gandolfi followed him, however, to the cafe and induced him to sign it, and we went on...."

There was no bridge over the Po in those days and carriages crossed on a ferry called a 'flying bridge', "....but its wings must have been very stiff for we were a long time going over," observed Florence. "A jolly, fat little officer crossed at the same time, who happened to be the head of the Austrian Dogana the other side; to this little man Gandolfi made himself so agreeable that he ran up the bank when we landed and told his men only to take down one box, and that whichever we liked..."

So on to Padua and Venice, but it was, when they arrived, "a miserable afternoon; everything looked wretched, even the graceful, gliding gondolas we thought looked like great coffins on boats". But next day was better: "Everything looked delightful", and the afternoon was spent on the Grand Canal in an open gondola. "Passing the railway, saw a gentleman violently waving his handkerchief... which gentleman proved on nearer inspection to be Mr Edwards". Without a courier, the Edwards party were already in difficulties and Florence could afford to be patronising. "We have rooms for you at the Hotel de Ville," she called out across the water.

"After dinner we repaired to the Piazza St. Marco where the Austrian band was playing" - no doubt voluptuous Viennese music, a subtle way of fostering indolence and curbing the rebellious impulses of the Venetians. Our English visitors were also infected by the general torpor, "....down the Grand Canal, passed the Edwards floating along like ourselves in the 'dolce fa niente'* fashion of lazy Venice," wrote Florence of the next day's events.

There were, of course, visits to the Doge's Palace and St. Mark's Cathedral, the sirocco permitting, for even then the lagoon was in the habit of slopping over the square, and to the glassworks at Murano where "....we saw them making beads for savages".

A thoroughly memorable trip was with Greville and Richard Orlebar to the island convent of the Armenian brothers, "....who were feeding some pretty yellow cats. A brother showed us the garden, library, cloisters etc. and church. Coming home fell in with a 'fiesta', the Austrian band and gondoliers taking it in turn to play and sing all down the Canale Grande; numbers of gondolas and coloured lamps.... it was so pretty...."

Apart from Mr Jeans, who was infatuated with Miss Osborne, the whole party was becoming increasingly bored with the Edwards, though of course Greville managed to conceal his true feelings. Wherever they went the Edwards seemed to be there, flaunting their wealth in a rather vulgar fashion. "....went to Boro the sculptors after dinner with Mamma, Greville, etc.," wrote Florence. "Boro is doing a head of Diana for Mr Alfred and has begun one of Emily...."

"That evening to the opera to see 'The Last Days of Suli'; very pretty, sweet little theatre; the Edwards had a box next to ours, but as they did not go the servants filled it, and Mr Alfred came into ours...." One suspects that Emily was having diplomatic vapours and Mr Alfred was getting the cold shoulder.

Florence's exasperation was mounting. "Went out with Greville and Mr Orlebar to choose something for Mamma's birthday, and settled at last upon a ring. Coming out met Mr Edwards, so asked his opinion of it. What must he do but at dinner ask Mamma what she thought of her ring - to her great astonishment. Of course, she was not to know anything about it till Tuesday, but then we had not told him that...."

On Sunday, Mr Jeans actually induced Miss Osborne into the same gondola for the concert on the Grand Canal. Florence remarked: "Saw two very pretty Russian girls - the rival beauties at Venice with Emily and Miss Osborne." But the dreamy days were passing and the party was breaking up.

* 'dolce fa niente' = sweetly doing nothing.

Monday, 19th, the Edwards left. "Emotion of Mr Jeans at breakfast!!" writes Florence. Their last event in Venice was the Fete of Corpus Christi on Thursday, 22nd May. "Went to the Square of St. Mark to see the procession, which issued from the Cathedral door at 10 precisely. We had very good seats: monks, priests, boys, elderly gentlemen, images, soldiers and tallow candles passed before us. An elderly gentleman in gay attire came up to Greville, I thought to shake hands, but it was to desire us all to kneel down as everyone else did.... however, I found the stone much too cold and soon got up again.... in the evening our last gondola but one - alas!"

The next day they left Venice: "The master of the house brought us up two lovely bouquets...." and they returned to Padua. Eliza and Mr Jeans did the Church of St. Justina and the others followed, protesting at the intense heat, and when "....threatened with the Cathedral, we three sat on the first seats that presented themselves...and steadfastly refused to go there.... Gandolfi left off his wig for the first time - he says it is too hot to wear it - he looks like a great, bald doll!"

Actually, Florence was hanging on to those last precious moments with Greville and Richard Orlebar, for the following day they set off for Treviso: "We shall not meet them again for ages, and shall miss them **extremely.**"

Although letters from Fanny at Ashton Court had been cheerful (one had been received at Naples "telling us of Jack....and pretty Guess Who?"), Eliza felt the time was approaching for a return. Uncle Arthur had also written, mailing cheques for their expenses and doubtless filling in with bits of news about the estate, the news and the weather.

On 21st April he wrote in his Day Book: "Consulted Mr Dowding at Bath on the possibility of a conservative candidate being returned for Bath at the next election. Mr Dowding did not think it possible after Mr Wateley's late defeat." With Greville's majority looming, Arthur Way was looking about for alternative diversion and the idea of his standing for Parliament had already entered his head.

30th April: "Discharged C. Phelps from Ashton Court gardens for insolence." 29th May: "This day was kept as a day of General Rejoycing throughout the Kingdom to celebrate the peace with Russia. I was in Bath with Mrs Way; the shops were closed, the weather bad and it seemed like a very dull Sunday...."

Greville and his companions did not return home until November. His Emily had long since been carried off to Redland Court where in the same month she gave birth to a son: he was given the name Greville. No doubts have ever been expressed about the paternity of Greville Edwards, but the choice of the name made devastatingly public an affair which could be hushed up no longer.

Greville had dallied on the Continent. The conclusion of the war with Russia had opened the door to exciting possibilities. The young and adventurous who had the means were now heading for Sebastapol to see the ruins of the Redan and Malakoff and to stroll over the battlefields of Balaclava and Inkerman, still strewn with cannon balls. Greville evidently had similar thoughts but Uncle Arthur, who for a few months longer still had his hands on the purse strings, would have to approve.

On 2nd July he wrote to Mr Jeans, "....to stop a visit to the Crimea," and Greville and his friends had to think again. No doubt Alpine torrents soon provided other opportunities for masculine and aristocratic pursuits, and the time passed quickly enough until the approaching coming of age.

We return to Florence's journal for the final stages of the Grand Tour. Deprived of male companionship, she entered wholeheartedly into the social chitchat of the table d'hôte, confiding her amusing and often penetrating observations to Mamma and the journal.

"At Verona we saw at the station a dear little French lady, about 18, and her husband - a cross, disagreeable-looking old man of 60. We had breakfasted and dined with them so often at Venice and the old wretch used to peep into the room of a morning in his dressing gown to see who was there before he would let her come in. I suppose he was jealous. Gandolfi says they are Carlists* and went to Venice to see the Duc de Bordeaux....

They were also very conscious of "....the Austrian Governor who sits at the head of the table with some other officers, all in uniform" - undoubtedly the hated, white-coated Tedeschi, whose strangle hold on North Italy was soon to be shattered, but Florence's sentiments were directed elswhere. "....who should be seated opposite but those 4 everlasting Miss Crossfields we got so **tired** of at Venice. We had decided they were American, but Gandolfi says they come from Liverpool...."

Monday, 26th: "Left Verona at 10; the Miss Crossfields, of course, left too...." and, horrible to relate, when dining at the Hotel de la Ville at Milan, they noticed the Miss Crossfields "....on the other side of the court, eating theirs...."

How they managed to shake off the unwanted attentions of Mr Alfred Edwards was cavalier to say the least, but as George and Emily had now returned home they were no longer obliged to put up with him. "In the evening (of their arrival in Milan) Mr Alfred came in but we were too tired to talk to him which, he perceiving, asked if he might come again in the morning; thankful to go to bed, we said 'Yes'. Next day he sent up to know if he might pay the promised visit. Mamma was unpacking in her room and I had forgotten all about it, so I told Gandolfi to explain that we were very busy. He went off that evening and we saw him no more."

* Supporters of Dom Carlos, pretender to the Spanish throne.

Milan in 1856 was bristling with Austrian troops, for her liberation, long dreamed of by the Milanese, was only three years away. "In the evening to the gay Corso, crowded with carriages, pretty dresses, gay uniforms, and two 4-in-hands belonging to the Hungarian cavalry...." wrote Florence. At the Arena where, going upstairs to a large room which had once been a cafe, they found it was now "....a kind of barrack room, and fitted with funny little beds all round the room, belonging to the Austrian soldiers". Two of them were in the room, "not in bed," she hastily added. Even the convent in whose refectory they saw 'The Last Supper' was now a barrack, and as for Leonardo's masterpiece, "....it is peeling off the walls and none of its original colour left".

At Como they crossed the lake by steamer and the extraordinary company they found at the table d'hote in the Hotel Genazzini, Bellagio, occupies several pages in Florence's journal.

"A merry old lady sat next to Mamma and talked without ceasing - her name is Mrs Payne; then there was an ugly lady in a white jacket, very badly made - her name is Miss Vance; then there was another maiden lady, Miss Williams, and another - very fat indeed - Miss Moreland, who had been to Egypt and Constantinople and Smyrna and I don't know where. Then there was Mr Rendle-Strong who was an American artist I think - long-haired, glaring-eyed and clever looking, and his wife - a nice, gentle little woman - they have a two year old called Mimmi. Last, but not least, there was the great Mr Grote, who wrote a history of Greece, and his wife." Florence was not to know it but 'great Mr Grote's' son Andrew later married her cousin Maria Way (Emily's sister). "The three maiden ladies are travelling with Mrs Payne. Mrs Payne and Miss Vance were very anxious to know what we were drinking, which was Muscat, so we gave them some...."

Florence and her mother were mystified by the sound of little bells which "....kept sounding over the lake. We thought thoy must be distant sheep bells, but find they are attached to the fishing nets, so when a fish gets into the net his struggles ring his little death knell and he is caught".

The next day they went across the lake to the Villa Semecina, "....belonging to the Princess Charlotte of Prussia, who is two years old and was having her hair combed at a window and kissed her hand affectionately to us in the garden".

The chatty Mrs Payne came to their room in the evening and told them all about her affairs, "....she had a son and daughter gone on a 'spree' to Constantinople and she had not heard from them for 6 weeks - **would** we be kind onough to enquire for her letters at Milan and bring them to her at Geneva?" She was back again next morning, "....bringing the 'Heiress of Houghton' for our edification, so we gave her 'Star Chamber' in exchange".

Back in Milan ("the Corso was gayer than ever: quite brilliant; a lady and gentleman bowed....") Florence and Gandolfi collected two letters for

Mrs Payne at the Poste Restante. But when, some days later, they enquired for Mrs Payne in Geneva, there was no sign of her, and the hotels had no knowledge of a lady of that name. Fortunately, while driving beside the Rhone one day they met Mr Rendle-Strong, the long-haired American artist. "We stopped the carriage and sent for the little man and asked him if he knew anything of Mrs Payne, for we still have her letters. He would be most happy to give Madame any information. He thought **Miss** Payne was to be found riding over the Tete Noir on a mule and might be expected at the Hotel de la Couronne in a few days. His wife passed and bowed and looked much amused." The lady in question eventually arrived and the letters were delivered, but she was now so busy spinning yarns to other travellers that she scarcely noticed Florence and her mother.

Before leaving Italy they visited Lake Maggiore and Isola Bella. "Splendid Palace and most enchanted island. Four priests went over it with us and listened to Gandolfi's remarks and explanations with most attentive admiration." They continued to the Simplon Pass: "Mamma was in a terrible fright owing to the eccentric conduct of the post-boy - he would not sit on his saddle like a Christian boy, but persisted in sitting on his Imperial and sliding about, the reins quite loose and in this dégagé manner driving four horses down the most fearful steep pitches and round the most abrupt corners...."

They slept at Sion, "....the conduct of the waiter there, to say the least, annoying; it was between 9 and 10; we were very tired; he took us up two stories and into so many rooms and talked about the view as if it mattered about the view - it was then quite dark and we were going on early next morning. Woke at 5 - overwhelmed with a feeling of Black Beetles, but could not find any. Mamma had seen two huge ones walking about the room the night before, with a cockroach!"

Switzerland. They spent three days at Vevey on Lake Geneva: "A nice, large, very clean and most comfortable house," wrote Florence. Excursions were made to Chillon, of course, to see "....the horrid oubliette and the black beam from which criminals were hung, and the rocky den in which the poor wretches passed their last night. Saw the prisoners of the present day, very different from being chained to a rock. They were playing at bowls in the garden; one had a mock croquet-green velvet cap on!"

At the table d'hote, Florence sat next to "....a handsome old lady - Miss Fane, who never speaks, but she told her maid who told Spurway, who told me in the evening, that she deeply regretted not being able to talk to me but is so very deaf that she does not like to". Also at the table d'hote was "....a very pretty boy" whom they later discovered to be the only son of Sir Michael Seymour, "....so his tutor informed Mamma under his breath. When the child asked for a spoon in English, the tutor told him to ask in

French, so he said a 'couller' which made us laugh...." ('Cuiller' = French for spoon).

They got into conversation with the tutor who was a Mr Ridley and had been curate at Devonport and knew James Furneaux. James Furneaux of Swilly, also a clergyman, was one of Greville's Oxford friends and a frequent visitor to Ashton Court.* He was a great favourite of the family on account of his irrepressible high spirits and comical stories, most of them directed at himself. He had written a little book of poems which he had presented to Eliza. One of them, entitled 'The Severed Heart', was a long-standing family joke and was evidently quite a hit elsewhere, for Mr Ridley had heard of it. He was astounded to hear Florence recite the verses by heart and begged to be allowed to see the whole written out:

"....And Oh! if you should meet the Severed Heart
Which once I deemed all mine
Never thought that I could lean upon too hardly
Till its patience snapped beneath my trying weight like a frail reed...."

Pretty bad stuff and lots of it; the joke was that no one ever seems to have discovered whose was 'the severed heart'. Nonetheless, James Furneaux and his antics seem to have been the principal topic of conversation until the steamer carried Florence and Eliza across the lake, while Mr Ridley and his charge watched and "waved their hats until we were out of sight".

At Geneva they walked about the town in search of a brown hat "....as my face is gradually becoming the colour of a dark brown berry," wrote Florence. A note of exasperation begins at this stage to enter her journal. A colonel, who is never mentioned by name, had begun to take an interest in Eliza, and forced his attentions on them all the way across Switzerland and back.

"Mamma's friend, Colonel ...., came in while we were at chicken," wrote Florence in Geneva. "Tiresome man; arriving with him a gentleman and a gaily dressed lady who was very proud of her hands. Certainly they were the prettiest things she had, except for the rings on them.... so we had to wait till they had the soup, fish and meat etc....", and a little later: "Mamma's horrid old colonel" sat next to her at dinner and talked across her to Eliza through the whole meal and then afterwards he "....would walk up and down the Colonnade with us till I was quite tired".

Gandolfi was also becoming rather tedious. Apparently he had been in Geneva many years before with Sir Humphrey Davy who 'had died in his arms'. They went to see his grave in the cemetery. "Gandolfi was **very** much affected at the remembrance; the grave was unkempt and uncared for;

* Later Rector of Lower Heyford, Oxon., and Fellow of Corpus Christi College, Oxford.

the name was almost obliterated. Gandolfi said he had often told Lady Davy the state it was in...." Next day he "....talked and explained a great deal (too much)" at the model of Mt. Blanc they went to look at in the garden, "....and was much admired by everyone except Mamma and myself". At Thun "....he asked if we were going to Interlaken tomorrow and, if so, he should not be able (nasty old man) to take a good dose of medicine, as he felt very bad - indeed bilious! So rather than he should suffer inconvenience when physic was so much needed, we told him we would delay Interlaken until Saturday."

The visit was worth the delay, "....drove through the lovely valley of Lauterbrunnen to the Staubbach cascade. Splendid scenery - coming back passed Mr Forbes, who used to preach so beautifully at Venice, lounging about a lane in a straw hat: he has the English church there."

Florence is at her best recording the droll, banal and ludicrous ways of her fellow travellers. At Berne she is much more amusing about "the perambulations of an elderly gentleman in a red dressing-gown opposite" than the great mechanical clock or the four live bears, and there is a touch of poetry in their last evening at Vevey where "....the moon was playing on the lake" and "....as the darkness came on, the gentlemen in the garden, emboldened by it, began to sing".

On the 25th July they came at last to Basle, crossed the frontier into France, and stayed at the Hotel de la Ville, where they entrusted the Chef of the Stables "....a particularly honest looking man" with the task of selling "....our dear comfortable carriage" which had accompanied them all the way from Nice.

En route

From Basle they returned to Paris by train, breaking the journey at Nancy. Another visitor broke his journey at Nancy the same night. "While we were at the table d'hoté," related Florence, "a handsome carriage drove under the archway. 'Would he dine at the table d'hote?' we asked, at which everybody laughed except ourselves, who did not understand the joke. Then came six more carriages and 13 splendid horses, and we found they belonged to the Emperor, who was going somewhere for Baths. I asked if he were ill, and the chambermaid replied she thought so, then to the stableyard to admire and criticise his carriages, as did all the good people of Nancy...."

No, the Emperor Napoleon III was not ill. Every year he indulged himself with a week or two at Plombieres, a spa in the Vosges, to get away from Eugenie, and the more easily to carry on his affair with the Duchess of Castiglione - a dazzling Italian beauty dangled before him, for largely political motives, by Cavour, the astute Prime Minister of Sardinia. At Plombieres, a year later, Cavour himself visited Napoleon III and there they contrived the great Italian War of Liberation which was, in 1859, to overturn the Italy that Florence, Eliza and Greville had come to know and love.

In the autumn of 1856 there was an atmosphere of mounting expectancy and excitement at Ashton Court. On the 15th November, Arthur Way wrote in his Day Book: "Gave orders to Dunning to prepare for festivities - Mr Smyth's coming of age". The wine cellars at Ashton Court were entirely rebuilt and restocked, and "....a step-piece coach with circular glass front, and a wagonette shooting carriage, were purchased from Messrs Edwards & Chamberlayne, Oxford Street".

On the 3rd November, Eliza and Florence went to Claridges for a few days for Florence to be bridesmaid to her friend Louisa Carew. She was married at St. George's, Hanover Square, to Sir Charles Pigott, "....who gave us all pretty presents," but Eliza lost her watch and Florence was totally unprepared for the new contrivance that had suddenly burst upon the fashionable world from Paris. "We had long dresses of white silk with pearl trimmings, and rather wide, swansdown edges, but no one had sent me a crinoline (that form of petticoat was just beginning to be universal) and I had none, so when I arrived at the house in Grosvenor Street to join the wedding party and go with them, I looked limp indeed. But kind Annie Maxwell, Louisa's most useful cousin, took me upstairs and put one on me so that I looked quite correct."

Florence's own marriage was being contemplated and that autumn she was passed around the great households, the ritual prescribed by high society for bringing the right young people together.

"One evening we went on an immensely long drive to a ball at Badminton, the Duke of Beaufort's. I do not remember anything particular about it, except some life-size pictures of cattle and horses in a passage. My mother could not bear to dance round dances, so I had to sit them out and, deeply as I respected her for all the plans for my good, I think the sitting out was a mistake. My favourite sitting out partner at the balls at that time was Mr Rogers, whose conversation had charms for me. Minnie and I went to the East Mendip Ball again that year, dressed as shepherdesses in white wigs with powdered hair, tiny hats and laced-up pink and blue and white skirts, and we joined a fancy quadrille. I had for my partner a Captain Cox, which I thought a most tiresome arrangement, for I should have preferred Mr Rogers. At one of the balls I met my dear future husband, Clement Cottrell-Dormer...."

19th November, Arthur Way wrote: "My dear wife taken ill and a little boy born to us at 11.30 p.m." He was christened Claude.

28th November. "Snow falling. Dear Greville returned to Ashton from his foreign travels, looking very well." It had been intended to ring the church bells to celebrate the event, but someone mistook his carriage and a joyful peal rang out the previous evening as Arthur returned from the audit of the Coalpit Heath Colliery accounts at the White Lion in Bristol.

Throughout December the preparations gathered momentum. Mr Niblett of the White Lion was engaged to dine 150 tenants at 6d a head; a dinner was ordered for the paupers at Bedminster Union; and there were long consultations with Eliza about a grand ball at Ashton Court.

"Heard about the bombardment of Canton," wrote Arthur Way on the 29th December 1856. It was the last but one entry in his Day Book, for two days later his nephew, Greville, celebrated his majority.

The Coming of Age

It was a great day for the House of Upton when, on 2nd January 1857, Greville Smyth celebrated his coming of age. The tenantry, marshalled by Uncle Arthur, laid on a week of rejoicing, which began with a salute of twenty-one guns fired at the stroke of midnight. This was followed by the pealing of bells from Long Ashton church. The gun salutes and bell-ringing continued at intervals through-out the day, and the towers and spires of St. Mary Redcliffe, St. Stephen's on the Quay, Christ Church, St. Nicholas, St. Mark, and half-a-dozen other city churches joined in jubilant discord.

The road to Ashton was spanned with triumphal arches, decked out in evergreens, flowers, flags and slogans. The first one, just outside Ashton Gate, bridged the highway between the Star Tavern and the hauling-way to Gummer's Colliery. The second one crossed the road near the Town Gate into the park, and was composed of laurels and ivy, on a framework of firs and larches, and bearing an inscription in silver, blue and crimson 'WELCOME TO THE HOME OF THY ANCESTORS'. At the Angel Inn was a third arch which proclaimed 'LONG LIFE TO HIM', and above the trees of the park the parapets of Somerset's longest house sported the St. George's ensign and "....flags of some score of friendly nations". The Illustrated London News reports that "The road from the Angel at Ashton to Redcliffe Hill exhibited an unbroken line of sight-seers", no doubt attracted by the promise of greater spectacles to come.

At ten in the morning the entire tenantry assembled at the Angel Inn and, attended by Hinton's Clifton Band, entered the park by the Lower Lodge Gate, and streamed in a great crowd to the west front. Greville appeared at the door, surrounded by his family and a considerable number of guests. A barrel was rolled up of "....strong beer specially made for the occasion", and he was hoisted upon it. Speeches were made and an address was handed to him, written on vellum, with an ivory mount:

> "We cannot permit the day on which, by attaining your majority, you enter into possession of one of the largest estates in the county, to pass over without tendering to you our warmest congratulations, and earnest wishes that you may live long to enjoy those riches with which it has pleased the Almighty to entrust you...."

So ran the pious sentiments, followed by the usual fulsome wishes for his happiness and hopes that he would be a "kind and considerate landlord", while the tenants pledged themselves in return "that nothing shall be wanting on our part to render our connection mutually beneficial". It was signed by 168 tenants and managers of the Bedminster Coal Company in neat columns - except in the last column where George Mathews, a farmer, made such a mess of his signature that it overflowed into the next two lines.

The ale was dispensed, the tenants drank the health of Mr Smyth and he drank a bumper to theirs. There was applause and the moment was recorded for posterity by an artist from the Illustrated London News who sketched the scene, and in due course an engraving appeared showing the west front looking much as it does today (reproduced at the beginning of this chapter.)

The procession then re-formed and proceeded to the tump on Ashton Hill for the purpose of partaking of the 'Tenants' Dinner', which was supplied by Mr F. E. Allen of the Angel Inn, in a spacious marquee erected for the purpose. Lifted into an open cart the young squire, landlord of more than 300 farmers, owner of 13,532,000 acres, with an annual income of £27,087*, the second wealthiest man in the county, was carried up to that vantage point from which he could say that everything, except the church and the glebe, belonged to him.

* Return of the owners of land, 1879:

1.	Viscount Portman	24,170,000 acres	£35,257
2.	Sir T. D. Acland	16,319,000 acres	£10,680
3.	Sir Greville Smyth	13,532,000 acres	£27,087

These figures are for their Somerset estates only.

"After the removal of the cloth," continues our reporter, "the chairman (Mr Shattock) gave the usual loyal and patriotic toasts which were drunk with honours. He then proposed the toast of the evening - their young landlord's good health (cheers) in the enjoyment of all happiness himself, and in the hearts of a prosperous and contented tenantry (cheers). He would give 'The health of Mr Smyth of Ashton Court'. The toast was received with great cheering, which was renewed upon a farmer with stentorian lungs calling out 'Long life and a good wife to him'.

There were further toasts to Mr Arthur Way, Mrs Upton and her family, and the chairman; after which 250 farmers, somewhat unsteady in the gaiters, joined their wives and children on the tump for the lighting of the bonfire. This was one of the most prodigious size ever seen. It measured 40 feet in height, was 111 feet in circumference, and was composed of 60 loads of wood, 1,500 bundles of faggots, 10 tons of coal, 50 tar barrels, and several waggon loads of other inflammable materials." No such blaze had been seen in the neighbourhood since July, 1588, when a former tenant had turned out to see the Armada beacons.

At 9 o'clock, Professor Burn, a distinguished pyrotechnist from the Zoological Gardens (his name was a euphemism, no doubt!) entertained an enormous crowd to a display of fireworks. The artist from the Illustrated London News was unable to do justice to it, but from the 'Official Programme of Rejoicings' we can imagine what sort of effect was produced, for example, by:

"ITEM 5: A CURIOUS TURNING PIECE, called Jim Crowe, or American Turnabout, with a wide variety of intricate changes, representing Revolving Fountains, Cascades etc., and concluding with a beautiful Palm Tree.

"ITEM 7: A GRAND SET PIECE, representing a large Star, formed of Saxon and five-pointed stars, commencing with a Vertical Wheel, illuminated with Crimson, Green and the beautiful Amethyst flame lately discovered by PROFESSOR BURN, and concluding with an extensive Star of Golden Fire, with reports.

"ITEM 9: An elegant BALLOON will ascend.

"ITEM 13: A Grand Aerial Effect of 50 Sky Rockets, completely filling the sky with Crimson light.

"ITEM 14: A Grand Illuminated Design of Bengal Lights, far surpassing the Drummond or Bude Light, which will give any Person in the neighbourhood of Clifton sufficient light to read a newspaper.

"ITEM 21: THE ERUPTION OF MOUNT VESUVIUS, discharging Three Horizontal Wheels, Sky Rockets, Sheels, Maroons, Tourbillions, Green, Crimson and Purple Roman Candles etc., concluding with a Large Mine of Serpents. This Piece is the Grand Finale of Mount Vesuvius, and is justly allowed to be the most intricate turning Piece ever displayed by any other Artist in England.

"ITEM 48: A SPLENDID BALLOON PIECE, an idea that has never in any Country been put into execution, viz: A Splendid Balloon, completely emblazoned in Fireworks, which after burning some as a Fixed Piece, will actually (by means of tremendous Sky Rockets and other Propelling Fireworks) ascend into the atmosphere with all its brilliancy, and when at its greatest altitude discharging an immense quantity of Carmine, Green and Purple Stars, with Rockets, Roman Candles, Jerbs, Mines, etc."

The extravagance of the language betrays something of the showmanship of the period; one only hopes Professor Burn's air rockets lived up to his name and his professional expertise. As for his concluding piece, even if it failed to get off the ground, its description alone is something of an achievement:

"This Magnificent Design, composed expressly for the occasion by PROFESSOR BURN, consisting of 200 Jets of Red, Green and Purple Lancets, with the words:

LONG LIFE TO J. H. G. S. Esq.

surmounted by a Grand Battery of Roman Candles discharging Green, Crimson and Purple Flames, the whole surrounded with fixed jerbs of Brilliant Fires, with loud reports, will conclude with a Grand Battery of Stars of every colour, and a Flight of Shells with 200 Sky Rockets, surpassing anything ever witnessed before in this Country, and the Artist pledges himself not to be surpassed by any pyrotechnist in England."

So, with a bursting of jerbs, jets of Golden Rain, and crimson sky rockets, recurring discharges of artillery, the clanging of church bells, and singing 'God Save the Queen', Greville Smyth came into his majority. It lasted forty-four years and his tenants were not disappointed. They had expressed in their address a wish that their young landlord would "....preside on the Bench, or assist in the legislation of the County, or simply fulfil the many duties of an English Country Gentleman". Although Greville resolutely refused to do any of these things, his reign at the Court was in many respects the most prosperous and memorable of the many regimes that had held sway there.

On a more personal note, the family rejoicing went on all week. That same night a vast company of guests attended a ball in the house. "All the apartments of the Court were brought into requisition," wrote one reporter. "The entrance halls, lobbies and staircases were lined with rare flowering shrubs, and the reception room, supper room, etc. were decorated with great elegance. The music hall was also thrown open, and Mr Frederick Huxtable presided at the great organ, and played with his known skill several fine compositions. The dancing took place in the Library, which Messrs Garraway, Hayes & Co. of the Durdham Down Nurseries, had dressed profusely with wreaths, festoons and ornaments of evergreens and flowers. Quadrilles, waltzes etc. followed each other in rapid succession until one o'clock, at which hour the ball supper was announced. It was provided by Warren of Clifton, and was of a most sumptuous and recherche character. The repast was laid in the great Dining Room, upon a semi-circular, a centre, and two side tables. The health of the youthful host was drunk with enthusiasm, and acknowledged by him. The company returned to the Ballroom and resumed the dance, which was kept up with spirit."

Perhaps never before or since was such an assemblage of notables gathered at Ashton Court. The county gentry predominated: the Duke & Duchess of Beaufort from Badminton; the Eltons from Clevedon Court; the Gore-Langtons from Newton Park; the Methuens from Corsham Court; the Berkeleys of Berkeley Castle; and the list of rank and quality filled a whole column of small print in the local and national press. There were seven Members of Parliament, three Bishops and two Deans!

Greville refuses the Shrievalty, 1857

If this prodigious gathering of notables was supposed to instil in the young John Henry Greville Smyth a true appreciation of his obligations to the community, it did not have the desired effect. Greville, from the start, showed an aversion for public life and, despite high expectations, played no part in local or national politics.

In November 1857, the Bristol City Council, anxious to renew its links with a family that had rendered such service to the city in the 18th Century, and perhaps with an eye to the lavishness of civic entertainment afforded by an income of £40,000 a yèar, appointed Greville Smyth sheriff. The Bristol Mercury (21st November) hinted that "....the subtle incense of venison and turtle rose upon their nostrils in an overpowering degree from the region of Ashton Court", but whatever the reason for their choice Greville had not been consulted beforehand and he categorically refused to serve. The duties of the office were not long, heavy or expensive: a week's attendance on the Judge during the annual Assize, attendance at executions and certain responsibilities in regard to city gaols were all that was expected. The post, in fact, was an honorary one, and in the Bristol Times (14 November) there was a very pointed reference to the fact that ".... a wealthy and intelligent city has paid the highest compliment to one whose large fortune and lineage entitled him to the distinction", and expressed the hope that, "Mr Smyth, who must be sensible of the honour done him.... will recall a refusal which we are satisfied he would regret, were it for a moment misconstrued as any want of respect on his part to those who have paid him a marked compliment".

Greville's refusal was unprecedented and placed the Council in a dilemma. They were not empowered to elect a substitute and had no choice but to compel obedience by recourse to the law - a proceeding they were reluctant to take. It was widely reported that Greville, who was at that time at Erchless, was unwilling to forego even a single day of his sport for tedious duties with civic dignitaries. It is a singular fact that the sheriff for the preceding year was George Oldham Edwards. What the public didn't appreciate was that Greville was having an affair with George Edwards' beautiful wife, Emily.

It is impossible to fathom the currents of emotion that sometimes overflow into public life. Had George Edwards hinted to the Council of Four that Greville would make a suitable successor, knowing full well the young man's abhorrence of public life? Did Greville refuse because he could not bring himself to step into the shoes of a man who was his chief rival? What neither probably realised was that Greville's refusal would oblige George Edwards to serve a second year by default.

Greville was adamant and impervious to the public censure which followed. He even secured the services of Sir Frederick Thesiger, the eminent barrister who had already got the family out of the Tom Provis imbroglio in 1853, in case of any legal action the City Council might take.

On 11th January 1858 the Times reported that the Queen's Bench had granted a rule nisi that Greville Smyth could be subject to criminal information "....for refusing to take and accept the office of High Sheriff of Bristol". The Court of Error pronounced a formal decision but the House of Lords refused to give it precedence, and so no verdict was reached that session. The Council did not pursue the matter on the grounds of cost and so no action was taken. George Edwards served a second year, which could not have improved relations between Ashton Court and Redland Court.

Uncle Arthur made up for his nephew's deficiency. In 1859 he defeated Sir William Tite in the Bath election, in spite of the latter's jovial battle cry: "Nail to your mast your cotton colours Tite, but don't get under Way!" and represented that Borough in Parliament for six years.

In one respect the majority was honourably consummated. In 1859 Greville sought and obtained a baronetcy - it was the third creation for the House of Smyth and it inaugurated the last great era in the history of the family.

MARRIAGE IN FASHIONABLE LIFE

"My Dearest Fanny

"One of our cursed old women, who is gone mad, is to be taken to St. Luke's and they cannot contrive to do this great deed without lugging me into the scrape...." wrote Charles Cottrell-Dormer to his intended - by way of an apology for not being able to accompany her for a walk in St. James's Park.

Fanny was Frances Strickland of Cokethorpe Park, Oxfordshire, and friend of Eliza Way during the Paris days, 1824-25. Fanny and Charles were married in 1826. He was the owner of Rousham, a castellated Jacobean mansion lying on the banks of the Cherwell, midway between Oxford and Banbury. It was the ancestral home of the Dormers, one of whom had driven great holes through his front door during the Civil War, so that his guns could be trained on the marauding Roundheads.

A later Dormer employed William Kent to lay out the park in the new style of landscape design and it remains the first and best preserved example of his work. In 1741 the estate passed to a cousin of the last Dormer, Sir Clement Cottrell, whose family had been Masters of Ceremonies at Court since the early 17th Century. The Master of Ceremonies was an inherited sinecure, and finally lapsed in the 1790s, but the Cottrell-Dormers, as they were known, continued to be county magnates, alternating the names Charles and Clement in the best aristocratic tradition.

The Charles who married Fanny Strickland in 1826 was a magistrate, Deputy Lieutenant and, in 1828, High Sheriff of the County. His fiery temperament, worthy of his Dormer ancestors, was directed in the 1840s to the machinations of the Great Western Railway, which projected a railroad through the Cherwell Valley, to connect Oxford and the south to the industrial Midlands. He marched down to the foreman's office at Heyford, demanded to see the plans, and promptly tore them up! The railway company prevailed in the end, and so did the Ministry of Defence, for not only do express trains shatter the calm of William Kent's Elysian Fields, but war planes roar out of Heyford Airfield not many miles further off. Even so, Rousham, its ancient house and lovely park, its dying Gaul and Temple of the Mill which formed part of Kent's design, remain little altered from the day when Florence. Upton arrived there in April 1858 on her marriage to Clement Cottrell-Dormer, son of the intrepid Charles.

The marriage of the younger sister of Mr Greville Smyth of Ashton Court, was an event of enormous interest to the neighbourhood. Greville's hopes of marrying the lady of his choice were remote, and the other sister, Fanny, was an incurable hypochondriac and unlikely to marry. The event was accorded several columns of small print in the local press, under a headline calculated to have maximum snob appeal: "Marriage in Fashionable Life".*

"The marriage of Miss Florence Anne Upton, sister to J. H. Greville Smyth Esq. of Ashton Court, to Clement Cottrell-Dormer Esq. of Rousham, Oxfordshire, was solemnised on Thursday at the parish church of Long Ashton. The ceremony was conducted in a manner becoming the rank of the parties and excited a large degree of interest, not only amongst the residents of Ashton and the surrounding neighbourhood, but amongst numbers who attended from this city. In the village the occasion was observed as quite a holiday, and there were many outward manifestations of rejoicing. The old cross (at that time outside the Angel Inn and not, as today, in the churchyard) was profusely decked with laurels, its broken column surmounted by a tapering fir tree. On the front of the village inn was an immense cluster of evergreens, while on each side of the avenue leading from the cross to the churchyard stood rows of fir trees whose roots had been imbedded for the occasion in the 'firm set earth'. A triumphal arch stretched across the entrance of the avenue; at about half-way down it, and in front of the parochial school, was a second arch.... intermingled with evergreens were gay coloured flowers and bridal knots and a tablet, doubtless an offering of the schoolchildren, but not the less to be valued on that account, inscribed 'May Health, Happiness and every other Blessing attend them through Life'. A third arch spanned the bottom of the drive, which bore upon it the names 'Dormer' and 'Upton' - the space between the two being filled by a colossal bridal favour. Upon a circlet was an inscription the precise meaning of which, as regards the neuter pronoun, we could not divine. 'May **it** be happy' (was our reporter being facetious?). The entrance

* Mercury & Western Courier, 27th April 1858.

to Mr Shattock's premises adjoining the church was very gaily decorated, there being clustered amongst the laurel and flowering shrubs with which it was dressed, many bridal knots and favours of pretty design, and a number of roses and other flowers, both real and artificial. An archway of laurel stood at the bottom of the church path next to the field and another spanned the carriageway in the park, about midway between the Court and the Lower Lodge, while at the principal entrance of the churchyard two arches were thrown up on either side of the gateway, the interval between the two being roofed, as it were, with laurel so as to form a complete sylvan canopy. From this point to the church the ground was covered with crimson cloth, flanked on each side the entire distance from the gate to the porch with rows of magnificent azaleas in the fullest and richest bloom. The porch itself was filled with choice ericas and other exotics from the Court gardens, while the old archway wore quite a gala aspect, so tastefully was it dressed with flowers. Besides the decorations we have noted there were many flags stretching in lines across the road, or waving upon the church tower, or from windows of the houses and, in one or two places, we observed floral devices exhibited on the house fronts of the villagers.

"There is an old ballad extant among the gossips of the South of England, the burthen of which runs thus:

The bride upon whose chaplet white
The sun doth shed its golden light,
A life of joy hath sure begun
Happy's the bride the sun shines on!

"If there is a grain of value in this prophecy, Mrs Florence Dormer may reasonably look forward - may it be realised say we - to a life of unbroken felicity. A more glorious day no one could desire. The sky was bright and cloudless; the earth clothed in its richest verdure, the flowers sprang up beneath the trees, and the trees were literally bursting with life"

....and there was a lot more banal stuff rhapsodising on the "high promise of nature's spring" and the usual observations about the absence of "cloakings and shawlings, and rushing in and out of carriages which on so many similar occasions have marred the general enjoyment, and tried and ruffled the tempers of mere lookers-on".

"The time fixed for the celebrations of the nuptials was a quarter past 11 o'clock. Upwards of an hour before that time crowds had begun to congregate at the church, and by half past ten the venerable edifice was filled to the fullest extent consistent with the increase of the bridal cortege. It had been arranged that the village schoolchildren should play their humble part in the ceremony and at 10 o'clock they assembled in the schoolroom, whence they were shortly afterwards marched to the churchyard and arranged in ranks on each side of the principal pathway. Subsequently (on the arrival of the bride and her party) they were admitted to the body of the church.

"Mr & Mrs Arthur Way were among the earliest arrivals at the church; shortly afterwards the Rev. H. Way and Mrs Henry, and the Misses Way (two of the bridesmaids) arrived and were soon followed by the bridegroom, Mr & Mrs Cottrell-Dormer, Mr & Mrs George Oldham Edwards and other members of the two families.

"It had been arranged that the ceremony should be performed by the Rev. Chancellor Law, assisted by the vicar, the Rev. J. Blackburne, and the curate, the Rev. W. M. Birch, and soon after 11 o'clock those divines, wearing full canonicals, entered the chancel. Full 20 minutes elapsed before the bride's party arrived from the Court, and as everybody was anxious and expectant, the time would probably have appeared tedious had it not been that the organist, Mr Flood, played a series of beautiful voluntaries on the recently erected organ. At length the joyous tones of the bells were heard reverberating through the vaulted building and there was a flutter amongst the party in the chancel. The clergymen passed within the rails of the communion table, and such of the bridesmaids and groomsmen as had not joined the party at the Court moved down the centre aisle to the porch. A few moments more and the nuptial cortege was seen making its way towards the altar. The bride, who was richly attired, leant on the arm of her brother, Mr Greville Smyth. She was attended by her mother, Mrs Upton, and by 6 bridesmaids, uniformly habited in dresses of white muslin trimmed with lilac coloured ruches, and wearing wreaths of white and coloured lilac. They were Miss Isabelle Way and Miss Maria Way of Henbury (Uncle Henry's daughters), Miss Fitzwilliam Way of Bath, Miss Dormer (Clement's sister Fanny), Miss Prior and Miss Georgiana Prior (Aunt Louisa's daughters). Among the groomsmen were Capt. Dashwood, Mr John Way (son of Uncle Henry), Mr Harvey, Mr Lysley, etc.

"The bride, having knelt in front of the altar, the bridegroom being on her right hand and Mr Greville Smyth (by whom she was given away), Mrs Upton and her sister, Miss Upton, on her left, the beautiful service prescribed by the ritual was impressively read by the Rev. Chancellor Law who, having declared the youthful couple man and wife, addressed to them with solemn earnestness the apostolic exhortation of love and obedience with which the service of the church is closed. The party then repaired to the vestry room where the contract was signed and the bridal favours distributed. Those worn by the gentlemen represented oak leaves in the proper colours, with acorns beautifully wrought in burnished and frosted silver; the ladies received white satin rosettes in the centres of which were small clusters of lilies of the valley and buds of the Persian rose. The organ then burst forth with Handel's sublime chorus 'The Glory of the Lord', after which it played Mendelssohn's grand wedding march and the National Anthem.

"The party now entered a long line of carriages in which they returned to the Mansion and partook of a magnificent dejeuner a la forchette. This repast provided by Warren of Clifton, and which was of a most costly and elegant description, was laid in the great dining room. The table was adorned by a costly silver plateau and numerous elegant ornaments in silver and gold, some of them filled with pines, peaches and other choice fruits. Towering above all, in the centre, was the bridal cake which was of large dimensions and profusely ornamented. It stood upon a handsome carved and gilded stand, and was surmounted by an Indian canopy of blue and white satin trimmed with silver. The adornments of the cake were chaste and appropriate: there were bridal knots and floral wreaths and a classic temple such as Hymen himself might have consecrated by his presence. The canopy was supported on 5 pillars en suite with the dome. From the top streamed half-a-dozen miniature flags of beautiful workmanship, and the apex of the dome was crowned with a small statuette of Hymen.

"The toast of the 'Bride & Bridegroom' was proposed in a feeling and appropriate speech by Captain Fitzway and, we need hardly say, was drunk with the greatest cordiality. The bridegroom responded. The healths of Mr Greville Smyth and Mrs Upton were likewise drunk with enthusiasm, as was 'The Bridesmaids' which was neatly proposed by Capt. Dashwood and acknowledged in a very humorous and telling speech by Mr Jeans (Greville's former tutor). At the close of the repast the bride and bridegroom took leave of their friends, and started on their wedding tour, proceeding to Oxford for a day or two, whence the purpose, we believe, of paying a somewhat lengthened visit to the Continent.

"We had well nigh committed what we are sure many a lady would have considered an 'unpardonable sin', id est closed our account of the wedding without having chronicled with becoming particularity the dresses of the bride and her attendant bridesmaids. The bride wore a robe of rich white glace silk with three skirts, trimmed with bouillances of tulle illusion, 2 deep flounces of Brussels lace and petite bouquets of orange blossoms and white lilacs. Her stomacher was ornamented with clusters of the same flowers, and she wore as a headdress a chaste and elegant wreath of orange blossoms with a flowing veil of white blonde. The bridesmaids had dresses of white muslin with 3 deep flounces trimmed with very broad ruches of mauve tarlatan. They wore wreaths of white and mauve crystallised lilac, with long tulle illusion veils.

"Connected with the festivities there have been some large dinner parties given at Ashton Court. Numerous guests were entertained there on Wednesday, Thursday and last night. We should not omit to state that the Clifton Band was stationed on the lawns in front of the Court on the wedding day, and played several popular marches and waltzes, and some pleasing selections from the operas. The 'creature comforts' of the schoolchildren were not overlooked, Mr Warren having been directed to send 5 or 6 large cakes for distribution among them."

Florence's own recollections of the event are far more humdrum. "My brother gave me away and after the ceremony we drove back to Ashton

Court. Presents were not so universal at that time; still I had some nice ones. Soon after the breakfast I put on a pearl grey silk, a brown cloak and a white bonnet and said goodbye to Darling Mother, and a crowd of friends and relations, and we drove off to Bristol station.

"We had not got out of sight of the house, however, before people called out after us. Old Turner, bumping along on the grey horses that had drawn so many of the family, stopped the carriage and we found that the maid, Cottier, a Swiss girl, was left behind. She was picked up onto the box, or rumble, and on we went again, arriving in course of time at Oxford, whence we drove on to Rousham along 12 miles of very ugly road."

It was, of course, an arranged marriage, projected by the mothers of the parties concerned, who had been close friends since the Paris days of 1824-5. In Florence's journal there is not even any reference to the formal courtship that usually preceded the matchmaking. "Among the guests...." at Erchless, the Scottish castle that Greville had taken for the season in 1857, she records, "....was a Mr Cottrell-Dormer, and whilst he was there our marriage was talked of. My mother, however, would not hear of its taking place for many months, though he was permitted to give me a ring." In the spring of 1858 Florence, accompanied by her mother, Greville, Mr Jeans and Mr Irby went to Paris to buy the wedding dress. The trip must have recalled many memories for Eliza, but Florence, not Eliza, is now the narrator and there is none of the lively repartee of earlier days - just the pedantic remark "....we had to pay duty on it (the wedding dress) after an awful tossing".

There is no reference in the local press or elsewhere to the good looks of the bridal pair. The fact is they were not very prepossessing. Clement was the country type, pensive and withdrawn, a model of filial obedience to the forthright Charles; and his portraits reveal a suitably bewhiskered profile and an expression both crushed and resigned, which rather increases over the years. Florence had brown and expressive eyes and, when young, shoulder length chestnut hair, but nothing could conceal the slab-like contour of her face, the straight nose and puckered chin. Beneath the stolid exterior was a large share of resilience and commonsense; and if she lacked the liveliness and good looks of her mother, she was no fool, and rode through a life beset with trials with her accustomed cheerfulness and wry sense of the ridiculous.

Married life at Rousham could not have been very easy. It was, in those days, a narrow, old-fashioned, draughty house, modelled on the H-plan: the hall and dining room the width of the house and forming the main thoroughfare. "The wing rooms were prepared for us," says Florence. "I very much enjoyed exploring the lovely grounds though I did not think much of the Cherwell after our rocky Lune." Augustus Hare, who visited Rousham the following year, wrote of Florence's in-laws:

"Mr & Mrs Dormer were quaint characters: he always insisting that he was a Roman Catholic in disguise, chiefly to plague his wife, and always reading through the whole of Pope's works in the large quarto edition once a year; she full of kind-heartedness, riding by herself about the property to manage the estate and cottagers, always welcoming you with a hearty: 'Well, to be sure, and how do **you** do?'."

The honeymoon began with a few days at Claridges, "then we went abroad with Cottier the maid and David the courier, for a nice long tour to Brussels, Cologne, Hamburg, Berlin, Dresden, Prague, Vienna, up the Danube to Linz, on to Salzburg and Traunstein, where we were joined by Mr Jeans, Mr Irby and Greville who were fishing there. The waiter was a very funny person who always spoke of women as 'trouts'. 'Two fine Trouts came in last night', etc. He often used to make me laugh. Traunstein was then a pretty little place and Clem used to drive me about in a pony carriage for I had been very ill at Vienna with a feverish attack, caught in the Saxon Switzerland, and felt pulled down to nothing...."

"We returned to Munich and Switzerland, where we sent Cottier for a week to her home. Her mother kept a cremerie near the Lake of Geneva and lying in her bed she could see Mt. Blanc. I went over the Wengen Alp - my one experience of mountain climbing, performed with the help of a mule, but very tiring. I was sorry, oh very sorry, when our tour came to an end.

"We stayed a few days at Paris and found Aunt Belinda and her husband, Mr Sampson, and Mary Prior - 'Perfect Loveliness' as she was called in those days. Also Mr Orlebar and his brother John, and old Monsieur Moreau who used to talk to us and say I had Persian eyes. (Was it a compliment?)"

On their return to Rousham Florence felt unwell and wrote, "It was decided that the beginning of a family was en route" - and what a family it was! In the next twenty-one years she had fourteen children, of whom two died in infancy. In some years she was pregnant twice and the childbearing only ceased with Clement's premature death. Of the twelve children that survived, five were daughters: Beatrice, 1859; Florence Augusta, 'Flo', 1862; Evelyn Hilda, 1869; Winnie Evelyn, 1876; Katherine Elizabeth, 'Kitty', 1877; and seven were sons: Charles Walter, 1860; Clement Adelmar, 1862; John Herbert, 1867; Maximilian, 1868; Aubrey Caesar, 1874; William Otway, 1878 and Humphrey Randall, 1881. Dorothy May, 1868, died at birth and Greville, 1864, died when he was twelve months, at Ashton Court. For each confinement, that is until her death in 1870, Eliza travelled up from Ashton and was an enormous comfort. As the family grew, Clement took rented houses and engaged an ever growing troop of nurses and governesses.

The first rented accommodation was 6 Beauchamp Square, Leamington Spa, taken especially to have the services of Dr. Middleton for Florence's first confinement, but he was found sadly wanting when the moment arrived.

"On the 16 Feb. 1859 I drove to Warwick and went over the curiosity shop at Redfern, 3 stories high. That night I felt rather uncomfortable and next morning we sent for Dr. Middleton. He said there was no immediate necessity for his presence and went calmly off to a broken leg 10 miles off. As we had come to Leamington to have the great benefit of his assistance at this time, this was rather too bad; in the course of the afternoon Dr. Busby, the parish doctor, had to be called in and speedily my dear Beatrice made her appearance.

"I had a horrible old nurse, Mrs Carey, who assured me the first day that in her opinion 'too much couldn't be done for the monthly nurse', and I wondered what she wanted. Dr. Middleton, who came back at midnight, was surprised and annoyed to see how well we had done without him. He said to me 'Sorry it's not a boy. Ah! but you don't know the comfort of an eldest daughter!'

"My bedroom was the back drawing room, a most inconvenient arrangement. Mrs Carey and the baby shared it with me; she snored and Bea occasionally roared, and I did not get enough sleep or fresh air. Altogether the house began to give us the horrors. (The owners had left full length portraits of themselves in the drawing room which did not add to our happiness for we were always meeting their gaze) and then Clement went down with measles. So, in the autumn of 1859, the family moved to an old house at Dundridge, near Totnes in Devon, the old home of the wife of Mr Orlebar, who kindly made it available.

"There, on 21 May 1860, dear Charlie made his appearance. He was rather peaky and delicate, so a Mrs Hill was engaged as his wet nurse. We had a certain amount of trouble and annoyance from her husband.

"We sometimes drove to Torquay, which was a lovely experience but an expensive drive, for it cost 5/- in turnpikes.* Once we went to a great

* The Turnpike Trusts were closed down, c.1862, when upkeep of roads was transferred to local government.

fete at Newton Abbot, in somebody's garden, to see Lord Churston presented with a great shield for some good deed. We lunched in a tent and listened to a lot of speeches by local bigwigs, but I felt that my bonnet was not up to date. Spoon bonnets had begun and mine was a trousseau relic.

"During my mother's lifetime we always stayed at Ashton Court either winter or summer or both for six weeks or two months at a time," wrote Florence. Greville was there less and less. Despite his tenants' hope that their young landlord would spend his time at Ashton, they saw very little of him during the next twenty to thirty years. He showed no interest in local or national affairs. In 1857 he even paid the statutory fine of £500 rather than serve as Sheriff of the County. The life style that characterised the years of his maturity was taking shape. He had unlimited means, boundless energy and lust for travel and

good company. In the 60s and 70s he was the playboy aristocrat: grouse shooting and deerstalking in the Scottish Highlands from August to November; Christmas was usually spent at Ashton Court in the grand manner, with open house for a wide circle of friends and relations. In the New Year he spread his wings and his quest for big game took him to the far corners of the British Empire. Uncle George Prior, ex-Indian Army and his travelling companion, once wrote:

"In America the bison he killed,
In Egypt the wild boar he slew.
In India the black buck and nilghau,
In Australia the far-famed emu."

Unfortunately the details of these journeys do not survive. We hear of his tutor, Mr Jeans, and dashing 'Duppa' - Captain Paul, an Anglo-Indian, a frequent guest of "this tenement baronial" who "walks and shoots and stalks in a way that's quite colonial".

We know from Florence's journal that Greville was away up the Nile in 1867, and there exists a remarkable photograph taken in Cairo that year of Greville and party. He is seated at a table, with a resolute, businesslike expression, between two pretty Way cousins, probably two of Emily's sisters, Maria and Isabella - substitutes, perhaps, for Emily herself. They look remarkably relaxed considering the climate and their stuffy, unhealthy clothes. Behind, standing, and attired in tropical gear, complete with pith helmet and mosquito nets, are Dr. Holman, companion of many journeys, and for much of his life resident physician at Ashton Court, and another gentleman who could be Mr Jeans.

The indiscriminate slaughtering of birds and animals on sight was still a noble pursuit, the hallmark of a gentleman. Perhaps in this way he sublimated his feelings for another man's wife, but the joys of the chase were combined with an intellectual interest in what was caught, and already a

Greville Smyth, Dr Holman L., Mr Jeans R., and two lady cousins in Cairo c. 1867.

stream of specimens were finding their way back to Ashton Court: butterflies, rare birds' eggs, nests, stuffed animals.

In 1870 he was in Ceylon with Captain Paul, investigating the jungle life of the Central Highlands. The abundance of tropical vegetation, insect and animal life, exercised a powerful attraction, and Greville returned to the island many times in the 1880s and 1890s. The long journeys by land and sea, the tossing about in P & O steamers, in three-masted windjammers, jostling with immigrants pushing westward into the American prairies, and diggers in New South Wales, produced a crop of lively stories and anecdotes; and at house parties at Ashton Court and in Scotland, Greville could be an entertaining host. "One day, in Australia, we arrived at an hotel and a friend of mine, who had a distinctly swanky air, got off the top of the coach and went into the hotel. There were two red-shirted Australian bushmen standing watching him and I heard one of them say as he went in 'Got a bit of side on 'im, ain't 'e, Bill?' and the other said 'Side! Why e's got a side on 'im like the Lord Mayor of 'ell!'

"In India I met an old Colonel who was always yarning about his shooting. He said, as one never knows what might rise at any moment, he always loaded one barrel with snipe shot and the other with bullet. One day a snipe and a tiger rose at the same moment, and he killed the snipe with the bullet and cut the tiger over with the snipe shot. Seeing one of his audience looking rather dubious, he added 'Yes, sir, I take my oath; it's the truth; and when I looked around there was my black servant as white as your shirt front...."*

Ashton Court during those years was left to his mother, to Uncle Arthur and to Florence and her growing family. "It was a very curious old house in those days," records Florence. "Most of the rooms were passage rooms, which was most inconvenient for if the occupant of one room chose to go to bed early, those using the next room must either pass through on the way to seek repose, or travel a long way round. The top bedroom on the top stairs to the right was my room, with 3 windows, and its only dressing room was a tiny closet inside, having no other outlet. Under this little closet was a secret chamber**.... in the next room to this, the oak-panelled room, was an enormous and melancholy looking bed with heavy green hangings, behind which there was a secret cupboard containing a rope bed. Then again, up in the attics, there was a mysterious room.... having no window, but with a stone floor in front of the fireplace much worn away as if some sad inmate had used it to walk up and down."

* These stories were later published in an anthology by his son-in-law, Gilbert Irby.

** Edgar Way, who spent part of his youth at Ashton Court, also refers to this "closet or dressing room, in the floor of which was a trap door which opened into a recess or hiding place".

The bedrooms had strange names like 'Kitty Fisher's Room' because a picture of Kitty Fisher hung there; and 'Drax's Kennel' was another, but who or what was Drax has never been disclosed. The drawing room was still 'The Great Chamber' above the Great Hall, which had a curious screen made of oak panels on the left of the fireplace, later removed to the staircase (1885).

The exterior was not very different from today, except that the main entrance on the south front was a modest Regency gatehouse, with a battlemented roofline, which rose no higher than the rest of the facade. The first photographs (1866) show that Sir John Hugh Smyth's pointed Neo-Gothic lights of the 1770s still filled the early 17th Century classical windows of the 'Inigo Jones' wing. What later (1885) became the Winter Garden was "....an open courtyard paved with flagstones, with musk growing between the stones, where once I kept a tame rabbit in a box under the central arch when a small boy," recalled Edgar Way.

Almost all the ground floor rooms were uninhabitable. The whole of what was later the museum and music room (a restaurant in 1988), was then stables. Sir John Hugh Smyth's splendid rococo-Gothic library was now "the new Dining Room", and, writes Florence, "....the portraits in it so realistic that it is reported that some old lady, a distant relation, being taken round, looked back at her daughters who were following her and said, 'My dears, lower your veils'".

"What later was the dining room was used for billiards and was far too small for the purpose, and the Long Gallery, 96 feet long with 8 windows, was hardly ever used. Greville's birthday ball, 1857, and my wedding, 1858, were the only exceptions that I remember, except when ladies of the family walked up and down it on wet days. It was furnished with fine old cabinets and a very dull brown chintz and was very dismal." A rare photograph of this period shows an appalling clutter of knobby and uncomfortable Beidemayer furniture, very much in vogue during the 1840s; the inevitable large cases of stuffed birds and fishes; and gas lamps.

In the absence of Greville, it was left to Florence to take the initiative in making the old house more comfortable. "My Aunt Belle (Mrs Fitzway) and I conceived the idea of making the Long Gallery into a really useful sitting room. Since only furniture was wanted, my Aunt and I received permission to do our worst, and we made it into a comfortable living room, which was immediately adopted with thankfulness by the family."

Florence and her family were at Ashton Court in December 1861 when, "The sad news came of the death of the Prince Consort. He died on a Saturday and at the Cathedral next day Clem saw an old citizen take out his pencil, on the event being announced from the pulpit, and deliberately scratch the poor Prince out of the Prayer Book. Partly owing to my vanity I, in a new black gown, caught a severe chill which turned to pleurisy. I was laid up at Ashton and was pretty bad for a few days. Dr. Budd of Clifton attended me and I soon got well again."

There were now three children, for Flo was born in August "....such a little, gentle, quiet baby", and in the summer of 1862 the old house at Dundridge was given up in favour of No. 14 Belvedere, Weymouth. "I had a fancy to spend a winter by the sea," wrote Florence candidly. It was this kind of fancy which, in course of time, became such an obsession that she sometimes uprooted the family and all the domestics several times a year. Greville was planning a world tour which would keep him away for the best part of two years, and visited Weymouth in the autumn of 1862 to say goodbye. "He bought me a lovely locket of enamel, carbuncle and pearl. (He did give me pretty things in those days - dear kind brother," she added in retrospect.) "I cried at his leaving for so long."

In November her second son, Clem, was born. Eliza came down as usual from Ashton and Mrs Cassidy, "....a funny old Irish nurse" was engaged. The winter by the sea didn't do much for Florence's spirits. The house was cold and draughty, and she felt depressed. It was a touch of the neurosis which we shall hear much more about later: "....then one night the Volunteers started playing 'Bonnie Dundee' and I enjoyed it and began to pick up again from that evening". Eliza, no longer obliged to 'keep house' for Greville, took herself off for several months to Spain, "....with only a courier and a maid, and returned, delighted with the beautiful cathedrals", just in time for Florence's fifth confinement at Bampton, a house put at their disposal by Clement's uncle, Walter Strickland of Cokethorpe, which was only five miles away.

In 1864 Greville returned home, and his mother and sister joined him at Erchless, where they were photographed in the doorway of the old castle. It is a remarkably telling photograph in which Eliza, seated, looks over her shoulder and winks engagingly at the camera, while Florence, standing, pouts. The enormous crinolines, then demanded by fashion, couldn't have helped and must have severely cramped the style of most highland activities.

In March 1865 when Florence and Clement were making a visit with the Stricklands to Torquay, Florence received a frantic letter from her mother at Ashton Court, "....to say that dear little Greville, then the youngest, just a year old and the sweetest and most engaging baby in the world, had been taken ill with internal bleeding. Of course we went by the next train to Bristol. He had never been a strong child so I felt frightfully anxious, though we had left him quite as well as usual a few days before. When we arrived it was evident that he was most seriously ill. He was then quite unconscious, and in a few hours the precious little life was gone. It was the first break in the family and a dreadful blow. He had only stood up for the first time a week or two before. He had a way of crawling to the door and peering round that was irresistible, and none of the others thought of doing it. In a few days he was taken to Henbury churchyard, and we went for a short time to Weston-super-Mare".

However, another child was on the way and in August, "....dear John came to gladden our hearts. Old Dr. Whittaker attended, as Mr Prickett was ill. He was very much disgusted and annoyed by the elder children running up to him when he called a day or two before the event and saying, 'Have you brought the baby? Have you brought the baby?' How they knew what was impending I cannot say.

"When John was a month old he and I and dear mother went to Brighton and stayed in the Grand Hotel, then quite new, and I went upstairs in a lift for the first time in my life. Our fellow passengers in it I well remember were a set of dwarfs who were performing at Brighton, General and Mrs Tom Thumb, Commodore Nutt, Minnie Warren, and a great tall man who showed them off. I saw General Tom Thumb once before when he performed on a table at Kendal, when he kissed me; but I didn't choose to remind him of it." In the autumn Florence was restless again. She and Clement went to Malvern for a "....cold water cure. Clement went to Dr. Gully's and I went to Dr. Marsden's, but I soon got very tired of it." Taking the waters - hot, cold, German, Belgian, Turkish - the more exotic the better, some years later became one of Florence's addictions; but in the 1860s she couldn't afford it. They were not exactly hard up. Her marriage settlement and Clement's allowance enabled them to live a life to which they were accustomed, and Uncle Strickland contributed £100 a year, and since 1863 had provided them with a house, rent free. But there was no money for extravagant extras and when, in the autumn of 1864, they went to the Blenheim Ball, Clement's mother gave her a new dress for it: "A pale grey moire antique," wrote Florence, some forty years after the event, with her usual unwavering memory for detail. Certain artifices were resorted to in order to keep up appearances of gentility. For example, "Joseph, our manservant, used to take away the luncheon, and then get on the box and drive me and the children in the carriage (on our outings to Burford or Faringdon), which was brought to the door by the gardener".

"But we were very happy," admits Florence, and then, "I think it was early February, 1867, on a Saturday afternoon, as Clement and I were pottering in our little greenhouse at Bampton, quite unconscious that anything was going to happen; all in a moment something did happen and it altered the whole of the rest of our lives."

Florence comes into a Fortune

The Rousham bailiff drove over fifteen miles to Bampton with a letter from Clement's mother, enclosing a telegram received that morning. He opened it and it contained these words, "John Upton Esq. is dead. I will write unless you come or send at once". John Upton, 'Big Nose', was Florence's half-uncle* and the telegram had come from Mr Whitley, the clerk in Hoares Bank who managed his affairs.

"We wondered in blank amazement what it could mean. I had not seen him for years, and Clement only once in his life," wrote Florence. In fact, only the previous December, Eliza, not having heard for many years of her old friend of Paris days, made a special trip to London to try to find him. Florence went with her. "We drove first to Cecil Street, Strand. This street being very narrow we left the carriage in the Strand, and proceeded on foot to the house where he had lodged when last heard of. The landlady received us civilly and seemed glad to talk, saying that she only wished she knew where he was, and would gladly have told us. She knew he must be alive for he kept on the rooms and the rent was punctually paid, though it was several years since he had used them. She told us what a kind friend he had been to her, paying for the children's schooling etc. She fancied he must be ill since he never came, but she knew nothing...."

It later transpired that a will had been prepared dividing his property between his doctor, lawyer and housekeeper, "....but to their great disappointment they had never been able to get him to sign it". If no other will was found, explained the family solicitor, then the whole of his considerable estate would pass to Florence, her brother and sister. Florence couldn't believe it. There must be a will somewhere.

"Clement decided to go up to London the following day, and he wrote to Mr Whitley to expect him. On his arrival he went, taking Mr Hulbert the family lawyer with him, to the house in Dorset Square where our uncle had breathed his last, and they saw the poor old gentleman in his coffin. Mr Bramley from Sedbergh also joined the party to look after my sister's interests. My brother being far away in Egypt was not represented."

Considerable quantities of watches, telescopes, and precious stones were discovered, whioh wcrc gathered up and deposited in the bank, but still

* Her father's half-brother: son of John Upton and Dorothy Wilson, b.1799.

no will was found. Meanwhile Uncle John had to be buried and the funeral was at Kensal Green cemetery.

"I strongly objected to Clement going up again for fear he should catch cold and as I could hardly believe that the money was really coming to us I added that he would not get enough to pay for a podophyllin pill! However, he thought he had better go. I begged that if circumstances looked like justifying the extravagance, to bring me a good box of chocolates and a new photograph album." He returned with both that evening, for still no will had been discovered.

Greville was still 'up the Nile' and could not give a lead in deciding how the property should be divided, whereupon Fanny, a confirmed neurotic, announced her intention of doing it. Clement objected and insisted that Florence should have a hand in it, and before anyone could stop it a blazing row broke out between the sisters. Fanny was furious. She was obliged to give in, but caused interminable delays by refusing to discuss it. For months their respective solicitors grappled with each other and the huge, rambling estate. The winter and spring (1868) passed, with letters and delays, and a great deal of unpleasantness, added to which Florence had to contend with a dishonest cook and tiresome servants, and another confinement! "March 1st. Max was born - in stormy times. I always put down poor Max's shaking hands to my nerves being so upset then."

At last the whole property of Uncle John was divided into three lots, A, B and C. Greville, who had at last come home, agreed with Florence that Fanny should have the first choice; she chose Lot C. Greville had so much anyway that he wasn't unduly bothered, so young Beatrice, aged eight, was given two pieces of paper with A on one and B on the other. Screwing them up into the palms of her hands she held them out and Greville and Florence drew lots. It made a very considerable difference to Florence's material circumstances and made possible quite another life style.

On the Continent en Famille

Florence and Clem decided to celebrate their good fortune with a trip to the Continent. They had not been abroad since their honeymoon ten years before, but there were now six children. "We never dreamt of not taking them all," recalled Florence, "it would certainly be an undertaking, but we began to look the journey in the face and plan where to go...."

The biggest problem was finding suitable servants who could cope with the needs of the children while travelling. Miss Barker, governess to the three eldest children, had lived in Paris, "....her French would be useful", noted Florence. Old Powe, the elderly widow who had come as a nurse for Max, had never been abroad, but she had proved invaluable in making and altering clothes, and generally helping with the children, and was willing to come. "A nursemaid was the next want; but good Amelia, the laundry maid who had always been so handy and good-natured, volunteered to come in that capacity, so our party was complete except for a courier." At last, Mrs Adams, the vicar's wife at Bampton, recommended Antonio. "He did his best," added Florence. "I wondered how he lived through the worries of the maids."

So, having boarded their Newfoundland dog 'Nip' and stored their furniture, the party of twelve set out early one bright, cold, October morning. Florence and Beatrice went up to London by an early train to buy Robb's biscuits for Max and sealskin travelling capes for the others. They joined the rest of the family, including Clem's parents, at the Charing Cross Hotel. Charles Cottrell-Dormer intended to travel on the Continent alone, and meet the rest of the family later, and Fanny came up to dine with them and say goodbye.

"I remember to this day," wrote Florence in 1903, "the troops of children and nurses getting out of the lift. It was an undertaking. Mrs Dormer had told her footman Joseph to come for her at a certain hour, but on enquiring he was not there, and Clem horrified his mother by suggesting that he might have gone to the play!"

The family crossed from Folkestone. "Charlie went to ground under some kind of rugs on deck, and Flo was very sick; a kind young man on his way to South America came forward to help her."

At Boulogne they put up at the Hotel des Baine, "....where Miss Barker distinguished herself and disappointed me by asking me to ask the chambermaid for some hot water. Her French couldn't even go as far as that".

They spent a few days in Paris, saw the Exhibition, and by slow degrees travelled to Marseilles via Lyons, Dijon and Macon . "Amelia was always bright and cheerful and obliging and enjoyed travelling," observed Florence, but, "I soon found that Miss Barker and Powe were not going to be of any use or comfort and we often longed to ship them both back home." There were problems too, with the children. At Marseilles Charlie had a bad attack of asthma; Max, the baby, spewed up the local milk. "We found that the cows were fed on orange and lemon leaves - anything but hay!", and John "....a fat English boy of 2½ on his first arrival at Cannes", was nearly eaten alive by mosquitoes. At Cannes they joined "Mother and Eliza Prior at the Grand Hotel" and a further halt of about a month was made at Nice. Since 1859 Nice was a French, not Italian town, having been traded by the King of Italy to the Emperor of the French, to the intense mortification of Garibaldi, who had been born there. Italy was, politically, more unified in 1868 than at Florence's last visit in 1857. Even so the Garibaldini were still at large and there were anxious consultations of the newspapers before venturing any further. It was decided that the state of the country was sufficiently settled to proceed and, "....two venturias were engaged and we drove off to Genoa - the second time I had passed the Corniche Road, and oh! how lovely it is! Clem and I sat on the raised seat in front of the first carriage; the nursery party inside our carriage and the schoolroom party inside the other. Once we heard shrieks from Amelia, 'Let I out, Antony; let I out!' but her fears were soon soothed, I think."

The children were horribly eaten by mosquitoes and the food ordered in advance by Antonio was horribly eaten by another family, "....the landlord thinking they were the people for whom the feast was ordered, and it had disappeared beyond recall. That family was always called in our family 'The Greedy Baillies'." At Pisa, Florence had to be left behind. She was pregnant again, but she soon recovered and joined the rest of the party at Florence, "....where I found them all in a yellow satin drawing room - Clem howling, poor child". He was only five. In Florence they watched the carnival from an upper room in company with the expatriate elite, and scattered confetti on those below - a custom which in due course made its way to England and has messed up churchyards ever since.

"On the evening of Shrove Tuesday we had a box at the opera house to see the masked ball, and we all had to wear masks, and at 12 precisely soldiers came in and stood at the top of the room, and slowly but steadily marched down, clearing all before them and quickly emptying the house."

That year Garibaldi and his Red Shirts made an heroic but futile attack on the last fragment of Italy still ruled by the Pope, Pio Nono, but he was defeated, wounded and captured by the French guardians of the papacy at the Battle of Mentana. Undeterred Clem, Florence and their tribe, with Amelia, Miss Barker, Old Powe and Antonio, pushed on to Rome and lodged at the Hotel des Iles Britanniques in the Piazza del Popolo, where they had stayed in 1857. Here they found Clem's father. At an early age he had been drenched in Italian culture, revolted from it, and gravitated to the congenial and ever so English sport of hunting. Clem and Florence dutifully went along to the meet. "On these occasions Clem sat on the edge of the seat looking on the ground. 'Clem, why are you looking on the ground? What are you looking at?' 'I was wondering which were father's horse's footmarks'."

One wonders why Florence found this remark worthy of her journal; if it was remarkable, then it doesn't say much for the level of their conversation. However, trips were made to the Catacombs, to the Colosseum to see it illuminated, and to Ostia, "....to see a curious mosaic pavement.... and while our horses rested we sat in a lovely wood full of evergreens in the grounds of the palace of Count Chigi". At Tivoli they went into the Church of St. Paul. "There I inadvertently wandered into the Cloisters and was driven from thence with shame and ignominy by furious monks, who declared they would have to purify the buildings my female feet had trod....!" This was, after all, the Patrimony of St. Peter's, the last of the Papal States, and ruled by a Council of Cardinals. Part of any English visitor's duty in Rome in those days was to seek an audience with His Holiness himself.

"On two occasions we went to the Vatican and stood round Pio Nono to hear the little address he gave to his visitors. This always happened on Sunday afternoons and once we took Beatrice and Charlie (aged 8 and 7) and Antonio and Clem knelt in the passage as His Holiness passed to the Audience Chamber. The last time we saw the dear old gentleman he stood in his white robe and white shoes and about 14 or 16 people stood in a circle while he talked. He told us of a saint whose Feast Day it would be tomorrow. Santa Francesca de Roma; of her holy life and good example...."

Three years later Pio Nono was driven from his Patrimony and imprisoned in the Vatican, but his Lateran Council of 1873 defined the doctrine of Papal Infallibility, and did much to transform the role of the Pope from secular to spiritual leader.

"Often we went out in the evening, and a little French hairdresser used to come and do my hair as Powe wasn't equal to doing up my locks for a party; and once I was taken for a Bride!" She had her portrait painted in Rome, a miniature; but it was not a success. She leans awkwardly in her crinoline against a pedestal, and wears an unbecoming black jacket, and the expression is vacuous and bovine.

"We made the acquaintance of the Champion of England and Mrs Dymoke. He has to do something (throw down the gauntlet, I think) at a Coronation, and was a mild old clergyman. His wife made up any deficiencies in appearance and was a very fine woman indeed!" - a polite way of saying that she looked like the back of a bus?

After two months in Rome the party returned via Florence, Turin and Mount Cenis. There was no railway tunnel then and all thirteen of them crossed the pass on sledges drawn by horses: "....so cold it was, and deep snow; the men who attended to us had icicles hanging on their eyelashes.... We left 14 of the party at Chambery and Clement and I went for a night or two to Geneva where I wanted to buy a musical box," - and so back to Paris and England.

Servant Problems

Florence was fated to have servant problems all her life. In this respect she fares probably no worse or better than most people of her class, as the standard jokes in 'Punch' of this period testify. The European tour of 1868-9 produced a major domestic crisis. "They were getting unbearable," wrote Florence in despair. "Even the faithful Amelia was terribly uppity, and as to Miss Barker...." Words failed her! She had created endless difficulties in Rome and, "....when it was suggested that it was a pity dear Beatrice always read on a journey instead of looking about her, Miss Barker instantly gave a peremptory order, 'Look at the mountains, Missy, look at the mountains'."

On the return home there was a clean sweep. In place of Miss Barker came Rose Stephenson, "an adult orphan", and Nurse Bodley replaced Amelia for the babies. Not long afterwards Florence was wailing about "....a good deal of trouble from the indoor servants". Nurse Bodley, "though devoted to the backbone", was untidy and careless. The undernurse scalded John in his bath while his parents were in Munich, which occasioned an anxious exchange of telegrams. She was later dismissed, whereupon she put on airs and graces and "....told the other servants that she was well-to-do, for when she got married her father would give her 'Fifty pounds and a feather bed'".

Miss Stephenson seems to have given satisfaction, but was much given to 'cottage visiting', or slumming as it was called later, when genteel ladies made condescending visits to their social inferiors. When she should have been coping with the unruly Cottrell-Dormer boys she was gossiping with "Mrs Cockerill who used to see visions; or Betsy Dunkerley, the blind carter's sister, and Annie Treane, a bedridden woman who used to hold poor Miss Stephenson's hand till it got deadly cold....", and so on. One suspects that Florence wasn't firm enough with them or her children, but both Nurse Bodley and Miss Stephenson stayed, for better or for worse, and the family continued to grow more numerous and less tractable.

BREEDING

In 1869 Florence and Clem, on their return from Italy, moved to a grand, stone house called Courtinhall, near Northampton. It was a fine example of late Georgian architecture* and was the property of Sir Hereward Wake, then a minor.

"The Wakes came over from Pitsford occasionally and we always got on very comfortably with them," wrote Florence. "Their tombstones were rather a trial in the Church - a marble figure of a tiny baby let into the wall and covered with glass was one of their memorials; also one of sweet Emily Wake, the pride of her home, and many others - the Church was full of sleeping Wakes.

"The vicar and his wife were a nice old couple, Mr & Mrs Leo (or Lea). They had a scapegrace son who had married (some say not married) an actress, Miss Julia Milson. She came and dined with us at Courtinhall once, and after-wards recited 'How we brought the good news from Aix' by Browning. One of my favourite bits was 'I sprang to the saddle, and Jones and he, I galloped, Dick Galloped, we galloped all three'. Many years after, she died suddenly in the Bois de Boulogne of an ice she was eating at one of the restaurants" - still reciting, very probably, 'I galloped, Dick galloped, we galloped all three'!

* Built in 1791-94 by Samuel Saxon.

Life at Courtinhall consisted of hobnobbing with the gentry and the usual country house pursuits. "Clement settled down to his hunting. He frequently went with the Duke of Grafton's hounds, but sometimes with the Pytchley.... He was made a magistrate for Northamptonshire and went to Northampton every Saturday to administer Justice and Mercy. I sometimes walked a long way to meet him...."

Occasionally Florence and Clem were invited to Wakefield Lawn, the home of the Duke of Grafton. They stayed there two nights in the spring of 1869 but "....the Duchess we only saw at meals and in the evenings; she was very delicate and devoted to the village when she did go out. Mr & Mrs Langton and Miss Berkeley were staying there, and a lot of men who were hunting all day, I suppose".

Florence's Brood

Florence and Clem stayed at Courtinhall for five years, during which another three children were born, and by 1875 there were nine little Cottrell-Dormers. Poor Florence had little joy from her numerous progeny. Her daughters were more of a worry than a comfort and her sons were a trial and later a torment.

Charlie, the eldest, was the most docile. He was sensitive and artistic. As a toddler he was deeply attached to Hart, Florence's lady's maid. "On one occasion, he screamed going up from the station in the carriage (and separate from Hart in the fly). He said to her afterwards: 'Harty Tarty, I sceem for 'oo'." Florence spoiled him. At the age of eight "....he was deposited at Miss Perry's school for boys at Clifton. I foolishly went to see him the very next day, when clinging arms went around my neck and a pitiful voice said, 'Do take me home again'." At home he was accustomed to address visitors in a precocious and almost impertinent manner; for example, he called the curate, who was a "very holy looking man, with a nice brisk wife" - Alick and Katie.

Clem, the second son, was a deceptively angelic looking child, and was painted by Corbould on 'Zingaro', his favourite dun coloured pony. The painting was exhibited in the Royal Academy in 1870. He was given to making devastating pronouncements. "Dear Clem never forgot how, on one occasion Old Powe, sitting in the carriage on the way to the station was wearing a bonnet trimmed with dark blue and crystal glass beads which dropped too near her red nose to be becoming. Clem, quite a little boy, but an observant one, looked at the poor woman for some time and then, to my horror, but to the delight of his father who quite agreed with him, said, 'Oh, Powe. How funny you do look!'." Young Clem had a wilful, intemperate streak. While on holiday at Brislington he smashed his sister Flo's finger with a stone, and his later escapades nearly broke his mother's heart.

John, five years younger than Clem, was not much better. He was headstrong and impulsive and showed an early and ultimately disastrous obsession with horses. "His delight was to lead the omnibus horses back to their stables on their return from their frequent journeys to the station," wrote Florence while at Spa in Belgium, where she was taking the waters in 1870. Arriving back in Dover at two or three in the morning, "....John, as usual, well to the front, making such a noise going up the stairs at the Lord Warden that I had to remind him that though he was so wide awake many others were asleep and preferred to remain so...."

That same year Florence was taken by Clem to Aberystwyth and Devil's Bridge for a change, after the death of her mother. The railway had just reached west Wales. "Coming home, the train stopped at Newtown and John, an impetuous child of nearly 5, took the opportunity to lean against the door, and fell right out betwoon the train and the platform. Dreadfully frightened we rushed out after him - the train fortunately at a standstill - and received the little wanderer who was unhurt. A kind, and I suppose convivial fellow traveller, came forward from another carriage and offered me some brandy at once as the only remedy for fright, but I was too pleased at the child's safety to need the well meant offer."

Clem and John quarrelled endlessly. "It was a pity how they used to fight," wrote Florence later, "it was nothing uncommon to find the effects of a bloody nose in the bath...." This was at Caledonia Place, Clifton, where Florence took a house at Christmas in order to join her brother's house parties at Ashton Court.

Max was the best looking and most talented. There exists a charming portrait of Florence with Max, then aged about three. The child, with a mass of brown curls, stares candidly at the viewer; his mother, her hair done up in the snood then in fashion, looks pensively to the right. At Courtinhall, Max took a header from his tricycle and "....cut his hand dreadfully". The good looks he lost later through licentious living; the talents, especially draughtsmanship, were never really put to good use.

There exists a solitary letter written by Florence about 1871 to her cousin Isabella Way of Denham, who was then part of Greville's house party at Erchless Castle in the Scottish Highlands. It was addressed South Cliff Villa, Filey, Yorks, where she and Clement had taken their young family sea bathing. It exudes all the verve and bounce of Florence in her prime.

"My dearest Izzie,

"I know it, so don't begin to scold. I **have** been a long time about writing and really time runs away so fast at the sea that one does think twice about a letter, but I know I shall not get one from you till I do write, so here goes. My dear Pussy Baby (Hilda was 18 months) has been so poorly that really we do not know what to do for her. Dr. says sea air is too exciting when double teeth are being cut, so we are going to take her to Courtinhall next week when we go there, and take Charlie back to school and try a few days home air for her and then back here. She is much better now.

"We all bathe (except Baby). John and Maxie look lovely little shrimps in the water and I thoroughly enjoy it. We often go to Scarborough to hear the band. Twice I have seen your Polly, Mrs Broth and her husband, but they were not near enough to speak to. I have not seen them very lately so I suppose they are gone. I have been so sorry for poor John and Carol and their boys (Cousin John Way, Vicar of Henbury). I have not heard for 2 days so hope they are better. Do tell me how the happy pair get on and all the Erchless news. I suppose you will stay all the time as you have your infant. I see your Aunt is dead in Berkeley Square, but I think she has been ill a long time. I want to know what's the matter with the Queen - can't be only a boil! I have not seen Mrs Duppa in the paper yet, but she must be nearly due and very uncomfortable I daresay - mind you tell me who is at Erchless now and what you all do with yourselves. We have had our photographs taken at Scarborough, but don't know till they come if satisfactory.

"Best love to G, (Greville)

"Ever yours, Flora C.D."

Florence, Miss Stephenson & 7 Children at Courtinhall.

Aubrey Caesar, born in 1874, was a "lovely baby" but turned out the oddest of the lot. He was a self-willed, belligerent child and repelled anyone who tried to show him affection. "I shall never forget Dot Platt, daughter of the Vicar of Sedbergh, advancing with lovely smiles upon Aubrey, a shy child of 3 or 4, and saying one of the pretty, kindly-meant nothings with which a maiden Lady propitiated a little boy. Aubrey, with extraordinary rudeness for so small a child, growled out 'Old Toad'. Miss Dot and I did not know which way to look."

Aubrey related much better to animals than to human beings. "In London he always took a biscuit in his perambulator for a cat, who, when this vehicle appeared in Green Park, always emerged from one of the back gardens in Arlington Street to receive from him this article of food, which he called a 'buck'." Later on Aubrey kept lizards and frogs in boxes which travelled around with the family and came more than once to Ashton Court. Aubrey remained a rebel all his life.

Charlie and Clem were sent to Eton, John to Wellington and Max to Radley. The daughters and younger sons were taught by a succession of tutors and governesses, some of whom were only engaged for the holidays. Harry Sparkham was one: "A most incompetent tutor," wrote Florence. "Very different to Charles Woodruffe, one of his predecessors - such a nice, really good and truly amiable young man. **He** was of some use, and would help me paste screens and read out loud" - an interesting comment on teaching methods employed in upper class Victorian homes. There was a succession of music mistresses for the girls. Miss Baber from Germany was one. Miss

Harild another - who played indefatigably on the drawing room piano whenever the family gave a dance. "The Swedish dance was one of our favourite performances," wrote Florence in 1876. The one whom everyone loved was Miss Pelzer from Switzerland.

"She was a **dear** little thing," wrote Florence. "She came first as a music mistress and jumped into all our hearts. Marie Theresa Conjunta Krotz Pelzer - we laughed at her many names and called her 'Pelly'. She often spent the holidays with us - ready to lead the donkey to the tea picnic or to join in anything that was going on - always bright and happy until in an evil moment she was persuaded to marry Mr Rooke. I believe he was very fond of her, and kind and all that, but we could see that she missed her music lessons and fun and felt like a bird in a cage. When I saw in the paper one day that she had a little daughter I had a dreadful feeling that I should see her name again lower down the page and there, sure enough, alas, it was, and dear Pelly Rooke, as we called her, had passed on. Her sister wrote about her end to me and once brought the little girl to see me."

Pelly taught Florence to play the concertina, but the high notes caused such torment to the family's pet pug, Puck, that he, "....would set up a howl of agony". Puck was one of a whole line of pugs; his mother was Lou-Lou; and before her was Pree, given to Flo by Lady Marie Spearman, and once lost when he accompanied Miss Harild, Beatrice and Flo to classes in London. Lady Spearman, "....on being informed of his loss, hunted him up and traced one clue after another and at last discovered the little dog and welcomed him to the bosom of our family - with wonderful energy."

The personalities of Florence's daughters do not emerge until much later. Beatrice and Flo were much older than the three younger ones, and Beatrice, the first-born, was her mother's special favourite. She was a gentle, good-natured girl. "I remember what a warm-hearted child Beatrice was," recalled her mother, years later. "If she saw an old woman picking up sticks in the avenue, she would rush out from luncheon and fill her apron with a jampot of food, higgledy-piggledy, pudding and meat all promiscuously, and run out to present her collection." Flo was a bit of a dark horse, with her mother's features, but a stronger personality. An amusing fragment survives, dated March 12, 1874, written by Flo, then twelve, to Beatrice who was fifteen:

"My dear Missy (a name evidently used by the servants and picked up by the children). I think that it would be useless to make poor Bijou eat a spider unless he has the symptoms of consumption, which I hope he has not. We did not go out this morning because it was so cold, but we have been out this afternoon. I know Babel does not eat apple but Bijou has generally liked it; please ask Ellen not to forget to put them together on Saturday in the small cage that Bijou is in now, to get used to each other.

"We have had a fire in our room all day since Monday. There is a school feast this afternoon at Hardwicke; only Hattie Thornhill and Miss Morland have gone to it. Trill and Rill are quite well. How is sweet Coco (the marmoset)?

"Miss Plaistow sends her love to you, and is much obliged for your letter. We are **so** happy here. I have read three very interesting books; there is a nice one about birds. There are several stories in it which are in Beaton.

"With best love to all (dearest Coco included),

"I remain your loving sister,

"Flo".

Flo, Beatrice & Charlie.

Florence and Clem were bewildered by their large number of children. They vaguely supposed that if sent to the right schools and provided with hosts of nannies and tutors, they would turn out well. It didn't occur to them to forego any of the pleasures to which their class was entitled just because there were small children to be left at home, and they went capering off to Spa, to Greville's shooting boxes in Scotland, to house parties at the homes of friends and relations - taking usually one or two of the smaller infants and a suitable number of nursemaids.

"I forget how we disposed of the children that autumn," wrote Florence, many years later, when trying to recall the events of 1874. But disposed of they were - that autumn and on innumerable other occasions when their parents saw fit to cavort on the Continent. Not that they were uncaring parents - if anything the children were heard as well as seen, were overindulged, and grand gestures made on their behalf were often misguided. One of these was 22 Berkeley Square. "I had never owned a London house before," wrote Florence, grandly, after she had come into money, "but we thought it would be good for the children." In 1872 they bought it from Algernon Strickland, Clem's uncle, and from then on there were prolonged trips to the capital. "A day or two after we got there was Saturday," wrote Florence of their first excursion to London en famille. "I, in fresh country innocence, thought it would be nice to go on the River, so off we went with some of our little tribe and embarked on a steam-boat. This, tolerably empty at first, gradually filled up till there was hardly standing room, and on and on we went. Then rumour went round that Harry Somebody, a champion winner, would presently be seen, and not only Harry but Miss Something would be there to; and sure enough the interesting couple before long were in full view on one side of the ship and, of course, all the people with one accord, and no thought, went over to that side to enjoy the sight of Mr & Miss, till it seemed really dangerous. The man was a mass of medals, but not at all worth running the risk of an upset; so I said the very next stop we'll get out - no matter which side - or where we were. The next stop soon took place and off we got, very thankful to be on dry land. The place was, I think, called Cherry Orchard, or Cherry Tree, but no sight of the fruit to be seen; only very dirty streets. Where were we? We asked the paper boy. Bermondsey he said. I think either a train or a convenient cab soon hove in sight and took us home again, and we decided that a Thames steamer on a Saturday afternoon in September - no, never again!"

Shah of Persia at the Opera.

In 1873 the London home made possible another kind of treat. "In the summer the Shah of Persia came over on a visit and stayed at Buckingham Palace, which must have wanted a good deal of cleaning. When he left many funny stories were told of his doings and sayings. Clement and I took stallsat the Opera for his grand appearance there; he always wore a black head-gear, apparently astrakhan, with a large diamond and garnet at the side; on this occasion the diamonds were in full force, and though the Princess of Wales was well covered in them, her sister the Princess Dagmar who sat with her husband* outshone them. Though not nearly as handsome as our Alexandra, she certainly had far finer stones. The Royalties and their ladies and gentlemen sat in the middle of the Grand Tier and made a very fine sight. Another night we had stalls in the Albert Hall to see the Shah again. We were on a level with him this time, so could look comfortably at his dark mysterious face, and he certainly looked at all the ladies in return. The crowd coming out was fearful, but one footman saw us and got the carriage with marvellous skill and quickness...."

Between these forays into London society, Florence brought her brood through their childish ailments with great dexterity. The slightest suspicion of a killer epidemic and she would uproot the family, servants and all, and decamp to a more healthy abode, regardless of expense or convenience. In 1870, for example, a Mrs Simpson who was staying with them at Courtinhall, "....did not feel quite the 'Thing', felt faint in church, and her throat sore. She mentioned that in the last house they had been staying in one of the children had scarlet fever - and sure enough the poor lady was soon down with the same complaint in our best bedroom. So we had to be bold and leave her and her family in possession. Rachel Orlebar, my great friend, was staying with us, and Hinwick House was empty and about 14 or 16 miles off. So we arranged with her brother, Richard Orlebar, the present owner, that we should take refuge there, and with the greatest kindness he said 'Come', and off we started with all the children, and what servants could be spared from the Simpsons. Our luggage was sent on in the morning and we had not gone on many miles when we passed it and its disconsolate driver - the cart having broken down by the way. We stayed a fortnight or 3 weeks at pretty Hinwick, with its lovely lime trees. Mrs Simpson was extremely ill, and her son was sent for, but she eventually recovered, and was able to leave Courtinhall, and while the paperer, painter and disinfectant man worked their pleasure, we went to Brighton till the house was fit for us to return to."

Florence's Ailments

Dr. Barr of Northampton was the family doctor - "a little, fat, pleasant man". He was so often summoned to Courtinhall that his horses knew the turning and turned of their own accord. Mostly it was to attend to the children's accidents; but after her sixth child Florence herself became a victim of ailments, mostly nervous disorders which afflicted her on and off for the rest of her life. At first it was boils, and Dr. Barr recommended a course of waters at Spa in Belgium. "It was no good for stopping the boils," wrote Florence, "but it was a pretty place - lovely woods and drives and

* Tsarevich, later Czar Alexander III of Russia.

walks." She had Flo aged eight and John aged four with her, and Clem's mother and sister joined them, "....and while we were there the French and German war broke out," (Franco-Prussian war), "and people every morning at the springs used to consult with each other: 'Is it safe to remain abroad, or had we better go home?'

"After 3 or 4 weeks we turned homewards once more. We saw groups of soldiers getting ready on the railway embankments, in case they should be wanted." They weren't. The Germans, in contrast to 1914 and 1940, respected Belgian neutrality, but easily trapped the French at Sedan and laid siege to Paris. "Pigeons used to fly away with notices which could only be read with a magnifying glass," related Florence, and the titled Bonapartist families who had fled to England consulted the Times daily, where there "....used to be several columns of notices to say where various French families would find their relatives, from whom the horrors of war had divided them".

Then came the Fall of Paris and the Revolt of the Communards, and "....dreadful women called Petroleuses used to throw paraffin down cellars and set alight to it". Many famous buildings were destroyed, including the Tuileries Palace where Florence's mother had seen Louis XVIII in 1824. "One night, on our return to Courtinhall, there was a curious red light all over the sky, and we all went out to see, but what it portended, I don't know."

Florence was next (1872) assailed with eczema, while in London, and Clement, in a panic, rushed to the nearest chemist (Godfrey & Cooke) to enquire for a doctor, who, on arriving, wrote out copious prescriptions for "scammony or julep, I forget which, or perhaps both together, for it was a dose the like of which I never had before, and devoutly hope I never shall again (colossal). Dr. Hawksley was most attentive in visiting me whenever I was in London, and never left without writing a prescription" - for Godfrey & Cooke, of course. Indeed, Godfrey & Cooke and Dr. Hawksley (two guineas a visit) did rather well out of Florence, as did fat little Dr. Barr.

Dr. Barr, on the strength of it, and a few other neurotic patients perhaps, owned a yacht called 'Coquette' of 70 tons, and prevailed upon Florence and Clem to accompany him on a cruise. "I told him what a bad sailor I was; he thought we should not leave the Thames, so one Saturday we repaired to Gravesend and went on board the pretty little ship. We had a most comfortable cabin, with 2 berths trimmed with rosebud chintz, and had a very cosy night, and I was just going to get up when Clement told me we were going out to sea, so I stayed in bed that long, weary, life-long day, too sick to move, my host occasionally coming in to see the havoc he had wrought, and his servant to remove the effects thereof. For some hours we were wind-bound with a great many other vessels off Walmer and we could hear the church bells and bugles summoning those fortunate enough to be on dry land to Church about 10 a.m...."

That experience lasted twenty-four hours and next summer (1873) Florence met again "....Dr. Barr and my old enemy 'Coquette'" at Le Havre, where she and Clem took their two eldest daughters on a bathing holiday. "We paid them a visit **in harbour.**" The sea bathing was much enjoyed: "French people make one so much more comfortable for the performance than our own countrymen; the little tent and hot water for one's feet, and an old sailor in a boat always ready to rescue the unwary or the nervous from any chance of a watery grave. Then, too, it is such a friendly, family arrangement; the papa sufficiently equipped for the purpose and with one or two children on his back swimming along easily, if not gracefully - with mamma by his side." Mixed bathing was then not permitted in England.

Florence went on to Paris to buy Beatrice and Flo: "Paris hats! Of brown straw trimmed with blue and white striped silk handkerchiefs". No mention of the destruction caused by the petroleuses, and Beatrice bought a marmoset "who lived some years, showing his white teeth when offended and requiring great care and warmth to keep him in health and good temper".

Fanny, Clement's mother, had inherited a large estate in Flamborough from her brother, Walter Strickland of Cokethorpe, and decided to build a mansion there. A huge, gaunt, Victorian pile called 'Dane's Dyke' began to grow on the cliffs and Florence and family went to Bridlington to watch the progress. When it was complete they went there for a holiday. "It was a very hot, dry year," (1874) wrote Florence, "and everything was burnt up to such an extent that to save the standing crops from being burnt by the sparks of the engines, men and women with things to beat out the fires (in the event of their being one) were stationed all along the line for miles and miles and miles."

During that holiday all her ailments returned, and some others appeared. Dr. Brett was tried, Dr. Hawksley again, and Dr. Barr with his horses. While Florence spent sleepless nights and had "uncomfortable feelings", the children explored the cliffs with Thomas Jeans, Clement's old tutor and Greville's travelling companion. Mr Jeans caused great excitement by reporting a cow having fallen over the cliff and having seen blue bottle-nosed whales out to sea - the rumours undoubtedly fabricated to keep little Cottrell-Dormers out of mischief.

Florence grew no better and the surfeit of doctors and doses made her worse. Dr. Hawksley had tried "every nerve tonic in the Pharmacopoeia" and she was becoming thoroughly neurotic. "Isabella* came to stay with me - she was not well owing to a coming event, and I was not well, and we both cried together and must have been a most melancholy couple."

* Isabella Way, wife of Benjamin Way of Denham.

Christmas 1874 at Courtinhall - it was their last one there - was excruciating. Florence had always enjoyed Christmases there in the past:

"....the old blind carter, Dunkerley, used to bring all the little flock of schoolchildren in their red Pryce Jones cloaks, into the hall or rather, I should think, they led him, and when they had arrived we always went down to listen to them singing 'Unto us a Son is born, unto us a child is given...'"

A conjuror was engaged every year for the schoolchildren's treat, but this year Florence couldn't sit it out. "Never again," and Miss Harild, the music teacher, almost drove her round the bend by saying 'Yars, Mrs Dormer' instead of 'Yes'; in fact everything was getting on her nerves. "I think if they (the doctors) had all left me alone after giving me a good scolding I should probably have recovered much sooner," she wrote, in retrospect.

In the end it was Rose Spencer who saved her from a complete breakdown. She was the vicar's daughter from Great Houghton who "rode over on her beloved mare Sylvia, and came to luncheon. I was not fond of her, but she was bright and cheerful and always brought a lot of gossip (not always of the kindest), but she thought I looked wretched and enquired what was being done, and never rested until she had brought us to promise to dismiss poor little Barr and try homeopathy....

"So a Dr. Ayerst was telegraphed for from London and duly appeared, and though he did not inspire me with much confidence, he completely routed all the nerve medicines and I began to feel better at once, and continued his treatment under Dr. Clifton of Northampton."

We shall hear a good deal more about Florence's ailments and their remedies, but in the meantime the death of three close relatives profoundly affected her means and status.

In 1870 her mother died. Eliza had always enjoyed good health and taken a lively interest in her family, travelling to Courtinhall for each of Florence's confinements and sometimes accompanying them to sea bathing resorts, or "....a course of waters at Ilkley". She lived out her last days at Ashton Court, devoted to Greville, who was very infrequently there, and embroidering for him his beloved stags into screens for his bedroom.

In 1869 Florence was with her mother at Ashton Court when the rest of the party had gone "to the play" when "she had a sudden attack in the evening after dinner, which was the beginning of a very serious illness. We had Dr. Day from the village and a succession of Clifton doctors. One day I said to one of them 'Dr. Beddoes, my mother does not seem to be getting any better'. 'Well, Mrs Dormer,' he said, 'I can assure you that everything is being done for her that can be done.' So I thought perhaps a change of doctors might do something and after consulting with the Aunts*, Dr., afterwards Sir, William Jenner was sent for from London. He came, and was most thorough in his attentions to the case for some hours, but he was not very hopeful that she could live very long; however, she picked up wonderfully after that and after some months I was able to leave her and Clement took me abroad with Clem (aged 7) and Palmer the maid, to the Loire and on by road to St. Moritz."

Next May, when Florence went to stay in Woodstock to see her husband's troop of Oxfordshire Yeomanry go through their paces in Blenheim Park, there came a telegram to say her mother was very ill. The visitors they had invited back to Courtinhall were put off and "I started at once, and got down to Ashton that evening. The housemaid had shut up earlier than she need have done that fine evening, the 1st of June, and the sight of the closed house frightened me as I drove up the steep hill from the station. However, the end was very near, and came that night. Aunt Louisa Prior and I were with her, and the Doctor, nurse and maid. She had caught a chill driving the day before.

"Her loss brought a great blank into my life, and was so dreadfully sudden and so great a shock. A few quiet days followed. Greville came back, and she was laid to rest in Arno's Vale Cemetery. Uncle Greg came to the funeral."

Arthur Way, who had so staunchly supported his sister during her early widowhood and the minority of her son, also died that year and was buried in the same grave.

Mistress of Rousham

In December 1874, Clement's father, who had steadily been growing more feeble, fell ill and died only a little while after moving into the new house at Flamborough. "Clement had been with him just before and had only gone out a few minutes when a servant came running after him and said, 'Poor Mr Dormer's gone, Sir'."

So Rousham, the ancestral home of the Cottrell-Dormers, came to Clement, and after much toing and froing it was decided to give up Courtinhall and settle in the old house. Sir Hereward Wake, owner of Courtinhall, had grown up and married a St. Aubyn of St. Michael's Mount, and was glad to have his house back.

"We left dear old Courtinhall one hot September day; we had been very happy there...." A last visit was made to 'The Spinney' that all the family were very attached to, for there was a stream and a summerhouse where there had been many happy picnics, but the last scanty meal was somewhat tarnished by the arrival of the Wakes.

* Louisa Prior and Belinda Sampson.

"I daresay they only meant it as a friendly farewell, but I **did** think that very tiresome of them," added Florence.

Rousham was found to be too small so an architect, Piers St. Aubyn, was engaged. "Well do I remember the first time he came and walked up through the pleasure grounds.... it was, of course, a most difficult house to alter, and I suppose he was right, according to his lights, when he said, 'Double it or do nothing'. There was nothing else to be done without spoiling some part of it, so plans and specifications began to make their appearance and we plunged into bricks and mortar for years....", during which time the family lived at their London home.

The result was not displeasing. From the front entrance no change was apparent and the new range of rooms at the back harmonised well with the rest.* As things turned out, the family never lived there long, for two years after inheriting the property Florence's sister Fanny died, and she found herself the mistress of Ingmire as well.

Fanny, a bright, good-looking girl, had never been out of the hands of doctors since her accident while at school in Clifton. When her father died she was left Ingmire, but noise caused her excessive distress, and when the navvies built a branch line to Sedbergh she fled and built herself a little chalet at Lilymere, overlooking a large artificial lake on the Kendal road. Nonetheless, she was sufficiently concerned with the spiritual needs of the navvies to build them the Vale of the Lune Chapel: "....a plain building of studied ugliness," wrote Florence, who later beautified it with fine panelling and pre-Raphaelite glass. Fanny installed an Anglican preacher who "....had been in the Crimea when the railways were building there, and was therefore accustomed to the navvies and their ways". This may have been the Mr Perkins whom Florence later sacked for drunkenness. She had gone there one Sunday to hear him preach "but strange to say old Mr Powell from Howgill officiated, and Mr Perkins was not there at all. So after the service I thanked Mr Powell for coming and asked him the reason why, but nothing could I get out of him but 'You will be informed in due course', and with that I was obliged to be content, 'til it transpired that poor Mr Perkins had been on an expedition to the Lakes with his godmother. Instead of helping him she had unintentionally proved his ruin. At meals he had stuck to Ginger Ale, till they got to some place where its excellent qualities had not been appreciated by the innkeeper, and there was none. 'Oh my dear,' said the godmamma, 'take a little brandy. It will warm you just as well as the Ginger', and this unfortunate advice had been followed, and the taste for strong drink had revived; and Mr Perkins lay a prostrate drunkard at his lodging in Sedbergh. He, of course, left at once and very difficult it was to replace him, for he had a 'way with him' and Perkins' lambs used to

* See Chapter 14: 'This Dreadful Year'.

flock to the Chapel in his time. Mr Perkins, of course, was not an habitual drunkard or he would not have stayed so long at the Chapel, but he had succumbed slightly before! But in response to an earnest appeal from the congregation I had him kept on that once, but as he well knew, never again. He has done, I believe, good work since and has often asked to preach once more, but I said not till he could show a clean bill of health (or rather sobriety) for several years, and so he has never preached again."

Fanny later moved to London, No. 22 Kensington Gardens - "a very dull house" - and Uncle Greg, who was like a father to her, made his home with her and cared for her with a dog-like devotion for many years. Florence, when in London, "used to drive across the Park nearly every day and have tea with her and try to amuse her...." but Fanny moved again to Wick Hall, Brighton, and there she died quite suddenly in her sleep. "This was a most unexpected shock, and knowing her habit of constantly taking things in her sleep, the first word I said was 'Chloral', but it was not that." Florence and Clement went to the funeral, but were almost prevented by "....one of the worst fogs I have ever known.... We tried to get to Victoria but had to go a foot pace with link boys and torches whom I could only see when close to them...." They found Wick Hall full of Petries - Uncle Greg's wife's relations - and were told of the last sad day of sister Fanny. "Uncle Greg was wonderfully well, though of course much cut up by the blow. She had been rather worse for some days, and there were two doctors in the house at the time only waiting for her to ring her bell (as she had been left to go to sleep). As she did not ring and it was long past her usual time, someone, Mrs Petrie I think, went in and found the sad, painful life ended. She had never enjoyed it, always ill or in some pain, and trying new remedies and had had so many different Doctors and yet passed away all alone. She was very clever and had she had good health might have done much...."

She was buried in Hove churchyard. Greville was at the funeral. Fanny had left everything to Uncle Greg, to be disposed of according to his directions - so Wick Hall went to Greville and Ingmire went to Florence.

CASTLE ERCHLESS

"Rightly named is Castle Erchless
For no where did I work less
Had I been compelled to work some
I should have called it Castle Irksome."

So wrote James Furneaux, one of Greville's guests at Erchless, in 1859. By the middle years of the 19th Century the English gentry had 'discovered' the Scottish Highlands. In 1848 Queen Victoria and Prince Albert bought the old fortress of Balmoral, and in the 1850s rebuilt it as an imposing country mansion. Their example was followed by the aristocracy, and the construction of railways enormously facilitated the removal of entire households to Scottish seats for the shooting season.

Between 1857 and 1877 Greville rented Erchless Castle from the Chisholm clan. It was the beginning of a long association between the Smyth family and the Scottish Highlands, which lasted up to 1946.

Erchless was a place full of romance and history. It was situated in Glen Cannich in the very heart of the Scottish Highlands. Through the glen ran the River Beauly, and at its head:

"....girt round with rocky mountains
The Loch Mullardoch lies,
In her blue heart reflected
Shine back the starry skies."

A. Stewart, 'Book of the Glen'.

Florence described the castle as "that strange, inconvenient, but beloved old house. It was a regular Scottish castle, gaunt and bare looking". Before reconstruction and modernisation in the 1880s, Erchless was a tall pele tower with pepper-pot turrets and steep steppered gables with corbie stones. Its walls were immensely thick; its rooms small, dark and vaulted. It dated mostly from the 16th Century. The eye of the approaching visitor, in the words of one of Greville's guests, is suddenly assailed:

"....old Erchless battlements it sees
Bosomed high in tufted trees
Where perhaps some beauty lies
To cheer the weary sportsman's eye.
Russet lawn and fallow bare
Good grounds for partridge and the hare...."

This comes from the famous 'Book of the Glen', an anthology put together by Greville from the jottings that his guests were required to write in the visitors' book. Often compelled unwillingly to contribute, their scribblings range from the banal to the sublime, but all agree in their love of Erchless, their affection for their host, referred to popularly as 'Grev', and the joy in each other's company in that wild and remote setting.

"But joy! Oh crowning joy of all!
He meets old Greville in the hall
And welcome, which can scarce be told
From him, and friends both new and old,
Such welcome as full well repays
The travel of two weary days."

The guests who contributed year after year to 'The Book of the Glen' saw in Grev a reincarnation of the lairds of Chisholm, who in days of yore had shown such prowess in war, and inspired such deep bonds of devotion from their clan.

"'Twas here in days now long gone by
The Chisholms held their sway.
No men more loved by vassal bold
Were found in North than they.
Where'er the fiery cross was sped
Through forest or through glen,
These chieftans bold, they rose in might
Like lions from their den,
And ever in the van of fight
They and their followers trod
Until on some unlucky raid
They gave their souls to God."

So wrote Mark J. Stewart, during a stalk in Corry Marm, 19th Sept. 1862.

"And now the chief who this day reigns
On lone Mullardoch's shore,
A lavish host, a friend sincere,
True to the very core.
With liberal hand and bounteous

'Tis his delight to give
As master kind and merciful
His motto 'Live, let live'....
His name, a southern one he boasts
It never was a myth.
It never was, much less is now,
'Tis Sir John Greville Smyth."

Praise indeed, from a Scotsman, when the highland clearances were driving thousands of wretched crofters across the Atlantic to gratify, among other things, the leisure pursuits of the English gentry. Florence says of the castle, "....there were lovely woods at the back and the family burial place was not far off, just an enclosed clearing in the wood".

This melancholy place, with its gaunt monuments, inspired more than one poem in 'The Book of the Glen':

"All hail to the home of the Chisholm,
The land of the free and the brave.
Yon column of granite denotes
Where they laid the young chief in his grave....

"His body so fragile, so weak
Lies low 'neath that soft mossy sod.
But his spirit, so gentle, so meek,
Has fled to his Saviour, his God!"

So wrote Arthur Waddilove on the grave of Alexander William Chisholm who died in 1838, aged 28. At the time of his death he was MP for Inverness-shire. When his brother and successor, William Macdonell died in 1857, the Glen Cannich book trots out, in quite a different vein:

"The people of Cannich
Will be minus a Bannock;
The Gillies of Aigus
Will be minus their Negus;
And the people of Struey
Feel quite 'Hulla-ballooey'."

The verse was not signed, which suggests that Greville himself wrote it.

The journey to Erchless was not without its trials. In 1857 the railway had not reached Inverness, and most of the guests left the railhead at Glasgow. Florence describes their first venture into the Highlands.

"In the beginning of August 1857, my mother and I, leaving Uncle Greg and Fanny to their waters and doctors at Malvern, started for Erchless.... We went to Glasgow, and then by Clyde and Caledonian Canal to Inverness, sleeping at Bonavie." The party presumably accomplished this part of the journey by paddle steamer. "The Captain of the steamer on one of the canals was a very funny little fellow, quite a character. At one of the stopping places of the ship he fed some sheep, and they danced and butted him for food. I was much pleased at the thoughts of the untried joys of the Highland shooting season, and everything seemed to me delightful. At another place the Ashton servants and carriage all came on board, and even my beautiful white Pomeranian dog - a present from Mr Orlebar - was of the party.

"When we reached Inverness, we stayed there a day or two, at the Caledonian Hotel, to get what would be wanted for Erchless Castle."

The carriage road to Glen Cannich was little more than a cart track:

"When I had gotten o'er the panic
Of the last ten miles to Glen Cannich
O'er roads - to speak in language forcible -
That really were scarce carriage-hors'able...."

F.S.D. Sept.13, 1860.

If we are to believe James Furneaux, carriage accidents were not infrequent:

"This morn from Erchless Castle went
A party, jovial-hearted.
In a dog-cart with horses twain
And waiting groom they started.

"Upon the driving seat was perched
Known as Arthur Pavis
A Welshman, up in horse's flesh
Hight, Mr Arthur Davies.

"And by his side, there sat his bride,
Who Sphinx-like, spun a riddle,
And just behind another pair
Were seated in the middle.

"Oh comely as a poplar tree
Was Miss Georgina Prior,
And sturdy as an ancient oak
Was I, the pilgrim friar.

"Insensible to all around
I sat, as in a dream,
For all my soul was in a bowl -
A bowl of cloutted cream.

"On the third seat, and at the back,
Groom William sat with B. Way *
And now I will proceed to tell
What fell out upon **the** Way."

He relates his misfortunes a la Ancient Mariner.

"All went on well as marriage bell,
Long as we kept the high road,
But griefs came thick when we branched off
Upon that horrid bye-road.

"We clambered up an awful hill
I could not view the scene
One eye was centred on the bowl
And one on the machine.

"But bad grew worse as we went down
Unto the river's bank.
The Water Kelpie all night long
Had been upon his pranks.

"And in the midst of deepest pool
The startled horses slid
And dragged the wheel upon a stone,
I shouted out 'Unskid'.

"Too late, too late, the toppling coach
Turned over on the wave
And all but I did straightway sink
Into a watery grave.

"The two behind they fought for life
As long as they were able,
The two before sank near the shore,
Smiling and comfortable.

"With soul of fire I caught Miss Prior
And bore her on my hand;
Two hours and more I strove for shore
But could not reach the strand.

"Reluctantly I loosed my grasp
She sank beneath the stream.
My other hand retained its hold,
And I saved the bowl of cream!"

Sept. 13, 1860

A tall story, one hopes; a brand of Devonshire humour. Colonel George Nelson Prior and his wife Maria, an aunt of Greville's, and for some years

* Benjamin Way, cousin of Greville Smyth, brother of Emily.

his housekeeper at Ashton, were frequent visitors at Erchless, and their daughters, Eliza Cotten, Georgina Scinde, Fanny Belinda and Mary Ann, came in for a lot of ragging.

Someone, perhaps Greville, wrote in the Glen Cannich book a letter which Fanny Belinda is supposed to have written home (Nov.10, 1869):

"I am off to Glen Cannich.
Could you see me Mamma
You would say 'Oh! My Fanny!
What a queer girl you are!'
Though it snow'd so thick round us
We could scarce feel our toes.
Yet what matter? Old Saunders*
Got the worst on his nose.

"But my thoughts cling to India
And I cannot get free
For I know there a Rajah
Is waiting for me.
With his emeralds and rubies
And diamonds so bright,
He is longing to meet me
On an elephant white.

"As I muse on the splendour
Of my Rajah so swell
All the balls go astray
When I play bagatelle.
Now this letter is ended
Sweet Mother, to thee
So Adieu - from the Begum
Of Trincomalee."

Pure jest, of course, or was it? The Prior girls had been born and brought up in India, and there may have been a grain of truth in the reference to Fanny's matrimonial intentions. In the end (1874), Fanny Belinda married Vice-Admiral Bythesea, VC - a gentleman many years her senior who had won his decoration interrupting Russian dispatches in the Baltic during the Crimean War; they had no children.

One of the photographs of the Erchless years to survive turned up in an album of Greville's cousin, Mrs Wilfred Way, which is now at Bacchus Marsh, Victoria, Australia. It is a studio portrait taken in 1875 by Collier and Park of Inverness, of four of the company in a mock rustic setting, with mountains on a painted backcloth. Standing at the back is Greville, who at forty was already portly and balding; on his left Mrs Wilfred Way, and seated in front of him, Eliza Cotten 'Tottie' Prior, looking coy; while at her feet sprawls, rather stiffly, John Smith Osbourne, who married her later that same year.

* Saunders, the coachman from Ashton Court.

The stalwarts of the company, whose names appear year after year on the pages of 'The Book of the Glen' were Greville's old college friends, and the companions of his forays into big game hunting in India, America and Australia. There was the reluctant deer-stalker, Edward R. King-Harman of Dublin, known familiarly as 'The King'; Mark J. Stewart, who bred enormous herds of Ayrshire cattle on his estate near Dumfries; 'Digger' Saunders-Davies, who had tried his luck in the 1850 Gold Rush; John Henry Buller, with his brandy flask, who was a relation of the famous soldier of Empire, Sir Redvers; 'Duppa' Paul from India - 'the scourge of tigers'; Philip 'The Apostle' Kington; and 'Saint' Clement Cottrell-Dormer of Rousham.)

Another college friend, whose house was also destined to be linked by marriage to that of Smyth, was 'Urbs' - Florance George Henry Irby of Hedsor, son of the 4th Baron Boston, and soon to succeed to that title. Also of the party was the latter's brother-in-law, Augustus Arthur Vansittart, who bravely began his poem:

"My name it is Vansittart
And I know I haven't wit, art
Or genius for inditing a sentimental lay...."

But he didn't do so badly, and his lay is worth repeating:

"I remember, I remember (apologies to Thomas Hood)
Those bright days of September.
I remember, but my memory's beginning to decay.
But yet Erchless hospitality
Its sport and joviality
All this surely I'll remember to my dying day.

"I remember Colonel Prior
Waited close at hand to fire
Till a Prior assignment called his stag away.
So to seek elsewhere its pleasure
Off it trotted at its leisure,
While the Colonel scored two wides, and then fainted in dismay.

"Kington, sly as Stonewall Jackson
(The American Civil War was much in the news.)
Said 'Stop here, Mark, I'll be back soon'.
Six hours Mark was green enough, his orders to obey,
You may fancy there was cursing

And swearing, there was nursing
Of wrath and writing poems in the pass that day.

"Of deer-stalking the true art
(Thus to himself said Stewart)
Is to watch for little openings and then make play.
So he thought his safest ticket
Was to polish off a pricket
But after seven misses the calf strolled away.

"No. I'll not forget the grub, or
The after dinner rubber
And how gaily Mrs Prior at the whist held sway.
My spirit half afraid is
To play against Bath ladies
But she trumps the Colonel's 13th which he says don't pay.

"I wish that I had fuller
Accounts of Paul and Buller
And Davies, the Commissioner (as some call him) yeh,
But I hope each may enjoy all
The rapture, when a royal
Is shot behind the shoulder and brought to bay.

"Least said is soonest mended
Last comes, what's most intended.
There's one sentiment we'll cherish and repeat for ages
For we finish with a toast
To our well-beloved host
Here's a bumper to Sir Greville and his friends - Hooray."

Greville (with binoculars) and friends - at Erchless

For Greville, the Erchless days were the happiest of his middle years. He was surrounded by his friends, and in their company he indulged the passion of his life, the pursuit of game. In July trout and salmon; in August the grouse; and well into November he was stalking the deer. But what filled his cup to over-flowing was that here, at Erchless, he was permitted to see his beloved Emily. She was, after all, his cousin, and at Erchless they could continue their romance, discreetly disguised under cover of a family reunion, for in the early days she brought with her, her father the vicar - ("The vicar whose skin must be tough as his breeches, likes to sit in the wood and kill millions of midges") and her brothers John Hugh, Bromley and Ben. Later, she and her life-long friend Zoe Rolt, graced the company as 'hostesses', and by all accounts she threw herself into the activities of the place with an abandon which would have been unthinkable at Redland Court. She painted, tramped and stalked, trailing crinoline and all through mountain, bog and fell.

"The lady of the golden hair
Kills roebuck without measure,
And when inclined to slay a hind
She shoots it at her pleasure."
Wrote Uncle George Prior, Oct. 11, 1862.

"Sir G. would laugh and shout with joy
To see so many deer destroy
And turning to Paul with knowing look
Would bid him record it in his book."

The rapture of those years is nowhere better caught than in the only verse that Greville himself ever committed to 'The Book of the Glen':

"Oh, Lancaster! Oh, Lancaster!
Under the greenwood tree,
Full many a time and often
Have I slain a deer with thee,
Have I slain the active roedeer
As he brushed away the dew,
And slain the stately red deer
I reckon not a few

"How often in Egypt
On the sandbanks of the Nile,
Have we slain the alligator
And the hideous crocodile.
How often when in India
Under the burning sky
Have we slain the wily black buck,
And the sleek blue bull nilgai.

"How often in the Prairies
We the bison did pursue.
Till from shooting them on horseback
My side was black and blue.
And lastly in Australia
We were dead on kangaroo
Where there's nothing else to shoot at
Save the bustard and emu."

The recklessness with which he slaughtered his prey would horrify conservationists of more modern times, but the stalking and killing of a full-grown stag was an achievement of consummate skill, and Greville reckoned to bag at least two during a season.

"Glen Cannich holds high revels
Free flows the mountain dew
For there the bold Sir Greville
Has shot a stag or two.
Three stags and eke a hind
Sir Greville has brought to bag
With brisket fat two inches deep
And one a hoop-horned stag.

"It's horns are hard as granite
It's neck is like a bull
It's face is as the planet
When she is at the full."

So wrote one of his 'Apostles', A.C.Paul.

"Though Assheton-Smith is dead*
The Smyth of Ashton lives.
All blessings on his head,
Paul no apostle gives
For Greville's a sportsman true
And a truer friend than he
Cannot be found the world around
So Vive La Compagnie."

The urge to hunt appealed to man's oldest and most basic needs, and among the men of Erchless, as among their beleaguered descendants of today, there was a mystique, a deadly earnestness in their tracking of the prey.

"When Loch Mullardoch's darken'd tide
Reflects the hills that clothe its side,
Where Lappich lifts his lofty head,
Sacred from all but stalker's tread,
Where torrents rush from crag to crag
There we stalk the noble stag."

Alfred Waddilove, in his epic poem 'The Death of the Monarch of Glen Cannich', recaptures for us, moment by moment, the stealthy movements of Greville and party, armed with Lancasters and clad in the deer-stalkers and tweeds that were to transform the casual wear of gentlemen for ever:

* Thomas Assheton-Smith, who died Sept. 13th 1858, was proprietor of the enormous Llanberis slate quarries in North Wales, but was more widely known for his prowess as a fox-hunter, for which he earned the title 'The British Nimrod'. He had a country seat at Tidworth in Hampshire and for many years was leader of the Melton Hunt. His daring and flamboyance in the field made him almost a legend in his lifetime.

"Up the corrie steep we go
Leaving behind the World below.
As we scale the mountainside
Lo! a herd of deer is spied.
Above it rise two antlers tall
Fit mark for our unerring ball....

"With cautious footsteps on we move
Clinging to the heights above
And now we crouch, and now we crawl,
Heedless alike of slip or fall.

"And now we creep on hand and knee
For should the herd but dimly see
Our form twixt them and light of day
As lightning quick, they're off - away!....

"We single out the antler's chief
There he stands in bold relief.
With steady aim and bated breath
Prepare to deal the blow of death.

"The bullet pings - loud, Duncan cries
'He's hit!' He staggers, drops and dies.
On with gladden'd step we rush
With our well-earned victory flushed.
There he lies - twelve points - a royal head,
Fit emblem of the mighty dead."

The splendid head and antlers no doubt made their way to the big house in Somerset to join trophies from four other continents. The Long Gallery could not contain them all, so the stables in the south front were converted into a museum, and eventually a spacious bungalow at the top of the park was built to house them.

It is a relief to note that Greville and his companions were not above seeing the funny side of their sport, and King-Harman, the reluctant stalker, was quick to seize upon any little happening that would turn the laughter against themselves.

Florence, recalling their nearest neighbours at Erchless Castle, writes, "Lord and Lady Lovatt and their handsome sons and daughters lived at Beaufort Castle, and my mother and I stayed there two nights that autumn (1857). But great were the lamentations when, in 1859, Lord Lovatt shot and killed the stag that Greville had been stalking for two months".

"Twas the laird of Erchless Castle sitting pensive and alone
Dark melancholy seemed to have marked him for her own.
By his side there lay his rifle forgot, neglected, spurned,
'Bell's Life' was spread before him unread, uncut, unturned.

"What ails thee, O Sir Greville? What means this look so sad?
Has the thunder turned the liquor (the ale thou lovest) bad?
Has the friend in whom thou trusteth repaid thy love with scorn,
Or sharper than a serpent's tooth, trod on thy fav'rite corn?

"Has soot come down the chimney and spoilt the meat below?
Or is it but the toothache that has stamp'd thy cheek with woe?
Does some circumstance to India* your visit disallow?
Come! Cheer up, I say, old buffer! and tell us what's the row.

"Thus we spoke, but he kept silence, scarce could he find words to
speak.
And we saw a tear, unbidden, coursing down his manly cheek.
And from forth his stalwart bosom burst a wild, heart-rending sob,
And I said 'Egad! he's crying he is, so help me Bob!'

"Then rose Sir Greville slowly from his seat upon the ground.
Sadly gazed he on his allies who stood wond'ringly around.
Like Niobe lamenting stood our loved and cherished chief,
And to all 'twas most apparent that somehow he'd come to grief.

"'Oh! my friends' (he spoke in accents of unutterable woe)
'Oh! my friends, whom I have cherished is'nt this a pretty go?
Little thought I when I bade ye share the pleasures of this place
That ye should be the partners of my sorrow and disgrace.

"'Better far, when Cunard's steamers bore me o'er the ocean wide,
I had fallen, with grog unsteadied, and sunk beneath the tide.
Better far in New York City or the plains of modern Troy
I had fallen, gorged and lifeless, 'neath some roaring Yankee bhoy.

"'Better far when youthful measles kept me helpless in my bed
That a drunken nurse had poisoned me with acetate of lead.
Better far some raging bison had 'pucked' me with his horn.
Better far, I rather fancy, that I never had been born.

"'Oh thunder! Oh thunder! Oh my uncle! Oh my aunt!
Oh ye gods and little fishes! Strength to bear this sorrow grant.
All the ills that flesh is heir to I had borne and never funked,
But the Lovatt is triumphant and Squaretoes is defunct.

"'Oh Squaretoes! Oh my ancient! whom I fondly hoped to slay,
After whom so many a bullet hath sped its fruitless way!
I have sought thee late and early and with many a faithful 'pal'
Wooed thee, as a Cockney lover, woos a deuced pretty gal!

"'But he the fiend who robbed me of the deer I loved so well,
Shall I curse him orthodoxly with candle, book and bell?
Shall I curse him as the navvies? But no: that won't be right:
Let the beast that he has slaughtered be avenged on him tonight.

"'And when he's gorged himself with venison from the haunch that
should be mine,
And sought the downy pillow overcome with sleep and wine,
Then avenge the woes of Erchless shade of the mighty dead!
Let him have a shocking nightmare ere he's half an hour
in bed.

* The Indian Mutiny, 1857-8.

"'As for me, first give me liquor for this talking makes me dry,
Then I'll hie me to my chamber and lay me down and die.
And the King shall write an elegy and put it on my grave:
Here lie the bones of Greville Smyth, the Generous, Good and
Brave'."

In 'The Book of the Glen' nearly all the popular classics were parodied. The 'Hero' of "How we brought the good news...." is Emily, in a poem of Harman's, part of which is quoted here, and called:

The New Consolation

"Oh, woman! Sir Walter has written, when anguish and pain rack the brow,
An angel to minister gently to grieved and oppressed ones art thou....

"The Clerk of the Weather was sulky and sent us sleet, wind, snow and rain,
And the tempest howled by 'till you'd fancy the Deluge was coming again.

"'Dear! dear!' then exclaimed Mrs Edwards as she sat by the fire so snug,
(She addressed Mrs Eyre who was sitting wrapped up in a rug).

"'Dear me! What a horrible evening! Just see what a terrible pour!
How I pity those suffering creatures who are tramping about in Treloar!

"'Do you think we can go out and meet them? I will, if you will - and I
say,
We can take them the New Consolation poor fellows, they'll want it today.'

"'Agreed,' says the other, 'I'll venture, there's nought could suit better my wish',
And they started directly in weather that would frighten a sensible fish.

"As for us, we were wet through and weary, we were sulky and heartsick beside,
And I think in another five minutes one or other must surely have died.

"But on nearing the boathouse, oh! wonder! Oh! moment of joy and surprise!
The vision angelic! seraphic! the ladies at length met our eyes.

"But when, as if seeing their faces was not for us rapture enough,
They pulled out the **New Consolation** and gave us all quantum stuff.

"Then our gratitude burst forth - 'Your kindness has snatched us,' we cried, 'from our graves,
You have saved all our lives, dearest ladies, henceforth we are wholly your slaves.'

"The taste of the New Consolation must soon from the palate depart
But the memory of those who have brought it shall ne'er be effaced from the heart.

"And the tale shall be told in the Tropics and the history rehearsed at the Poles.
How you brought forth the Apricot Brandy to sooth our poor suffering souls."

The regime at Erchless was tough. Emily, 'the hostess', expected all the guests to be up and breakfasted by nine. The 'King' found this particularly hard to bear.

"This book, as you see, is filled up for the most
With praises for Erchless, and words for the host;
I agree in the main, but make one protest small
There's one thing I don't like about them at all.

"For kindness there's none with the hostess can vie
And Greville himself wouldn't injure a fly,
What cause then for groans, and complainings so deep
Why! They breakfast before you've got well off to sleep!

"You're off all day either 'grousing' or stalking
(Uncommon good sport, but uncommon hard walking).
It's three ere you lunch, and past eight ere you dine
Yet they coolly expect you to breakfast by NINE.

"Yet the lateness of dinner is not the sole grief
The way that we're fed really passes belief.
When you're charged to the muzzle with venison and wine
How CAN they expect you to breakfast at NINE?

"'Oh! come!' I hear somebody say (what a beast)
'You can always get turned in by midnight, at least.'
Get turned in by midnight? Oh yes! Pretty joke,
Why what's to become of our whisky and smoke?

"So it happens at eight that we're dragged from our beds
With eyes red as ferrets, that burn in our heads.
And the first thing I hear, ere I pull on my shirt, is
Paul yelling for brandy and soda to Curtis.*

"'Tis hard to be called from your pillow to rise
When you fancy you scarcely have shut up your eyes.
'Tis hard when you hear ere you're out of your tub
By the clatter of knives, Ben is hard at the grub.

"'Tis hard when the table at length meets your eye
To find nothing left, but hard crust of a pie.
'Tis hard as you swear how the ladies all laugh
And instead of condolence, give hard-hearted chaff.

"'Tis hard writing this, and I fear me indeed
That you will complain that it's harder to read.
But with these hardships described by my pen
The hardship I hate most is - leaving the Glen!"

However, there were Sundays, and the regime slackened a little. Those who wished attended church. "The service was that of the Scottish church," said Florence, "and the collie dogs came as a matter of course with their masters, seldom disturbing the congregation." But even churchgoing to the merry throng at Erchless became a source of hilarity.

"For our Sunday recreation we indulge in tuneful song,
And Miss Prior accompanies the **Hymn** so clear and strong,
That if she'll be advised by me, she'll certainly endeavour
To wed a singing husband, and stick to **HIM** for ever."

After Sunday luncheon, the 'quiet Sunday walk' often ended with unseemly romps with the ladies....

"Through planting road and meadow go the merry little crowd
Feet and tongues go patter clatter, Babel wasn't half as loud.
When a brawling stream, and broken bridge all further progress baulk
'Here's an end,' says Mrs Lewis, 'to our Quiet Sunday Walk'.

"'Pooh! Nonsense!' cry the gentlemen, 'a truce to false alarms,
We sons of toil will ford the stream the ladies in our arms.'
Each lady quickly raised aloft not heeding scream or squawk
And landed on the other side pursues her Sunday walk.

"Shall we tell how Paul, while carrying his precious burden o'er
Let her dress fall draggling in the stream before he reached the shore?
And the lady screamed 'Good gracious!' How the Digger answered 'Lawk!'
Why that's nothing when you're going on a Quiet Sunday Walk."

The last two poems did not appear in the printed edition of 'The Book of the Glen'. No doubt they were considered too indecorous. Nor did the following two, and for more obvious reasons.

"One misty day two ladies fair one **Irby** named, the other **Eyre**,
Made a request that I would write something that in the Glen Book might
Without offence be placed, and though little of making rhymes I know
I fairly promised there and then to write their adventures at the Glen.

* Greville's valet.

"They started in the wagonette the day and date I quite forget.
But this I know, indeed, that when they reached the cottage of the Glen
Tho' draped in silks and grand as queens they soon took off their crinolines,
And when again the two came out the one was **thin**, the other **stout**.

"I asked politely would they go and walk with me, a mile or so.
They only answered with a laugh 'We mean to go and have a **bath**'.
'Take care,' I cried, 'the loch is deep.' 'Gammon,' they said, 'you go to sleep.'
At this rebuke I straight retired but sudden, with a bright thought fired
I ran down quickly through the pass and seized upon my spying glass,
Then seated on a rock, looked round to see that neither one was drowned...."

....and it goes on to say what he saw through his 'spying glass'. When Greville published 'The Book of the Glen' in 1870 the author of this poem had become the 5th Baron Boston, and may well have requested that these verses be suppressed.

Stalking the ladies when they should have been stalking the deer is a frequent source of ribaldry in 'The Book of the Glen', and the following is an excerpt from another expurgated poem on the subject, by Philip Kington.

"Have you heard how Nowell Way discovered what's o'clock?
When the Ladies of the Glen Cannich talked of bathing in the loch?
Benstickets Hill he straight went up, so modestly inclined
And mindful of Mrs Lot, he never looked behind.
I am told the fish were jealous and reduced to grim despair
At the **Mermaid** in the water with her flowing chestnut hair...."

Greville formed the Erchless Castle Cricket Eleven and they played local teams, and even one from Cambridge staying in the neighbourhood. On that occasion (28th August 1866) the Erchless eleven defeated the visitors by 60 runs; Greville scored 6 and was run out. Tommy Eyre (whose wife had been scrutinised by 'Urbs' sporting naked in the loch) scored 25, and also bowled out four of the opposing team.

Evening diversions were varied. The ladies collected ferns to press; they exercised Emily's little dog 'Bijou', and they sang to the banjo. 'King' Harman was so busy scribbling verses into 'the Book' that he was usually late for dinner.

"'Tis hard when you get rather late in to dine
To find Tommy Eyre has just finished the wine.
And if there's one thing that could make your case harder
'Tis to find out that nothing is left in the larder."

And after dinner, Scottish reels or cards:

"The rain poured down with wind and sleet
But inside all was snug and bright
The dinner good, the toddy sweet
And gay the games of cards at night."

....especially when the ladies cheated!

"'Tis hard to win money at night you'll perceive
When a lady keeps all the Court cards in her sleeve.
And it's hard to express one's opinion in rhyme
Of a lady who turns up the King every time!

"'Tis hard when your smoking and grog you begin
To find all declaring it's time to turn in.
And 'twixt whist and fear of disturbing the Eyres
It's uncommonly hard climbing up those steep stairs."

After the ladies retired, the grog not infrequently got out of hand, and the revelry reached bacchanalian proportions:

"To Sir Greville of Ashton 'twas Juddkins who spoke,
Ere (Eyre) my crown goes to rest there are crowns to be broke.
Then let each jolly pal who would wish for a spree
Come follow downstairs and play billiards with me!
Come fill up my cup! Come fill up my can!
When I'm drunk as a lord then I feel I'm a man.
Throw the billiard room open and let me go free,
And its room for bold Juddkins who's out on a spree.

"On the table he's mounted and (wonderful feat)
He declares that himself in a pocket he'll seat.
Then away with the pool balls, the cues and the rest,
Smash the lamps and behave like a Baronet's guest.
Base Buller beware or you shortly shall see
I'm a dangerous man when I'm out for a spree.
Come fill up my cup! Come fill up my can!
Though he's drunk as a lord fill his goblet again.
Throw the billiard room open and drink, three times three,
To the health of bold Juddkins who's out for a spree!"

This is one of Irby's best. It was entitled 'The Raid of Judcock' (air: 'Bonnie Dundee'), and was clearly inspired by Judd's weakness for port.

The undignified termination of these proceedings is described in another poem:

"They raised him up from off the floor
He staggered off to bedwards.
And murmured as he reached the door
Of Mesdames Rolt and Edwards."

It was unfortunate that nothing much rhymed with 'Edwards' except 'bedwards'. For Greville it meant the same thing. With the women in bed and the company drunk in the billiard room, Greville sought out Emily. In August 1863 Emily's second child, Esme, was born. In November 1862 she had been at Erchless. Although Esme always passed herself off as an Edwards, it was known to almost everyone that she was Greville's child.

Near Loch Mullardoch's head you'll see
Close by the waterside
A shooting lodge, a wild retreat
In midst of forest wide." (A. Stewart)

This was five miles up the glen from the castle, and Greville and his companions often spent whole days there together, to be closer to their quarry. It was a fine spot in good weather, but when a Scottish mist descended it was a gloomy, desolate place.

Greville and 'Urbs' (Irby) were alone there, on one occasion, determined to stalk whatever the weather:

"Early we woke in the morning
For we were determined to stalk,
Though the mist on the hills gave us a warning
It intended our efforts to baulk.
'This weather,' cried Grev, 'is past bearing
I'm hanged if I think it will clear.'
'What's the object,' cried I, 'of your swearing
Will that get you a shot at a deer?
Turn up, men, a truce to your snoring
Already my foot's in a sock,
Though the rain just at present be pouring
It may clear yet, by twelve of the clock....'

"Grev jumped up, my lecture on hearing
And quickly was dressed to his boots,
While I, with a comb, was still tearing
The hair from my head by the roots.
'Well, old fellow, I said I'd be ready
Before you'd half finished to dress.'
'My Maxim,' cried I, 'is sure and steady,
But I shan't be long after, I guess.'

"Our breakfast we rapidly finished,
Then gave a look out at the sky.
But we found that our chance was diminished
We should never be able to spy.
For the mist on the hills kept increasing
Loch Mullardoch was covered in foam,
The rain it poured down without ceasing
And we a long distance from home.
So sadly we peeped from our hovel
And fervently wished it would clear,
While Greville sat down to his novel
And I to my pipe and my beer.

"Thus slowly we passed through the morning
On the hill-tops mist heavily lay,
So we said we'd return to the Castle
Nor uselessly longer delay.
And wrapping our things in a parcel
Prepared to set out on our way,
Then tighter we folded our plaidies
And in mind were at Erchless again.
And the thought of rejoining the ladies
Made us heedless of wind and of rain,
For we knew they would feel for our sorrows
And kindly pity us, when
We related our manifold horrors
Of a shocking wet day at the Glen."

Many years later, Irby's son married Greville's daughter.

Grev and 'Urbs' were not usually defeated by the weather, and on a further celebrated occasion (Oct. 1868) they decided to sit out the storm at the 'hovel' on Loch Mullardoch, come what may. The company this time consisted of Greville, Tommy Eyre, King Harman, Digger Paul and one other who remains nameless, but who decided to monitor events daily, for the benefit of the readers of 'The Book of the Glen'.

Greville, companions and crofters' wives at the shooting box, Loch Mullardoch.

"**Wednesday, Oct. 28:** Left Erchless in perfect sobriety and a violent storm. Little Samuel in immediate requisition. Heavy snowstorm off 'Denham Cottage'. Flasks out and whisky all round. Reached Cannich wet but joyous. Replenished flasks and inner man. Met Duncan at Mochra Bridge. Liquor all round to celebrate the event. Met Campbell further on. Celebrate the event as before. Heard of a stag - further celebration. Continued in frequent intervals till the Cottage is reached. Investigate the cupboard and discover liquor. Celebrate the event. Happy thought - send to Erchless for Apricot Brandy - celebrate the thought all round. Festive evening. Old Maid - conducive to thirst. Turn in, all hands drunk. Paul in his boots. Tommy Eyre put to bed in the bath.

"**Thursday, Oct. 29:** Coppers (sic) in the morning all round, liquor ditto ditto. Wet and snowy outside; depression of spirits and liquor all round to raise them. John Campbell arrives with news of a stag - celebrate the event. Grev starts in pursuit, liquor all round to wish him luck. Water Ousel visible to the naked eye - celebrate the event. Depression of spirits of frequent occurrence - the draught as before to raise them. The Baronet kills a stag - celebrate the event several times. Festive evening as before. Old Maid more thirsty than usual. Turn in as before. Tommy in his boots and Paul in the bath.

"**Friday, Oct. 30:** Curious thirst all round. Liquor ditto to allay it. A large quantity of things about the house - active but hopeless pursuit, no one can catch them. Liquor all round to quell disappointment. Snow and rain outside, lots of sherry inside - inside preferable. Arrival of Apricot Brandy - taste it. Grev kills a stag. Celebrate the event. Festive evening - Old Maid wonderfully thirsty. Turn in as before. Paul and Tommy both in their boots in the bath.

"**Sat. Oct. 31:** Remarkable thirst and depression of spirits all round. Liquor strongly recommended as an antidote. Curious entomological specimens about the house - flies, beetles, spiders and a black thing with a tail - pursuit as before but without success - disappointment got rid of in usual manner. Duncan arrived with news of a stag - celebrate the event. Digger goes in pursuit, but is driven back by a blue dog with orange spots which follows him into the house. Liquor all round to condole with him; wind, snow and rain. Whisky invaluable.

"**Sunday, Nov. 1:** Damp, thirsty and blowing. Liquor all round. Beetles, flies etc. as before. Curious quantities of rats and mice constantly running under the door and out of the window. Fruitless pursuit. Liquor all round to console us. News of deer. Tommy goes in pursuit. Wish him luck in the usual manner. General loss of appetite at lunch. Liquor allowed to fill up the vacuum. Tommy returns remembering it is Sunday; commend his scruples and celebrate the event. Grev finds curious dog under the table, black, with yellow tail and ears. King finds another in his bedroom, green picked out in red. Celebrate both events. Festive evening. Turn in early. Sunday a remarkably thirsty day. Grev, King, Tommy, Digger and all the dogs in the bath.

"**Monday, November 2nd:** Unexampled depression in the house. Paul weeping for his grandmother. King crying over the days when he was a happy child. Liquor all round to restore equanimity. Tommy tries t he tub - can't do it. Full of crocodiles. Condole the event. Dogs grown wonderfully. News of deer on the hill. Celebrate the event frequently. No use going after deer - larger game nearer hand. Lions, tigers, scorpions, boa constrictors, and a green beast with a flaming eye in its tail, running about the house. General chase without result. Liquor all round to remove depression. Festive, not to say noisy evening, and general turn-in on the floor among the fragments of furniture.

"**Tuesday, November 3rd:** Awful day. Fearful depression. Liquor all gone. Flies, dogs, snakes, and beasts as before. Blue devil in Grev's room; pink ditto in King's; yellow ditto in Tommy's; striped ditto in sitting room. Howls, yells and general combat of all the devils. Opportune arrival of carriage with four doctors, four straight waistcoats and eight Keepers. General melee.

Ow! Bow, wow, wow!!!"

There are several acrostics in 'The Book of the Glen'. It is fitting to close this chapter with two of them. The characters mentioned in them have all been mentioned before and need no introduction.

A for **Albert,** who picks up each stag that he shoots,
B for **Bucking Blink Bonny,** and **Buller's** bad Boots.
C for **Chisholm,** who now as a parent doth figure,
D for John **Davis,** and also for **Digger.**
E for old **Erchless,** a time-honoured place,
F for **Fred** Wright, with his merry round face,
G for Sir **Greville,** and also for **Glen,**
H for King **Harman,** so glib with his pen.
I for **Irby,** who now has a house and can stock it,
J for **Judd,** who can screw himself into a pocket.
K for **Kington,** who has been a traveller afloat,
L for the **Lysleys,** the kid and the goat.
M for **Macrae,** that deer stalker true,
N stands for **Nothing** I know of, do you?
O for the **Old Port** that sets Judd on fire,
P for the **Pricket,** so **peppered** by **Prior.**
Q for the **Quizzing,** at Erchless there's much of it,
R for John **Rolt,** who sometimes gets a touch of it.
S for you'll observe, **sir,** for **Sargeant** must **stand,**
T for **Tod** (Fox), slain by a certain fair hand.
U for **Upton,** a name that we all of us honour,
V for Mrs **Vansittart,** who likes frogs upon her.
W for **Way,** Ben, Brum and the Vicar,
X for unknown quantity (probably liquor).
Y for **You,** gentle reader, is clearly designed,
Z by the **Zeal** of the three, undersigned.

T.E. (Tommy Eyre)
J.P. (John Paul)
P.K. (Philip Kington)

And lastly:

Guests at jolly old Erchless, whoever you be
Read this little acrostic, and then you will see
Engraven a name, that, without any boast,
Very truly I saw in itself is a 'Host'.
I abstain from an eulogy ever so brief
Lest when I am gone he may tear out the leaf.
Let me only predict, that when we forget Greville
Erchless Castle itself will have gone to the Devil.

Philip V. Kington.

The Erchless years came to an end about 1880. The old castle was altered and modernised about 1884, which suggests that the Chisholm clan had claimed it back. Greville and party had long since moved on to fresh hunting grounds; but all later castles and shooting lodges lacked the romance of old Erchless; and the company was never again quite so scintillating. The house parties of later years never managed to recapture the spirit of the 60s, but that might have something to do with the vastly changed status of the host, Greville Smyth.

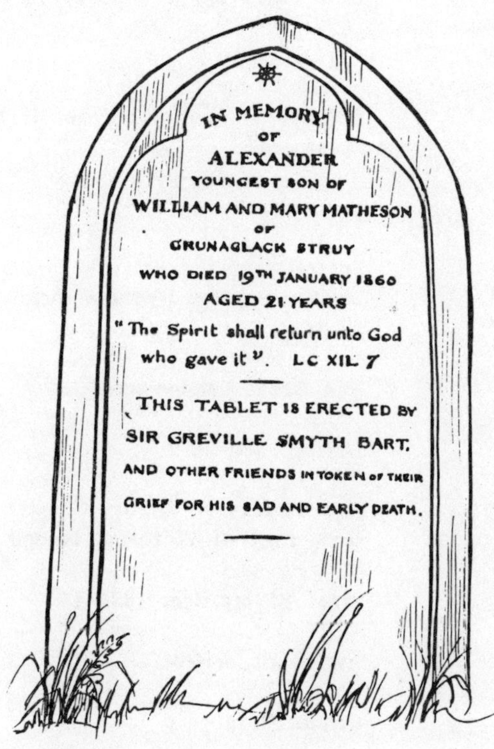

In the churchyard, Struy.

BIBLIOGRAPHY

A M W Stirling	The Ways of Yesterday: Thornton Butterworth, 1930
Thomas Provis calling himself Sir Richard Smyth	The Victim of Fatality of the Claimant of Ashton Court: J Hewitt, Bristol. c.1853 Bristol Bibliography
Sir Bernard Burke	Vicissitudes of Families, Vol. II, 1864.
O Woodall	The Trial of the action of Smyth v. Smyth relating to the Ashton Court Estate, at the Gloucester Summer Assizes, Aug. 8.9.10.1853 in a collection of celebrated trials, Vol. I, 1873
	Smyth v. Smyth Special Jury: tried at Gloucester Assizes before Mr Justice Coleridge
	Upton v. Abbot, 1854
Jane Evans	Portraits of the Smyth-Piggott family Leisure Service Department, Woodspring District Council
John Bateman	The Great Landowners, 1879
Rosina Sharples	Diary, 1803-36
Richard Davey	The Smyths of Ashton Court: How typical were they of Victorian landed society
Augustus Hare	Story of my life, 1896-1906
Latimer	Annals of Bristol
Census Returns	Bristol Reference Library

PORTRAITS

The photographs included in this book are reproduced from the following sources.

Lewis Way) Mrs Lewis Way) Four of the children) of Lewis Way)	"The Ways of Yesterday" by A. M. W. Stirling, 1930
The Rev. Henry Hugh Way	"History of the Way Family" by W. L. Herbert, 1914
Sir Richard Smyth and title page	"The Victim of Fatality of the Claimant of Ashton Court" by Thomas Provis, calling himself Sir Richard Smyth (c.1853)
George Oldham Edwards	"History of Banking in Bristol from 1750 to 1899" by C. H. Cave
Thomas Upton) John Upton) Greville Upton as) an undergraduate) Eliza Upton) Clement Cottrell Dormer)	by kind permission of Dorothy North of Melling, Carnforth, Lancs.
Emily Way) Greville Smyth)	by kind permission of Susan Graham of Ringwood, Hants.
Florence Upton) Fanny Upton)	by kind permission of Thomas Cottrell Dormer of Rousham, Oxon.

****

Drawings in this book are taken from portraits in Woodspring Museum, Weston-super-Mare and in Bristol City Museum; and from photographs kindly loaned by Judith Harris of Bacchus Marsh, Victoria, Australia; Mr Moat of Witney, Oxon.; Dorothy North of Melling, Carnforth, Lancs; Bill Perry, Long Ashton, Bristol; and Major Parish, Walcot Hall, Salop.

Negatives of all portraits and photographs are held by the Malago Society.

Index

A

B

C

H

I

J

K

L

M

N

R

S

X Y Z